BEST-
LOVED
TALKS
OF THE LDS
PEOPLE

BEST-
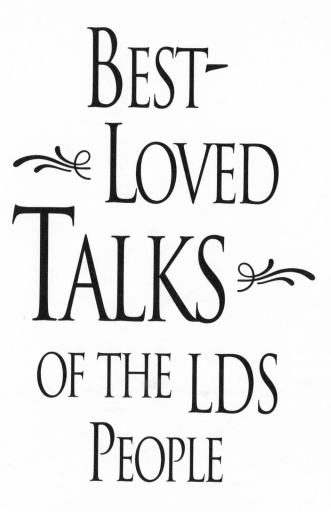
~ LOVED
TALKS ~
OF THE LDS
PEOPLE

EDITED BY JAY A. PARRY,

JACK M. LYON, AND

LINDA RIRIE GUNDRY

**DESERET
BOOK**

SALT LAKE CITY, UTAH

Also available from Deseret Book

BEST-LOVED POEMS OF THE LDS PEOPLE

BEST-LOVED HUMOR OF THE LDS PEOPLE

BEST-LOVED STORIES OF THE LDS PEOPLE, VOLUME 1

BEST-LOVED STORIES OF THE LDS PEOPLE, VOLUME 2

BEST-LOVED STORIES OF THE LDS PEOPLE, VOLUME 3

BEST-LOVED CHRISTMAS STORIES OF THE LDS PEOPLE

Library of Congress Cataloging-in-Publication Data

Best-loved talks of the LDS people / [edited by] Jay A. Parry, Jack M. Lyon, Linda Ririe Gundry.
     p.   cm.
  Includes bibliographical references and index.
  ISBN 1-57008-824-1 (alk. paper)
  1. Christian life—Mormon authors.   2. Church of Jesus Christ of Latter-day Saints—Doctrines.   I. Parry, Jay A.   II. Lyon, Jack M.   III. Gundry, Linda Ririe.

BX8656 .B48 2002
252'.09332—dc21   2002004598

Printed in the United States of America   72076-30022
Publishers Printing, Salt Lake City, UT

10   9   8   7   6   5   4   3   2

⁓ꝫ ꝫ⁓

Contents

~❧ ❧~

PREFACE

A great talk can change your life. Remember President Spencer W. Kimball's exhilarating admonition to "lengthen your stride"? How about Elder Bruce R. McConkie's final address and powerful testimony of the Savior? Church leaders have given hundreds of inspiring talks over the years, speaking the word of the Lord for our instruction and edification.

All too often it is difficult to locate classic talks by Church leaders. Where can you find President J. Reuben Clark Jr.'s monumental address on teaching in the Church? Or President Lorenzo Snow's inspiring discourse on tithing? Or President David O. McKay's memorable talk on love at home? These and many other outstanding addresses have been collected in this volume.

Of course, this collection is far from complete. Many talks had to be excluded because:

- There simply was not room for everything.
- We wanted to provide an overview of addresses from many different speakers rather than try to include every outstanding talk from a single Church leader.
- We were limited by copyright restrictions.

We are grateful to those who gave their permission to include talks that are still under copyright. Their generosity has made it possible to republish several important addresses that would not otherwise be readily available.

We have categorized the talks under different subjects to make using the book easier, especially for preparing talks and lessons. Under each subject, the talks are arranged chronologically, from earliest to latest. For purposes of clarity and consistency, we have occasionally modified paragraphing, capitalization, spelling, punctuation, and the style used in the citation of scriptures and other sources. If a talk was originally published with subheads, we have left those subheads in place.

We thank those at Deseret Book Company who have helped to turn this collection into a finished book: Sheri Dew, Jana Erickson, Michael Morris, Tom Hewitson, and Kent Minson. Their "behind the scenes" work has been truly invaluable.

We hope you enjoy *Best-Loved Talks of the LDS People*.

ADVERSITY

❧ ❧

TRAGEDY OR DESTINY?

SPENCER W. KIMBALL

In "Tragedy or Destiny?" given to students at Brigham Young University on December 5, 1955, Elder Spencer W. Kimball, then a member of the Quorum of the Twelve, spoke of the trials of mortality and of our feeble attempts to make sense of them. His audience may not have fully realized the adversity he had experienced personally, including heart disease that often threatened his life. Had they done so, his words would have acquired an added poignancy: "The Lord is omnipotent, with all power to control our lives, save us pain, prevent all accidents, drive all planes and cars, feed us, protect us, save us from labor, effort, sickness, even from death, if he will. But he will not. . . . Is there not wisdom in his giving us trials that we might rise above them, responsibilities that we might achieve, work to harden our muscles, sorrows to try our souls? Are we not exposed to temptations to test our strength, sickness that we might learn patience, death that we might be immortalized and glorified?"

The daily newspaper screamed the headlines: "Plane Crash Kills 43. No Survivors of Mountain Tragedy," and thousands of voices joined in a chorus: "Why did the Lord let this terrible thing happen?"

Two automobiles crashed when one went through a red light, and six people were killed. Why would God not prevent this?

Why should the young mother die of cancer and leave her eight children motherless? Why did not the Lord heal her?

A little child was drowned; another was run over. Why?

A man died one day suddenly of a coronary occlusion as he climbed a stairway. His body was found slumped on the floor. His wife cried out in agony, "Why? Why would the Lord do this to me? Could he not have considered my three little children who still need a father?"

A young man died in the mission field and people critically questioned: "Why did not the Lord protect this youth while he was doing proselyting work?"

I wish I could answer these questions with authority, but I cannot. I am sure that sometime we'll understand and be reconciled. But for the present we must seek understanding as best we can in the gospel principles.

Was it the Lord who directed the plane into the mountain to snuff out the lives of its occupants, or were there mechanical faults or human errors?

Did our Father in Heaven cause the collision of the cars that took six people into eternity, or was it the error of the driver who ignored safety rules?

Did God take the life of the young mother or prompt the child to toddle into the canal or guide the other child into the path of the oncoming car?

Did the Lord cause the man to suffer a heart attack? Was the death of the missionary untimely? Answer, if you can. I cannot, for though I know God has a major role in our lives, I do not know how much he causes to happen and how much he merely permits. Whatever the answer to this question, there is another I feel sure about.

Could the Lord have prevented these tragedies? The answer is, Yes. The Lord is omnipotent, with all power to control our lives, save us pain, prevent all accidents, drive all planes and cars, feed us, protect us, save us from labor, effort, sickness, even from death, if he will. But he will not.

We should be able to understand this, because we can realize how unwise it would be for us to shield our children from all effort, from disappointments, temptations, sorrows, and suffering.

The basic gospel law is free agency and eternal development. To force us to be careful or righteous would be to nullify that fundamental law and make growth impossible.

> And the Lord spake unto Adam, saying: Inasmuch as thy children are conceived in sin, even so when they begin to grow up, sin conceiveth in their hearts, and they taste the bitter, that they may know to prize the good.
>
> And it is given unto them to know good from evil; wherefore they are agents unto themselves. . . . (Moses 6:55–56.)

> . . . Satan rebelled against me, and sought to destroy the agency of man, which I, the Lord God, had given him. (Moses 4:3.)

If we looked at mortality as the whole of existence, then pain, sorrow, failure, and short life would be calamity. But if we look upon life as an eternal thing stretching far into the premortal past and on into the eternal post-death future, then all happenings may be put in proper perspective.

Is there not wisdom in his giving us trials that we might rise above them, responsibilities that we might achieve, work to harden our muscles, sorrows to try our souls? Are we not exposed to temptations to test our strength, sickness that we might learn patience, death that we might be immortalized and glorified?

If all the sick for whom we pray were healed, if all the righteous were protected and the wicked destroyed, the whole program of the Father would be annulled and the basic principle of the gospel, free agency, would be ended. No man would have to live by faith.

If joy and peace and rewards were instantaneously given the

doer of good, there could be no evil—all would do good but not because of the rightness of doing good. There would be no test of strength, no development of character, no growth of powers, no free agency, only satanic controls.

Should all prayers be immediately answered according to our selfish desires and our limited understanding, then there would be little or no suffering, sorrow, disappointment, or even death, and if these were not, there would also be no joy, success, resurrection, nor eternal life and godhood.

> For it must needs be, that there is an opposition in all things . . . righteousness . . . wickedness . . . holiness . . . misery . . . good . . . bad. . . . (2 Nephi 2:11.)

Being human, we would expel from our lives physical pain and mental anguish and assure ourselves of continual ease and comfort, but if we were to close the doors upon sorrow and distress, we might be excluding our greatest friends and benefactors. Suffering can make saints of people as they learn patience, long-suffering, and self-mastery. The sufferings of our Savior were part of his education.

> Though he were a Son, yet learned he obedience by the things which he suffered;
> And being made perfect, he became the author of eternal salvation unto all them that obey him. (Hebrews 5:8–9.)

I love the verse of "How Firm a Foundation"—

> When through the deep waters I call thee to go,
> The rivers of sorrow shall not thee o'erflow
> For I will be with thee, thy troubles to bless,
> And sanctify to thee thy deepest distress.
> —Hymns, no. 85

And Elder James E. Talmage wrote: "No pang that is suffered by man or woman upon the earth will be without its compensating effect . . . if it be met with patience."

On the other hand, these things can crush us with their mighty impact if we yield to weakness, complaining, and criticism.

No pain that we suffer, no trial that we experience is wasted. It ministers to our education, to the development of such qualities as patience, faith, fortitude and humility. All that we suffer and all that we endure, especially when we endure it patiently, builds up our characters, purifies our hearts, expands our souls, and makes us more tender and charitable, more worthy to be called the children of God . . . and it is through sorrow and suffering, toil and tribulation, that we gain the education that we come here to acquire and which will make us more like our Father and Mother in heaven. . . . (Orson F. Whitney)

There are people who are bitter as they watch loved ones suffer agonies and interminable pain and physical torture. Some would charge the Lord with unkindness, indifference, and injustice. We are so incompetent to judge!

I like also the words of these verses, the author of which I do not know:

Pain stayed so long I said to him today,
"I will not have you with me any more."
I stamped my foot and said, "Be on your way,"
And paused there, startled at the look he wore.

"I, who have been your friend," he said to me,
"I, who have been your teacher—all you know
Of understanding love, of sympathy,
And patience, I have taught you. Shall I go?"

He spoke the truth, this strange unwelcome guest;
I watched him leave, and knew that he was wise.
He left a heart grown tender in my breast,
He left a far, clear vision in my eyes.

I dried my tears, and lifted up a song—
Even for one who'd tortured me so long.

The power of the priesthood is limitless but God has wisely placed upon each of us certain limitations. I may develop priesthood power as I perfect my life, yet I am grateful that even through the priesthood I cannot heal all the sick. I might heal people who should die. I might relieve people of suffering who should suffer. I fear I would frustrate the purposes of God.

Had I limitless power, and yet limited vision and understanding, I might have saved Abinadi from the flames of fire when he was burned at the stake, and in doing so I might have irreparably damaged him. He died a martyr and went to a martyr's reward—exaltation.

I would likely have protected Paul against his woes if my power were boundless. I would surely have healed his "thorn in the flesh." And in doing so I might have foiled the Lord's program. Thrice he offered prayers, asking the Lord to remove the "thorn" from him, but the Lord did not so answer his prayers. Paul many times could have lost himself if he had been eloquent, well, handsome, and free from the things that made him humble. Paul speaks:

> And lest I should be exalted above measure through the abundance of the revelations, there was given to me a thorn in the flesh, the messenger of Satan to buffet me, lest I should be exalted above measure.
>
> And he said unto me, My grace is sufficient for thee: for my strength is made perfect in weakness. Most gladly therefore will I rather glory in my infirmities, that the power of Christ may rest upon me.
>
> Therefore I take pleasure in infirmities, in reproaches, in necessities, in persecutions, in distresses for Christ's sake: for when I am weak, then am I strong. (2 Corinthians 12:7, 9–10.)

I fear that had I been in Carthage Jail on June 27, 1844, I might have deflected the bullets that pierced the body of the Prophet and the Patriarch. I might have saved them from the sufferings and agony, but lost to them the martyr's death and reward. I am glad I did not have to make that decision.

With such uncontrolled power, I surely would have felt to

protect Christ from the agony in Gethsemane, the insults, the thorny crown, the indignities in the court, the physical injuries. I would have administered to his wounds and healed them, giving him cooling water instead of vinegar. I might have saved him from suffering and death, and lost to the world his atoning sacrifice.

I would not dare to take the responsibility of bringing back to life my loved ones. Christ himself acknowledged the difference between his will and the Father's when he prayed that the cup of suffering be taken from him; yet he added, "Nevertheless not my will, but thine, be done." (Luke 22:42.)

For the one who dies, life goes on and his free agency continues, and death, which seems to us such a calamity, could be a blessing in disguise just as well for one who is not a martyr.

Melvin J. Ballard wrote:

> I lost a son six years of age and I saw him a man in the spirit world after his death, and I saw how he had exercised his own freedom of choice and would obtain of his own will and volition a companionship, and in due time to him and all those who are worthy of it, shall come all of the blessings and sealing privileges of the house of the Lord. . . . (*Three Degrees of Glory.*)

If we say that early death is a calamity, disaster, or tragedy, would it not be saying that mortality is preferable to earlier entrance into the spirit world and to eventual salvation and exaltation? If mortality be the perfect state, then death would be a frustration, but the gospel teaches us there is no tragedy in death, but only in sin. "Blessed are the dead that die in the Lord." (D&C 63:49.)

We know so little. Our judgment is so limited. We judge the Lord's ways from our own narrow view.

I spoke at the funeral service of a young Brigham Young University student who died during World War II. There had been hundreds of thousands of young men rushed prematurely into eternity through the ravages of that war, and I made the statement that I believed this righteous youth had been called to the spirit world to preach the gospel to these deprived souls. This may not be true of all who die, but I felt it true of him.

In his vision of "The Redemption of the Dead" President Joseph F. Smith saw this very thing. He sat studying the scriptures on October 3, 1918, particularly the statements in Peter's epistle regarding the antediluvians. He writes:

> . . . As I pondered over these things which are written, the eyes of my understanding were opened, and the Spirit of the Lord rested upon me, and I saw the hosts of the dead. . . .
>
> While this vast multitude of the righteous waited and conversed, rejoicing in the hour of their deliverance . . . the Son of God appeared, declaring liberty to the captives who had been faithful, and there He preached to them the . . . redemption of mankind from the fall, and from individual sins on conditions of repentance. But unto the wicked he did not go, and among the ungodly and the unrepentant who had defiled themselves while in the flesh, His voice was not raised, neither did the rebellious who rejected the testimonies and the warnings of the ancient prophets behold his presence, nor look upon his face. . . .
>
> And as I wondered . . . I perceived that the Lord went not in person among the wicked and the disobedient who had rejected the truth . . . but behold, from among the righteous He organized his forces . . . and commissioned them to go forth and carry the light of the gospel. . . .
>
> . . . our Redeemer spent His time . . . in the world of spirits, instructing and preparing the faithful spirits . . . who had testified of Him in the flesh, that they might carry the message of redemption unto all the dead unto whom He could not go personally because of their rebellion and transgression.
> . . .
>
> Among the great and mighty ones who were assembled in this vast congregation of the righteous were Father Adam . . . Eve, with many of her faithful daughters . . . Abel, the first martyr . . . Seth, . . . Noah, . . . Shem, the great High Priest; Abraham, . . . Isaac, Jacob, and Moses . . . Ezekiel, . . .

Daniel. . . . All these and many more, even the prophets who dwelt among the Nephites. . . . The Prophet Joseph Smith, and my father, Hyrum Smith, Brigham Young, . . . and other choice spirits . . . in the spirit world. I observed that they were also among the noble and great ones who were chosen in the beginning to be rulers in the Church of God. . . .

I beheld that the faithful elders of this dispensation, when they depart from mortal life, continue their labors in the preaching of the gospel of repentance and redemption. (Joseph F. Smith, *Gospel Doctrine*, 472–76.)

Death, then, may be the opening of the door to opportunities, including that of teaching the gospel of Christ. There is no greater work.

Despite the fact that death opens new doors, we do not seek it. We are admonished to pray for those who are ill and use our priesthood power to heal them.

And the elders of the church, two or more, shall be called, and shall pray for and lay their hands upon them in my name; and if they die they shall die unto me, and if they live they shall live unto me.

Thou shalt live together in love, insomuch that thou shalt weep for the loss of them that die, and more especially for those that have not hope of a glorious resurrection.

And it shall come to pass that those that die in me shall not taste of death, for it shall be sweet unto them;

And they that die not in me, wo unto them, for their death is bitter.

And again, it shall come to pass that he that hath faith in me to be healed, and is not appointed unto death, shall be healed. (D&C 42:44–48.)

We are assured by the Lord that the sick will be healed if the ordinance is performed, if there is sufficient faith, and if the ill one is "not appointed unto death." But there are three factors, all of which should be satisfied. Many do not comply with the ordinances, and great numbers are unwilling or incapable of exercising sufficient faith. But the other factor also looms important: If they are not appointed unto death.

Everyone must die. Death is an important part of life. Of course, we are never quite ready for the change. Not knowing when it should come, we properly fight to retain our life. Yet we ought not be afraid of death. We pray for the sick, we administer to the afflicted, we implore the Lord to heal and reduce pain and save life and postpone death, and properly so, but not because eternity is so frightful.

The Prophet Joseph Smith confirmed:

> The Lord takes many away even in infancy, that they may escape the envy of man and the sorrows and evils of this present world; they were too pure, too lovely, to live on this earth. Therefore, if rightly considered, instead of mourning we have reason to rejoice as they are delivered from evil and we shall have them again. The only difference between the old and the young dying is, one lives longer in heaven and eternal light and glory than the other, and is freed a little sooner from this miserable world.

Just as Ecclesiastes (3:2) says, I am confident that there is a time to die, but I believe also that many people die before "their time" because they are careless, abuse their bodies, take unnecessary chances, or expose themselves to hazards, accidents, and sickness.

Of the antediluvians, we read:

> Hast thou marked the old way which wicked men have trodden?
>
> Which were cut down out of time, whose foundation was overflown with a flood. (Job 22:15–16.)

In Ecclesiastes 7:17 we find this statement:

> Be not over much wicked, neither be thou foolish: why shouldest thou die before thy time?

I believe we may die prematurely but seldom exceed our time

very much. One exception was Hezekiah, 25-year-old king of Judah who was far more godly than his successors or predecessors.

> In those days was Hezekiah sick unto death. And the prophet Isaiah . . . came to him, and said unto him, Thus saith the Lord, Set thine house in order; for thou shalt die, and not live.

Hezekiah, loving life as we do, turned his face to the wall and wept bitterly, saying:

> . . . Remember now how I have walked before thee in truth and with a perfect heart, and have done that which is good in thy sight. . . .

The Lord yielded unto his prayers.

> . . . I have heard thy prayer, I have seen thy tears: behold I will heal thee. . . .
> And I will add unto thy days fifteen years; and I will deliver thee and this city out of the hand of the king of Assyria. . . . (2 Kings 20:1, 3, 5–6.)

A modern illustration of this exceptional extension of life took place in November 1881.

My uncle, David Patten Kimball, left his home in Arizona on a trip across the Salt River desert. He had fixed up his books and settled accounts and had told his wife of a premonition that he would not return. He was lost on the desert for two days and three nights, suffering untold agonies of thirst and pain. He passed into the spirit world and described later, in a letter of January 8, 1882, to his sister, what happened there. He had seen his parents. "My father . . . told me I could remain there if I chose to do so, but I pled with him that I might stay with my family long enough to make them comfortable, to repent of my sins, and more fully pre-pare myself for the change. Had it not been for this, I never should have returned home, except as a corpse. Father finally told me I could remain two years and to do all the good I could during that time, after which he would come for me. . . . He mentioned four others that he would come for also. . . ." Two years to the day from that experience on the desert he died easily and apparently without pain. Shortly before he died he looked up and called, "Father, Father." Within approximately a year of his death the other four men named were also dead.

God has many times preserved the lives of his servants until they could complete their work—Abinadi, Enoch, the sons of Helaman, and Paul.

And God will sometimes use his power over death to protect us. Heber C. Kimball was subjected to a test which, like the one given Abraham, was well-nigh unthinkable. Comfortless and in great perplexity he importuned the Prophet Joseph to inquire of the Lord, and the Prophet received this revelation: "Tell him to go and do as he has been commanded, and if I see that there is any danger of his apostatizing, I will take him to myself." (Orson F. Whitney, *Life of Heber C. Kimball*.)

God controls our lives, guides and blesses us, but gives us our agency. We may live our lives in accordance with his plan for us or we may foolishly shorten or terminate them.

I am positive in my mind that the Lord has planned our destiny. Sometime we'll understand fully, and when we see back from the vantage point of the future, we shall be satisfied with many of the happenings of this life that are so difficult for us to comprehend.

We sometimes think we would like to know what lies ahead, but sober thought brings us back to accepting life a day at a time and magnifying and glorifying that day. Sister Ida Allredge gave us a thought-provoking verse:

I cannot know the future, nor the path I shall have trod,
But by that inward vision, which points the way to God.
I would not glimpse the beauty or joy for me in store,
Lest patience ne'er restrain me from thrusting wide the door.

I would not part the curtains or cast aside the veil,
Else sorrows that await me might make my courage fail;
I'd rather live not knowing, just doing my small mite;
I'd rather walk by faith with God, than try alone the light.

We knew before we were born that we were coming to the earth for bodies and experience and that we would have joys and sorrows, ease and pain, comforts and hardships, health and sickness, successes and disappointments, and we knew also that after a period of life we would die. We accepted all these eventualities with a glad heart, eager to accept both the favorable and unfavorable. We eagerly accepted the chance to come earthward even though it might be for only a day or a year. Perhaps we were not so much concerned whether we should die of disease, of accident, or of senility. We were willing to take life as it came and as we might organize and control it, and this without murmur, complaint, or unreasonable demands.

In the face of apparent tragedy we must put our trust in God, knowing that despite our limited view his purposes will not fail. With all its troubles life offers us the tremendous privilege to grow in knowledge and wisdom, faith and works, preparing to return and share God's glory.

BYU Speeches of the Year, December 6, 1955.

~&e &~

GOD IS THE GARDENER

HUGH B. BROWN

Elder Hugh B. Brown first told the story of the gardener and the currant bush in the form of a parable in the *Improvement Era,* July 1943. This version of the talk was given at a graduation exercise at Brigham Young University on May 31, 1968. Elder Brown prefaced his address by saying, with his characteristic humor, "It is indeed a daring, if not a reckless venture, for an octogenarian to undertake to speak across a void of sixty years to a group of vibrant young students who are graduating. But knowing of your four years of training, especially in patience and endurance in your classes, I think you'll have some sympathy for me if I attempt to address you from the far side of life."

I want to speak about humor for just a minute. Golden Kimball is reported to have said that "the Lord himself must like a joke or he wouldn't have made some of you people." I hope none of you will take that personally. . . .

Now I'd like to bring to your attention one of the oldest subjects known to man, timeless in interest, always up-to-date, and imperative in its appeal. It is a subject on which the Savior spent much time, one with which philosophers have wrestled and on which scientists have ventured great, learned, and thoughtful opinions. From the beginning of time right down to this space and atomic age, this has been a lively subject, imperative in its demands. It is a topic vitally important to each and all of us from the time we enter this world until we leave it, and then on throughout eternity. The subject I wish to discuss, briefly but reverently, is God and man's relationship to Him.

In the tenth chapter of Luke we read, "Thou shalt love the Lord thy God with all thy heart, and with all thy soul, and with all thy strength, and with all thy mind." (v. 27.) Can a man love God with his mind, or is the mind limited to those cold processes of reasoning only?

You young men and women have already begun to study and to marvel at the wonders of your universe. Your maturing and inquiring minds have caused you to ask, "Who was in control when all this was set in motion?" I would rather you'd find a reverent and truthful answer to that question than to be able to read in Greek and Hebrew or to read the planet's or nature's story in stone and earth and plant. In other words, I would have you put first things first and begin your education at the center of your heart.

As these convictions grow, you will hunger and thirst after knowledge, even as a plant thirsts for water. You'll come to realize that all the knowledge which is obtainable in the best universities, without some underlying synthesis or some understandable meaning and purpose, without these it would be incomplete and wholly inadequate. I'm pleading for you to take note of the underlying truths having to do with our universe, with our lives, and with our purpose in life, and then to live as though we believe what we say when we say we believe in God.

Jesus said that if you'd have life eternal, you must know God. As we progressively come to know Him, we'll be prompted to emulate Him, and that's the thing I'd like to leave with this graduating class and call to the attention of all of us—that as we progressively come to know God, we will undeniably and constantly be reminded of the possibility of our emulating Him and thereby becoming more like Him.

I was in Colorado Springs recently. A guest of the Air Force

Academy and a speaker to the cadets, I was taken by the commanding officer on a tour of the facility and the campus there. We came to a wonderful monument, topped by a falcon with spreading wings. On the base of this monument I read these words: "Man's flight through life is sustained by the power of his knowledge." And I asked myself the question, "What knowledge? Which phase of knowledge, which branch of learning, will most definitely and inspiringly take care of man's flight through life?"

I concluded that man's life and his flight through life are sustained most by a knowledge of God and of man. I submit to you that faith in a personal God, one who can be referred to as Father, gives one a sense of dignity and holds before one an ideal toward which to strive. He is real, as you and I are real. And I want to impress that on the minds of you young students as you go out into the world—that you have someone greater than yourself dwelling with you and on whom you can call.

In the story of the Creation, these words are recorded in Genesis, "So God created man in his own image, in the image of God created he him; male and female created he them." (Genesis 1:27.) It was doubtless this thought of man being in God's image, in a godlike status, that prompted the Apostle John to say, "Now are we the sons of God, and it doth not yet appear what we shall be: but we know that, when he shall appear, we shall be like him; for we shall see him as he is." (1 John 3:2.) Across the centuries, no experience has been more universal and helpful in the sense of someone caring for us, near enough to be called upon, responsive enough to understand. He is real and He is personal and should be idealized but also realized. We must not only possess the idea of God, but we should be possessed by it. Men do not believe in God because they have proved Him. Rather they try endlessly to prove Him because they can't help believing in Him. He has established that in the hearts of His children. . . .

Now you have been taught, young people, to believe that God

and man belong to a society of eternal intelligences. Differences exist, of course, indescribably great, but more of degree rather than of kind. The idea of a supreme being is indelibly stamped on the inner-consciousness of men. Though man is to some extent master of his destiny, he is conscious of the supreme source of his existence.

Dr. James E. Talmage sums up the discussion of creation and the universe as follows: "What is man in this boundless setting of sublime splendor? I answer you, potentially now, but actually to be, man is greater and grander, more precious in the arithmetic of God than all the planets and suns of space. For him they were created."

I'm reading this because I'd like you to feel the dignity of man. . . . In this world, man is given dominion over a few things; it is his privilege to achieve supremacy over many things. The heavens declare the glory of God, and the firmament shows his handiwork, incomprehensibly grand as are the physical creations of the earth and space. They have been brought into existence as a means to an end, necessary to the realization of the supreme purpose, which in the words of the Creator is thus declared, "Behold, this is my work and my glory—to bring to pass the immortality and eternal life of man." (Moses 1:39.)

Some theologians tell us that God is incomprehensible. But He says that to know Him is life eternal. The one view takes hope out of life, the other is an eternal beacon. Sometimes young people say we older ones are behind the times, and they're probably right. They're certainly right. But, during the time that is behind me— and I bring this to you as a testimony—during the time that is behind me, I have developed a faith in a personal, living God, which I consider to be the most priceless possession.

It has been my glorious privilege, progressively, to know Him. Such faith gives order, meaning, stimulus, and direction to life. We cannot know Him by the intellect alone nor with bodily senses alone nor by only reading scripture, but by inspiration, the illumination of the soul, such as was experienced by Peter when he replied to the question of Christ, "Whom say ye that I am?" And he said, without hesitation, though it was a surprise to him what he said, "Thou art the Christ, the Son of the Living God." And Christ replied to him, "Flesh and blood hath not revealed it unto thee, but my Father which is in Heaven." (Matthew 16:15–17.)

If you'll always keep in mind that you are actually the children of your Heavenly Father, that there is something of Him in you, that you may aspire to become something like that from which you came, and to cooperate with Him in the unfinished work of creation, you will remember that His plan for the salvation of His children has purpose behind it—a design to be carried out. If you keep these great truths in mind, you'll be fortified and sustained, whatever life may hold for you.

It is important not only that you keep growing but also that you be versatile, adaptive, and unafraid to venture. In other words, be up-to-date. Seek to obtain a certain flexibility of mind, which will inspire you to listen, to learn, and to adapt as you move forward into a new and ever-expanding universe. Of the cowardice that shrinks from new truths, someone has said, "From the laziness that is content with half-truth, from the arrogance that thinks it knows all the truth, Oh, God of Truth, deliver us!" In the process of self-discovery you will sometimes stand amazed at what you've progressively become aware of, having to do with your potential range and your abilities. You will not then be discouraged by a failure or two along the way, as long as you are learning and growing. I leave with you my humble testimony in respect to these things.

Now some of you as you go forward are going to meet with disappointment, perhaps many disappointments, some of them crucial. Sometimes you will wonder whether God has forgotten you. Sometimes you may even wonder if He lives and where He has gone. But in these times when so many are saying God is dead, and where so many are denying His existence, I think I could not leave with you a better message than this: God is aware of you individually. He knows who you are and what you are, and, furthermore, He knows what you are capable of becoming. Be not discouraged then, if you do not get all the things you want just when you want them. Have the courage to go on and face your life and if necessary reverse it to bring it into harmony with His law.

Could I tell you just a quick story out of my own experience in life? Sixty-odd years ago, I was on a farm in Canada. I had purchased the farm from another who had been somewhat careless in keeping it up, and I went out one morning and found a currant bush, at least six feet high. I knew that it was going all to wood; there was no sign of blossom or of fruit. I had had some experience in pruning trees before we left Salt Lake to go to Canada, as my father had a fruit farm. So I got my pruning shears and went to work on the currant bush, and I clipped it and cut it and cut it down until there was nothing left but a little clump of stumps. And as I looked at them, I yielded to an impulse, which I often have, to talk with inanimate things and have them talk to me. It's a ridiculous habit, one I can't overcome.

As I looked at this little clump of bushes, stumps, there seemed to be a tear on each one, and I said, "What's the matter, currant bush? What are you crying about?"

And I thought I heard that currant bush speak. It seemed to say, "How could you do this to me? I was making such wonderful growth. I was almost as large as the fruit tree and the shade tree, and now you've cut me down. And all in the garden will look upon me with contempt and pity. How could you do it? I thought you were the gardener here."

I thought I heard that from the currant bush. I thought it so much that I answered it. I said, "Look, little currant bush, I *am* the gardener here, and I know what I want you to be. If I let you go the way you want to go, you'll never amount to anything. But, someday, when you are laden with fruit, you're going to think back and say, 'Thank you, Mr. Gardener, for cutting me down, for loving me enough to hurt me.'"

Ten years passed, and I found myself in Europe. I had made some progress in the First World War in the Canadian Army. In fact I was a field officer, and there was only one man between me and the rank of general, which I had cherished in my heart for years. Then he became a casualty. And the day after, I received a telegram from London. General Turner, in charge of all Canadian officers, said, "Be in my office tomorrow morning at ten o'clock."

I puffed up. I called my special servant. (We called them "Batmen" over there.) I said, "Polish my boots and my buttons. Make me look like a general because I'm going up tomorrow to be appointed." He did the best he could with what he had to work on, and I went to London.

I walked into the office of the general. I saluted him smartly, and he replied to my salute, as higher officers usually do to juniors: sort of a "Get out of the way, worm." Then he said, "Sit down, Brown." I was deflated. I sat down. And he said, "Brown, you're entitled to this promotion, but I cannot make it. You've qualified, passed the regulations, you've had the experience, you're entitled to it in every way, but I cannot make this appointment." Just then he went into the other room to answer a phone call, and I did what most every officer and man in the army would do under those circumstances: I looked over on his desk to see what my personal history sheet showed. And I saw written on the bottom of that history sheet in large, capital letters, "THIS MAN IS A MORMON."

Now at that time, we were hated heartily in Britain, and I knew why he couldn't make the appointment. Finally he came back and said, "That's all, Brown." I saluted him, less heartily than before, and went out.

On my way back to Shorencliff, a hundred and twenty miles away, I thought every turn of the wheel that clacked across the rails was saying, "You're a failure. You must go home and be called a coward by those who do not understand." And bitterness rose in my heart until when I arrived, finally, in my tent, I rather vigorously threw my cap on the cot, together with my Sam Brown belt. I clenched my fist, and I shook it at heaven, and I said, "How could you do this to me, God? I've done everything that I knew how to do to uphold the standards of the Church. I was making such wonderful growth and now you've cut me down. How could you do it?"

And then I heard a voice. It sounded like my own voice, and the voice said, "I'm the gardener here, I know what I want you to be. If I let you go the way you want to go, you'll never amount to anything. And, someday, when you are ripened in life, you're going to shout back across the time, and say, 'Thank you, Mr. Gardener, for cutting me down, for loving me enough to hurt me.'"

But those words, which I recognize now as my words to the currant bush, which had become God's word to me, drove me to my knees, where I prayed for forgiveness for my arrogance and my ambition.

As I was praying there I heard some Mormon boys in an adjoining tent singing the closing number to an M.I.A. session, which I usually attended with them. And I recognized these words, which all of you have memorized: "It may not be on the mountain height or over the stormy sea; It may not be at the battle's front my Lord will have need of me; . . . So trusting my all to thy tender care, and knowing thou lovest me, I'll do thy will with a heart sincere; I'll be what you want me to be."

My young friends and brothers and sisters, will you remember that little experience, which changed my whole life? Had the Gardener not taken control and done for me what was best for me, or if I had gone the way I wanted to go, I would have returned to Canada as a senior commanding officer of Western Canada. I would have raised my family in a barracks. My six daughters would have had little chance to marry in the Church. I myself would probably have gone down and down; I do not know what might have happened. But this I know, and this I say to you and to Him in your presence, looking back over sixty years, "Thank you, Mr. Gardener, for cutting me down."

Now I leave with you my testimony, and I received this testimony from the same source which Jesus said inspired Peter, when the chief Apostle said, "Thou art the Christ!" Whatever undertakings may demand of you and your attention, I tell you, young men, young women, you cannot make a better resolution today than this: "I am going to keep close to the Lord. I am going to understand Him better, and understanding Him, I will understand myself and will try to put my life into harmony with His." For I have come to know that every man, every woman, has potential godhood dwelling in him or her, for God is in reality the Father of us all.

I leave you my blessing: God bless these young people. They're looking forward hopefully and gleefully to the experiences of life. Oh, Father, be with and sustain them, uphold them, deepen their testimonies, keep them true to the faith and true to themselves. Father, bless them that they may live up to the best traditions of our country and be proud of the fact that they graduated from a Church-owned and -operated school where they were taught these precious truths concerning the purpose of their life and their relationship to Deity, I pray in the name of Jesus Christ, amen.

From a transcript of a tape recording of the address.

AN ANCHOR TO THE
SOULS OF MEN

HOWARD W. HUNTER

Howard W. Hunter was serving as president of the Quorum of the Twelve Apostles when he delivered this talk on February 7, 1993, at a nineteen-stake fireside at Brigham Young University. President Hunter had just stood to begin his speech when an assailant leaped onto the stage, claiming to have a bomb and threatening those present. President Hunter responded with courage and coolness while BYU security officers subdued the assailant. Then he calmly began his address, noting as he said the first line, "Life has a fair number of challenges in it—as demonstrated!"

Life has a fair number of challenges in it, and that's true of life in the 1990s. Indeed, you may be feeling that you have more than your share of problems. These concerns may be global difficulties, such as the devastating famine we see in Africa and other places in the world, or the incessant sounds of war in the former Yugoslavia, or the Middle East, or India, or Ireland, or so many other locations round the world. Unfortunately, some of these wars have religious or ethnic overtones, and that makes them even more tragic, if that is possible.

These past few years, we have seen our fair share of economic difficulties and recession in every nation. Sometimes those economic challenges get translated into very immediate problems for college students and those trying to earn a living, and perhaps start a family, in their early adult years.

Years ago there was a popular music group formed at Brigham
Young University named the Three D's. They took that name from
their three singers' first names. My fear is that if in the nineties our
young people were to form a popular singing group, they might still
call themselves the Three D's, but that could be for Despair,
Doom, and Discouragement.

Despair, Doom, and Discouragement are not acceptable views
of life for a Latter-day Saint. However high on the charts they are
on the hit parade of contemporary news, we must not walk on our
lower lip every time a few difficult moments happen to confront
us.

I am just a couple of years older than most of you, and in those
few extra months I have seen a bit more of life than you have. I
want you to know that there have always been some difficulties in
mortal life, and there always will be. But knowing what we know,
and living as we are supposed to live, there really is no place, no
excuse, for pessimism and despair.

In my lifetime I have seen two world wars, plus Korea, plus
Vietnam and all that you are currently witnessing. I have worked
my way through the Depression and managed to go to law school
while starting a young family at the same time. I have seen stock
markets and world economics go crazy, and I have seen a few
despots and tyrants go crazy, all of which caused quite a bit of
trouble around the world in the process.

So I hope you won't believe all the world's difficulties have
been wedged into your decade, or that things have never been
worse than they are for you personally, or that they will never get
better. I reassure you that things have been worse and they *will*
always get better. They always do—especially when we live and
love the gospel of Jesus Christ and give it a chance to flourish in
our lives.

Here are some actual comments that have been passed on to
me in recent months:

This comes from a fine returned missionary: "Why should I date and get serious with a girl? I am not sure I even want to marry and bring a family into this kind of world. I am not very sure about my own future. How can I take the responsibility for the future of others whom I would love and care about and want to be happy?"

Here's another from a high school student: "I hope I die before all these terrible things happen that people are talking about. I don't want to be on the earth when there is so much trouble."

This from a recent college graduate: "I am doing the best I can, but I wonder if there is much reason to even plan for the future, let alone retirement. The world probably won't last that long anyway."

Well, my, my, my. Isn't that a fine view of things? Sounds like we all ought to go eat a big plate of worms.

Contrary to what some might say, you have every reason in this world to be happy and to be optimistic and to be confident. Every generation since time began has had some things to overcome and some problems to work out. Furthermore, every individual person has a particular set of challenges that sometimes seem to be earmarked for us personally. We understood that in our premortal existence.

Prophets and apostles of the Church have faced some of those personal difficulties. I acknowledge that I have faced a few, and you will undoubtedly face some of your own now and later in your life. When these experiences humble us and refine us and teach us and bless us, they can be powerful instruments in the hands of God to make us better people, to make us more grateful, more loving, and more considerate of other people in their own times of difficulty.

Yes, we all have difficult moments, individually and collectively, but even in the most severe of times, anciently or in modern times, those problems and prophecies were never intended to do anything but bless the righteous and help those who are less righteous move toward repentance. God loves us, and the scriptures tell us he "gave his only begotten Son, that whosoever believeth in him should not perish, but have everlasting life. For God sent not his Son into the world to condemn the world; but that the world through him might be saved." (John 3:16–17.)

The scriptures also indicate that there will be seasons of time when the whole world will have some difficulty. We know that in our dispensation, unrighteousness will, unfortunately, be quite evident, and it will bring its inevitable difficulties and pain and punishment. God will cut short that unrighteousness in his own due time, but our task is to live fully and faithfully and not worry ourselves sick about the woes of the world or when it will end. Our task is to have the gospel in our lives and to be a bright light, a city set on the hill, that reflects the beauty of the gospel of Jesus Christ and the joy and happiness that will always come to every people in every age who keep the commandments.

In this last dispensation there will be great tribulation. We know that there will be wars and rumors of wars and that the whole earth will be in commotion. All dispensations have had their perilous times, but our day will include genuine peril. Evil men will flourish, but then evil men have very often flourished. Calamities will come and iniquity will abound. (See Matthew 24:21; D&C 45:26–27; 2 Timothy 3:1, 13.)

Inevitably the natural result of some of these kinds of prophecies is fear, and that is not fear limited to a younger generation. It is fear shared by those of any age who don't understand what we understand.

But I want to stress that these feelings are not necessary for faithful Latter-day Saints, and they do not come from God. To ancient Israel, the great Jehovah said: "Be strong and of a good courage, fear not, nor be afraid of them: for the Lord thy God, he it is that doth go with thee; he will not fail thee, nor forsake thee. . . . And the Lord, he it is that doth go before thee; he will be with thee, he will not fail thee, neither forsake thee: fear not, neither be dismayed." (Deuteronomy 31:6, 8.)

And to the Saints in modern Israel, the Lord has given this wonderful reassurance: "Fear not, little children, for you are mine, and I have overcome the world, and you are of them that my Father hath given me." (D&C 50:41.) "Verily I say unto you my friends, fear not, let your hearts be comforted; yea, rejoice evermore, and in everything give thanks." (D&C 98:1.)

In light of such counsel, I think it is incumbent upon us to rejoice a little more and despair a little less, to give thanks for what we have and for the magnitude of God's blessings to us, and to talk a little less about what we may not have or what anxiety may accompany difficult times in this or any generation.

For Latter-day Saints this is a time of great hope and excitement—one of the greatest eras in the Restoration and therefore one of the greatest eras in any dispensation, inasmuch as ours is the greatest of all dispensations. We need to have faith and hope, two of the great fundamental virtues of any discipleship of Christ. We must continue to exercise confidence in God, inasmuch as that is the first principle in our code of belief. We must believe that God has all power, that he loves us, and that his work will not be stopped or frustrated in our individual lives or in the world generally. He will bless us as a people because he always has blessed us as a people. He will bless us as individuals because he always has blessed us as individuals.

Listen to this marvelous counsel given by President Joseph F. Smith nearly ninety years ago. It sounds as if people in that day might have been a little anxious about their future as well. I quote:

"You do not need to worry in the least, the Lord will take care of you and bless you. He will also take care of His servants, and will bless them and help them to accomplish His purposes; and all the powers of darkness combined in earth and in hell cannot prevent it. . . . He has stretched forth His hand to accomplish his purposes,

and the arm of flesh cannot stay it. He will cut His work short in
righteousness, and will hasten His purposes in His own time. It is
only necessary for us to try with our might to keep pace with the
onward progress of the work of the Lord, then God will preserve
and protect us, and will prepare the way before us, that we shall
live and multiply and replenish the earth and always do His will."
(Conference Report, October 1905, 5–6.)

More recently, Elder Marion G. Romney, then of the Quorum
of the Twelve, counseled the Church in 1966, when the world also
knew some difficulty. An American president had been assassinated, communism was alive and menacing, and a war was beginning to widen in Southeast Asia. My sons had some of the same
anxieties young adults today have about life and marriage and the
future. Here's what President Romney said then:

"Naturally, believing Christians, even those who have a
mature faith in the gospel, are concerned and disturbed by the low-
ering clouds on the horizon. But they need not be surprised or fran-
tic about their portent, for, as has already been said, at the very
beginning of this last dispensation the Lord made it abundantly
clear that through the tribulations and calamity that he foresaw
and foretold and that we now see coming upon us, there would be
a people who, through acceptance and obedience to the gospel,
would be able to recognize and resist the powers of evil, build up
the promised Zion, and prepare to meet the Christ and be with
him in the blessed millennium. And we know further that it is possible for every one of us, who will, to have a place among those
people. It is this assurance and this expectation that give us understanding of the Lord's admonition, 'Be not troubled.'" (Conference
Report, October 1966, 53–54.)

Let me offer a third example from yet another moment of difficulty in the world. In the midst of the most devastating international conflagration the modern world has ever seen, Elder John
A. Widtsoe of the Council of the Twelve counseled people who

were worried. Nazism was on the march, there was war in the Pacific, and nation after nation seemed to be drawn into war. This is what Brother Widtsoe said in 1942:

"Above the roar of cannon and airplane, the maneuvers and plans of men, the Lord always determines the tide of battle. So far and no farther does He permit the evil one to go in his career to create human misery. The Lord is ever victorious; He is the Master to whose will Satan is subject. Though all hell may rage, and men may follow evil, the purposes of the Lord will not fail." (Conference Report, April 1942, 34.)

I promise you in the name of the Lord whose servant I am that God will always protect and care for his people. We will have our difficulties the way every generation and people have had difficulties. But with the gospel of Jesus Christ, you have every hope and promise and reassurance. The Lord has power over his Saints and will always prepare places of peace, defense, and safety for his people. When we have faith in God, we can hope for a better world—for us personally, and for all mankind. The prophet Ether taught anciently (and he knew something about troubles): "Wherefore, whoso believeth in God might with surety hope for a better world, yea, even a place at the right hand of God, which hope cometh of faith, maketh an anchor to the souls of men, which would make them sure and steadfast, always abounding in good works, being led to glorify God." (Ether 12:4.)

Disciples of Christ in every generation are invited, indeed commanded, to be filled with a perfect brightness of hope. (See 2 Nephi 31:20.)

This faith and hope of which I speak is not a Pollyanna-like approach to significant personal and public problems. I don't believe we can wake up in the morning and simply by drawing a big "happy face" on the chalkboard believe that is going to take care of the world's difficulties. But if our faith and hope are anchored in Christ, in his teachings, commandments, and promises, then we are able to count on something truly remark-able, genuinely miraculous, which can part the Red Sea and lead modern Israel to a place "where none shall come to hurt or make afraid." (*Hymns*, no. 30.) Fear, which can come upon people in dif-ficult days, is a principal weapon in the arsenal Satan uses to make mankind unhappy. He who fears loses strength for the combat of life in the fight against evil. Therefore the power of the evil one always tries to generate fear in human hearts. In every age and in every era, mankind has faced fear.

As children of God and descendants of Abraham, Isaac, and Jacob, we must seek to dispel fear from among people. A timid, fearing people cannot do their work well, and they cannot do God's work at all. The Latter-day Saints have a divinely assigned mission to fulfill that simply must not be dissipated in fear and anxiety.

Elder Widtsoe said, "The key to the conquest of fear has been given through the Prophet Joseph Smith. 'If ye are prepared ye shall not fear.' (D&C 38:30.) That divine message needs repeat-ing today in every stake and ward." (Conference Report, April 1942, 33.)

Are we prepared to surrender to God's commandments? Are we prepared to achieve victory over our appetites? Are we prepared to obey righteous law? According to Elder Widtsoe, if we can hon-estly answer yes to those questions, we can bid fear to depart from our lives. Surely the degree of fear in our hearts may well be meas-ured by our preparation to live righteously—living in a way that should characterize every Latter-day Saint in every age and time.

Let me close with one of the greatest statements I have ever read from Joseph Smith, who faced such immense difficulties in his life and who, of course, paid the ultimate price for his victory. But he *was* victorious, and he was a happy, robust, optimistic man. Those who knew him felt his strength and courage, even in the darkest of times. He did not sag in spirits, or remain long in any despondency.

He said about our time that ours is the moment "upon which prophets, priests and kings [in ages past] have dwelt with peculiar delight; [all these ancient witnesses for God] have looked forward with joyful anticipation to the day in which we live; and fired with heavenly and joyful anticipations they have sung and written and prophesied of this our day; . . . we are the favored people that God has [chosen] to bring about the Latter-day glory." (*History of the Church*, 4:609–10.)

What a privilege! What an honor! What a responsibility! And what joy! We have every reason in time and eternity to rejoice and give thanks for the quality of our lives and the promises we have been given.

That We Might Have Joy, 89–96.

BOOK OF MORMON

THE BOOK OF MORMON — KEYSTONE OF OUR RELIGION

EZRA TAFT BENSON   .

Turning the hearts of Latter-day Saints to the Book of Mormon was one of the dominant themes of the presidency of Ezra Taft Benson. He focused on the Book of Mormon in several addresses and often referred to it on other occasions. Two years after giving this talk during general conference in November 1996, President Benson summarized some of his feelings for this great gift:

"Sister Benson and I have a great love for the Book of Mormon and we try to read it every day.

"The Book of Mormon is the instrument that God has designed to 'sweep the earth as with a flood, to gather out His elect unto the New Jerusalem.' (Moses 7:62.)

"This sacred volume of scripture has not been, nor is it yet, central in our preaching, our teaching, and our missionary work. We have not adequately used 'the most correct of any book on earth.'

"Presently the Book of Mormon is studied in our Sunday School and seminary classes every fourth year. This four-year pattern, however, must *not* be followed by Church members in their personal study of the standard works. All scripture is not of equal value. The book that is the 'keystone of our religion' and that will get a man 'nearer to God by abiding by its precepts, than by any other book' needs to be studied constantly. (*History of the Church*, 4:461.)

"In section 84 of the Doctrine and Covenants, the Lord declares that the whole Church and all the children of Zion are under condemnation because of the way we have treated the Book of Mormon. (Verses 54–58.) This condemnation has not been lifted, nor will it be until we repent.

"The Lord states that we must not only *say* but we must *do*. We have neither said enough nor have we done enough with this divine instrument—the key to conversion. As a result, as individuals, as families, and as the Church, we sometimes have felt the scourge and judgment God said would be 'poured out upon the children of Zion' because of our neglect of this book.

"The Lord inspired His servant Lorenzo Snow to reemphasize the principle of tithing to redeem the Church from financial bondage. In those days the General Authorities took that message to the members of the Church. So too in our day. The Lord has inspired His servants to reemphasize the Book of Mormon to get the Church and all the children of Zion out from under condemnation—the scourge and judgment. (See D&C 84:54–58.) This message must be carried to the members of the Church throughout the world.

"We invite each member of the Church to read again and again the Book of Mormon. Those who teach or speak in Church meetings should carefully and prayerfully use the Book of Mormon to strengthen and enhance their messages and presentations.

"I bless you with increased *understanding* of the Book of Mormon. I promise you that from this moment forward, if we will daily sup from its pages and abide by its precepts, God will pour out upon each child of Zion and the Church a blessing hitherto unknown. And we will plead to the Lord that He will begin to lift the condemnation—the scourge and judgment. Of this I bear solemn witness.

"I promise you that as you more diligently study modern revelation on gospel subjects, your power to teach and preach will be magnified and you will so move the cause of Zion that added numbers will enter into the house of the Lord as well as the mission field.

"I bless you with increased desire to flood the earth with the Book of Mormon, to gather out from the world the elect of God who are yearning for the truth but know not where to find it." (A *Witness and a Warning*, vii–ix.)

My beloved brethren and sisters, today I would like to speak about one of the most significant gifts given to the world in modern times. The gift I am thinking of is more important than any of the inventions that have come out of the industrial and technological revolutions. This is a gift of greater value to mankind than even the many wonderful advances we have seen in modern medicine. It is of greater worth to mankind than the development of flight or space travel. I speak of the gift of the Book of Mormon, given to mankind 156 years ago.

This gift was prepared by the hand of the Lord over a period of more than a thousand years, then hidden up by Him so that it would be preserved in its purity for our generation. Perhaps there is nothing that testifies more clearly of the importance of this modern book of scripture than what the Lord Himself has said about it.

By His own mouth He has borne witness (1) that it is true (D&C 17:6), (2) that it contains the truth and His words (D&C 19:26), (3) that it was translated by power from on high (D&C 20:8), (4) that it contains the fulness of the gospel of Jesus Christ (D&C 20:9; 42:12), (5) that it was given by inspiration and confirmed by the ministering of angels (D&C 20:10), (6) that it gives evidence that the holy scriptures are true (D&C 20:11), and (7) that those who receive it in faith shall receive eternal life (D&C 20:14).

A second powerful testimony to the importance of the Book of Mormon is to note where the Lord placed its coming forth in the timetable of the unfolding Restoration. The only thing that preceded it was the First Vision. In that marvelous manifestation, the Prophet Joseph Smith learned the true nature of God and that God had a work for him to do. The coming forth of the Book of Mormon was the next thing to follow.

Think of that in terms of what it implies. The coming forth of the Book of Mormon preceded the restoration of the priesthood. It was published just a few days before the Church was organized. The Saints were given the Book of Mormon to read before they were given the revelations outlining such great doctrines as the three degrees of glory, celestial marriage, or work for the dead. It came before priesthood quorums and Church organization. Doesn't this tell us something about how the Lord views this sacred work?

Once we realize how the Lord feels about this book, it should not surprise us that He also gives us solemn warnings about how we receive it. After indicating that those who receive the Book of Mormon with faith, working righteousness, will receive a crown of eternal glory (see D&C 20:14), the Lord follows with this warning: "But those who harden their hearts in unbelief, and reject it, it shall turn to their own condemnation." (D&C 20:15.)

In 1829, the Lord warned the Saints that they are not to trifle with sacred things (see D&C 6:12). Surely the Book of Mormon is a sacred thing, and yet many trifle with it, or in other words, take it lightly, treat it as though it is of little importance.

In 1832, as some early missionaries returned from their fields of labor, the Lord reproved them for treating the Book of Mormon lightly. As a result of that attitude, he said, their minds had been darkened. Not only had treating this sacred book lightly brought a loss of light to themselves, it had also brought the whole Church under condemnation, even all the children of Zion. And then the Lord said, "And they shall remain under this condemnation until they repent and remember the new covenant, even the Book of Mormon." (D&C 84:54–57.)

Has the fact that we have had the Book of Mormon with us for over a century and a half made it seem less significant to us today? Do we remember the new covenant, even the Book of Mormon? In the Bible we have the Old Testament and the New Testament. The word *testament* is the English rendering of a Greek word that can also be translated as *covenant*. Is this what the Lord meant when He called the Book of Mormon the "new covenant"? It is indeed another testament or witness of Jesus. This is one of the reasons why we have recently added the words "Another Testament of Jesus Christ" to the title of the Book of Mormon.

If the early Saints were rebuked for treating the Book of Mormon lightly, are we under any less condemnation if we do the same? The Lord Himself bears testimony that it is of eternal significance. Can a small number of us bring the whole Church under condemnation because we trifle with sacred things? What will we say at the Judgment when we stand before Him and meet His probing gaze if we are among those described as forgetting the new covenant?

There are three great reasons why Latter-day Saints should make the study of the Book of Mormon a lifetime pursuit.

The *first* is that the Book of Mormon is the keystone of our religion. This was the Prophet Joseph Smith's statement. He testified that "the Book of Mormon was the most correct of any book on earth, and the keystone of our religion." (Introduction to the Book of Mormon.) A keystone is the central stone in an arch. It holds all the other stones in place, and if removed, the arch crumbles.

There are three ways in which the Book of Mormon is the

keystone of our religion. It is the keystone in our witness of Christ. It is the keystone of our doctrine. It is the keystone of testimony.

The Book of Mormon is the keystone in our witness of Jesus Christ, who is Himself the cornerstone of everything we do. It bears witness of His reality with power and clarity. Unlike the Bible, which passed through generations of copyists, translators, and corrupt religionists who tampered with the text, the Book of Mormon came from writer to reader in just one inspired step of translation. Therefore, its testimony of the Master is clear, undiluted, and full of power. But it does even more. Much of the Christian world today rejects the divinity of the Savior. They question His miraculous birth, His perfect life, and the reality of His glorious resurrection. The Book of Mormon teaches in plain and unmistakable terms about the truth of all of those. It also provides the most complete explanation of the doctrine of the Atonement. Truly, this divinely inspired book is a keystone in bearing witness to the world that Jesus is the Christ (see title page of the Book of Mormon).

The Book of Mormon is also the keystone of the doctrine of the Resurrection. As mentioned before, the Lord Himself has stated that the Book of Mormon contains the "fulness of the gospel of Jesus Christ." (D&C 20:9.) That does not mean it contains every teaching, every doctrine ever revealed. Rather, it means that in the Book of Mormon we will find the fulness of those doctrines required for our salvation. And they are taught plainly and simply so that even children can learn the ways of salvation and exaltation. The Book of Mormon offers so much that broadens our understandings of the doctrines of salvation. Without it, much of what is taught in other scriptures would not be nearly so plain and precious.

Finally, the Book of Mormon is the keystone of testimony. Just as the arch crumbles if the keystone is removed, so does all the Church stand or fall with the truthfulness of the Book of Mormon.

The enemies of the Church understand this clearly. This is why they go to such great lengths to try to disprove the Book of Mormon, for if it can be discredited, the Prophet Joseph Smith goes with it. So does our claim to priesthood keys, and revelation, and the restored Church. But in like manner, if the Book of Mormon be true—and millions have now testified that they have the witness of the Spirit that it is indeed true—then one must accept the claims of the Restoration and all that accompanies it.

Yes, my beloved brothers and sisters, the Book of Mormon is the keystone of our religion—the keystone of our testimony, the keystone of our doctrine, and the keystone in the witness of our Lord and Savior.

The *second* great reason why we must make the Book of Mormon a center focus of study is that it was written for our day. The Nephites never had the book; neither did the Lamanites of ancient times. It was meant for us. Mormon wrote near the end of the Nephite civilization. Under the inspiration of God, who sees all things from the beginning, he abridged centuries of records, choosing the stories, speeches, and events that would be most helpful to us.

Each of the major writers of the Book of Mormon testified that he wrote for future generations. Nephi said: "The Lord God promised unto me that these things which I write shall be kept and preserved, and handed down unto my seed, from generation to generation." (2 Nephi 25:21.) His brother Jacob, who succeeded him, wrote similar words: "For [Nephi] said that the history of his people should be engraven upon his other plates, and that I should preserve these plates and hand them down unto my seed, from generation to generation." (Jacob 1:3.) Enos and Jarom both indicated that they too were writing not for their own peoples but for future generations (see Enos 1:15–16; Jarom 1:2).

Mormon himself said, "Yea, I speak unto you, ye remnant of the house of Israel." (Mormon 7:1.) And Moroni, the last of the inspired writers, actually saw our day and time. "Behold," he said, "the Lord hath shown unto me great and marvelous things concerning that which must shortly come, at that day when these things shall come forth among you.

"Behold, I speak unto you as if ye were present, and yet ye are not. But behold, Jesus Christ hath shown you unto me, and I know your doing." (Mormon 8:34–35.)

If they saw our day and chose those things which would be of greatest worth to us, is not that how we should study the Book of Mormon? We should constantly ask ourselves, "Why did the Lord inspire Mormon (or Moroni or Alma) to include that in his record? What lesson can I learn from that to help me live in this day and age?"

And there is example after example of how that question will be answered. For example, in the Book of Mormon we find a pattern for preparing for the Second Coming. A major portion of the book centers on the few decades just prior to Christ's coming to America. By careful study of that time period, we can determine why some were destroyed in the terrible judgments that preceded His coming and what brought others to stand at the temple in the land of Bountiful and thrust their hands into the wounds of His hands and feet.

From the Book of Mormon we learn how disciples of Christ live in times of war. From the Book of Mormon we see the evils of secret combinations portrayed in graphic and chilling reality. In the Book of Mormon we find lessons for dealing with persecution and apostasy. We learn much about how to do missionary work. And more than anywhere else, we see in the Book of Mormon the dangers of materialism and setting our hearts on the things of the world. Can anyone doubt that this book was meant for us and that in it we find great power, great comfort, and great protection?

The *third* reason why the Book of Mormon is of such value to Latter-day Saints is given in the same statement by the Prophet

Joseph Smith cited previously. He said, "I told the brethren that the Book of Mormon was the most correct of any book on earth, and the keystone of our religion, and a man would get nearer to God by abiding by its precepts, than by any other book." (*History of the Church*, 4:461.) That is the third reason for studying the book. It helps us draw nearer to God. Is there not something deep in our hearts that longs to draw nearer to God, to be more like Him in our daily walk, to feel His presence with us constantly? If so, then the Book of Mormon will help us do so more than any other book.

It is not just that the Book of Mormon teaches us truth, though it indeed does that. It is not just that the Book of Mormon bears testimony of Christ, though it indeed does that, too. But there is something more. There is a power in the book which will begin to flow into your lives the moment you begin a serious study of the book. You will find greater power to resist temptation. You will find the power to avoid deception. You will find the power to stay on the strait and narrow path. The scriptures are called "the words of life" (D&C 84:85), and nowhere is that more true than it is of the Book of Mormon. When you begin to hunger and thirst after those words, you will find life in greater and greater abundance.

Our beloved brother, President Marion G. Romney, who celebrated his eighty-ninth birthday last month and who knows of himself of the power that resides in this book, testified of the blessings that can come into the lives of those who will read and study the Book of Mormon. He said:

"I feel certain that if, in our homes, parents will read from the Book of Mormon prayerfully and regularly, both by themselves and with their children, the spirit of that great book will come to permeate our homes and all who dwell therein. The spirit of reverence will increase; mutual respect and consideration for each other will grow. The spirit of contention will depart. Parents will counsel their children in greater love and wisdom. Children will be more responsive and submissive to the counsel of their parents. Righteousness will increase. Faith, hope, and charity—the pure love of Christ—will abound in our homes and lives, bringing in their wake peace, joy, and happiness." (*Ensign*, May 1980, 67.)

These promises—increased love and harmony in the home, greater respect between parent and child, increased spirituality and righteousness—are not idle promises, but exactly what the Prophet Joseph Smith meant when he said the Book of Mormon will help us draw nearer to God.

Brethren and sisters, I implore you with all my heart that you consider with great solemnity the importance of the Book of Mormon to you personally and to the Church collectively.

Over ten years ago I made the following statement regarding the Book of Mormon:

"Do eternal consequences rest upon our response to this book? Yes, either to our blessing or our condemnation.

"Every Latter-day Saint should make the study of this book a lifetime pursuit. Otherwise he is placing his soul in jeopardy and neglecting that which could give spiritual and intellectual unity to his whole life. There is a difference between a convert who is built on the rock of Christ through the Book of Mormon and stays hold of that iron rod, and one who is not." (*Ensign*, May 1975, 65.)

I reaffirm those words to you this day. Let us not remain under condemnation, with its scourge and judgment, by treating lightly this great and marvelous gift the Lord has given to us. Rather, let us win the promises associated with treasuring it up in our hearts.

In the Doctrine and Covenants, section 84, verses 54 to 58, we read:

"And your minds in times past have been darkened because of unbelief, and because you have treated lightly the things you have received—

"Which vanity and unbelief have brought the whole church under condemnation.

"And this condemnation resteth upon the children of Zion, even all.

"And they shall remain under this condemnation until they repent and remember the new covenant, even the Book of Mormon and the former commandments which I have given them, not only to say, but to do according to that which I have written—

"That they may bring forth fruit meet for their Father's kingdom; otherwise there remaineth a scourge and judgment to be poured out upon the children of Zion."

Since last general conference, I have received many letters from Saints, both young and old, from all over the world who accepted the challenge to read and study the Book of Mormon.

I have been thrilled by their accounts of how their lives have been changed and how they have drawn closer to the Lord as a result of their commitment. These glorious testimonies have reaffirmed to my soul the words of the Prophet Joseph Smith that the Book of Mormon is truly "the keystone of our religion" and that a man and woman will "get nearer to God by abiding by its precepts, than by any other book."

This is my prayer, that the Book of Mormon may become the keystone of our lives, in the name of Jesus Christ, amen.

Ensign, November 1986, 4–7.

CHANGE OF HEART

~❧ ❧~

THE MEANING OF REPENTANCE

THEODORE M. BURTON

What is true repentance? That is the question posed in this enlightening talk. In answering, Elder Theodore M. Burton said it might be easier to describe what repentance is *not*. "Suffering, punishment, confession, remorse, and sorrow may sometimes accompany repentance, but they are not repentance. . . .

"The Old Testament teaches time and again that we must turn from evil and do instead that which is noble and good. This means that we must not only change our ways, we must change our very thoughts, which control our actions."

Elder Burton described the steps involved in true repentance, and he issued this caution: "As you undergo the process of repentance, be patient. Be active with positive, righteous thoughts and deeds so that you can become happy and productive again."

Theodore M. Burton served as an Assistant to the Quorum of the Twelve and as a member of the First Quorum of the Seventy. He delivered this address at Brigham Young University on March 26, 1985, while serving in the First Quorum of the Seventy.

The most basic principles of the gospel are sometimes those least understood. And one of the most fundamental gospel principles is repentance. Repentance is a mechanism for personal growth and development. So fundamental is the principle that the Lord stressed its importance seventy-one times in the Doctrine and Covenants. Two of those revelations, one following the other in the Doctrine and Covenants, are identical and conclude with these words:

"And now, behold, I say unto you, that the thing which will be of the most worth unto you will be to *declare repentance unto this people*, that you may bring souls unto me, that you may rest *with them* in the kingdom of my Father." (D&C 15:6; 16:6; italics added.)

Why would the Lord give two *identical* revelations and have them published in the Doctrine and Covenants, one following the other? The Lord is the Master Teacher; he knows the value of repetition in learning. It may be that these revelations were intended not only for those to whom they were given, but also for all of us. If these revelations do indeed apply to all of us, they help us understand that what is of greatest worth to each of us is to declare repentance to others and to practice it ourselves.

Just what *is* repentance? Actually, in some ways it is easier to understand what repentance is *not* than to understand what it *is*.

As a General Authority, I have prepared information for the First Presidency to use in considering applications to readmit repentant transgressors into the Church and to restore priesthood and temple blessings. Many times a bishop will write, "I feel he has suffered enough!" But suffering is not repentance. Suffering comes from *lack* of complete repentance. A stake president will write, "I feel he has been punished enough!" But punishment is not repentance. Punishment *follows* disobedience and *precedes* repentance. A husband will write, "My wife has confessed everything!" But confession is not repentance. Confession is an admission of guilt that occurs as repentance begins. A wife will write, "My husband is filled with remorse!" But remorse is not repentance. Remorse and sorrow continue because a person has *not* yet fully repented. Suffering, punishment, confession, remorse, and sorrow may sometimes accompany repentance, but they are not repentance. What, then, *is* repentance?

To find the answer to this question, we must go to the Old Testament. The Old Testament was originally written in Hebrew, and the word used in it to refer to the concept of repentance is *shube*. We can better understand what *shube* means by reading a passage from Ezekiel and inserting the word *shube*, along with its English translation. To the "watchmen" appointed to warn Israel, the Lord says:

"When I say unto the wicked, O wicked man, thou shalt surely die; if thou dost not speak to warn the wicked from his way, that wicked man shall die in his iniquity; but his blood will I require at thine hand.

"Nevertheless, if thou warn the wicked of his way to turn from [*shube*] it; if he do not turn from [*shube*] his way, he shall die in his iniquity; but thou hast delivered thy soul. . . .

"Say unto them, As I live, saith the Lord God, I have no pleasure in the death of the wicked; but that the wicked turn from [*shube*] his way and live." (Ezekiel 33:8–11.)

I know of no kinder, sweeter passage in the Old Testament than those beautiful lines. In reading them, can you think of a kind, wise, gentle, loving Father in Heaven pleading with you to *shube*, or turn back to him—to leave unhappiness, sorrow, regret, and despair behind and turn back to your Father's family, where you can find happiness, joy, and acceptance among his other children?

That is the message of the Old Testament. Prophet after prophet writes of *shube*—that turning back to the Lord, where we can be received with joy and rejoicing. The Old Testament teaches time and again that we must turn from evil and do instead that which is noble and good. This means that we must not only change our ways, we must change our very thoughts, which control our actions.

The concept of *shube* is also found in the New Testament, which was written in Greek. The Greek writers used the Greek word *metaneoeo* to refer to repentance. *Metaneoeo* is a compound word. The first part, *meta-*, is used as a prefix in our English vocabulary. It refers to change. The second part of the word *metaneoeo* can be spelled various ways. The letter *n*, for instance, is sometimes transliterated as *pn*, and can mean air, the mind, thought, thinking, or spirit—depending on how it is used.

In the context in which *meta-* and *-neoeo* are used in the New Testament, the word *metaneoeo* means a change of mind, thought, or thinking so powerful that it changes one's very way of life. I think the Greek word *metaneoeo* is an excellent synonym for the Hebrew word *shube*. Both words mean thoroughly changing or turning from evil to God and righteousness.

Confusion came, however, when the New Testament was translated from Greek into Latin. Here an unfortunate choice was made in translation; the Greek word *metaneoeo* was translated into the Latin word *poenitere*. The Latin root *poen* in that word is the same root found in our English words *punish, penance, penitent,* and *repentance*. The beautiful meaning of the Hebrew and Greek words was thus changed in Latin to a meaning that involved hurting, punishing, whipping, cutting, mutilating, disfiguring, starving, or even torturing! It is no small wonder, then, that people have come to fear and dread the word *repentance*, which they understand to mean repeated or unending punishment.

The meaning of repentance is not that people be punished, but rather that they change their lives so that God can help them escape eternal punishment and enter into his rest with joy and rejoicing. If we have this understanding, our anxiety and fears will be relieved. *Repentance* will become a welcome and treasured word in our religious vocabulary.

We can learn more about the meaning of repentance from the thirty-third chapter of Ezekiel, where we read, "If the wicked restore the pledge, give again that he had robbed, walk in the statutes of life, without committing iniquity; he shall surely live, he shall not die." (v. 33:15.)

Let us analyze these three steps of repentance. The first is commitment—to "restore the pledge." This is the most difficult step in the repentance process. What does "restoring the pledge" mean?

To restore or renew a pledge means to renew one's covenant with the Lord. We must forget all excuses and recognize fully, exactly, what we have done. We must not say, "If I hadn't been so angry," "If my parents had only been more strict," "If my bishop had only been more understanding," "If my teachers had only taught me better," "If it hadn't been so dark!" There are hundreds of such excuses—none of which matters much in the final analysis.

To truly repent, we must forget all such rationalizations. We must kneel down before God and openly and honestly admit that what we did was wrong. As we do so, we open our hearts to our Heavenly Father and commit ourselves completely to him.

To really *commit* oneself to God and to changing one's life— and to *mean* it—is the beginning of repentance. Our Savior's great commitment to his Father is exemplified best by his terrible trial in the Garden of Gethsemane, where he suffered in agony of spirit and shed great drops of blood.

Before this experience, he had always had ready communica- tion with his Father. But now he was left alone to carry the bur- den of the world's sins. It was as if the heavens over his head were made of brass and he couldn't get through!

As he struggled in prayer and suffered horribly under the strain, he asked that the cup might pass and that some other path might be found. It is true that he added the words, "Thy will be done," but there was no answer to his request, and his soul con- tinued to be filled with anguish.

Three times he pleaded for release, and all three times the answer was the same. (See Matthew 26:36–44.)

Yet Christ had fully committed himself to do what he had been appointed to do. He was *willing,* and he went forward! Though it cost him tremendous suffering, he had made up his mind and committed himself to be obedient in every particular, regardless of the cost.

Our struggles to repent may cost us agony of mind and body also, but our commitment to our Heavenly Father to do his will will make repentance possible and bearable for us. In our repentance, we should remember that the Lord does not punish us for our sins; he simply withholds his blessings. We punish ourselves. The scriptures tell us again and again that the wicked are punished by the wicked. A simple illustration can show how we do this.

Suppose my mother told me not to touch a hot stove because it would burn me. She would only be stating the law. Suppose I should forget or deliberately touch that hot stove. I would be burned. I could cry and complain of my hurt, but who would be responsible for the hurt I received? Not my mother. Certainly not the hot stove! *I* would be responsible. I would have punished myself.

This illustration, however, disregards the important element of mercy, which I will try to make clear in discussing a second step in the process of repentance—restitution, or to "give again that [which we have] robbed." (Ezekiel 33:15.) If you have stolen money or goods, you can repay them—even sizable amounts, in time. But what if you have robbed yourself of virtue? Is there *anything* you can do, of yourself, to restore your virtue? Even if you gave your very life, you could not restore your virtue. But—perish the thought—does that then mean that it is useless to attempt restitution by performing significant good works or that your sin is unforgivable? No!

Jesus Christ has paid for your sin and has thus satisfied justice.

Therefore, he will extend mercy to you—*if* you repent. True repentance on your part, including a change in your lifestyle, enables Christ, in mercy, to forgive your sin.

The more serious the sin, the greater the effort it takes to repent. But if we work daily at turning completely to the Lord, we can stand blameless before the Savior. The key is to allow the Lord to complete the healing process without reopening the wound. Just as it takes time for a wound of the body to heal, so it takes time for a wound of the soul to heal.

If I cut myself, for example, the wound will gradually heal. But as it heals, it may begin to itch, and if I scratch it, it may open up again and take longer to heal. But there is a greater danger. If I scratch the wound, it may become infected from the bacteria on my fingers. I may poison the wound and lose that part of my body or even my life!

We must allow injuries to follow their prescribed healing course. If they are serious, we must see a doctor for skilled help. So it is with injuries to the soul. Allow the injury to follow its prescribed healing course without "scratching" it through vain regrets. If the transgression requires ecclesiastical confession, go to your bishop and get spiritual help. It may hurt as he disinfects the wound and sews it back together, but it will heal properly that way.

As you undergo the process of repentance, be patient. Be active with positive, righteous thoughts and deeds so that you can become happy and productive again.

As long as we dwell on sin or evil and refuse to forgive ourselves, we will be subject to return again to our sins. But if we turn from our problems and sins and put them behind us in both thought and action, we can concentrate on good and positive things. As we become fully engaged in good causes, sin will no longer be such a great temptation for us.

Now we come to a third step of repentance—forsaking sin, or striving to "walk in the statutes of life, without committing iniquity." We must forsake our sins, one by one. If we do this, the Lord has promised: "None [not even one] of his sins that he hath committed shall be mentioned unto him: he hath done that which is lawful and right; he shall surely live." (Ezekiel 33:15–16.)

In our day, the Lord told the Prophet Joseph Smith, "Behold, he who has repented of his sins, the same is forgiven, and I, the Lord, remember them no more."

How do we know if a man or a woman has repented of his or her sins? The Lord answers that question in the next verse: "By this ye may know if a man repenteth of his sins—behold, he will confess them and forsake them." (D&C 58:42–43.)

Naturally, the confession that precedes repentance for serious sins should be made to a bishop or stake president who has the authority to hear such confession. Confessions to others—particularly confessions repeated in open meetings, unless the sin has been a public sin requiring public forgiveness—only demean both the confessor and the hearer. Repenting of serious sins takes time and effort. But whether the sin is small or great, the final step of repentance—forsaking sin—means that we do not repeat that transgression.

How grateful we should be for a kind, wise, loving Savior who will help us overcome our faults, our mistakes, and our sins. He loves and understands us and is sympathetic to the fact that we face temptations.

In the Book of Mormon, King Benjamin explains one way we can show our gratitude to the Lord for his great mercy and his sacrifice for our sins: "Behold, I tell you these things that ye may learn wisdom: that ye may learn that when ye are in the service of your fellow beings ye are only in the service of your God." (Mosiah 2:17.) God's work and glory is to redeem his children. If we participate in redemptive service to others, we can, in some small measure, repay him for his blessings.

God is merciful; he has provided a way for us to apply the

principle of repentance in our lives and thus escape the bondage of pain, sorrow, suffering, and despair that comes from disobedience. After all is said and done, we are God's sons and daughters. And for those who understand its true meaning, repentance is a beautiful word and a marvelous refuge.

Ensign, August 1988, 7–9.

~e ~

BORN OF GOD

EZRA TAFT BENSON

Ezra Taft Benson gave this masterful November 1985 conference address while serving as president of the Quorum of the Twelve Apostles. He became president of the Church only one month later.

"Christ changes men, and changed men can change the world," he said. "Men changed for Christ will be captained by Christ. Like Paul they will be asking, 'Lord, what wilt thou have me to do?' (Acts 9:6.) Peter stated, they will 'follow his steps.' (1 Peter 2:21.) John said they will 'walk, even as he walked.' (1 John 2:6.)"

Those captained by Christ would die for the Lord, but even more important, President Benson said, "they want to live for Him."

This was not a new theme for President Benson. In 1983 he published a book titled *Come Unto Christ*, which carried the same emphasis.

———————————

What think ye of Christ?" (Matthew 22:42.) That question, posed by our Lord, has challenged the world for centuries.

Fortunately for us, God has provided modern scripture, another testament, even the Book of Mormon, for the convincing of the world that Jesus is the Christ. Anyone who will read the Book of Mormon and put it to the divine test that Moroni proposes (see Moroni 10:3–5) can be convinced that Jesus is the Christ. Once that conviction is gained, then comes the question

"Will we choose to follow Him?" The devils believe that Jesus is the Christ, but they choose to follow Lucifer. (See James 2:19; Mark 5:7.)

Throughout the ages prophets have exhorted the people to make up their minds. "Choose you this day whom ye will serve," pled Joshua. (Joshua 24:15.)

Elijah thundered, "How long halt ye between two opinions? If the Lord be God, follow him." (1 Kings 18:21.)

When you choose to follow Christ, you choose the Way, the Truth, the Life—the right way, the saving truth, the abundant life. (See John 14:6.)

"I would commend you to seek this Jesus," states Moroni. (Ether 12:41.)

When you choose to follow Christ, you choose to be changed.

"No man," said President David O. McKay, "can sincerely resolve to apply in his daily life the teachings of Jesus of Nazareth without sensing a change in his own nature. The phrase 'born again' has a deeper significance than many people attach to it. This *changed feeling* may be indescribable, *but it is real*." (Conference Report, April 1962, 7.)

Can human hearts be changed? Why, of course! It happens every day in the great missionary work of the Church. It is one of the most widespread of Christ's modern miracles. If it hasn't happened to you—it should.

Our Lord told Nicodemus that "except a man be born again, he cannot see the kingdom of God." (John 3:3.) Of these words President Kimball said, "This is the simple total answer to the weightiest of all questions. . . . To gain eternal life there must be a rebirth, a transformation." (Conference Report, April 1958, 14.)

President McKay said that Christ called for "an entire revolution" of Nicodemus's "inner man." "His manner of thinking, feeling, and acting with reference to spiritual things would have to undergo a fundamental and permanent change." (Conference Report, April 1960, 26.)

Besides the physical ordinance of baptism and the laying on of hands, one must be spiritually born again to gain exaltation and eternal life.

Alma states: "And the Lord said unto me; Marvel not that all mankind, yea, men and women, all nations, kindreds, tongues and people, must be born again; yea, born of God, changed from their carnal and fallen state, to a state of righteousness, being redeemed of God, becoming his sons and daughters;

"And thus they become new creatures; and unless they do this, they can in nowise inherit the kingdom of God." (Mosiah 27:25–26.)

The "change of heart" and "born again" processes are best described in the keystone of our religion, the Book of Mormon.

Those who had been born of God after hearing King Benjamin's address had a mighty change in their hearts. They had "no more disposition to do evil, but to do good continually." (See Mosiah 5:2, 7.)

The fourth chapter of Alma describes a period in Nephite history when "the church began to fail in its progress." (Alma 4:10.) Alma met this challenge by resigning his seat as chief judge in government "and confined himself wholly to the high priesthood" responsibility which was his. (Alma 4:20.)

He bore "down in pure testimony" against the people (see Alma 4:19), and in the fifth chapter of Alma he asks over forty crucial questions.

Speaking frankly to the members of the Church, he declared, "I ask of you, my brethren of the church, have ye spiritually been born of God? Have ye received his image in your countenances? Have ye experienced this mighty change in your hearts?" (Alma 5:14.)

He continued, "If ye have experienced a change of heart, and if ye have felt to sing the song of redeeming love, I would ask, can ye feel so now?" (Alma 5:26.)

Would not the progress of the Church increase dramatically today with an increasing number of those who are spiritually reborn? Can you imagine what would happen in our homes? Can you imagine what would happen with an increasing number of copies of the Book of Mormon in the hands of an increasing number of missionaries who know how to use it and who have been born of God? When this happens, we will get the harvest President Kimball envisions. It was the "born of God" Alma who as a missionary was so able to impart the word that many others were also born of God. (See Alma 36:23–26.)

The Lord works from the inside out. The world works from the outside in. The world would take people out of the slums. Christ takes the slums out of people, and then they take themselves out of the slums. The world would mold men by changing their environment. Christ changes men, who then change their environment. The world would shape human behavior, but Christ can change human nature.

"Human nature *can* be changed, here and now," said President McKay, and then he quoted the following:

"You can change human nature. No man who has felt in him the Spirit of Christ even for half a minute can deny this truth. . . .

"You do change human nature, your own human nature, if you surrender it to Christ. Human nature can be changed here and now. Human nature has been changed in the past. Human nature must be changed on an enormous scale in the future, unless the world is to be drowned in its own blood. And only Christ can change it.

"Twelve men did quite a lot to change the world [nineteen hundred] years ago. Twelve simple men." (Quoting Beverly Nichols, in *Stepping Stones to an Abundant Life*, comp. Llewelyn R. McKay [Salt Lake City: Deseret Book, 1971], 23, 127.)

Yes, Christ changes men, and changed men can change the world.

Men changed for Christ will be captained by Christ. Like Paul they will be asking, "Lord, what wilt thou have me to do?" (Acts 9:6.) Peter stated, they will "follow his steps." (1 Peter 2:21.) John said they will "walk, even as he walked." (1 John 2:6.)

Finally, men captained by Christ will be consumed in Christ. To paraphrase President Harold B. Lee, they set fire in others because they are on fire. (*Stand Ye in Holy Places* [Salt Lake City: Deseret Book, 1974], 192.)

Their will is swallowed up in His will. (See John 5:30.)

They do always those things that please the Lord. (See John 8:29.)

Not only would they die for the Lord, but more important they want to live for Him.

Enter their homes, and the pictures on their walls, the books on their shelves, the music in the air, their words and acts reveal them as Christians.

They stand as witnesses of God at all times, and in all things, and in all places. (See Mosiah 18:9.)

They have Christ on their minds, as they look unto Him in every thought. (See D&C 6:36.)

They have Christ in their hearts as their affections are placed on Him forever. (See Alma 37:36.)

Almost every week they partake of the sacrament and witness anew to their Eternal Father that they are willing to take upon them the name of His Son, always remember Him, and keep His commandments. (See Moroni 4:3.)

In Book of Mormon language, they "feast upon the words of Christ" (2 Nephi 32:3), "talk of Christ" (2 Nephi 25:26), "rejoice in Christ" (2 Nephi 25:26), "are made alive in Christ" (2 Nephi 25:25), and "glory in [their] Jesus." (See 2 Nephi 33:6.)

In short, they lose themselves in the Lord, and find eternal life. (See Luke 17:33.)

President David O. McKay tells of a singular event that happened to him. After falling asleep, he said he "beheld in vision something infinitely sublime." He saw a beautiful city, a great concourse of people dressed in white, and the Savior.

"The city, I understood, was his. It was the City Eternal; and the people following him were to abide there in peace and eternal happiness.

"But who were they?

"As if the Savior read my thoughts, he answered by pointing to a semicircle that then appeared above them, and on which were written in gold the words:

> *"These Are They Who Have Overcome the World—*
> *Who Have Truly Been Born Again!*

"When I awoke, it was breaking day." (*Cherished Experiences from the Writings of President David O. McKay*, comp. Clare Middlemiss [Salt Lake City: Deseret Book, 1976], 59–60.)

When we awake and are born of God, a new day will break and Zion will be redeemed.

May we be convinced that Jesus is the Christ, choose to follow Him, be changed for Him, captained by Him, consumed in Him, and born again I pray in the name of Jesus Christ, amen.

Ensign, November 1985, 5–7.

CHURCH GOVERNMENT

❦ ❧

THE KEYS OF THE KINGDOM

WILFORD WOODRUFF

In these remarks, President Wilford Woodruff recalls his feelings about the martyrdom of Joseph and Hyrum Smith, and he shares his witness that Joseph delivered the keys of the kingdom to the Twelve before his death. "'But,' he said, after having done this, 'ye apostles of the Lamb of God, my brethren, upon your shoulders this kingdom rests; now you have got to round up your shoulders and bear off the kingdom.' And he also made this very strange remark, 'If you do not do it you will be damned.'" This address was given at a conference of the Young Men's Mutual Improvement Association on Sunday, June 2, 1889.

———————

Before the close of this conference there is a subject upon which I wish to bear my testimony. . . . I am . . . the only one living in the flesh who was with [Brigham Young] and Joseph Smith, the Prophet of God, when he gave to the Twelve Apostles their charge concerning the Priesthood and the keys of the kingdom of God; and as I myself shall soon pass away like other men, I want to leave my testimony to these Latter-day Saints.

I was sitting with Brigham Young in the depot in the city of Boston at the time when the two prophets were martyred. Of course we had no telegraphs and no fast reports as we have today to give communication over the land. During that period Brother Young was waiting there for a train of cars to go to Peterborough.

Whilst sitting there we were overshadowed by a cloud of darkness and gloom as great as I ever witnessed in my life under almost any circumstances in which we were placed. Neither of us knew or understood the cause until after the report of the death of the prophets was manifested to us.

Brother Brigham left; I remained in Boston, and next day took passage for Fox Islands, a place I had visited some years before, and baptized numbers of people and organized branches upon both those islands. My father-in-law, Ezra Carter, carried me on a wagon from Scarborough to Portland. I there engaged passage on board of a steamer. I had put my trunk on board and was just bidding my father-in-law farewell, when a man came out from a shop—a shoemaker—holding a newspaper in his hand. He said, "Father Carter, Joseph and Hyrum Smith have been martyred—they have been murdered in Carthage jail!"

As soon as I looked at the paper, the Spirit said to me that it was true. I had no time for consultation, the steamer's bell was ringing, so I stepped on board and took my trunk back to land. As I drew it off, the plank was drawn in. I told Father Carter to drive me back to Scarborough. I there took the car for Boston, and arrived at that place on the Saturday night.

On my arrival there I received a letter which had been sent from Nauvoo, giving us an account of the killing of the prophets. I was the only man in Boston of the Quorum of the Twelve.

I had very strange feelings, as, I have no doubt, all the Saints had. I attended a meeting on the following day in Boydston's Hall, where a vast number of the inhabitants of Boston and some three hundred Latter-day Saints had assembled. Hundreds of men came to that meeting to see what the "Mormons" were going to do now that their prophets were dead. I felt braced up; every nerve, bone, and sinew within me seemed as though made of steel. I did not shed a tear. I went into that hall, though I knew not what I was going to say to that vast audience. I opened the Bible [randomly] and opened to the words of St. John where he saw under the altar the souls of them that were slain for the word of God, and heard them cry, "How long, O Lord, holy and true, dost thou not judge and avenge our blood on them that dwell on the earth?" The Lord informed them that they must wait a little season, until their brethren were slain as they were. I spoke on those words.

Next day I met Brigham Young in the streets of Boston, he having just returned, opposite to Sister Voce's house. We reached out our hands, but neither of us was able to speak a word. We walked into Sister Voce's house. We each took a seat and veiled our faces. We were overwhelmed with grief and our faces were soon bathed in a flood of tears. I felt then that I could talk, though I could not do so before—that is, to Brother Brigham. After we had done weeping we began to converse together concerning the death of the prophets. In the course of the conversation, he smote his hand upon his thigh and said, "Thank God, the keys of the kingdom are here." . . .

All that President Young or myself or any member of the Quorum need have done in the matter was to have referred to the last instructions at the last meeting we had with the Prophet Joseph before starting on our mission. I have alluded to that meeting many times in my life.

The Prophet Joseph, I am now satisfied, had a thorough presentiment that that was the last meeting we would hold together here in the flesh. We had had our endowments; we had had all the blessings sealed upon our heads that were ever given to the apostles or prophets on the face of the earth. On that occasion the Prophet Joseph rose up and said to us: "Brethren, I have desired to live to see this temple built. I shall never live to see it, but you will. I have sealed upon your heads all the keys of the kingdom of God. I have sealed upon you every key, power, principle that the God of heaven has revealed to me. Now, no matter where I may go or what I may do, the kingdom rests upon you."

Now, don't you wonder why we, as apostles, could not have understood that the prophet of God was going to be taken away from us? But we did not understand it. The apostles in the days of Jesus Christ could not understand what the Savior meant when He told them "I am going away; if I do not go away the Comforter will not come!" Neither did we understand what Joseph meant. "But," he said, after having done this, "ye apostles of the Lamb of God, my brethren, upon your shoulders this kingdom rests; now you have got to round up your shoulders and bear off the kingdom." And he also made this very strange remark, "If you do not do it you will be damned."

I am the last man living who heard that declaration. He told the truth, too; for would not any of the men who have held the keys of the kingdom of God or an apostleship in this Church have been under condemnation, and would not the wrath of God have rested upon them if they had deserted these principles or denied and turned from them and undertaken to serve themselves instead of the work of the Lord which was committed to their hands?

When the Lord gave the keys of the kingdom of God, the keys of the Melchizedek Priesthood, of the apostleship, and sealed them upon the head of Joseph Smith, He sealed them upon his head to stay here upon the earth until the coming of the Son of Man. Well might Brigham Young say, "The keys of the kingdom of God are here." They were with him to the day of his death. They then rested upon the head of another man—President John Taylor. He held those keys to the hour of his death. They then fell by turn, or in the providence of God, upon Wilford Woodruff.

I say to the Latter-day Saints the keys of the kingdom of God are here, and they are going to stay here, too, until the coming of the Son of Man. Let all Israel understand that. They may not rest upon my head but a short time, but they will then rest on the head of another apostle, and another after him, and so continue until the coming of the Lord Jesus Christ in the clouds of heaven to "reward every man according to the deeds done in the body."

I want to add another thing, because I feel it my duty to say it to the Latter-day Saints. There is a feeling—it was so in the days of Joseph Smith—that he was not the man to lead the Church. Even his bosom friends, men with whom he saw angels of God, Oliver Cowdery and others, considered him a fallen prophet and thought they ought to lead the Church. This history is before you and before the world. The same feeling was manifested in the days of Brigham Young when he was called to hold the keys of the Presidency of the Church. There were other men who thought they should be appointed to that office. But the God of heaven manifested to you, and to me, and to all men, who were in Nauvoo, upon whom the mantle had fallen. Brigham Young took his place, and led the Church and kingdom of God up to the day of his death.

There are men today, there will be men till the coming of the Son of Man, I expect, who feel as though they ought to lead the Church, as though it is not going right—that this, that, and the other is wrong. I say to all Israel at this day, I say to the whole world, that the God of Israel, who organized this Church and kingdom, never ordained any President or Presidency to lead it astray. Hear it, ye Israel, no man who has ever breathed the breath of life can hold these keys of the kingdom of God and lead the people astray.

We talk of revelation. There has been a feeling of wonder many times as to why Brigham Young did not have revelation, why John Taylor did not have revelation, why Wilford Woodruff does not have revelation, why any other apostle does not have revelation. I hold in my hand a book of revelations, enough to lead this Church into the celestial kingdom of God. Anybody who will obey that law will have all the revelation that he can fulfill on earth. We are not without revelation. The heavens are full of it, so is the holy priesthood.

I know the destiny of this people; it is revealed by the God of Israel, and left on record. I know the destiny of this kingdom, and I want to say, let us try to unite together and fulfill the law of God. You need not trouble about the kingdom God has established. He will take care of it. The same God who has organized this Zion and gathered one hundred and fifty thousand people here from the nations of the earth has his eye over you. He is watching over you, and He will take care of you when you do your duty. Zion is not going to be moved out of her place. The Lord will plead with her strong ones, and if she sins He will chastise her until she is purified before the Lord.

I do not pretend to tell how much sorrow you or I are going to meet with before the coming of the Son of Man. That will depend upon our conduct.

With regard to the keys of the kingdom of God, they were placed on the earth to remain, and they will remain until Jesus Christ comes in the clouds of heaven. But I and other men, the apostles, and all who are called to officiate in the name of the Lord need the faith and prayers of the Latter-day Saints.

By way of closing I will say that Brigham Young, John Taylor, Wilford Woodruff, these Twelve Apostles around me, and every one of the Seventies, High Priests, High Councilors, Presidents of Stakes, the Melchizedek and all the Aaronic Priesthood, and all the Latter-day Saints—all will get what they labor for. Whatsoever we sow, whether good or evil, of that we will reap the fruit.

But in the morning of the resurrection you will find Joseph Smith holding the keys of this kingdom and dispensation at the head of all Israel who belong to this dispensation; he will hold them to the endless ages of eternity, notwithstanding that we shall all get our reward for what we do. The keys of the kingdom were given to Joseph Smith. They were placed on the heads of other men to make use of on earth for a short time; and when we get through we shall all have our reward.

Let us make up our minds to serve and honor God. Do not have any fears concerning the kingdom; the Lord will lead that aright; and if Brother Woodruff or any of the Presidency of this Church should take any course to lead you astray, the Lord will remove us out of the way. We are in the hands of the Lord, and those keys will be held and taken care of by the God of Israel until He comes whose right it is to reign.

God bless you all. Amen.

[At the evening session President Woodruff made the following additional remarks]

Before dismissing this assembly I feel it my duty to say a few words. I addressed the Saints a short time this afternoon upon a certain subject, and that was in bearing my testimony to the keys of the kingdom of God, which the Lord gave to Joseph Smith, and the retaining of those keys upon the earth through their bestowal upon the heads of the apostles. I did not pretend to dwell upon the organization of the Priesthood or of the Church in these remarks. My only object was to bear my testimony upon that subject. After the meeting I began to reflect, from remarks which I made, that perhaps many of the people might get an entirely wrong idea of my views with regard to the kingdom of God. I referred to the Doctrine and Covenants—a code of revelations which the Lord gave to Joseph Smith. This book contains some of the most glorious revelation upon doctrine, upon principle, upon government, upon the kingdom of God and the different glories, and upon a great many things which reach into the eternal worlds. My leaving this subject there, perhaps, might lead my friends to suppose that I did not believe in any more revelation. This would be a great mistake. For if we had before us every revelation which God ever gave to man; if we had the Book of Enoch; if we had the untranslated plates before us in the English language; if we had the records of the Revelator St. John which are sealed up, and all other revelations, and they were piled up here a hundred feet high, the Church and kingdom of God could not grow, in this or any other age of the world, without the living oracles of God.

The Presidency of the Church is composed of three men—the President and his Counselors; and not only does the President of the Church need revelation daily, in order to pass through the labor, the care and the business that rests upon him, but his Counselors need it. Every one of the Twelve Apostles need it in all their administrations throughout the world; and not only the Twelve Apostles, but the Seventies, the High Priests, the Bishops, the Elders, and all who belong to the Melchizedek or Aaronic Priesthood—all need it in their administrations in the world. No man can go forth and lift up his voice and declare the gospel of Jesus Christ without revelation. He needs the holy priesthood with him every day of his life. I do not wish to be misunderstood in this matter. Every man or woman that has ever entered into the Church of God and been baptized for the remission of sins has a right to revelation, a right to the Spirit of God, to assist them in their labors, in their administrations to their children, in coun-seling their children and those over whom they are called upon to preside. The Holy Ghost is not restricted to men, nor to apostles or prophets; it belongs to every faithful man and woman, and to every child who is old enough to receive the gospel of Christ.

I am very much opposed to false doctrine, either preaching it myself or having anybody else preach it. I, therefore, wish to make this correction if there is any need of it. God never had a Church or a people, in any age of the world, that were governed and con-trolled except by revelation. The living oracles of God were among them—those who held the keys of the kingdom, and they had to receive revelation to assist them in all their work. The Elders of Israel, when they go abroad to the nations of the earth, need the

Spirit of God, to tell them to go here, or go there, that they may search out the honest in heart. Let us all understand this, so that we may not be divided in our views and sentiments.

_____

Collected Discourses, vol. 1, June 2, 1889.

EDUCATION

~ ❧ ~

THE CHARTED COURSE OF THE CHURCH IN EDUCATION

J. REUBEN CLARK JR.

On August 8, 1938, President J. Reuben Clark Jr. gave this address, with the approval of the First Presidency, to Church seminary and institute leaders. In it he outlined the essential attributes of an effective teacher of the gospel, focusing on such basic matters as a testimony and the moral courage to express it. "Your chief interest," he said, "your essential and all but sole duty, is to teach the Gospel of the Lord Jesus Christ as that has been revealed in these latter days." He also explained what it means to teach—and be taught—by the Spirit. This powerful address has been widely quoted and remains as important as ever for anyone who is called to teach the gospel.

As a schoolboy I was thrilled with the great debate between those two giants, [Daniel] Webster and [Robert] Hayne. The beauty of their oratory, the sublimity of Webster's lofty expression of patriotism, the forecast of the civil struggle to come for the mastery of freedom over slavery, all stirred me to the very depths. The debate began over the Foot Resolution concerning the public lands. It developed into consideration of great fundamental problems of constitutional law. I have never forgotten the opening paragraph of Webster's reply, by which he brought back to its place of beginning this debate that had drifted so far from its course. That paragraph reads:

Mr. President: When the mariner has been tossed for many days in thick weather, and on an unknown sea, he naturally avails himself of the first pause in the storm, the earliest glance of the sun, to take his latitude, and ascertain how far the elements have driven him from his true course. Let us imitate this prudence, and, before we float farther on the waves of this debate, refer to the point from which we departed, that we may at least be able to conjecture where we now are. I ask for the reading of the resolution.

Now I hasten to express the hope that you will not think that I think this is a Webster-Hayne occasion or that I think I am a Daniel Webster. If you were to think those things—or either of them—you would make a grievous mistake. I admit I am old, but I am not that old. But Webster seemed to invoke so sensible a procedure for occasions where, after a wandering on the high seas or in the wilderness, effort is to be made to get back to the place of starting, that I thought you would excuse me if I invoked and in a way used this same procedure to restate some of the more outstanding and essential fundamentals underlying our Church school education.

The following are to me those fundamentals:

The Church is the organized Priesthood of God. The Priesthood can exist without the Church, but the Church cannot exist without the Priesthood. The mission of the Church is first, to teach, encourage, assist, and protect the individual member in his striving to live the perfect life, temporally and spiritually, as laid down in the Gospel: "Be ye perfect, even as your Father which is in Heaven is perfect," said the Master. Secondly, the Church is to maintain, teach, encourage, and protect, temporally and spiritually, the membership as a group in its living of the Gospel. And thirdly, the Church is militantly to proclaim the truth, calling upon all men to repent, and to live in obedience to the Gospel, "for every knee must bow and every tongue confess."

In all this there are for the Church and for each and all of its members, two prime things which may not be overlooked, forgotten, shaded, or discarded:

First: That Jesus Christ is the Son of God, the Only Begotten of the Father in the flesh, the Creator of the world, the Lamb of God, the Sacrifice for the sins of the world, the Atoner for Adam's transgression; that He was crucified; that His spirit left His body; that He died; that He was laid away in the tomb; that on the third day His spirit was reunited with His body, which again became a living being; that He was raised from the tomb a resurrected being, a perfect Being, the First Fruits of the Resurrection; that He later ascended to the Father; and that because of His death and by and through His resurrection every man born into the world since the beginning will be likewise literally resurrected. This doctrine is as old as the world. Job declared: "And though after my skin worms destroy this body, yet in my flesh shall I see God, whom I shall see for myself and mine eyes shall behold, and not another." (Job 19:26, 27.)

The resurrected body is a body of flesh and bones and spirit, and Job was uttering a great and everlasting truth. These positive facts, and all other facts necessarily implied therein, must all be honestly believed, in full faith, by every member of the Church.

The second of the two things to which we must all give full faith is: That the Father and the Son actually and in truth and very deed appeared to the Prophet Joseph in a vision in the woods; that other heavenly visions followed to Joseph and to others; that the Gospel and the holy Priesthood after the Order of the Son of God were in truth and fact restored to the earth from which they were lost by the apostasy of the Primitive Church; that the Lord again set up His Church, through the agency of Joseph Smith; that the Book of Mormon is just what it professes to be; that to the Prophet came numerous revelations for guidance, upbuilding, organization, and encouragement of the Church and its members; that the Prophet's successors, likewise called of God, have received revelations as the needs of the Church have required, and that they will continue to receive revelations as the Church and its members, living the truth they already have, shall stand in need of more; that this is in truth The Church of Jesus Christ of Latter-day Saints; and that its foundation beliefs are the laws and principles laid down in the Articles of Faith. These facts also, and each of them, together with all things necessarily implied therein or flowing therefrom, must stand, unchanged, unmodified, without dilution, excuse, apology, or avoidance; they may not be explained away or submerged. Without these two great beliefs the Church would cease to be the Church.

Any individual who does not accept the fulness of these doctrines as to Jesus of Nazareth or as to the restoration of the Gospel and Holy Priesthood, is not a Latter-day Saint; the hundreds of thousands of faithful, God-fearing men and women who compose the great body of the Church membership do believe these things fully and completely; and they support the Church and its institutions because of this belief.

I have set out these matters because they are the latitude and longitude of the actual location and position of the Church, both in this world and in eternity. Knowing our true position, we can change our bearings if they need changing; we can lay down anew our true course. And here we may wisely recall that Paul said: "But though we, or an angel from heaven, preach any other Gospel unto you than that which we have preached unto you, let him be accursed." (Galatians 1:8.)

Returning to the Webster-Hayne precedent, I have now finished reading the original resolution.

As I have already said, I am to say something about the religious education of the youth of the Church. I shall bring together what I have to say under two general headings—the student and the teacher. I shall speak very frankly, for we have passed the place where we may wisely talk in ambiguous words and veiled phrases.

We must say plainly what we mean, because the future of our youth, both here on earth and in the hereafter, as also the welfare of the whole Church, are at stake.

The youth of the Church, your students, are in great majority sound in thought and in spirit. The problem primarily is to keep them sound, not to convert them.

The youth of the Church are hungry for things of the spirit; they are eager to learn the Gospel, and they want it straight, undiluted.

They want to know about the fundamentals I have just set out—about our beliefs; they want to gain testimonies of their truth; they are not now doubters but inquirers, seekers after truth. Doubt must not be planted in their hearts. Great is the burden and the condemnation of any teacher who sows doubt in a trusting soul.

These students crave the faith their fathers and mothers have; they want it in its simplicity and purity. There are few indeed who have not seen the manifestations of its divine power; they wish to be not only the beneficiaries of this faith, but they want to be themselves able to call it forth to work.

They want to believe in the ordinances of the Gospel; they wish to understand them so far as they may.

They are prepared to understand the truth which is as old as the Gospel and which was expressed thus by Paul (a master of logic and metaphysics unapproached by the modern critics who decry all religion):

> For what man knoweth the things of a man, save the spirit of the man which is in him? even so the things of God knoweth no man but the Spirit of God.
>
> Now we have received, not the spirit of the world, but the spirit which is of God: that we might know the things that are freely given to us of God. (1 Corinthians 2:11, 12.)
>
> For they that are after the flesh do mind the things of the flesh; but they that are after the Spirit the things of the Spirit. (Romans 8:5.)

This I say then, walk in the Spirit, and ye shall not fulfil the lust of the flesh.

For the flesh lusteth against the Spirit, and the Spirit against the flesh; and these are contrary the one to the other; so that ye cannot do the things that ye would.

But if ye be led of the Spirit, ye are not under the law. (Galatians 5:16–18.)

Our youth understand, too, the principle declared in modern revelation:

Ye cannot behold with your natural eyes, for the present time, the design of your God concerning those things which shall come hereafter, and the glory which shall follow after much tribulation. (D&C 58:3.)

By the power of the Spirit our eyes were opened and our understandings were enlightened, so as to see and understand the things of God. . . .

And while we meditated upon these things, the Lord touched the eyes of our understandings and they were opened and the glory of the Lord shone round about.

And we beheld the glory of the Son, on the right hand of the Father, and received of his fulness;

And saw the holy angels, and them who are sanctified before his throne, worshiping God, and the Lamb, who worship him for ever and ever. (D&C 76:12, 19–21.)

And now, after the many testimonies which have been given of him, this is the testimony, last of all, which we give of him: That he lives!

For we saw him, even on the right hand of God; and we heard the voice bearing record that he is the Only Begotten of the Father.

That by him, and through him, and of him, the worlds are and were created, and the inhabitants thereof are begotten sons and daughters unto God.

And while we were yet in the Spirit, the Lord commanded us that we should write the vision. (D&C 76:22–24, 28.)

These students are prepared, too, to understand what Moses meant when he declared:

> But now mine eyes have beheld God; but not my natural, but my spiritual eyes, for my natural eyes could not have beheld; for I should have withered and died in his presence; but his glory was upon me; and I beheld his face, for I was transfigured before him. (Moses 1:11.)

These students are prepared to believe and understand that all these things are matters of faith, not to be explained or understood by any process of human reason, and probably not by any experiment of known physical science.

These students (to put the matter shortly) are prepared to understand and to believe that there is a natural world and there is a spiritual world; that the things of the natural world will not explain the things of the spiritual world; that the things of the spiritual world cannot be understood or comprehended by the things of the natural world; that you cannot rationalize the things of the spirit, because first, the things of the spirit are not sufficiently known and comprehended, and secondly, because finite mind and reason cannot comprehend nor explain infinite wisdom and ultimate truth.

These students already know that they must be honest, true, chaste, benevolent, virtuous, and do good to all men, and that "if there is anything virtuous, lovely, or of good report or praiseworthy, we seek after these things"—these things they have been taught from very birth. They should be encouraged in all proper ways to do these things which they know to be true, but they do not need to have a year's course of instruction to make them believe and know them.

These students fully sense the hollowness of teachings which would make the Gospel plan a mere system of ethics, they know that Christ's teachings are in the highest degree ethical, but they also know they are more than this. They will see that ethics relate primarily to the doings of this life, and that to make of the Gospel a mere system of ethics is to confess a lack of faith, if not a disbelief, in the hereafter. They know that the Gospel teachings not only touch this life, but the life that is to come, with its salvation and exaltation as the final goal.

These students hunger and thirst, as did their fathers before them, for a testimony of the things of the spirit and of the hereafter, and knowing that you cannot rationalize eternity, they seek faith, and the knowledge which follows faith. They sense by the spirit they have, that the testimony they seek is engendered and nurtured by the testimony of others, and that to gain this testimony which they seek for, one living, burning, honest testimony of a righteous God-fearing man that Jesus is the Christ and that Joseph was God's prophet, is worth a thousand books and lectures aimed at debasing the Gospel to a system of ethics or seeking to rationalize infinity.

Two thousand years ago the Master said: "Or what man is there of you, whom if his son ask bread, will he give him a stone? Or if he ask a fish, will he give him a serpent?" (Matthew 7:10, 11.)

These students, born under the Covenant, can understand that age and maturity and intellectual training are not in any way or to any degree necessary to communion with the Lord and His Spirit. They know the story of the youth Samuel in the temple; of Jesus at twelve years confounding the doctors in the temple; of Joseph at fourteen seeing God the Father and the Son in one of the most glorious visions ever beheld by man. They are not as were the Corinthians, of whom Paul said: "I have fed you with milk and not with meat; for hitherto ye were not able to bear it, neither yet now are ye able." (1 Corinthians 3:2.)

They are rather as was Paul himself when he declared to the same Corinthians: "When I was a child, I spake as a child, I understood as a child, I thought as a child: but when I became a man, I put away childish things." (1 Corinthians 13:11.)

These students as they come to you are spiritually working towards a maturity which they will early reach if you but feed them the right food. They come to you possessing spiritual knowledge and experience the world does not know.

So much for your students and what they are and what they expect and what they are capable of. I am telling you the things that some of you teachers have told me, and that many of your youth have told me.

May I not say now a few words to you teachers?

In the first place, there is neither reason nor is there excuse for our Church religious teaching and training facilities and institutions, unless the youth are to be taught and trained in the principles of the Gospel, embracing therein the two great elements that Jesus is the Christ and that Joseph was God's prophet. The teaching of a system of ethics to the students is not a sufficient reason for running our seminaries and institutes. The great public school system teaches ethics. The students of seminaries and institutes should of course be taught the ordinary canons of good and righteous living, for these are part, and an essential part, of the Gospel. But there are the great principles involved in eternal life, the Priesthood, the resurrection, and many like other things, that go way beyond these canons of good living. These great fundamental principles also must be taught to the youth; they are the things the youth wish first to know about.

The first requisite of a teacher for teaching these principles is a personal testimony of their truth. No amount of learning, no amount of study, and no number of scholastic degrees, can take the place of this testimony, which is the *sine qua non* of the teacher in our Church school system. No teacher who does not have a real testimony of the truth of the Gospel as revealed to and believed by the Latter-day Saints, and a testimony of the Sonship and Messiahship of Jesus, and of the divine mission of Joseph Smith— including in all its reality the First Vision—has any place in the

Church school system. If there be any such, and I hope and pray there are none, he should at once resign; if the Commissioner knows of any such and he does not resign, the Commissioner should request his resignation. The First Presidency expects this pruning to be made.

This does not mean that we would cast out such teachers from the Church—not at all. We shall take up with them a labor of love, in all patience and long-suffering, to win them to the knowledge to which as Godfearing men and women they are entitled. But this does mean that our Church schools cannot be manned by unconverted, untestimonied teachers.

But for you teachers the mere possession of a testimony is not enough. You must have besides this, one of the rarest and most precious of all the many elements of human character—moral courage. For in the absence of moral courage to declare your testimony, it will reach the students only after such dilution as will make it difficult if not impossible for them to detect it; and the spiritual and psychological effect of a weak and vacillating testimony may well be actually harmful instead of helpful.

The successful seminary or institute teacher must also possess another of the rare and valuable elements of character—a twin brother of moral courage and often mistaken for it—I mean intellectual courage—the courage to affirm principles, beliefs, and faith that may not always be considered as harmonizing with such knowledge—scientific or otherwise—as the teacher or his educational colleagues may believe they possess.

Not unknown are cases where men of presumed faith, holding responsible positions, have felt that, since by affirming their full faith they might call down upon themselves the ridicule of their unbelieving colleagues, they must either modify or explain away their faith, or destructively dilute it, or even pretend to cast it away. Such are hypocrites to their colleagues and to their co-religionists.

An object of pity (not of scorn, as some would have it) is that man or woman, who having the truth and knowing it, finds it necessary either to repudiate the truth or to compromise with error in order that he may live with or among unbelievers without subjecting himself to their disfavor or derision as he supposes. Tragic indeed is his place, for the real fact is that all such discardings and shadings in the end bring the very punishments that the weak-willed once sought to avoid.

For there is nothing the world so values and reveres as the man, who, having righteous convictions, stands for them in any and all circumstances; there is nothing towards which the world turns more contempt than the man who, having righteous convictions, either slips away from them, abandons them, or repudiates them. For any Latter-day Saint psychologist, chemist, physicist, geologist, archaeologist, or any other scientist, to explain away, or misinterpret, or evade or elude, or most of all, to repudiate or to deny, the great fundamental doctrines of the Church in which he professes to believe, is to give the lie to his intellect, to lose his self-respect, to bring sorrow to his friends, to break the hearts and bring shame to his parents, to besmirch the Church and its members, and to forfeit the respect and honor of those whom he has sought, by his course, to win as friends and helpers.

I prayerfully hope there may not be any such among the teachers of the Church school system, but if there are any such, high or low, they must travel the same route as the teacher without the testimony. Sham and pretext and evasion and hypocrisy have, and can have, no place in the Church school system or in the character building and spiritual growth of our youth.

Another thing which must be watched in our Church institutions is this: It must not be possible for men to keep positions of spiritual trust who, not being converted themselves, being really unbelievers, seek to turn aside the beliefs, education, and activities of our youth, and our aged also, from the ways they should follow, into other paths of education, beliefs, and activities, which (though leading where the unbeliever would go) do not bring us to the places where the Gospel would take us. That this works as a conscience-balm to the unbeliever who directs it is of no importance. This is the grossest betrayal of trust; and there is too much reason to think it has happened.

I wish to mention another thing that has happened in other lines, as a caution against the same thing happening in the Church educational system. On more than one occasion our Church members have gone to other places for special training in particular lines; they have had the training which was supposedly the last word, the most modern view, the *ne plus ultra* of up-to-dateness; then they have brought it back and dosed it upon us without any thought as to whether we needed it or not. I refrain from mentioning well-known and, I believe, well-recognized instances of this sort of thing. I do not wish to wound any feelings.

But before trying on the newest fangled ideas in any line of thought, education, activity, or what not, experts should just stop and consider that however backward they think we are, and however backward we may actually be in some things, in other things we are far out in the lead, and therefore these new methods may be old, if not worn out, with us.

In whatever relates to community life and activity in general, to clean group social amusement and entertainment, to closely knit and carefully directed religious worship and activity, to a positive, clear-cut, faith-promoting spirituality, to a real, everyday, practical religion, to a firm-fixed desire and acutely sensed need for faith in God, we are far in the van of on-marching humanity. Before effort is made to inoculate us with new ideas, experts should kindly consider whether the methods, used to spur community spirit or build religious activities among groups that are decadent and maybe dead to these things, are quite applicable to us, and whether their effort to impose these upon us is not a rather crude, even gross anachronism.

For example, to apply to our spiritually minded and religiously alert youth a plan evolved to teach religion to youth having no interest or concern in matters of the spirit, would not only fail in meeting our actual religious needs, but would tend to destroy the best qualities which our youth now possess.

I have already indicated that our youth are not children spiritually; they are well on towards the normal spiritual maturity of the world. To treat them as children spiritually, as the world might treat the same age group, is therefore and likewise an anachronism. I say once more there is scarcely a youth that comes through your seminary or institute door who has not been the conscious beneficiary of spiritual blessings, or who has not seen the efficacy of prayer, or who has not witnessed the power of faith to heal the sick, or who has not beheld spiritual outpourings, of which the world at large is today ignorant. You do not have to sneak up behind this spiritually experienced youth and whisper religion in his ears; you can come right out, face-to-face, and talk with him. You do not need to disguise religious truths with a cloak of worldly things; you can bring these truths to him openly, in their natural guise. Youth may prove to be not more fearful of them than you are. There is no need for gradual approaches, for "bed-time" stories, for coddling, for patronizing, or for any of the other childish devices used in efforts to reach those spiritually inexperienced and all but spiritually dead.

You teachers have a great mission. As teachers you stand upon the highest peak in education, for what teaching can compare in priceless value and in far-reaching effect with that which deals with man as he was in the eternity of yesterday, as he is in the mortality of today, and as he will be in the forever of tomorrow. Not only time but eternity is your field. Salvation of yourself not only, but of those who come within the purlieus of your temple, is the blessing you seek, and which, doing your duty, you will gain. How brilliant will be your crown of glory, with each soul saved an encrusted jewel thereon.

But to get this blessing and to be so crowned, you must, I say once more, you must teach the Gospel. You have no other function and no other reason for your presence in a Church school system.

You do have an interest in matters purely cultural and in matters of purely secular knowledge; but, I repeat again for emphasis, your chief interest, your essential and all but sole duty, is to teach the Gospel of the Lord Jesus Christ as that has been revealed in these latter days. You are to teach this Gospel using as your sources and authorities the Standard Works of the Church, and the words of those whom God has called to lead His people in these last days. You are not, whether high or low, to intrude into your work your own peculiar philosophy, no matter what its source or how pleasing or rational it seems to you to be. To do so would be to have as many different churches as we have seminaries—and that is chaos.

You are not, whether high or low, to change the doctrines of the Church or to modify them, as they are declared by and in the Standard Works of the Church and by those whose authority it is to declare the mind and will of the Lord to the Church. The Lord has declared he is "the same yesterday, today, and forever."

I urge you not to fall into that childish error, so common now, of believing that merely because man has gone so far in harnessing the forces of nature and turning them to his own use, that therefore the truths of the spirit have been changed or transformed. It is a vital and significant fact that man's conquest of the things of the spirit has not marched side by side with his conquest of things material. The opposite sometimes seems to be true. Man's power to reason has not matched his power to figure. Remember always and cherish the great truth of the Intercessory Prayer: "And this is life eternal, that they might know thee the only true God, and Jesus Christ, whom thou hast sent." This is an ultimate truth; so are all spiritual truths. They are not changed by the discovery of a new element, a new ethereal wave, nor by clipping off a few seconds, minutes, or hours of a speed record.

You are not to teach the philosophies of the world, ancient or modern, pagan or Christian, for this is the field of the public schools. Your sole field is the Gospel, and that is boundless in its own sphere.

We pay taxes to support those state institutions whose function and work it is to teach the arts, the sciences, literature, history, the languages, and so on through the whole secular curriculum. These institutions are to do this work. But we use the tithes of the Church to carry on the Church school system, and these are impressed with a holy trust. The Church seminaries and institutes are to teach the Gospel.

In thus stating this function time and time again, and with such continued insistence as I have done, it is fully appreciated that carrying out the function may involve the matter of "released time" for our seminaries and institutes. But our course is clear. If we cannot teach the Gospel, the doctrines of the Church, and the Standard Works of the Church, all of them, on "released time," in our seminaries and institutes, then we must face giving up "released time" and try to work out some other plan of carrying on the Gospel work in those institutions. If to work out some other plan be impossible, we shall face the abandonment of the seminaries and institutes and the return to Church colleges and academies. We are not now sure, in the light of developments, that these should ever have been given up. We are clear upon this point, namely, that we shall not feel justified in appropriating one further tithing dollar to the upkeep of our seminaries and institutes unless they can be used to teach the Gospel in the manner prescribed. The tithing represents too much toil, too much self-denial, too much sacrifice, too much faith, to be used for the colorless instruction of the youth of the Church in elementary ethics. This decision and situation must be faced when the next budget is considered. In saying this, I am speaking for the First Presidency.

All that has been said regarding the character of religious teaching, and the results which in the very nature of things must follow a failure properly to teach the Gospel, applies with full and equal force to seminaries, to institutes, and to any and every other educational institution belonging to the Church school system.

The First Presidency earnestly solicits the whole-hearted help and co-operation of all you men and women who, from your work on the firing line, know so well the greatness of the problem which faces us and which so vitally and intimately affects the spiritual health and the salvation of our youth, as also the future welfare of the whole Church. We need you, the Church needs you, the Lord needs you. Restrain not yourselves, nor withhold your helping hand.

In closing I wish to pay a humble but sincere tribute to teachers. Having worked my own way through school, high school, college, and professional school, I know something of the hardship and sacrifice this demands; but I know also the growth and satisfaction which come as we reach the end. So I stand here with a knowledge of how many, perhaps most of you, have come to your present place. Furthermore, for a time I tried, without much success, to teach school, so I know also the feelings of those of us teachers who do not make the first grade and must rest in the lower ones. I know the present amount of actual compensation you get and how very sparse it is—far, far too sparse. I wish from the bottom of my heart we could make it greater; but the drain on the Church income is already so great for education that I must in honesty say there is no immediate prospect of betterment. Our budget for this school year is $860,000, or almost seventeen percent of the estimated total cost of running the whole Church, including general administration, stakes, wards, branches, and mission expenses, for all purposes, including welfare and charities. Indeed, I wish I felt sure that the prosperity of the people would be so ample that they could and would certainly pay tithes enough to keep us going as we are.

So I say I pay my tribute to your industry, your loyalty, your sacrifice, your willing eagerness for service in the cause of truth, your faith in God and in His work, and your earnest desire to do the things that our ordained leader and Prophet would have you do. And I entreat you not to make the mistake of thrusting aside your leader's counsel, or of failing to carry out his wish, or of refusing to follow his direction. David of old, privily cutting off only the skirt of Saul's robe, uttered the cry of a smitten heart: "The Lord forbid that I should do this thing unto my master, the Lord's anointed, to stretch forth mine hand against him, seeing he is the anointed of the Lord." (1 Samuel 24:6.)

May God bless you always in all your righteous endeavors, may He quicken your understanding, increase your wisdom, enlighten you by experience, bestow upon you patience, charity, and, as among your most precious gifts, endow you with the discernment of spirits that you may certainly know the spirit of righteousness and its opposite as they come to you; may He give you entrance to the hearts of those you teach and then make you know that as you enter there you stand in holy places, that must be neither polluted nor defiled, either by false or corrupting doctrine or by sinful misdeed; may He enrich your knowledge with the skill and power to teach righteousness; may your faith and your testimonies increase, and your ability to encourage and foster them in others grow greater every day—all that the youth of Zion may be taught, built up, encouraged, heartened, that they may not fall by the wayside, but go on to eternal life, that these blessings coming to them, you through them may be blessed also. And I pray all this in the name of Him who died that we might live, the Son of God, the Redeemer of the world, Jesus Christ. Amen.

———————————

Charge to Religious Educators, 11–17.

F A I T H

~❧ ❧~

The Sacrifice of All Things

Joseph Smith

This talk is taken from the *Lectures on Faith*, a series of lessons given in the Kirtland School of the Elders during the winter of 1834–35. These lectures were published as the first section in the first edition of the Doctrine and Covenants, printed in the fall of 1835, and they continued to be published in subsequent editions until 1921. They were finally removed because Church leaders were concerned about doctrinal ambiguity in Lecture 5, and because the lectures were not to be considered as direct revelations from God.

Joseph Smith was not the only author of the *Lectures on Faith*; they were written by a committee composed of Joseph Smith, Oliver Cowdery, Sidney Rigdon, and Frederick G. Williams. The Prophet certainly would have had the prevailing voice in the committee, however, and he approved their publication in the Doctrine and Covenants. Because the concepts and principles in the lectures undoubtedly come from Joseph Smith, he is generally considered their primary author.

———————

Having treated in the preceding lectures of the ideas, of the character, perfections, and attributes of God, we next proceed to treat of the knowledge which persons must have, that the course of life which they pursue is according to the will of God, in order that they may be enabled to exercise faith in him unto life and salvation.

2. This knowledge supplies an important place in revealed religion; for it was by reason of it that the ancients were enabled to endure as seeing him who is invisible. An actual knowledge to any person, that the course of life which he pursues is according to the will of God, is essentially necessary to enable him to have that confidence in God without which no person can obtain eternal life. It was this that enabled the ancient saints to endure all their afflictions and persecutions, and to take joyfully the spoiling of their goods, knowing (not believing merely) that they had a more enduring substance. (Hebrews 10:34.)

3. Having the assurance that they were pursuing a course which was agreeable to the will of God, they were enabled to take, not only the spoiling of their goods, and the wasting of their substance, joyfully, but also to suffer death in its most horrid forms; knowing (not merely believing) that when this earthly house of their tabernacle was dissolved, they had a building of God, a house not made with hands, eternal in the heavens. (2 Corinthians 5:1.)

4. Such was, and always will be, the situation of the saints of God, that unless they have an actual knowledge that the course they are pursuing is according to the will of God they will grow weary in their minds, and faint; for such has been, and always will be, the opposition in the hearts of unbelievers and those that know not God against the pure and unadulterated religion of heaven (the only thing which insures eternal life), that they will persecute to the uttermost all that worship God according to his revelations, receive the truth in the love of it, and submit themselves to be guided and directed by his will; and drive them to such extremities that nothing short of an actual knowledge of their being the favorites of heaven, and of their having embraced the order of things which God has established for the redemption of man, will enable them to exercise that confidence in him, necessary for them to overcome the world, and obtain that crown of glory which is laid up for them that fear God.

5. For a man to lay down his all, his character and reputation, his honor, and applause, his good name among men, his houses, his lands, his brothers and sisters, his wife and children, and even his own life also—counting all things but filth and dross for the excellency of the knowledge of Jesus Christ—requires more than mere belief or supposition that he is doing the will of God; but actual knowledge, realizing that, when these sufferings are ended, he will enter into eternal rest, and be a partaker of the glory of God.

6. For unless a person does know that he is walking according to the will of God, it would be offering an insult to the dignity of the Creator were he to say that he would be a partaker of his glory when he should be done with the things of this life. But when he has this knowledge, and most assuredly knows that he is doing the will of God, his confidence can be equally strong that he will be a partaker of the glory of God.

7. Let us here observe, that a religion that does not require the sacrifice of all things never has power sufficient to produce the faith necessary unto life and salvation; for, from the first existence of man, the faith necessary unto the enjoyment of life and salvation never could be obtained without the sacrifice of all earthly things. It was through this sacrifice, and this only, that God has ordained that men should enjoy eternal life; and it is through the medium of the sacrifice of all earthly things that men do actually know that they are doing the things that are well pleasing in the sight of God. When a man has offered in sacrifice all that he has for the truth's sake, not even withholding his life, and believing before God that he has been called to make this sacrifice because he seeks to do his will, he does know, most assuredly, that God does and will accept his sacrifice and offering, and that he has not, nor will not seek his face in vain. Under these circumstances, then, he can obtain the faith necessary for him to lay hold on eternal life.

8. It is in vain for persons to fancy to themselves that they are heirs with those, or can be heirs with them, who have offered their all in sacrifice, and by this means obtain faith in God and favor with him so as to obtain eternal life, unless they, in like manner, offer unto him the same sacrifice, and through that offering obtain the knowledge that they are accepted of him.

9. It was in offering sacrifices that Abel, the first martyr, obtained knowledge that he was accepted of God. And from the days of righteous Abel to the present time, the knowledge that men have that they are accepted in the sight of God is obtained by offering sacrifice. And in the last days, before the Lord comes, he is to gather together his saints who have made a covenant with him by sacrifice. Psalm 50:3–5: "Our God shall come, and shall not keep silence: a fire shall devour before him, and it shall be very tempestuous round about him. He shall call to the heavens from above, and to the earth, that he may judge his people. Gather my saints together unto me; those that have made a covenant with me by sacrifice."

10. Those, then, who make the sacrifice, will have the testimony that their course is pleasing in the sight of God; and those who have this testimony will have faith to lay hold on eternal life, and will be enabled, through faith, to endure unto the end, and receive the crown that is laid up for them that love the appearing of our Lord Jesus Christ. But those who do not make the sacrifice cannot enjoy this faith, because men are dependent upon this sacrifice in order to obtain this faith: therefore, they cannot lay hold upon eternal life, because the revelations of God do not guarantee unto them the authority so to do, and without this guarantee faith could not exist.

11. All the saints of whom we have account, in all the revelations of God which are extant, obtained the knowledge which they had of their acceptance in his sight through the sacrifice which they offered unto him; and through the knowledge thus

obtained their faith became sufficiently strong to lay hold upon the promise of eternal life, and to endure as seeing him who is invisible; and were enabled, through faith, to combat the powers of darkness, contend against the wiles of the adversary, overcome the world, and obtain the end of their faith, even the salvation of their souls.

12. But those who have not made this sacrifice to God do not know that the course which they pursue is well pleasing in his sight; for whatever may be their belief or their opinion, it is a matter of doubt and uncertainty in their mind; and where doubt and uncertainty are there faith is not, nor can it be. For doubt and faith do not exist in the same person at the same time; so that persons whose minds are under doubts and fears cannot have unshaken confidence; and where unshaken confidence is not there faith is weak; and where faith is weak the persons will not be able to contend against all the opposition, tribulations, and afflictions which they will have to encounter in order to be heirs of God, and joint heirs with Christ Jesus; and they will grow weary in their minds, and the adversary will have power over them and destroy them.

Lectures on Faith, 6:1–12.

~℘ ℘~

MIRACLES

MATTHEW COWLEY

Elder Matthew Cowley's miraculous experiences among the Saints in the Pacific Islands, as related here, have become legendary. This talk was delivered at Brigham Young University on February 18, 1953. Elder Cowley died later that same year at the relatively young age of fifty-six. Elder Cowley's humor, seen throughout his talks, is evident in his introduction to his remarks: "I feel very humble this morning, and sometimes when I'm introduced, I get the idea that others feel that I'm untouchable, but I want you to know that I'm neither untouchable nor unteachable. And since I've been in this position in the Church, I have learned some very fine things from some of the members of the Church, generally in anonymous letters. I don't know why they don't sign those letters because almost invariably what they say is true, especially when I look it up in the books."

When I was invited to come here, President [Ernest] Wilkinson suggested that I might talk a little bit about miracles. Well, it will be a miracle if I do. I had a particular assignment or instruction from President George Albert Smith when I was called to this position. He called me into his office one day and took hold of my hand, and while he was holding my hand and looking at me he said, "I want to say something to you, Brother Cowley."

I said, "Well, I'm willing to listen."

"This is just a particular suggestion to you, not to all the brethren but to you." He said, "Never write a sermon. Never write down what you are going to say."

I said, "What on earth will I do?"

He said, "You tell the people what the Lord wants you to tell them while you are standing on your feet."

I said, "That certainly is putting some responsibility on the Lord."

But I've tried to live up to that instruction. And I've had some great experiences. There have been times when the Lord has forsaken me. But when he hasn't, I've had some miraculous—well, I shouldn't say miraculous—it is the normal experience of the priesthood, of having the inspiration of the Holy Spirit. I can bear witness to you . . . that God can work through his priesthood and that he does work through it. I know that without any question of doubt. I've had too many experiences. I'm an expert witness about these things.

A few weeks ago I was called to the County Hospital in Salt Lake City by a mother. I didn't know her. She said her boy was dying from polio and asked if I would come down and give that boy a blessing. So I picked up a young bishop whom I generally take with me, for I think his faith is greater than mine, and I always like him along. We went down there, and here was this young lad in an iron lung, unconscious, his face rather a blackish color, with a tube in his throat, and they said he had a tube lower down in his abdomen. He had been flown in from an outlying community. The mother said to me, "This is an unusual boy. Not because he's my child, but he is an unusual boy." I think he was eight or nine years of age. After they put the usual coverings on us, we went in, and we blessed that boy. It was one of those occasions when I knew as I laid my hands upon that lad that he was an unusual boy, and he had faith. Having faith in his faith, I blessed him to get well and promised him he would. I never heard any more about him until last Sunday. I was on my way to Murray to conference; I dropped in the County Hospital, and I asked if I might see the lad. The nurse said, "Certainly. Walk right down the hall." As I walked down the hall, out came the boy running to meet me. He ran up and asked, "Are you Brother Cowley?"

And I said, "Yes."

He said, "I want to thank you for that prayer." He added, "I was unconscious then, wasn't I?"

I replied, "You certainly were."

He said, "That's the reason I don't recognize you." Then he asked, "Come in my room; I want to talk to you." He was an unusual boy. Well, we went in the room. He still had a tube in his throat. I said, "How long are you going to have that tube there?"

He said, "Oh, two weeks. Two more weeks, and then I'm all well. How about another blessing?"

So I said, "Certainly." I blessed him again. I was in a hurry. I wanted to get out to my conference. But he stopped me and asked, "Hey, how about my partner in the next bed?" There was a young fellow about sixteen or seventeen.

I said, "What do you mean?"

He said, "Don't go without blessing him. He's my partner."

I said, "Sure." Then I asked the boy, "Would you like a blessing?"

He said, "Yes, sir. I'm a teacher in the Aaronic Priesthood in my ward." I blessed him, and then my little friend went and brought another fellow in. Here was another partner. And I blessed him.

Now, except ye believe as a child, you can't receive these blessings. We have to have the faith of a child in order to believe in these things, especially when you reach college age, and your minds are so full of skepticism and doubt. I guess there are some things that you should doubt. But you can become as little children in these things. Miracles are commonplace, brothers and sisters.

In 1851 or 1852, Parley P. Pratt wrote a book called *The Key to [the Science of] Theology*. In that book he said the day would come (these were not his exact words), when man would not be satisfied with going along the surface of the earth at the rate of sixty, seventy, eighty or ninety miles an hour, but we would use the air and go at the rate of a thousand miles an hour. Now in 1852 when he wrote that he was "crazy," wasn't he? He was "mad"—but he was a prophet. Today it is commonplace. Since the first time I flew from San Francisco to Australia the flying time has been decreased twelve hours. I see in the paper where they are going to have a jet plane from Vancouver to Tokyo, Japan, which will require only eight hours for that long journey. Now, are they miracles? No, they are just commonplace—just commonplace!

The boy prophet went into the grove and prayed—a young lad with simple faith. He opened up his heart to God. He apparently reached out and by prayer got under his control the proper channels, and God and the Son came down and appeared to him. A few weeks ago I sat in my front room and had Dwight Eisenhower come right into my front room. I saw him sworn in as President of the United States. I saw the parade over other people's shoulders—all of this right in my own front room, and the same thing in millions of homes! Now there was no wire connecting me or my home with Washington, D.C., just these channels, or whatever Brother [Harvey] Fletcher and others call them out there, air waves, or whatever they are. But through those channels I brought into my home the President of the United States and the inaugural ceremonies. If I'd have told you twenty-five years ago that this would be done in this year 1953, I know what you'd have told me.

Well, no man invented those elements out there. Man has invented instruments whereby he harnesses those elements, but he never invented the elements; they are eternal; they've been there all the time, and if I can turn a little gadget and bring the President of the United States into my front room, God can bring

himself within the vision of man. The Master can come down
within the range of man's vision because he has more control over
those elements out there than man does himself. The Prophet
Joseph said that Moroni appeared to him in his bedroom. I've been
back there to that house. I've stood there and wondered how he
got through those walls, how he came in. Now I don't doubt any
more about the Angel Moroni coming into the Prophet's home.
Man hasn't yet harnessed all of these elements. He's working at it
and meeting with great success.

I was on an island down in French Oceania one Sunday afternoon. I started fooling with the radio; I don't know whether
you're supposed to play radios on Sunday afternoon or not, but I
started turning the dials, and all of a sudden I heard the voice of
Richard L. Evans from the Tabernacle in Salt Lake City. The
strange thing about it was that I wasn't in contact with Salt Lake
City, I was in tune with a station in Houston, Texas. That station
was getting the program from Salt Lake City, and I was picking it
up from Houston. I can't explain these things. Some of you fellows can. But I had an instrument there which man had invented
so that he could bring under his control and direction these elements out there.

I was over in Samoa. I couldn't sleep, worrying about the cen-
tipedes, and so forth. So I got up. It was three o'clock in the
morning. I went in the room where they had the radio. I started
turning the dials, and all of a sudden I heard a voice say, "Station
KSL, Salt Lake City. Songs of Harry Clarke." I sat there and listened to Harry Clarke sing for fifteen minutes. Then I had to get
up the next morning at three o'clock because I'd sent him a cable
and I wanted to see if he got it. He had. He mentioned it over the
air. So I listened to him sing for another fifteen minutes. You
know, the strange thing about it was I was hearing him sing four
hours before he actually sang. And you talk about miracles. . . .

The missionaries down in Samoa didn't have a president for a few months. I was the president but by remote control. I used to go to a Chinaman's home in Honolulu and tell him to tune in one of our natives down in Samoa, then tell that native to round up all the missionaries and have them come there, as I wanted to give them some instruction.

So he'd tune in down there and get this young Samoan with his ham radio, and I'd sit there in that Chinese home and talk to these missionaries down in Samoa and give whatever instructions I wanted to give them. But being the usual missionaries, I don't think they paid any attention. I telephoned one day from Honolulu to my home, and I asked the engineer there at the radio-phone place, "How can I talk confidentially to my wife? I send this message out into the air, and anybody with a ham radio can reach out and pick it up."

He said, "Yes, that's right, but they won't understand it."

I said, "Well, why not?"

He said, "Well, when your words go out of this transmitter we jumble them up; there is no meaning to them. But when they go into the receiver on the mainland they are all straightened out again, and your wife will understand them just as you spoke them."

My, I'm glad of that. I'll tell you why. I get my prayers so jumbled up sometimes that I'm glad there's a receiving set over on the other side that will straighten out the things I'm trying to say. And I believe that, I'm just simple enough to believe that. I'm simple enough to believe that if man can talk to man across the ocean and across the world with these instruments, that man can talk to God, that God has as much power as man, as much control over the elements. And so, brothers and sisters of the Church, God has his priesthood here upon the earth, his power, and with that power we can be used by God for the accomplishment of his purpose. Don't ever forget that. I've had these experiences. I know.

I've learned a lot from these islanders that I see scattered around here. I see Albert Whaanga from New Zealand in the audience; I wish he'd teach you people how to rub noses. That's what we do down in New Zealand, you know. We don't really rub. You just press your forehead and your nose against the nose and forehead of the other person. It's a wonderful thing. You can always tell when they're keeping the Word of Wisdom down there. All you have to do is walk up and greet them and sniff a little bit, and you've got 'em! It would be a good practice to have over here, maybe even with some of our BYU students. So if I ever come up to one of you some day and say I'd like to rub noses with you, you'll know I'm suspecting something.

These natives live close to God. They have some kind of power. I guess it's just because they accept miracles as a matter of course. They never doubt anything. They used to scare me. Someone would come up and say, "Brother Cowley, I've had a dream about you."

I'd say, "Don't tell me. I don't want to hear about it."

"Oh, it was a good one."

"All right. Tell me."

And they'd tell me something. Now I remember when President Rufus K. Hardy of the First Council of the Seventy passed away. I was walking along the street of one of the cities in New Zealand, and one of our native members came up—a lady.

She said to me, "President Hardy is dead."

I said, "Is that so? Have you received a wire?"

She said, "No. I received a message, but I haven't received any wire." She repeated, "He's dead. I know."

Well, I always believed them when they told me those things. When I got back to headquarters, I wasn't there long when here came a cablegram which said that President Hardy had passed away the night before. But she knew that without any cablegram. She told me about it.

I got out of my car once in the city. I got out to do some window-shopping to get a little rest from driving. I walked around, and finally I went around a corner, and there stood a native woman and her daughter. The mother said to the daughter, "What did I tell you?"

I said, "What's going on here?"

The daughter said, "Mother said if we'd stand here for fifteen minutes you'd come around the corner." Now she didn't have any radio set with her, just one in her heart where she received the impression.

After President Hardy died, we had a memorial service for him. I'll never forget the native who was up speaking, saying what a calamity it was to the mission to lose this great New Zealand missionary who could do so much for them as one of the Authorities of the Church. He was talking along that line, and all of a sudden he stopped and looked around at me and said, "Wait a minute. There's nothing to worry about. When President Cowley gets home, he'll fill the first vacancy in the Council of the Twelve Apostles, and we'll still have a representative among the Authorities of the Church." Then he went on talking about President Hardy. When I arrived home the following September, I filled the first vacancy in the Quorum of the Twelve. Now did that just happen by chance? Oh, I might have thought so if it had been one of you white Gentiles that had prophesied that, but not from the blood of Israel. Oh, no, I could not deny, I couldn't doubt it.

And so, remember we have great opportunities. Great opportunities to bless. Sometimes I wonder if we do enough in our administration of the sick. You know when the Apostles tried to cast out an evil spirit, they couldn't do it or they didn't do it. The Master came along, and he immediately cast out the dumb spirit. Then the Apostles said, "Why could not we cast him out?" And what did Christ say? "This kind goeth not out but by prayer and by fasting." (Matthew 17:21.)

Sometimes we rush in, administer to a person, rush out, and

say, "Well, he won't make it. I know he won't." Of course, we have to, in case of an emergency, go immediately. Sometimes I wonder, if we have a little time, if we shouldn't do a little fasting. "This kind cometh not out save by prayer and by fasting."

A little over a year ago a couple came into my office carrying a little boy. The father said to me, "My wife and I have been fasting for two days, and we've brought our little boy up for a blessing. You are the one we've been sent to."

I said, "What's the matter with him?"

They said he was born blind, deaf, and dumb, had no coordination of his muscles, couldn't even crawl at the age of five years. I said to myself, this is it. I had implicit faith in the fasting and the prayers of those parents. I blessed that child, and a few weeks later I received a letter: "Brother Cowley, we wish you could see our little boy now. He's crawling. When we throw a ball across the floor, he races after it on his hands and knees. He can see. When we clap our hands over his head, he jumps. He can hear." Medical science had laid the burden down. God had taken over. The little boy was rapidly recovering or really getting what he'd never had.

I went into a hospital one day in New Zealand to bless a woman who didn't belong to the Church. She was dying. We all knew she was dying. Even the doctor said so. She was having her farewell party. Ah, that's one thing I like about the natives. When you go, they give you a farewell party. They all gather around. They send messages over to the other side. "When you get over there, tell my mother I'm trying to do my best; I'm not so good, but I'm trying. Tell her to have a good room fixed for me when I get over there—plenty of fish, good meals." My, it's wonderful how they send you off. Well, there they were, all gathered around this poor sister. She was about to be confined, and the doctor told her it would kill her. She was tubercular from head to foot. I had with me an old native, almost ninety. She was his niece. He stood up at the head of the bed, and he said, "Vera, you're dead. You're dead because the doctor says you're dead. You're on your way out. I've been to you, your home, your people, my relatives. I'm the only one that has joined the Church. None of you has ever listened to me. You're dead now; if you're going to live," he turned to me and said, "is it all right if we kneel down and pray?"

I said, "Yes." So we knelt down. Everybody around there knelt down. And after the prayer we blessed her. The last time I was in New Zealand she had her fifth child and she's physically well from head to foot. She has not joined the Church yet. That's the next miracle I'm waiting for.

Well, now, this is just psychological effect, isn't it? There's nothing to this priesthood business. It's only psychological effect. But where was the psychological effect on that little boy in the County Hospital who was so unconscious he didn't even know we were praying over him? He wasn't even conscious of what we were doing.

I was called to a home in a little village in New Zealand one day. There the Relief Society sisters were preparing the body of one of our Saints. They had placed his body in front of the Big House, as they call it, the house where the people came to wail and weep and mourn over the dead, when in rushed the dead man's brother.

He said, "Administer to him."

And the young natives said, "Why, you shouldn't do that; he's dead."

"You do it!"

This same old man that I had with me when his niece was so ill was there. The younger native got down on his knees, and he anointed the dead man. Then this great old sage got down and blessed him and commanded him to rise. You should have seen the Relief Society sisters scatter. And he sat up, and he said, "Send for the elders; I don't feel very well." Now, of course, all of that was just psychological effect on that dead man. Wonderful, isn't it—

this psychological effect business? Well, we told him he had just been administered to, and he said: "Oh, that was it." He said, "I was dead. I could feel life coming back into me just like a blanket unrolling." Now, he outlived the brother that came in and told us to administer to him.

I've told the story about the little baby nine months old who was born blind. The father came up with him one Sunday and said, "Brother Cowley, our baby hasn't been blessed yet; we'd like you to bless him."

I said, "Why have you waited so long?"

"Oh, we just didn't get around to it."

Now, that's the native way; I like that. Just don't get around to doing things! Why not live and enjoy it? I said, "All right, what's the name?" So he told me the name, and I was just going to start when he said, "By the way, give him his vision when you give him a name. He was born blind." Well, it shocked me, but then I said to myself, why not? Christ told his disciples when he left them they could work miracles. And I had faith in that father's faith. After I gave that child its name, I finally got around to giving it its vision. That boy's about twelve years old now. The last time I was back there I was afraid to inquire about him. I was sure he had gone blind again. That's the way my faith works sometimes. So I asked the branch president about him. And he said, "Brother Cowley, the worst thing you ever did was to bless that child to receive his vision. He's the meanest kid in the neighborhood, always getting into mischief." Boy, I was thrilled about that kid getting into mischief!

God does have control of all of these elements. You and I can reach out, and if it's his will, we can bring those elements under our control for his purposes. I know that God lives. I know that Jesus is the Christ. I know that Joseph Smith was a prophet of God. And if there ever was a miracle in the history of mankind that miracle is this Church which has grown to its present greatness in the earth.

And your institution here stems from the prayer of a boy who was persecuted, who was driven from pillar to post, whose life was taken, who has been branded as the greatest fraud that ever lived on the American continent. This Church from that kind of fraud is the greatest miracle of modern history. And it's a miracle of God our Father. May you all have an inward witness that Joseph Smith was a prophet, that God used him to bring about his purposes in this Dispensation of the Fulness of Times. May we always be loyal, devoted, and simple in our faith, I pray in the name of Jesus Christ. Amen.

BYU Speeches of the Year, February 18, 1953.

FAITHFULNESS

～ ～

GENERAL CHARGE TO THE TWELVE

OLIVER COWDERY

On February 14, 1835, in Kirtland, Ohio, Joseph Smith called a meeting to organize the first twelve Apostles of this dispensation. As directed by a previous revelation (D&C 18:37), the Three Witnesses to the Book of Mormon sought the inspiration of the Spirit and named, in that meeting, the twelve who were to serve as Apostles. On February 14 and 15, the Three Witnesses ordained nine of the twelve to the apostleship; three were out of town and received their ordinations later. Joseph Smith then confirmed the ordination with the laying on of hands. During these meetings, Oliver Cowdery issued this charge to the Twelve.

Elder Bruce R. McConkie wrote of this charge: "It follows that everything stated by Elder Oliver Cowdery in his charge to the apostles could also be given as a charge to all elders. Every elder is entitled and expected to seek and obtain all the spiritual blessings of the gospel, including the crowning blessing of seeing the Lord face to face." (*Promised Messiah*, 595.)

———————

Dear Brethren—Previous to delivering the charge, I shall read a part of a revelation. It is known to you, that previous to the organization of this Church in 1830, the Lord gave revelations, or the Church could not have been organized. The people of this Church were weak in faith compared with the ancients. Those who embarked in this cause were desirous to know how the work was to be conducted. They read many things in the

Book of Mormon concerning their duty, and the way the great work ought to be done; but the minds of men are so constructed that they will not believe, without a testimony of seeing or hearing. The Lord gave us a revelation that, in process of time, there should be twelve men chosen to preach His Gospel to Jew and Gentile. Our minds have been on a constant stretch, to find who these twelve were; when the time should come we could not tell; but we sought the Lord by fasting and prayer to have our lives prolonged to see this day, to see you, and to take a retrospect of the difficulties through which we have passed; but having seen the day, it becomes my duty to deliver to you a charge; and first, a few remarks respecting your ministry. You have many revelations put into your hands—revelations to make you acquainted with the nature of your mission; you will have difficulties by reason of your visiting all the nations of the world. You will need wisdom in a tenfold proportion to what you have ever had; you will have to combat all the prejudices of all nations.

[He then read the revelation (Doctrine and Covenants 18), and said:] Have you desired this ministry with all your hearts? If you have desired it you are called of God, not of man, to go into the world.

[He then read again, from the revelation, what the Lord said unto the Twelve.] Brethren, you have had your duty presented in this revelation. You have been ordained to this holy Priesthood, you have received it from those who have the power and authority from an angel; you are to preach the Gospel to every nation. Should you in the least degree come short of your duty, great will be your condemnation; for the greater the calling the greater the transgression. I therefore warn you to cultivate great humility; for I know the pride of the human heart. Beware, lest the flatterers of the world lift you up; beware, lest your affections be captivated by worldly objects. Let your ministry be first. Remember, the souls of men are committed to your charge; and if you mind your calling, you shall always prosper.

You have been indebted to other men, in the first instance, for evidence; on that you have acted; but it is necessary that you receive a testimony from heaven for yourselves; so that you can bear testimony to the truth of the Book of Mormon, and that you have seen the face of God. That is more than the testimony of an angel. When the proper time arrives, you shall be able to bear this testimony to the world. When you bear testimony that you have seen God, this testimony God will never suffer to fall, but will bear you out; although many will not give heed, yet others will. You will therefore see the necessity of getting this testimony from heaven.

Never cease striving until you have seen God face to face. Strengthen your faith; cast off your doubts, your sins, and all your unbelief; and nothing can prevent you from coming to God. Your ordination is not full and complete till God has laid His hand upon you. We require as much to qualify us as did those who have gone before us; God is the same. If the Savior in former days laid His hands upon His disciples, why not in latter days?

With regard to superiority, I must make a few remarks. The ancient apostles sought to be great; but lest the seeds of discord be sown in this matter; understand particularly the voice of the Spirit on this occasion. God does not love you better or more than others. You are to contend for the faith once delivered to the Saints. Jacob, you know, wrestled till he had obtained. It was by fervent prayer and diligent search that you have obtained the testimony you are now able to bear. You are as one; you are equal in bearing the keys of the Kingdom to all nations. You are called to preach the Gospel of the Son of God to the nations of the earth; it is the will of your Heavenly Father, that you proclaim His Gospel to the ends of the earth and the islands of the sea.

Be zealous to save souls. The soul of one man is as precious as the soul of another. You are to bear this message to those who consider themselves wise; and such may persecute you—they may seek your life. The adversary has always sought the life of the servants of

God; you are therefore to be prepared at all times to make a sacrifice of your lives, should God require them in the advancement and building up of His cause. Murmur not at God. Be always prayerful; be always watchful. You will bear with me while I relieve the feelings of my heart. We shall not see another day like this; the time has fully come—the voice of the Spirit has come—to set these men apart.

You will see the time when you will desire to see such a day as this, and you will not see it. Every heart wishes you peace and prosperity, but the scene with you will inevitably change. Let no man take your bishopric, and beware that you lose not your crowns. It will require your whole souls, it will require courage like Enoch's.

The time is near when you will be in the midst of congregations who will gnash their teeth upon you. The Gospel must roll forth, and it will until it fills the whole earth. Did I say congregations would gnash their teeth at you? Yea, I say, nations will oppose you—you will be considered the worst of men. Be not discouraged at this. When God pours out His Spirit, the enemy will rage; but God, remember, is on your right hand, and on your left. A man, though he be considered the worst, has joy, who is conscious that he pleases God.

The lives of those who proclaim the true Gospel will be in danger; this has been the case ever since the days of righteous Abel. The same opposition has been manifest whenever man came forward to publish the Gospel. The time is coming when you will be considered the worst of men by many, and by some the best. The time is coming when you will be perfectly familiar with the things of God. This testimony will make those who do not believe your testimony, seek your lives; but there are whole nations who will receive your testimony. They will call you good men. Be not lifted up when ye are called good men. Remember you are young men, and ye shall be spared. I include the other three [not in attendance]. Bear them in mind in your prayers—carry their cases to the throne of grace; although they are not present, yet you and they are equal. This appointment is calculated to create for you an affection for each other, stronger than death. You will travel to other nations; bear each other in mind. If one or more be cast into prisons, let the others pray for them, and deliver them by their prayers. Your lives shall be in great jeopardy; but the promise of God is, that you shall be delivered.

Remember, you are not to go to other nations till you receive your endowments. Tarry at Kirtland until you are endowed with power from on high. You need a fountain of wisdom, knowledge and intelligence such as you never had. Relative to the endowment, I make a remark or two that there may be no mistake. The world cannot receive the things of God. He can endow you without worldly pomp or great parade. He can give you that wisdom, that intelligence, and that power, which characterized the ancient Saints, and now characterizes the inhabitants of the upper world.

The greatness of your commission consists in this: you are to hold the keys of this ministry; you are to go to the nations afar off—nations that sit in darkness. The day is coming when the work of God must be done. Israel shall be gathered: the seed of Jacob shall be gathered from their long dispersion. There will be a feast to Israel, the elect of God. It is a sorrowful tale, but the Gospel must be preached, and God's ministers rejected: but where can Israel be found and receive your testimony, and not rejoice? Nowhere! The prophecies are full of great things that are to take place in the last days. After the elect are gathered out, destructions shall come on the inhabitants of the earth; all nations shall feel the wrath of God, after they have been warned by the Saints of the Most High. If you will not warn them, others will, and you will lose your crowns.

You must prepare your minds to bid a long farewell to Kirtland, even till the great day come. You will see what you never expected to see; you will need the mind of Enoch or Elijah, and the faith of the brother of Jared; you must be prepared to walk by faith, how-ever appalling the prospect to human view; you, and each of you, should feel the force of the imperious mandate, Son, go labor in my vineyard, and cheerfully receive what comes; but in the end you will stand while others will fall. You have read in the revela-tion concerning ordination: Beware how you ordain, for all nations are not like this nation; they will willingly receive the ordinances at your hands to put you out of the way. There will be times when nothing but the angels of God can deliver you out of their hands.

We appeal to your intelligence, we appeal to your understand-ing, that we have so far discharged our duty to you. We consider it one of the greatest condescensions of our Heavenly Father, in pointing you out to us; you will be stewards over this ministry; you have a work to do that no other men can do; you must proclaim the Gospel in its simplicity and purity; and we commend you to God and the word of His grace. You have our best wishes, you have our most fervent prayers, that you may be able to bear this testi-mony, that you have seen the face of God. Therefore call upon Him in faith in mighty prayer till you prevail, for it is your duty and your privilege to bear such testimony for yourselves. We now exhort you to be faithful to fulfill your calling; there must be no lack here; you must fulfill in all things; and permit us to repeat, all nations have a claim on you; you are bound together as the Three Witnesses were; notwithstanding you can part and meet, and meet and part again, till your heads are silvered over with age.

[He then took them separately by the hand, and said, "Do you with full purpose of heart take part in this ministry, to proclaim the Gospel with all diligence, with these your brethren, according to the tenor and intent of the charge you have received?" Each of them answered in the affirmative.]

History of the Church, 2:194–95.

"BE YE AS PERFECT AS YE CAN"

BRIGHAM YOUNG

This discourse was delivered in the Old Tabernacle in Salt Lake City on December 18, 1853. In this address, President Brigham Young taught this comforting doctrine: "When we are doing as well as we know how in the sphere and station which we occupy here, we are justified in the justice, righteousness, mercy, and judgment that go before the Lord of heaven and earth. We are as justified as the angels who are before the throne of God. The sin that will cleave to all the posterity of Adam and Eve is that they have not done as well as they knew how."

We all occupy diversified stations in the world, and in the kingdom of God. Those who do right, and seek the glory of the Father in Heaven, whether their knowledge be little or much, or whether they can do little or much, if they do the very best they know how, they are perfect.

It may appear strange to some of you, and it certainly does to the world, to say it is possible for a man or woman to become perfect on this earth. It is written "Be ye therefore perfect, even as your Father which is in heaven is perfect." Again, "If any man offend not in word, the same is a perfect man, and able also to bridle the whole body." This is perfectly consistent to the person who understands what perfection really is.

If the first passage I have quoted is not worded to our understanding, we can alter the phraseology of the sentence, and say, "Be ye as perfect as ye can," for that is all we can do, though it is written, be ye perfect as your Father who is in heaven is perfect.

To be as perfect as we possibly can, according to our knowledge, is to be just as perfect as our Father in Heaven is. He cannot be any more perfect than He knows how, any more than we. When we are doing as well as we know how in the sphere and station which we occupy here, we are justified in the justice, righteousness, mercy, and judgment that go before the Lord of heaven and earth. We are as justified as the angels who are before the throne of God. The sin that will cleave to all the posterity of Adam and Eve is that they have not done as well as they knew how.

I will apply this to myself, and it will apply to you, and to every man and woman upon the earth; of course including brother [Isaac] Morley, who spoke to you this morning. If he has done the best he could in the late Indian difficulties in the district where he lives, and acted according to the judgment and light of the spirit of revelation in him, he is as justified as an angel of God.

Though we may do the best we know how at this time, can there be no improvement made in our lives? There can. If we do wrong ignorantly, when we learn it is wrong, then it is our duty to refrain from that wrong immediately and for ever, and the sin of ignorance is winked at, and passes into oblivion.

An inquiry was made this morning, if we know who we are, what our situation is, and the relationship we sustain to each other, to our God, and the position we occupy to the human family. I can answer the question. No, we do not. Do the people understand all the obligations they are under to each other and to their God? They do not. Again, do they try to know, as far as it is in their power? They do not. Are there individuals among us who seek with all their hearts to know and understand the will of God? Yes, many. But as a people, do they, with an undivided heart, endeavor to know the will of God in preference to everything else upon earth? They do not.

There is a reason for this. Brother Morley wanted to know if we had learned ourselves. We have not. When he referred to the spirits in the world, and what we could witness in the infant child in its mother's lap, at this moment like a little seraph, and in the next, more like a demon with passion and rage, I thought we need not confine ourselves to the child for example, for this picture of good and evil is exhibited as frequently in the parent, and even in the grey-headed sire, as in the child. If men and women understood perfectly their position before God, angels, and men, the place they occupy, and the sphere they act in, they would know they are as independent in their organization as the angels, or as the Gods. Yet, in consequence of sin entering into the world, darkness, wretchedness, folly, weakness of every kind, and the power of temptation surround the children of men, as well as the power of God. I say the grey-headed father, and the aged matron will give way to the power of evil, when it comes upon them, as readily, in many instances, as the infant child upon its mother's lap.

I speak what I know, and say, shame on those who are subject to such weakness, when they have had time and opportunity to learn better. . . . When men and women give way to these wicked spirits, it is a proof they have not learned their organization, and what they were made for.

As for this people knowing their true position before God, in the midst of the nations of the earth, it is certain they have not yet learned it. Shall we ever learn it? We shall. And further, *we shall be obliged to learn it*; and further still, *we shall be* COMPELLED *to learn it*. How? By flattery? By blessings? By the kind smiles of Providence? By the bountiful fulness of the invisible hand of our Heavenly Father bestowing every blessing upon us? Now some of us are ready to say, this will not bring us to an understanding of our true position, and prepare us for what is before us. If the mercies and blessings of our kind and indulgent heavenly Parent will not produce the desired effects upon His people, He will certainly chasten them, and make them know, by what they suffer, how to govern and sanctify themselves before Him. . . .

Do you inquire if I think we are about to be afflicted? If we are not good children, we shall be. We must learn to love righteousness, and hate iniquity, and then we can chasten ourselves, and bring ourselves to the sphere we were designed to fill in our existence, and govern and control ourselves in it, preparatory to power being put into our hands. We should never have but one desire, but one determination; our will should be perfectly centered upon the one object, viz., to find out the will of God, and do it. Let every individual thus school, chasten, prove, view, and review himself, taking himself into custody as a prisoner to be subjected to a severe examination, until his will is perfectly subservient to the will of God in every instance, and you can say, "No matter what it is, let us know the will of the Father in Heaven, and that is our will." Then we shall be able to train, school, and practice upon ourselves, until we can control, and bring under subjection, the wicked influences that surround us; we can then begin to pave the way, or throw up an highway of holiness to the rising generation.

This we have to do. It is our business. It is the labor of the Latter-day Saints, which, if carried out, will run through all the various changing scenes of mortal life. It is in every act and dealing, both with ourselves, our families, and strangers. It fills every avenue of human life, from beginning to end. To gain the spiritual ascendancy over ourselves, and the influences with which we are surrounded, through a rigid course of self-discipline, is our first consideration, it is our first labor, before we can pave the way for our children to grow up without sin unto salvation.

No man, in a short hour or two, can tell everything that is in his heart, when it is filled by the inspiration of the Holy Ghost. But I will continue my remarks, and give you a little more.

All persons are surrounded with circumstances peculiar to their location, station, and situation in life. A portion of our old associates believe we are controlled entirely by circumstances; but this people have learned enough to know they have the ability and

power to control circumstances, to a certain extent; they will control us more or less, but not entirely. We can lay the foundation in
the midst of this people for a train of circumstances to surround
the rising generation with a divine influence. We can also produce
a train of circumstances that will work their certain destruction.
This is in our power, and the first is the labor of the Latter-day
Saints.

Some, when their minds are opened to behold the purity of a
God of eternity—the purity of heaven, and understand that no
impure thing can enter there; when they can realize the perfection
of the redeemed and glorified Zion, and then look at the people
now, and their actions, and how they are overcome with their
weaknesses, how they cannot go out and come in without coming
in contact, in some way, with their neighbors; when they look at
the universal sinfulness of mortal man; are ready to exclaim, "We
shall all go to destruction, salvation is impossible." I do not believe
a word of it. If we do the best we know how, and yet commit many
acts that are wrong, and contrary to the counsel given to us, there
is hope in our case.

The Savior has warned us to be careful how we judge, forgiving
each other seven times seventy in a day, if we repent, and confess
our sins one to another. Can we be more merciful and forgiving
than our Father in Heaven? We cannot. Therefore let people do
the best they can, and they will pave the way for the rising generation to walk up into the light, wisdom, and knowledge of the
angels, and of the redeemed from this earth, to say nothing of
other earths, and they will be prepared to enjoy in the resurrection
all the blessings which are for the faithful, and enjoy them in the
flesh.

It is our duty, and to this we are called so to frame and control circumstances in our lifetime, as to bring blessings upon the
rising generation, which we can never attain to while we are in
the flesh. But when the vision of our minds is opened to behold

the immaculate purity, perfection, light, beauty, and glory of Zion, the heaven of eternity, the place where Saints and angels dwell in the eternal worlds, then salvation for us poor erring mortals seems almost impossible; it seems that we shall hardly be saved. This, however, is verily true, we shall hardly be saved. There never was any person over saved; all who have been saved, and that ever will be in the future, are only just saved, and then it is not without a struggle to overcome, that calls into exercise every energy of the soul.

It is good for us to follow the example of those who have attained unto salvation; consequently if I wish to be saved, and be an instrument of pointing out the way to others, let me not only preach the doctrine of salvation, but set the example in my conduct, and plead with them to follow it. If our faith is one, and we are united to gain one grand object, and I, as an individual, can possibly get into the celestial kingdom, you and every other person, by the same rule, can also enter there.

Though our interest is one as a people, yet remember, salvation is an individual work; it is every person for themselves. I mean more by this than I have time to tell you in full, but I will give you a hint. There are those in this Church who calculate to be saved by the righteousness of others. They will miss their mark. They are those who will arrive just as the gate is shut, so in that case you may be shut out; then you will call upon someone, who, by their own faithfulness, through the mercy of Jesus Christ, has entered in through the celestial gate, to come and open it for you; but to do this is not their province. Such will be the fate of those persons who vainly hope to be saved upon the righteousness and through the influence of brother Somebody. I forewarn you therefore to cultivate righteousness and faithfulness in yourselves, which is the only passport into celestial happiness. . . .

As it respects the wicked actions of the people, . . . I could tell you things about some men, that you would not want to hear. To satisfy my own feelings by way of comparison, I will give you a faint idea of how they look to me.

Imagine all the carcasses of the people who have died of the cholera, and of other loathsome diseases, heaped up to rot in one general mass, under the rays of a southern sun, and the stench of such a mass of corruption would not begin to offend my nostrils, and the nostrils of every righteous man, so much as those men do. On the other hand, if every man will do the best he can, and as far as he knows how, it will be well with him, and he will be blessed until there is not room to contain the blessings which will be poured upon him. Sin consists in doing wrong when we know and can do better, and it will be punished with a just retribution, in the due time of the Lord. . . .

Are those who are drinking and carousing today (and there may be some doing so who profess to be brethren) obliged to break the Sabbath, and make themselves drunkards and gluttons? No. If the brethren who profess to be Saints, and do wrong, would reveal the root of the matter, and tell the whole truth, it would be, "I have a desire to do a great deal of good, but the devil is always at my elbow, and I always like to keep the old gentleman so that I can put my hand upon him, for I want to use him sometimes." That is the reason why men and women are overcome with evil.

Again, I can charge you with what you will all plead guilty of, if you would confess the truth, viz., you dare not quite give up all your hearts to God, and become sanctified throughout, and be led by the Holy Ghost from morning until evening, and from one year's end to another. I know this is so, and yet few will acknowledge it. I know this feeling is in your hearts, as well as I know the sun shines. . . .

If I were to ask you individually, if you wished to be sanctified throughout, and become as pure and holy as you possibly could live, every person would say yes; yet if the Lord Almighty should give a revelation instructing you to be given wholly up to Him, and to His cause, you would shrink, saying, "I am afraid He will take away some of my darlings." That is the difficulty with the majority of this people.

It is for you and I to wage war with that principle [of evil] until it is overcome in us, then we shall not entail it upon our children. It is for us to lay a foundation so that everything our children have to do with, will bring them to Mount Zion, and unto the city of the living God, the heavenly Jerusalem, and to an innumerable company of angels, to the general assembly and church of the first-born, which are written in heaven, and to God the Judge of all, and to the spirits of just men made perfect, and to Jesus the mediator of the new covenant, and to the blood of sprinkling that speaketh better things than the blood of Abel. If we lay such a foundation with all good conscience, and labor as faithfully as we can, it will be well with us and our children in time and in eternity.

What kind of a sensation would it produce in my heart, should I hear at the close of this meeting that the Lord had suffered the devil to destroy my houses, [and my family], and committed every particle of my property to the devouring flames—that I am left destitute, and alone in the world? I wish you all to apply this interrogation to yourselves. . . .

Or suppose, when you arrive at home from this meeting, you find your neighbors have killed your horses and destroyed your property, how would you feel? You would feel like taking instant vengeance on the perpetrator of the deed. But it would be wrong for you to encourage the least particle of feeling to arise in your bosom like anger, or revenge, or like taking judgment into your own hands, until the Lord Almighty shall say, "Judgment is yours, and for you to execute."

Brother Morley wished to know if anyone could tell the origin of thought. The origin of thought was planted in our organization at the beginning of our being. This is not telling you how it came there, or who put it there. Thought originated with our individual being, which is organized to be as independent as any being in eternity. When you go home, and learn that your neighbors have committed some depredation on your property, or in your family, and anger arises in your bosom, then consider, and know that it arises in yourselves.

On the other hand, suppose some person has blessed you when you return home, brought you a bag of flour, for instance, in a time of great scarcity, and some butter, milk, and vegetables, thoughts would at once spring up to bless the giver. The origin of thought and reflection is in ourselves. We think, because we are, and are made susceptible of external influences, and to feel our relationship to external objects. Thus thoughts of revenge, and thoughts of blessing will arise in the same mind, as it is influenced by external circumstances.

If you are injured by a neighbor, the first thought of the unregenerate heart is for God to damn the person who has hurt you. But if a person blesses you, the first thought that arises in you is, God bless that man; and this is the disposition to which we ought to cleave. But dismiss any spirit that would prompt you to injure any creature that the Lord has made, give it no place, encourage it not, and it will not stay where you are. You can let the [evil] man, or the [good] man into your house, as you please; you can say, "Walk in," to both of them.

This is a figure. When the [good] man presents himself, you know him at once by his [countenance]; the same when you see darkness and blackness advancing, you know it is from beneath, and you can command it to leave your house. When the good man comes, he brings with him a halo of kindness which fills you with peace and heavenly comfort; invite him into your house, and make him your constant guest.

I have often told you from this stand, if you cleave to holy, godlike principles, you add more good to your organization, which is made independent in the first place, and the good spirit and influence which come from the Father of lights, and from Jesus Christ, and from the holy angels add good to it. And when you have been proved, and when you have labored and occupied sufficiently upon that, it will become, in you, what brother Joseph Smith told Elder [John] Taylor, if he would adhere to the Spirit of the Lord strictly, it should become in him, viz., a fountain of revelation. That is true. After a while the Lord will say to such, "My son, you have been faithful, you have clung to good, and you love righteousness, and hate iniquity, from which you have turned away, now you shall have the blessing of the Holy Spirit to lead you, and be your constant companion, from this time henceforth and forever." Then the Holy Spirit becomes your property, it is given to you for a profit, and an eternal blessing. It tends to addition, extension, and increase, to immortality and eternal lives.

If you suffer the opposite of this to take possession of your tabernacles, it will hurt you, and all that is associated with you, and blast, and strike with mildew, until your tabernacle, which was created to continue throughout an endless duration, will be decomposed, and go back to its native elements, to be ground over again like the refractory clay that has spoiled in the hand of the potter, it must be worked over again until it shall become passive, and yield to the potter's wish.

One power is to add, to build up, and increase; the other to destroy and diminish; one is life, the other is death. Let us, then, lay a foundation for the rising generation to grow up without being trammeled and hindered in their onward course to glory and happiness by the superstitions, tradition, and ignorance that have blinded and hurt us. Let us do the best we can, and if we make a mistake once, seven times, or seventy times seven in a day, and are honest in our confessions, we shall be forgiven freely. As we expect to obtain mercy, so let us have mercy upon each other. And when the evil spirit comes let him find no place in you.

I recollect telling the Latter-day Saints that no man could judge the nature of a spirit without first testing it; until then, he is not capable to judge of it. Brethren, love righteousness, and hate iniquity.

May God bless you for ever. Amen.

Journal of Discourses, 2:129–36.

~❧ ❦~

The Lord's Side of the Line

George Albert Smith

President George Albert Smith often spoke of his grand-father's counsel to "stay on the Lord's side of the line." In this talk, delivered during the priesthood session of general conference, October 1945, he emphasized the significance of that advice: "There is a line of demarcation well defined between the Lord's territory and the devil's territory. If you will remain on the Lord's side of the line, the adversary cannot come there to tempt you. You are perfectly safe as long as you stay on the Lord's side of the line."

―――――――――――

My brethren, you have been very patient for the last two days; you have been in meeting very much of the time. Ordinarily, one would become exceedingly weary, but if we enjoy the Spirit of the Lord, it relieves us of that weariness and we are happy.

Incidents from Missionary Life

I remember as a young man and missionary in the Southern States, the first conference I attended. It was out in the woods on a farm in Mississippi. We didn't have comfortable seats to sit on. The brethren had been permitted to cut down a few trees and lay the trunks of those trees across the stumps which were left. We balanced ourselves on those or else sat on the ground.

Our meeting started right after breakfast time, and we didn't even think it was necessary to have anything more to eat until evening. We stayed and enjoyed the inspiration of the Almighty, and we certainly were blessed, notwithstanding the inconveniences and discomforts which surrounded us. At that time there was considerable hostility manifested in Mississippi and other states in the South, but we just felt as if we had walked into the presence of our Heavenly Father, and all fear and anxiety left. That was my first experience in the mission field attending a conference, and from that time until now I have appreciated the fact that the companionship of the Spirit of the Lord is an antidote for weariness, for hunger, for fear, and all those things that sometimes overtake us in life.

We sang [in this meeting] "Do What Is Right." When I was in the mission field first, I went into a section of country where that hymn was known to the community, apparently. Two humble missionaries, after walking until late in the afternoon in the sun, in the heat of summer, came to a small house that was at the bottom of a hill. When the missionaries arrived, they found friends who invited them in to partake of their meager refreshment. And then they were asked to go outside in the cool of the afternoon shade, on one of those comfortable, open southern porches between two rooms and sing some hymns. The people were not members of the Church, but they enjoyed Latter-day Saint hymns.

The missionaries had been threatened in that section. One of the men who had threatened them had kept watch of the road and in that way learned when they arrived. He sent word to his associates who saddled their horses and took their guns, and rode to the top of the hill overlooking the little house. The missionaries knew nothing about it; they did not know that right over their heads, not very far away, were a considerable number of armed horsemen. But they had the Spirit of the Lord, and as they sat there in the cool of the afternoon and sang hymns, the one hymn that seemed to have been prepared for the occasion was, "Do What Is Right." They happened to be good singers, and their voices went out into the quiet air. They had only sung one verse when the leader of the mob took off his hat. They sang another verse, and he got off his horse, and the others got off their horses, and by the time the last verse had been sung, those men were repentant. Upon the advice of their leader, they rode away without making their presence known. The leader was so impressed with what he heard the missionaries sing that he said to his associates: "We made a mistake. These are not the kind of men we thought they were. Wicked men can't sing like angels, and these men sing like angels. They must be servants of the Lord."

The result was that this man became converted to the Church and later was baptized. And I never hear that hymn sung but I think of that very unusual experience when two missionaries, under the influence of the spirit of God, turned the arms of the adversary away from them and brought repentance into the minds of those who had come to destroy them. . . .

Exhortation to Faithfulness

I am grateful to see so many of you here tonight, leaving aside other things that might have been done. You have been busy in many cases all day, and yet when the priesthood is called together you come as if to say, "Here, Lord, am I." If we in our homes shall so live that the Spirit of the Lord abides with us, we will always be prepared to say when the call comes, "Here, Lord, am I."

Tonight, I congratulate myself with you, that in the peaceful quiet of these everlasting hills, in the comfort of this great house of God, we are permitted to assemble ourselves together, not to plan our financial uplift, our social uplift, but to plan how we may find our place in the kingdom of heaven, to dwell there eternally with Jesus Christ, our Lord. We will all be tempted; no man is free from temptation. The adversary will use every means possible to deceive us; he tried to do that with the Savior of the world without success. He has tried it on many other men who have possessed divine authority, and sometimes he finds a weak spot and the individual loses what might have been a great blessing if he had been faithful.

So I want to plead with you, my brethren, be as anchors in the community in which you live that others may be drawn to you and feel secure. Let your light so shine that others seeing your good works will have a desire in their hearts to be like you. Wherever you go, keep in mind the fact that you represent him who is the author of our being. The priesthood that you hold is not the priesthood of Joseph Smith, or Brigham Young, or any other men who have been called to leadership of the Church at home or abroad. The priesthood that you hold is the power of God, conferred upon you from on high. Holy beings had to be sent to earth a little over a hundred years ago in order to restore that glorious blessing that had been lost to the earth for hundreds of years. Surely we ought to be grateful for our blessings.

Remember that as long as we seek the Lord, and keep his commandments as best we know, the adversary will have no power over us to lead us into transgression that may forfeit for us our place in the celestial kingdom.

The Line of Demarcation Between Good and Evil

I think I would like to repeat something I have told many times as a guide to some of these younger men. It was an expression of advice of my grandfather for whom I was named. He said: "There is a line of demarcation well defined between the Lord's territory and the devil's territory. If you will remain on the Lord's side of the line, the adversary cannot come there to tempt you. You are perfectly safe as long as you stay on the Lord's side of the line. But," he said, "if you cross onto the devil's side of the line, you are in his territory, and you are in his power, and he will work on you to get you just as far from that line as he possibly can, knowing that he can only succeed in destroying you by keeping you away from the place where there is safety."

All safety, all righteousness, all happiness are on the Lord's side of the line. If you are keeping the commandments of God by observing the Sabbath day, you are on the Lord's side of the line. If you attend to your secret prayers and your family prayers, you are on the Lord's side of the line. If you are grateful for food and express that gratitude to God, you are on the Lord's side of the line. If you love your neighbor as yourself, you are on the Lord's side of the line. If you are honest in your dealing with your fellow men, you are on the Lord's side of the line. If you observe the Word of Wisdom, you are on the Lord's side of the line. And so I might go on through the Ten Commandments and the other commandments that God has given for our guidance and say again, all that enriches our lives and makes us happy and prepares us for eternal joy is on the Lord's side of the line.

Finding fault with the things that God has given to us for our guidance is not on the Lord's side of the line. Setting one's self up as a receiver of dreams and visions to guide the human family is not on the Lord's side of the line; and when men, as they have sometimes done in order to win their success along some line or another, have come to an individual or individuals and said, "I have had this dream and this is what the Lord wants us to do," you may know that they are not on the Lord's side of the line. The dreams and visions and revelations of God to the children of men have always come through his regularly appointed servant. You may have dreams and manifestations for your own comfort and for your own satisfaction, but you will not have them for the Church unless God appoints you to take the place that he gave to his prophets of old and in our day, and unless you have been divinely commissioned to do the thing he wants you to do.

So, brethren, we need not be deceived—it will be easy to be deceived—but we need not be deceived if we will honor God by honoring ourselves and our families and loved ones and our associates in the places which they occupy in righteousness.

The Gospel to Be Preached

It is a wonderful day and age in which we live. It will not be long until the servants of the Lord will go again to the nations of the earth in great numbers. I have been asked within the last few hours, "Are we going to open the European Mission?" I may say to you the European Mission has never been closed. We had to call home many of those who were there, but we left men holding divine authority. By appointment they have been ministering to the faithful, and the work of the Lord is still anchored in those lands. It will not be long before there will go forth from the headquarters of the Church, leadership to set in order everything that needs to be set in order, in power and might and faith, giving to those people over there another opportunity, in many cases opportunities they had neglected in the past, and in some cases opportunities they have never yet enjoyed.

We must preach the gospel to the South American countries which we have scarcely touched. We must preach the gospel to every African section that we haven't been in yet. We must preach the gospel to Asia. And I might go on and say in all parts of the world where we have not yet been permitted to go. I look upon Russia as one of the most fruitful fields for the teaching of the gospel of Jesus Christ. And if I am not mistaken, it will not be long before the people who are there will desire to know something about this work which has reformed the lives of so many people. We have some few from that land, who belong to the Church—fine, capable individuals who may be called to go, when the time comes, back to the homeland of their parents, and deliver the message that is so necessary to all mankind.

Our most important obligation, my brethren, is to divide with our Father's children all those fundamental truths, all his rules and regulations which prepare us for eternal life, known as the gospel of Jesus Christ. Until we have done that to the full limit of our power, we will not receive all the blessings which we might otherwise have. So let us set our own homes in order, prepare our boys and our girls, and ourselves, so that if we are called to go to the various parts of the earth, we will be prepared to go. This will be our great mission.

Joy in Work in the Church

I want to thank you again for the joy I have had in your companionship during my long ministry. I have been laboring many years. My first ordination to an office in the Aaronic Priesthood was to that of a deacon, within two blocks of where I now stand. I was baptized in City Creek within one block from here. I was confirmed a member of the Church within two blocks from here. But since that time and since I received that gift from my Heavenly Father, for which I have no words to express my gratitude, he has called me to go to many parts of the earth, and more than a million miles have been traversed since I was called into the ministry. I have traveled in many lands and climes, and wherever I have gone I have found good people, sons and daughters of the living God who are waiting for the gospel of Jesus Christ, and there are thousands, hundreds of thousands, millions of them, who would be accepting the truth if they only knew what we know.

Brethren, let us be humble, let us be prayerful, let us be generous with our means, let us be unselfish in our attitude towards our fellows. Let our lives be such that our homes will always be the abiding place of prayer and thanksgiving, and the Spirit of the Lord will always be there.

Promises Made to the Faithful

In conclusion, let me say, wherever we are, let us remember that there has been conferred upon us a portion of divine authority, and therefore we represent the Master of heaven and earth. And so far as we honor that fine and wonderful blessing we will continue to grow in grace before the Lord; our lives will continue to be enriched; and in the end, eternal happiness in the celestial kingdom will be our reward. That's what the gospel is for. Let us live to be worthy of it every day of our lives, and I pray that when the time comes for us to go, we will not feel as though we have neglected any of our own dear ones, any of our neighbors and friends, by failing to divide with them that which is more precious than anything that the world can give, because it is the gift of God himself.

I pray that peace and love and happiness may abide in your hearts and in your homes, and that we may go forward with renewed determination to be worthy of peace because it can only dwell with us when we ourselves are living the commandments of our Heavenly Father and honoring him.

May peace abide with you and with your loved ones, and brethren, surround your families by the arms of your love and unite them together in that bond of affection which will insure eternal happiness.

I invoke upon you the favor of our Heavenly Father in the name of Jesus Christ. Amen.

Conference Report, October 1945, 115–20.

"STAND YE IN HOLY PLACES"

HAROLD B. LEE

In this address, delivered during general conference in April 1973, President Harold B. Lee bore powerful testimony: "I come to you today, with no shadow of doubting in my mind that I know the reality of the person who is presiding over this church, our Lord and Master, Jesus Christ. I know that he is. I know that he is closer to us than many times we have any idea. They are not an absentee Father and Lord. They are concerned about us, helping to prepare us for the advent of the Savior, whose coming certainly isn't too far away."

W e are grateful to all who have contributed to the success and inspiration of this conference, especially to our General Authorities who have delivered such timely, inspired messages. Sitting where we do as the First Presidency, we have been aware these last six months that there has been such a feeling of need to have questions answered, to have spoken from this pulpit at this conference things that are needed by so many in this mixed-up world, to help them to set guidelines for their own lives.

I believe I have never known when the General Authorities have so completely covered the various areas where we have had great concern. If you want to know what the Lord has for this people at the present time, I would admonish you to get and read the discourses that have been delivered at this conference; for what these brethren have spoken by the power of the Holy Ghost is the mind of the Lord, the will of the Lord, the voice of the Lord, and the power of God unto salvation. I am sure all who have listened, if they have been in tune, have felt the sincerity and the deep conviction from those who have spoken so appropriately and so effectively.

My soul is filled with joy as I think of these great men whom the Lord has brought to the service of the Church as General Authorities and all others who have served, our Regional Representatives of the Twelve, our Mission Representatives of the Twelve and the First Council of Seventy, and all who serve in the various organizations. As we have seen them being brought into key positions, we have marveled as to how, when we have need of a man or person for a particular office, the man of the hour seems to have been brought to us, almost in a miraculous way.

As I have listened to the brethren, and feeling the concern that has been so frequently referred to, I have remembered the instruction that was given by the prophet Alma as a group of those who had been converted waited on the banks for baptism; and as he explained to them the nature of the covenant in which they were to enter as baptized members, he said:

" . . . as ye are desirous to come into the fold of God, and to be called his people, and are willing to bear one another's burdens, that they may be light;

"Yea, and are willing to mourn with those that mourn; yea, and comfort those that stand in need of comfort, and to stand as witnesses of God at all times and in all things, and in all places that ye may be in, . . .

"Now I say unto you, if this be the desire of your hearts, what have you against being baptized in the name of the Lord, as a witness before him that ye have entered into a covenant with him, that ye will serve him and keep his commandments, that he may pour out his Spirit more abundantly upon you?" (Mosiah 18:8–10.)

I call your attention to one of these requirements, particularly that which has been stressed by direct and indirect words in this conference: "are willing to bear one another's burdens that they may be light." If I were to ask you what is the heaviest burden one may have to bear in this life, what would you answer? The heaviest burden that one has to bear in this life is the burden of sin. How do you help one to bear that great burden of sin, in order that it might be light?

Some years ago, President Romney and I were sitting in my office. The door opened and a fine young man came in with a troubled look on his face, and he said, "Brethren, I am going to the temple for the first time tomorrow. I have made some mistakes in the past, and I have gone to my bishop and my stake president, and I have made a clean disclosure of it all; and after a period of repentance and assurance that I have not returned again to those mistakes, they have now adjudged me ready to go to the temple. But, brethren, that is not enough. I want to know, and how can I know, that the Lord has forgiven me also?"

What would you answer one who would come to you asking that question? As we pondered for a moment, we remembered King Benjamin's address contained in the book of Mosiah. Here was a group of people who now were asking for baptism, and they said they viewed themselves in their carnal state:

" . . . And they all cried aloud with one voice, saying: O have mercy, and apply the atoning blood of Christ that we may receive forgiveness of our sins, and our hearts may be purified; . . .

" . . . after they had spoken these words the Spirit of the Lord came upon them, and they were filled with joy, having received a remission of their sins, and having peace of conscience. . . ." (Mosiah 4:2–3.)

There was the answer.

If the time comes when you have done all that you can to repent of your sins, whoever you are, wherever you are, and have made amends and restitution to the best of your ability; if it be something that will affect your standing in the Church and you have gone to the proper authorities, then you will want that con-firming answer as to whether or not the Lord has accepted of you. In your soul-searching, if you seek for and you find that peace of conscience, by that token you may know that the Lord has accepted of your repentance. Satan would have you think other-wise and sometimes persuade you that now having made one mis-take, you might go on and on with no turning back. That is one of the great falsehoods. The miracle of forgiveness is available to all of those who turn from their evil doings and return no more, because the Lord has said in a revelation to us in our day: " . . . go your ways and sin no more; but unto that soul who sinneth [mean-ing again] shall the former sins return, saith the Lord your God." (D&C 82:7.) Have that in mind, all of you who may be troubled with a burden of sin.

And to you who are teachers, may you help to lift that great burden from those who are carrying it, and who have their con-science so seared that they are kept from activity, and they don't know where to go to find the answers. You help them to that day of repentance and restitution, in order that they too may have that peace of conscience, the confirming of the Spirit of the Lord that he has accepted of their repentance.

The great call has come now in the sermons of the brethren to aid those who are in need of aid, not just temporal aid but also spiri-tual aid. The greatest miracles I see today are not necessarily the healing of sick bodies, but the greatest miracles I see are the healing of sick souls, those who are sick in soul and spirit and are down-hearted and distraught, on the verge of nervous breakdowns. We are reaching out to all such, because they are precious in the sight of the Lord, and we want no one to feel that they are forgotten.

I read again and again the experience of Peter and John, as they went through the Gate Beautiful on the way to the temple. Here was one who had never walked, impotent from his birth, beg-ging alms of all who approached the gate. And as Peter and John approached, he held out his hand expectantly, asking for alms. Peter, speaking for this pair of missionaries—church authorities—said, "Look on us." And, of course, that heightened his expectation. "Then Peter said, Silver and gold have I none; but such as I have give I thee: In the name of Jesus Christ of Nazareth rise up and walk." (Acts 3:4, 6.)

Now in my mind's eye I can picture this man, what was in his mind. "Doesn't this man know that I have never walked? He commands me to walk." But the biblical record doesn't end there. Peter just didn't content himself by commanding the man to walk, but he "took him by the right hand, and lifted him up." (Acts 3:7.)

Will you see that picture now of that noble soul, that chiefest of the apostles, perhaps with his arms around the shoulders of this man, and saying, "Now, my good man, have courage, I will take a few steps with you. Let's walk together, and I assure you that you can walk, because you have received a blessing by the power and authority that God has given us as men, his servants." Then the man leaped with joy.

You cannot lift another soul until you are standing on higher ground than he is. You must be sure, if you would rescue the man, that you yourself are setting the example of what you would have him be. You cannot light a fire in another soul unless it is burning in your own soul. You teachers, the testimony that you bear, the spirit with which you teach and with which you lead, is one of the most important assets that you can have, as you help to strengthen those who need so much, wherein you have so much to give. Who of us, in whatever station we may have been in, have not needed strengthening?

May I impose upon you for a moment to express appreciation for something that happened to me some time ago, years ago. I was suffering from an ulcer condition that was becoming worse and worse. We had been touring a mission; my wife, Joan, and I were impressed the next morning that we should get home as quickly as possible, although we had planned to stay for some other meetings.

On the way across the country, we were sitting in the forward section of the airplane. Some of our Church members were in the next section. As we approached a certain point en route, someone laid his hand upon my head. I looked up; I could see no one. That happened again before we arrived home, again with the same experience. Who it was, by what means or what medium, I may never know, except I knew that I was receiving a blessing that I came a few hours later to know I needed most desperately.

As soon as we arrived home, my wife very anxiously called the doctor. It was now about eleven o'clock at night. He called me to come to the telephone, and he asked me how I was; and I said, "Well, I am very tired. I think I will be all right." But shortly thereafter, there came massive hemorrhages which, had they occurred while we were in flight, I wouldn't be here today talking about it.

I know that there are powers divine that reach out when all other help is not available. We see that manifest down in the countries we speak of as the underprivileged countries where there is little medical aid and perhaps no hospitals. If you want to hear of great miracles among these humble people with simple faith, you will see it among them when they are left to themselves. Yes, I know that there are such powers.

As I came to realize the overwhelming magnitude of the responsibility that now has been given to me, if I were to have sat down and tried to think of the burden, I would have been devastated and wholly incapable of carrying it. But when I was guided by the Spirit to name two noble men, whose powerful words of teaching and testimony you have heard today, President N. Eldon Tanner and President Marion G. Romney, I realized that mine was not the responsibility to carry these responsibilities alone. And then as we meet week by week in the temple and look across the room and see twelve stalwart men, men chosen from out the world and given the power of the holy apostleship, I am aware that no greater men walk the earth than these men. . . .

The other day we met in the seminar for Regional Representatives of the Twelve. These are men who are fanning out over the whole earth now, to every corner of the earth. Newly baptized members who know little about the gospel and much less about the disciplines of the Church must be taught if the Church is to be safely led. These men who have been chosen from out of the strongest men we have in the Church now are going out now under the direction of the Council of the Twelve. And there are also the Mission Representatives of the Twelve and the First Council of the Seventy associated with them. They are going out to the humblest everywhere and teaching them these fundamental principles, teaching them, as the Prophet Joseph answered when asked, "How do you govern your people?" His answer was, "I teach them correct principles, and they govern themselves."

They are not going out to do the work themselves. As we have said to them, they are standing as "coaches" rather than as "quarterbacks" on the football team, teaching the quarterbacks how to direct, teaching them correct principles. They are men of faith. And how grateful we are for all these auxiliary workers who have gone out, likewise at great expense, great travel, and sacrifice on the part of their businesses and their families.

To you great leaders, stake presidencies, mission presidencies, bishoprics, priesthood quorum leaders, all of you, the faithful Saints everywhere, you who pray for us, I want you to know that we pray earnestly at the altars of the temple for all of you faithful who pray for us. How grateful we are for you!

As I come to you at the closing moments of this conference, I would like to take you back now to just one incident, and I am sorry that I can tell you only a part of it because of the limitations of some things contained therein.

It was just before the dedication of the Los Angeles Temple.

We were all preparing for that great occasion. It was something new in my life, when along about three or four o'clock in the morning, I enjoyed an experience that I think was not a dream, but it must have been a vision. It seemed that I was witnessing a great spiritual gathering, where men and women were standing up, two or three at a time, and speaking in tongues. The spirit was so unusual. I seemed to have heard the voice of President David O. McKay say, "If you want to love God, you have to learn to love and serve the people. That is the way you show your love for God." And there were other things then that I saw and heard.

And so I come to you today, with no shadow of doubting in my mind that I know the reality of the person who is presiding over this church, our Lord and Master, Jesus Christ. I know that he is. I know that he is closer to us than many times we have any idea. They are not an absentee Father and Lord. They are concerned about us, helping to prepare us for the advent of the Savior, whose coming certainly isn't too far away because of the signs that are becoming apparent.

All you need to do is to read the scriptures, particularly the inspired translation of Matthew, the twenty-fourth chapter, found in the writings of Joseph Smith in the Pearl of Great Price, where the Lord told his disciples to stand in holy places and be not moved, for he comes quickly, but no man knows the hour nor the day. That is the preparation.

Go home now to your people, I pray you, and say as did Joshua of old: " . . . as for me and my house, we will serve the Lord." (Joshua 24:15.) Teach your families in your family home evening, teach them to keep the commandments of God, for therein is our only safety in these days. If they will do that, the powers of the Almighty will descend upon them as the dews from heaven, and the Holy Ghost will be theirs. . . . That can be our guide, and that kind of Spirit shall guide us and direct us to his holy home.

And so as it is my privilege to do, I give you faithful members of the Church everywhere my blessing. God bless you, take care of you, preserve you as you travel home, that there may be no accident or no untoward experience. Take to your people out in the far reaches the feeling of love that we have for all of them; and indeed, as the missionaries go out, that love extends not only to those of our Father's children who are already members of the Church, but those who are our Father's children to whom he would have us bring the gospel of truth; make them also to enjoy all the blessings that we now have.

May the Lord help us so to understand and do, and fill our stations, and not be found wanting in the day of judgment that we have not done all we know how to do to advance his work in righteousness, I humbly pray in the name of the Lord Jesus Christ. Amen.

Ensign, July 1973, 121–24.

The False Gods We Worship

Spencer W. Kimball

In this thought-provoking address, President Spencer W. Kimball notes, "The Lord has blessed us as a people with a prosperity unequaled in times past. The resources that have been placed in our power are good, and necessary to our work here on the earth. But I am afraid that many of us have been surfeited with flocks and herds and acres and barns and wealth and have begun to worship them as false gods, and they have power over us." Then he asks, "Do we have more of these good things than our faith can stand?"

I have heard that the sense most closely associated with memory is the sense of smell. If this is true, then perhaps it explains the many pleasing feelings that overtake me these mornings when I am able to step outdoors for a few moments and breathe in the warm and comfortable aromas that I have come to associate over the years with the soil and vegetation of this good earth.

Now and then, when the moment is right, some particular scent—perhaps only the green grass, or the smell of sage brought from a distance by a breeze—will take me back to the days of my youth in Arizona. It was an arid country, yet it was fruitful under the hands of determined laborers.

We worked with the land and the cattle in all kinds of weather, and when we traveled it was on horseback or in open wagons or carriages, mostly. I used to run like the wind with my brothers and sisters through the orchards, down the dusty lanes, past rows of corn, red tomatoes, onions, squash. Because of this, I suppose it is natural to think that in those days we were closer to elemental life.

Some time ago I chanced to walk outdoors when the dark and massive clouds of an early afternoon thunderstorm were gathering; and as the large raindrops began to drum the dusty soil with increasing rapidity, I recalled the occasional summer afternoons when I was a boy when the tremendous thunderheads would gather over the hills and bring welcome rain to the thirsty soil of the valley floor. We children would run for the shed, and while the lightning danced about we would sit and watch, transfixed, marveling at the ever-increasing power of the pounding rainfall. Afterward, the air would be clean and cool and filled with the sweet smells of the soil, the trees, and the plants of the garden.

There were evenings those many years ago, at about sunset, when I would walk in with the cows. Stopping by a tired old fence post, I would sometimes just stand silently in the mellow light and the fragrance of sunflowers and ask myself, "If you were going to create a world, what would it be like?" Now with a little thought the answer seems so natural: "Just like this one."

So on this day while I stood watching the thunderstorm, I felt—and I feel now—that this is a marvelous earth on which we find ourselves: and when I thought of our preparations for the United States Bicentennial celebration I felt a deep gratitude to the Lord for the choice land and the people and institutions of America. There is much that is good in this land, and much to love.

Nevertheless, on this occasion of so many pleasant memories another impression assailed my thoughts. The dark and threatening clouds that hung so low over the valley seemed to force my mind back to a theme that the Brethren have concerned themselves with for many years now—indeed a theme that has often occupied the attention of the Lord's chosen prophets since the world began. I am speaking of the general state of wickedness in

which we seem to find the world in these perilous yet crucially
momentous days; and thinking of this, I am reminded of the general principle that where much is given, much is expected. (See
Luke 12:48.)

The Lord gave us a choice world and expects righteousness and
obedience to his commandments in return. But when I review the
performance of this people in comparison with what is expected,
I am appalled and frightened. Iniquity seems to abound. The
Destroyer seems to be taking full advantage of the time remaining
to him in this, the great day of his power. Evil seems about to
engulf us like a great wave, and we feel that truly we are living
in conditions similar to those in the days of Noah before the
Flood.

I have traveled much in various assignments over the years,
and when I pass through the lovely countryside or fly over the vast
and beautiful expanses of our globe, I compare these beauties with
many of the dark and miserable practices of men, and I have the
feeling that the good earth can hardly bear our presence upon it. I
recall the occasion when Enoch heard the earth mourn, saying,
"Wo, wo is me, the mother of men; I am pained, I am weary,
because of the wickedness of my children. When shall I rest, and
be cleansed from the filthiness which is gone forth out of me?"
(Moses 7:48.)

The Brethren constantly cry out against that which is intoler-
able in the sight of the Lord: against pollution of mind, body, and
our surroundings; against vulgarity, stealing, lying, pride, and blasphemy; against fornication, adultery, homosexuality, and all other
abuses of the sacred power to create; against murder and all that is
like unto it; against all manner of desecration.

That such a cry should be necessary among a people so blessed
is amazing to me. And that such things should be found even
among the Saints to some degree is scarcely believable, for these
are a people who are in possession of many gifts of the Spirit, who

have knowledge that puts the eternities into perspective, who have been shown the way to eternal life.

Sadly, however, we find that to be shown the way is not necessarily to walk in it, and many have not been able to continue in faith. These have submitted themselves in one degree or another to the enticings of Satan and his servants and joined with those of "the world" in lives of ever-deepening idolatry.

I use the word *idolatry* intentionally. As I study ancient scripture, I am more and more convinced that there is significance in the fact that the commandment "Thou shalt have no other gods before me" is the first of the Ten Commandments.

Few men have ever knowingly and deliberately chosen to reject God and his blessings. Rather, we learn from the scriptures that because the exercise of faith has always appeared to be more difficult than relying on things more immediately at hand, carnal man has tended to transfer his trust in God to material things. Therefore, in all ages when men have fallen under the power of Satan and lost the faith, they have put in its place a hope in the "arm of flesh" and in "gods of silver, and gold, of brass, iron, wood, and stone, which see not, nor hear, nor know" (Daniel 5:23)—that is, in idols. This I find to be a dominant theme in the Old Testament. Whatever thing a man sets his heart and his trust in most is his god; and if his god doesn't also happen to be the true and living God of Israel, that man is laboring in idolatry.

It is my firm belief that when we read these scriptures and try to "liken them unto [our]selves," as Nephi suggested (1 Nephi 19:24), we will see many parallels between the ancient worship of graven images and behavioral patterns in our very own experience.

The Lord has blessed us as a people with a prosperity unequaled in times past. The resources that have been placed in our power are good, and necessary to our work here on the earth. But I am afraid that many of us have been surfeited with flocks and herds and acres and barns and wealth and have begun to worship them as false gods, and they have power over us. Do we have more of these good things than our faith can stand? Many people spend most of their time working in the service of a self-image that includes sufficient money, stocks, bonds, investment portfolios, property, credit cards, furnishings, automobiles, and the like to *guarantee* carnal security throughout, it is hoped, a long and happy life. Forgotten is the fact that our assignment is to use these many resources in our families and quorums to build up the kingdom of God—to further the missionary effort and the genealogical and temple work; to raise our children up as fruitful servants unto the Lord; to bless others in every way, that they may also be fruitful. Instead, we expend these blessings on our own desires, and as Moroni said, "Ye adorn yourselves with that which hath no life, and yet suffer the hungry, and the needy, and the naked, and the sick and the afflicted to pass by you, and notice them not." (Mormon 8:39.)

As the Lord himself said in our day, "They seek not the Lord to establish his righteousness, but every man walketh in his own way, and after the image of his own God, whose image is in the likeness of the world, and *whose substance is that of an idol*, which waxeth old and shall perish in Babylon, even Babylon the great, which shall fall." (D&C 1:16; italics added.)

One man I know of was called to a position of service in the Church, but he felt that he couldn't accept because his investments required more attention and more of his time than he could spare for the Lord's work. He left the service of the Lord in search of Mammon, and he is a millionaire today.

But I recently learned an interesting fact: If a man owns a million dollars worth of gold at today's prices, he possesses approximately one 27-billionth of all the gold that is present in the earth's thin crust alone. This is an amount so small in proportion as to be inconceivable to the mind of man. But there is more to this: The Lord who created and has power over all the earth created many other earths as well, even "worlds without number" (Moses 1:33); and when this man received the oath and covenant of the priesthood (D&C 84:33–44), he received a promise from the Lord of "all that my Father hath" (v. 38). To set aside all these great promises in favor of a chest of gold and a sense of carnal security is a mistake in perspective of colossal proportions. To think that he has settled for so little is a saddening and pitiful prospect indeed; the souls of men are far more precious than this.

One young man, when called on a mission, replied that he didn't have much talent for that kind of thing. What he was good at was keeping his powerful new automobile in top condition. He enjoyed the sense of power and acceleration, and when he was driving, the continual motion gave him the illusion that he was really getting somewhere.

All along, his father had been content with saying, "He likes to do things with his hands. That's good enough for him."

Good enough for a son of God? This young man didn't realize that the power of his automobile is infinitesimally small in comparison with the power of the sea, or of the sun; and there are many suns, all controlled by law and by priesthood, ultimately—a priesthood power that he could have been developing in the service of the Lord. He settled for a pitiful god, a composite of steel and rubber and shiny chrome.

An older couple retired from the world of work and also, in effect, from the Church. They purchased a pickup truck and camper and, separating themselves from all obligations, set out to see the world and simply enjoy what little they had accumulated the rest of their days. They had no time for the temple, were too busy for genealogical research and for missionary service. He lost contact with his high priests quorum and was not home enough to work on his personal history. Their experience and leadership were sorely needed in their branch, but, unable to "endure to the end," they were not available.

I am reminded of an article I read some years ago about a group of men who had gone to the jungles to capture monkeys. They tried a number of different things to catch the monkeys, including nets. But finding that the nets could injure such small creatures, they finally came upon an ingenious solution. They built a large number of small boxes, and in the top of each they bored a hole just large enough for a monkey to get his hand into. They then set these boxes out under the trees and in each one they put a nut that the monkeys were particularly fond of.

When the men left, the monkeys began to come down from the trees and examine the boxes. Finding that there were nuts to be had, they reached into the boxes to get them. But when a monkey would try to withdraw his hand with the nut, he could not get his hand out of the box because his little fist, with the nut inside, was now too large.

At about this time, the men would come out of the underbrush and converge on the monkeys. And here is the curious thing: When the monkeys saw the men coming, they would shriek and scramble about with the thought of escaping; but as easy as it would have been, they would not let go of the nut so that they could withdraw their hands from the boxes and thus escape. The men captured them easily.

And so it often seems to be with people, having such a firm grasp on things of the world—that which is telestial—that no amount of urging and no degree of emergency can persuade them to let go in favor of that which is celestial. Satan gets them in his grip easily. If we insist on spending all our time and resources building up for ourselves a worldly kingdom, that is exactly what we will inherit.

In spite of our delight in defining ourselves as modern, and our tendency to think we possess a sophistication that no people in the past ever had—in spite of these things, we are, on the whole, an idolatrous people—a condition most repugnant to the Lord.

We are a warlike people, easily distracted from our assignment of preparing for the coming of the Lord. When enemies rise up, we commit vast resources to the fabrication of gods of stone and steel—ships, planes, missiles, fortifications—and depend on them for protection and deliverance. When threatened, we become anti-enemy instead of pro-kingdom of God; we train a man in the art of war and call him a patriot, thus, in the manner of Satan's counterfeit of true patriotism, perverting the Savior's teaching:

"Love your enemies, bless them that curse you, do good to them that hate you, and pray for them which despitefully use you, and persecute you; that ye may be the children of your Father which is in heaven." (Matthew 5:44–45.)

We forget that if we are righteous the Lord will either not suffer our enemies to come upon us—and this is the special promise to the inhabitants of the land of the Americas (see 2 Nephi 1:7)—or he will fight our battles for us (Exodus 14:14; D&C 98:37, to name only two references of many). This he is able to do, for as he said at the time of his betrayal, "Thinkest thou that I cannot now pray to my Father, and he shall presently give me more than twelve legions of angels?" (Matthew 26:53.) We can imagine what fearsome soldiers they would be. King Jehoshaphat and his people were delivered by such a troop (see 2 Chronicles 20), and when Elisha's life was threatened, he comforted his servant by saying, "Fear not: for they that be with us are more than they that be with them." (2 Kings 6:16.) The Lord then opened the eyes of the servant, "And he saw: and, behold, the mountain was full of horses and chariots of fire round about Elisha." (2 Kings 6:17.)

Enoch, too, was a man of great faith who would not be distracted from his duties by the enemy: "And so great was the faith of Enoch, that he led the people of God, and their enemies came to battle against them; and he spake the word of the Lord, and the earth trembled, and the mountains fled, even according to his command; and the rivers of water were turned out of their course;

and the roar of the lions was heard out of the wilderness; and all nations feared greatly, so powerful was the word of Enoch." (Moses 7:13.)

What are we to fear when the Lord is with us? Can we not take the Lord at his word and exercise a particle of faith in him? Our assignment is affirmative: to forsake the things of the world as ends in themselves; to leave off idolatry and press forward in faith; to carry the gospel to our enemies, that they might no longer be our enemies.

We must leave off the worship of modern-day idols and a reliance on the "arm of flesh," for the Lord has said to all the world in our day, "I will not spare any that remain in Babylon." (D&C 64:24.)

When Peter preached such a message as this to the people on the day of Pentecost, many of them "were pricked in their heart, and said unto Peter and to the rest of the apostles, Men and brethren, what shall we do?" (Acts 2:37.)

And Peter answered: "Repent, and be baptized every one of you in the name of Jesus Christ for the remission of sins, and . . . receive the Holy Ghost." (v. 38.)

As we near the year 2000, our message is the same as that which Peter gave. And further, that which the Lord himself gave "unto the ends of the earth, that all that will hear may hear:

"Prepare ye, prepare ye for that which is to come, for the Lord is nigh." (D&C 1:11–12.)

We believe that the way for each person and each family to prepare as the Lord has directed is to begin to exercise greater faith, to repent, and to enter into the work of his kingdom on earth, which is The Church of Jesus Christ of Latter-day Saints. It may seem a little difficult at first, but when a person begins to catch a vision of the true work, when he begins to see something of eternity in its true perspective, the blessings begin to far outweigh the cost of leaving "the world" behind.

Herein lies the only true happiness, and therefore we invite and welcome all men, everywhere, to join in this work. For those who are determined to serve the Lord at all costs, this is the way to eternal life. All else is but a means to that end.

Ensign, June 1976, 3–6.

⁓ ❦ ⁓

"No Less Serviceable"

Howard W. Hunter

"Tens of thousands of unseen people make possible our opportunities and happiness every day," said President Howard W. Hunter in this address, delivered at Brigham Young University on September 2, 1990. "As the scriptures state, they are 'no less serviceable' than those whose lives are on the front pages of newspapers."

Howard W. Hunter knew something of the lives of "unseen people." Born in 1907 to a part-member family, he spent an unremarkable childhood in Boise, Idaho. But he grew to be a remarkable man, successful in business and family life and in Church service

After becoming president of the Church in June 1994, following the death of President Ezra Taft Benson, President Hunter told members of the press, "I have shed many tears and have sought my Father in Heaven in earnest prayer with a desire to be equal to the high and holy calling which is now mine."

———————

It was said of the young and valiant Captain Moroni: "If all men had been, and were, and ever would be, like unto Moroni, behold, the very powers of hell would have been shaken forever; yea, the devil would never have power over the hearts of the children of men." (Alma 48:17.)

What a compliment to a famous and powerful man! I can't imagine a finer tribute from one man to another. Two verses later is a statement about Helaman and his brethren, who played a less conspicuous role than Moroni: "Now behold, Helaman and his brethren were no less serviceable unto the people than was Moroni." (Alma 48:19.)

In other words, even though Helaman was not as noticeable or conspicuous as Moroni, he was as serviceable; that is, he was as helpful or useful as Moroni.

Obviously, we could profit greatly by studying the life of Captain Moroni. He is an example of faith, service, dedication, commitment, and many other godly attributes. Rather than focusing on this magnificent man, however, I have chosen to look instead at those who are not seen in the limelight, who do not receive the attention of the world, yet who are "no less serviceable," as the scripture phrased it.

Not all of us are going to be like Moroni, catching the acclaim of our colleagues all day every day. Most of us will be quiet, relatively unknown folks who come and go and do our work without fanfare. To those of you who may find that lonely or frightening or just unspectacular, I say, you are "no less serviceable" than the most spectacular of your associates. You, too, are part of God's army.

Consider, for example, the profound service a mother or father gives in the quiet anonymity of a worthy Latter-day Saint home. Think of the Gospel Doctrine teachers and Primary choristers and Scoutmasters and Relief Society visiting teachers who serve and bless millions but whose names will never be publicly applauded or featured in the nation's media.

Tens of thousands of unseen people make possible our opportunities and happiness every day. As the scriptures state, they are "no less serviceable" than those whose lives are on the front pages of newspapers.

The limelight of history and contemporary attention so often focuses on the *one* rather than on the *many*. Individuals are frequently singled out from their peers and elevated as heroes. I acknowledge that this kind of attention is one way to identify that which the people admire or hold to be of some value. But some-times that recognition is not deserved, or it may even celebrate the wrong values.

We must choose wisely our heroes and examples, while also giving thanks for those legions of friends and citizens who are not so famous but who are "no less serviceable" than the Moronis of our lives.

Perhaps you could consider with me some interesting people from the scriptures who did not receive the limelight of attention but who, through the long lens of history, have proven themselves to be truly heroic.

Many who read the story of the great prophet Nephi almost completely miss another valiant son of Lehi whose name was Samuel. Nephi is one of the most famous figures in the entire Book of Mormon. But Sam? Sam's name is mentioned there only ten times. When Lehi counseled and blessed his posterity, he said to Sam:

"Blessed art thou, and thy seed; for thou shalt inherit the land like unto thy brother Nephi. And thy seed shall be numbered with his seed; and thou shalt be even like unto thy brother, and thy seed like unto his seed; and thou shalt be blessed in all thy days." (2 Nephi 4:11.)

Sam's role was basically one of supporting and assisting his more acclaimed younger brother, and he ultimately received the same blessings promised to Nephi and his posterity. Nothing prom-ised to Nephi was withheld from the faithful Sam, yet we know very little of the details of Sam's service and contribution. He was an almost unknown person in life, but he is obviously a triumphant leader and victor in the annals of eternity.

Many make their contributions in unsung ways. Ishmael trav-eled with the family of Nephi at great personal sacrifice, suffering "much affliction, hunger, thirst, and fatigue." (1 Nephi 16:35.) Then in the midst of all of these afflictions, he perished in the wilderness. Few of us can even begin to understand the sacrifice of such a man in those primitive times and conditions. Perhaps if we were more perceptive and understanding, we too would mourn, as his daughters did in the wilderness, for what a man like this gave— and gave up!—so that we could have the Book of Mormon today.

The names and memories of such men and women who were "no less serviceable" are legion in the Book of Mormon. Whether it be Mother Sariah or the maid Abish, servant to the Lamanite queen, each made contributions that were unacknowledged by the eyes of men but not unseen by the eyes of God.

We have only twelve verses of scripture dealing with the life of Mosiah, king over the land of Zarahemla and father of the famous King Benjamin. Yet his service to the people was indispensable. He led the people "by many preachings and prophesyings" and "admonished [them] continually by the word of God." (Omni 1:13.) Limhi, Amulek, and Pahoran—the latter of whom had the nobility of soul not to condemn when he was very unjustly accused—are other examples of people who served selflessly in the shadow of others' limelight.

The soldier Teancum, who sacrificed his own life, or Lachonius, the chief judge who taught people to repent during the challenge of the Gadiantons, or the virtually unmentioned missionaries Omner and Himni, were all "no less serviceable" than their companions, yet they received very little scriptural attention.

We don't know much about Shiblon, the faithful son of Alma whose story is sandwiched between those of Helaman, the future leader, and Corianton, the transgressor; but it is significant that he is described as a "just man [who] did walk uprightly before God." (Alma 63:2.) The great prophet Nephi, mentioned in the book of Helaman, had a brother named Lehi, who is seemingly mentioned only in passing but is noted as being "not a whit behind him [Nephi] as to things pertaining to righteousness." (See Helaman 11:18–19.)

Of course, there are examples of these serviceable individuals in our dispensation as well. Oliver Granger is the kind of quiet, supportive individual in the latter days that the Lord remembered in section 117 of the Doctrine and Covenants. Oliver's name may be unfamiliar to many, so I will take the liberty to acquaint you with this early stalwart.

Oliver Granger was eleven years older than Joseph Smith and, like the Prophet, was from upstate New York. Because of severe cold and exposure when he was thirty-three years old, Oliver lost much of his eyesight. Notwithstanding his limited vision, he served three full-time missions. He also worked on the Kirtland Temple and served on the Kirtland high council.

When most of the Saints were driven from Kirtland, Ohio, the Church left some debts unsatisfied. Oliver was appointed to represent Joseph Smith and the First Presidency by returning to Kirtland to settle the Church's business. Of this task, the Doctrine and Covenants records: "Therefore, let him contend earnestly for the redemption of the First Presidency of my Church, saith the Lord." (D&C 117:13.)

He performed this assignment with such satisfaction to the creditors involved that one of them wrote: "Oliver Granger's management in the arrangement of the unfinished business of people that have moved to the Far West, in redeeming their pledges and thereby sustaining their integrity, has been truly praiseworthy, and has entitled him to my highest esteem, and every grateful recollection." (Horace Kingsbury, as cited in Joseph Smith, *History of the Church*, 3:174.)

During Oliver's time in Kirtland, some people, including disaffected members of the Church, were endeavoring to discredit the First Presidency and bring their integrity into question by spreading false accusations. Oliver Granger, in very deed, "redeemed the First Presidency" through his faithful service. In response, the Lord said of Oliver Granger: "His name shall be had in sacred remembrance from generation to generation, forever and ever." (D&C 117:12.) "I will lift up my servant Oliver, and beget for him a great name on the earth, and among my people, because of the integrity of his soul." (*History of the Church*, 3:350.)

When he died in 1841, even though there were but few Saints remaining in the Kirtland area and even fewer friends of the Saints, Oliver Granger's funeral was attended by a vast concourse of people from neighboring towns.

Though Oliver Granger is not as well known today as other early leaders of the Church, he was nevertheless a great and important man in the service he rendered to the kingdom. And even if no one but the Lord had his name in remembrance, that would be a sufficient blessing for him—or for any of us.

I think we should be aware that there can be a spiritual danger to those who misunderstand the singularity of always being in the spotlight. They may come to covet the notoriety and thus forget the significance of the service being rendered.

We must not allow ourselves to focus on the fleeting light of popularity or substitute that attractive glow for the substance of true but often anonymous labor that brings the attention of God, even if it does not get coverage on the six o'clock news. In fact, applause and attention can become the spiritual Achilles' heels of even the most gifted among us.

If the limelight of popularity should fall on you sometime in your life, it might be well for you to follow the example of those in the scriptures who received fame. Nephi is one of the great examples. After all he accomplished traveling in the wilderness with his family, his attitude was still fixed on the things that matter most. He said:

"And when I desire to rejoice, my heart groaneth because of my sins; nevertheless, I know in whom I have trusted.

"My God hath been my support; he hath led me through mine

afflictions in the wilderness; and he hath preserved me upon the waters of the great deep.

"He hath filled me with his love, even unto the consuming of my flesh.

"He hath confounded mine enemies, unto the causing of them to quake before me." (2 Nephi 4:19–22.)

The limelight never blinded Nephi as to the source of his strength and his blessings.

At times of attention and visibility, it might also be profitable for us to answer the question, Why do we serve? When we understand why, we won't be concerned about where we serve.

President J. Reuben Clark Jr., taught this vital principle in his own life. At general conference in April 1951, President David O. McKay was sustained as President of the Church after the passing of President George Albert Smith. Up to that time, President Clark had served as the First Counselor to President Heber J. Grant and then to President George Albert Smith. President McKay had been the Second Counselor to both men.

During the final session of conference when the business of the Church was transacted, Brother Stephen L Richards was called to the First Presidency and sustained as First Counselor. President J. Reuben Clark Jr., was then sustained as the Second Counselor. After the sustaining of the officers of the Church, President McKay explained why he had chosen his counselors in that order. He said:

"I felt that one guiding principle in this choice would be to follow the seniority in the Council [of the Twelve]. These two men were sitting in their places in that presiding body in the Church, and I felt impressed that it would be advisable to continue that same seniority in the new quorum of the First Presidency." (In Conference Report, April 9, 1951, 151.)

President Clark was then asked to speak following President McKay. His remarks on this occasion were brief but teach a powerful lesson: "In the service of the Lord, it is not where you serve but how. In The Church of Jesus Christ of Latter-day Saints, one takes the place to which one is duly called, which place one neither seeks nor declines. I pledge to President McKay and to President Richards the full loyal devoted service to the tasks that may come to me to the full measure of my strength and my abilities and so far as they will enable me to perform them, however inadequate I may be." (Ibid., 154.)

The lesson that President Clark taught is expressed in another way in this poem by Meade McGuire, which has been repeated many times:

> "Father, where shall I work today?"
> And my love flowed warm and free.
> Then He pointed out a tiny spot
> And said, "Tend that for me."
> I answered quickly, "Oh no; not that!
> Why, no one would ever see,
> No matter how well my work was done;
> Not that little place for me."
> And the word He spoke, it was not stern;
> He answered me tenderly:
> "Ah, little one, search that heart of thine.
> Art thou working for them or for me?
> Nazareth was a little place,
> And so was Galilee."
> (*Ensign*, May 1986, 39.)

King Benjamin declared: "Behold, I say unto you that because I said unto you that I had spent my days in your service, I do not desire to boast, for I have only been in the service of God. And behold, I tell you these things that ye may learn wisdom; that ye may learn that when ye are in the service of your fellow beings ye are only in the service of your God." (Mosiah 2:16–17.)

President Ezra Taft Benson said recently: "Christlike service exalts. . . . The Lord has promised that those who lose their lives serving others will find themselves. The Prophet Joseph Smith told us that we should 'wear out our lives' in bringing to pass His purposes. (D&C 123:13.)" (*Ensign*, November 1989, 5–6.)

If you feel that much of what you do does not make you very famous, take heart. Most of the best people who ever lived weren't very famous, either. Serve and grow, faithfully and quietly. Be on guard regarding the praise of men. Jesus said in the Sermon on the Mount:

"Take heed that ye do not your alms before men, to be seen of them: otherwise ye have no reward of your Father which is in heaven.

"Therefore when thou doest thine alms, do not sound a trumpet before thee, as the hypocrites do in the synagogues and in the streets, that they may have glory of men. Verily I say unto you, They have their reward.

"But when thou doest alms, let not thy left hand know what thy right hand doeth:

"That thine alms may be in secret: and thy Father which seeth in secret himself shall reward thee openly." (Matthew 6:1–4.)

May our Father in Heaven so reward you always.

Ensign, April 1992, 64–67.

GOD

❧ ❧

THE ATTRIBUTES OF GOD

JOSEPH SMITH

This address was the fourth in the series called *Lectures on Faith*. (For background comments on the *Lectures on Faith*, see "The Sacrifice of All Things" on page 85.) Each lecture included a summary, in question-and-answer form, of the teachings immediately preceding it. For instance, following Lecture 4 we read the following:

"What was shown in the third lecture? It was shown that correct ideas of the character of God are necessary in order to exercise faith in him unto life and salvation; and that without correct ideas of his character, men could not have power to exercise faith in him unto life and salvation, but that correct ideas of his character, as far as his character was concerned in the exercise of faith in him, lay a sure foundation for the exercise of it. (Lecture 4:1.)

"What object had the God of Heaven in revealing his attributes to men? That through an acquaintance with his attributes they might be enabled to exercise faith in him so as to obtain eternal life. (Lecture 4:2.)

"Could men exercise faith in God without an acquaintance with his attributes, so as to be enabled to lay hold of eternal life? They could not. (Lecture 4:2–3.)

"What account is given of the attributes of God in his revelations? First, Knowledge; secondly, Faith or Power; thirdly, Justice; fourthly, Judgment; fifthly, Mercy; and sixthly, Truth. (Lecture 4:4–10.) . . .

"Is the idea of the existence of these attributes in the Deity necessary in order to enable any rational being to exercise faith in him unto life and salvation? It is.

"How do you prove it? By the eleventh, twelfth, thirteenth, fourteenth, fifteenth and sixteenth paragraphs in this lecture. [Let the student turn and commit these paragraphs to memory.] . . ."

Having shown, in the third lecture, that correct ideas of the character of God are necessary in order to the exercise of faith in him unto life and salvation; and that without correct ideas of his character the minds of men could not have sufficient power with God to the exercise of faith necessary to the enjoyment of eternal life; and that correct ideas of his character lay a foundation, as far as his character is concerned, for the exercise of faith, so as to enjoy the fullness of the blessing of the gospel of Jesus Christ, even that of eternal glory; we shall now proceed to show the connection there is between correct ideas of the attributes of God, and the exercise of faith in him unto eternal life.

2. Let us here observe, that the real design which the God of heaven had in view in making the human family acquainted with his attributes, was, that they, through the ideas of the existence of his attributes, might be enabled to exercise faith in him, and, through the exercise of faith in him, might obtain eternal life; for without the idea of the existence of the attributes which belong to God the minds of men could not have power to exercise faith in him so as to lay hold upon eternal life. The God of heaven, understanding most perfectly the constitution of human nature, and the weakness of men, knew what was necessary to be revealed, and what ideas must be planted in their minds in order that they might be enabled to exercise faith in him unto eternal life.

3. Having said so much, we shall proceed to examine the attributes of God, as set forth in his revelations to the human family and to show how necessary correct ideas of his attributes are

to enable men to exercise faith in him; for without these ideas being planted in the minds of men it would be out of the power of any person or persons to exercise faith in God so as to obtain eternal life. So that the divine communications made to men in the first instance were designed to establish in their minds the ideas necessary to enable them to exercise faith in God, and through this means to be partakers of his glory.

4. We have, in the revelations which he has given to the human family, the following account of his attributes:

5. First—Knowledge. Acts 15:18: "Known unto God are all his works from the beginning of the world." Isaiah 46:9–10 (italics added): "Remember the former things of old: for I am God, and there is none else; I am God, and there is none like me, *declaring the end from the beginning,* and from ancient times the things that are not yet done, saying, My counsel shall stand, and I will do all my pleasure."

6. Secondly—Faith or power. Hebrews 11:3: "Through faith we understand that the worlds were framed by the word of God." Genesis 1:1: "In the beginning God created the heaven and the earth." Isaiah 14:24, 27: "The Lord of hosts hath sworn, saying, Surely as I have thought, so shall it come to pass; and as I have purposed, so shall it stand. . . . For the Lord of hosts hath purposed, and who shall disannul it? and his hand is stretched out, and who shall turn it back?"

7. Thirdly—Justice. Psalm 89:14: "Justice and judgment are the habitation of thy throne." Isaiah 45:21: "Tell ye, and bring them near; yea, let them take counsel together: who hath declared this from ancient time? . . . have not I the Lord? and there is no God else beside me; a just God and a Saviour." Zephaniah 3:5: "The just Lord is in the midst thereof." Zechariah 9:9: "Rejoice greatly, O daughter of Zion; shout, O daughter of Jerusalem: behold, thy King cometh unto thee: he is just, and having salvation."

8. Fourthly—Judgment. Psalm 89:14: "Justice and judgment

are the habitation of thy throne." Deuteronomy 32:4: "He is the Rock, his work is perfect: for all his ways are judgment: a God of truth and without iniquity, just and right is he." Psalm 9:7: "But the Lord shall endure for ever: he hath prepared his throne for judgment." Psalm 9:16: "The Lord is known by the judgment which he executeth."

9. Fifthly—Mercy. Psalm 89:14: "Mercy and truth shall go before thy face." Exodus 34:6: "And the Lord passed by before him, and proclaimed, The Lord, the Lord God, merciful and gracious." Nehemiah 9:17: "But thou art a God ready to pardon, gracious and merciful."

10. And sixthly—Truth. Psalm 89:14: "Mercy and truth shall go before thy face." Exodus 34:6: "Long-suffering; and abundant in goodness and truth." Deuteronomy 32:4: "He is the Rock, his work is perfect: for all his ways are judgment: a God of truth and without iniquity, just and right is he." Psalm 31:5: "Into thine hand I commit my spirit: thou hast redeemed me, O Lord God of truth."

11. By a little reflection it will be seen that the idea of the existence of these attributes in the Deity is necessary to enable any rational being to exercise faith in him; for without the idea of the existence of these attributes in the Deity men could not exercise faith in him for life and salvation; seeing that without the knowledge of all things God would not be able to save any portion of his creatures; for it is by reason of the knowledge which he has of all things, from the beginning to the end, that enables him to give that understanding to his creatures by which they are made partakers of eternal life; and if it were not for the idea existing in the minds of men that God had all knowledge it would be impossible for them to exercise faith in him.

12. And it is not less necessary that men should have the idea of the existence of the attribute power in the Deity; for unless God had power over all things, and was able by his power to control all things, and thereby deliver his creatures who put their trust in him

from the power of all beings that might seek their destruction, whether in heaven, on earth, or in hell, men could not be saved. But with the idea of the existence of this attribute planted in the mind, men feel as though they had nothing to fear who put their trust in God, believing that he has power to save all who come to him to the very uttermost.

13. It is also necessary, in order to the exercise of faith in God unto life and salvation, that men should have the idea of the existence of the attribute justice in him; for without the idea of the existence of the attribute justice in the Deity men could not have confidence sufficient to place themselves under his guidance and direction; for they would be filled with fear and doubt lest the judge of all the earth would not do right, and thus fear or doubt, existing in the mind, would preclude the possibility of the exercise of faith in him for life and salvation. But when the idea of the existence of the attribute justice in the Deity is fairly planted in the mind, it leaves no room for doubt to get into the heart, and the mind is enabled to cast itself upon the Almighty without fear and without doubt, and with the most unshaken confidence, believing that the Judge of all the earth will do right.

14. It is also of equal importance that men should have the idea of the existence of the attribute judgment in God, in order that they may exercise faith in him for life and salvation; for without the idea of the existence of this attribute in the Deity, it would be impossible for men to exercise faith in him for life and salvation, seeing that it is through the exercise of this attribute that the faithful in Christ Jesus are delivered out of the hands of those who seek their destruction; for if God were not to come out in swift judgment against the workers of iniquity and the powers of darkness, his saints could not be saved; for it is by judgment that the Lord delivers his saints out of the hands of all their enemies, and those who reject the gospel of our Lord Jesus Christ. But no sooner is the idea of the existence of this attribute planted in the minds

of men, than it gives power to the mind for the exercise of faith and confidence in God, and they are enabled by faith to lay hold on the promises which are set before them, and wade through all the tribulations and afflictions to which they are subjected by reason of the persecution from those who know not God, and obey not the gospel of our Lord Jesus Christ, believing that in due time the Lord will come out in swift judgment against their enemies, and they shall be cut off from before him, and that in his own due time he will bear them off conquerors, and more than conquerors, in all things.

15. And again, it is equally important that men should have the idea of the existence of the attribute mercy in the Deity, in order to exercise faith in him for life and salvation; for without the idea of the existence of this attribute in the Deity, the spirits of the saints would faint in the midst of the tribulations, afflictions, and persecutions which they have to endure for righteousness' sake. But when the idea of the existence of this attribute is once established in the mind it gives life and energy to the spirits of the saints, believing that the mercy of God will be poured out upon them in the midst of their afflictions, and that he will compassionate them in their sufferings, and that the mercy of God will lay hold of them and secure them in the arms of his love, so that they will receive a full reward for all their sufferings.

16. And lastly, but not less important to the exercise of faith in God, is the idea of the existence of the attribute truth in him; for without the idea of the existence of this attribute the mind of man could have nothing upon which it could rest with certainty— all would be confusion and doubt. But with the idea of the existence of this attribute in the Deity in the mind, all the teachings, instructions, promises, and blessings, become realities, and the mind is enabled to lay hold of them with certainty and confidence, believing that these things, and all that the Lord has said, shall be fulfilled in their time; and that all the cursings, denunciations, and

judgments, pronounced upon the heads of the unrighteous, will also be executed in the due time of the Lord: and, by reason of the truth and veracity of him, the mind beholds its deliverance and salvation as being certain.

17. Let the mind once reflect sincerely and candidly upon the ideas of the existence of the before-mentioned attributes in the Deity, and it will be seen that, as far as his attributes are concerned, there is a sure foundation laid for the exercise of faith in him for life and salvation. For inasmuch as God possesses the attribute knowledge, he can make all things known to his saints necessary for their salvation; and as he possesses the attribute power, he is able thereby to deliver them from the power of all enemies; and seeing, also, that justice is an attribute of the Deity, he will deal with them upon the principles of righteousness and equity, and a just reward will be granted unto them for all their afflictions and sufferings for the truth's sake. And as judgment is an attribute of the Deity also, his saints can have the most unshaken confidence that they will, in due time, obtain a perfect deliverance out of the hands of all their enemies, and a complete victory over all those who have sought their hurt and destruction. And as mercy is also an attribute of the Deity, his saints can have confidence that it will be exercised towards them, and through the exercise of that attribute towards them comfort and consolation will be administered unto them abundantly, amid all their afflictions and tribulations. And, lastly, realizing that truth is an attribute of the Deity, the mind is led to rejoice amid all its trials and temptations, in hope of that glory which is to be brought at the revelation of Jesus Christ, and in view of that crown which is to be placed upon the heads of the saints in the day when the Lord shall distribute rewards unto them, and in prospect of that eternal weight of glory which the Lord has promised to bestow upon them, when he shall bring them in the midst of his throne to dwell in his presence eternally.

18. In view, then, of the existence of these attributes, the faith of the saints can become exceedingly strong, abounding in righteousness unto the praise and glory of God, and can exert its mighty influence in searching after wisdom and understanding, until it has obtained a knowledge of all things that pertain to life and salvation.

19. Such, then, is the foundation which is laid, through the revelation of the attributes of God, for the exercise of faith in him for life and salvation; and seeing that these are attributes of the Deity, they are unchangeable—being the same yesterday, today, and for ever—which gives to the minds of the Latter-day Saints the same power and authority to exercise faith in God which the Former-day Saints had; so that all the saints, in this respect, have been, are, and will be, alike until the end of time; for God never changes, therefore his attributes and character remain forever the same. And as it is through the revelation of these that a foundation is laid for the exercise of faith in God unto life and salvation, the foundation, therefore, for the exercise of faith was, is, and ever will be, the same; so that all men have had, and will have, an equal privilege.

Lectures on Faith, 4:1–19.

THE TRUE CHARACTER OF GOD AND MAN

ORSON PRATT

This address was delivered in the Tabernacle in Salt Lake City on November 12, 1876. "There is nothing pertaining to the things of this present life that is worthy of being named, in contrast with the riches of eternal life," Elder Orson Pratt taught. " . . . There is nothing so precious, nothing of so great importance, as that of securing, in this life, the salvation of our souls in the world to come. Far better is it if we can gain salvation by passing through various scenes of affliction and persecution in this world, than to give way to its pleasures and vanities, which can only be enjoyed for a season, and afterwards lose that eternal reward which God has in store for the righteous."

We, as a people, have passed through many scenes trying and afflicting to our natures, which we have endured because of the anxiety of our hearts to obtain salvation. People who are sincere will manifest their sincerity in undergoing great tribulation, if necessary, for the sake of being saved. This mortal life is of small consideration, compared with eternal salvation in the kingdom of the Father. There is nothing pertaining to the things of this present life that is worthy of being named, in contrast with the riches of eternal life. Jesus, in speaking upon this subject when he was on the earth, asks this question: "For what is a man profited, if he gain the whole world, and lose his own soul? Or what shall a man give in exchange for his soul?" There is nothing so precious, nothing of so great importance, as that of securing, in this life, the salvation of our souls in the world to come. Far better is it if we can gain salvation by passing through various scenes of affliction and persecution in this world, than to give way to its pleasures and vanities, which can only be enjoyed for a season, and afterwards lose that eternal reward which God has in store for the righteous.

It is true we look upon our future reward in quite a different light from the religious world generally. We look for something tangible, something we can form some degree of rational conception of, having a resemblance in some measure to the present life. But how very imaginary are the ideas of the religious world! . . . If you ask these people about the future state of man, some will give you one idea and some another, all more or less, perhaps, differing from each other, but in the main they all agree, namely, that it is a state entirely spiritual, that is, unconnected with anything tangible like this present life, an existence which cannot be conceived of by mortals. . . .

The Latter-day Saints believe that there is a true and living God, that this true and living God consists of three separate, distinct persons, which have bodies, parts, and passions. . . . We believe that God, the Eternal Father, who reigns in yonder heavens, is a distinct personage from Jesus Christ, as much so as an earthly father is distinct in his existence from his son. That is something I can comprehend, which I conceive to be the doctrine of revelation. We read about Jesus having been seen, after he arose from the dead. Stephen the Martyr, just before he was stoned to death, testified to the Jewish people that were standing before him at the time, saying, "Behold, I see the heavens opened, and the Son of Man standing on the right hand of God." Here, then, the Father and Jesus, two distinct personages, were seen, and both had bodies. . . .

We have it recorded too in this sacred Bible, that God was seen by ancient men of God. Jacob testifies as follows: "for I have seen

God face to face." I know that there are other passages of Scripture, which would seem to militate against this declaration. For instance, there is one passage which reads, "No man hath seen God at any time." This is in direct contradiction to the testimony of Jacob. The way I reconcile this is that no *natural* man can see the face of God the Father and live, it would overpower him; but one quickened by the spirit, as old father Jacob was, could look upon God, and converse with him face to face, as he says he did; he must have seen a personage, a being, in his general outlines like unto himself; man, as Moses informs us, having been created in the image of God.

We might refer to many other passages of Scripture, bearing on this subject. The Prophet Isaiah saw God; he saw not only the Lord, but also a great congregation in connection with him, so that his train filled the Temple. He is always represented by those who have seen him as a personage in the form of a man.

Having cited a very few evidences, let us inquire into the character and being of God, the Eternal Father. We are the offspring of the Lord, but the rest of animated nature is not; we are just as much the sons and daughters of God as the children in this congregation are the sons and daughters of their parents. We were begotten by him. When? Before we were born in the flesh; this limited state of existence is not our origin, it is merely the origin of the tabernacle in which we dwelt. The mind we are possessed of, the being that is capable of thinking and reflecting, that is capable of acting according to the motives presented to it, that being which is immortal, which dwells within us, which is capable of reasoning from cause to effect, and which can comprehend, in some measure, the laws of its Creator, as well as trace them out as exhibited in universal nature, that being, which we call the Mind, existed before the tabernacle.

But says one, "That does not look reasonable." Why not? Do you not believe that the Spirit will endure forever? O, yes. You may ask, "What becomes of the spirit, separated from the body of flesh and bones, when this body lies in the grave? Has it life and intelligence and power to think and reflect?" Let us hear what was said by those who sat under the altar, who were slain for the word of God, and for the testimony which they held, as seen and heard by John while on Patmos. "And they cried with a loud voice, saying, How long, O Lord, holy and true, dost thou not judge and avenge our blood on them that dwell on the earth?" The Lord tells them that they should "rest yet for a little season." These faithful servants of God are anxiously awaiting the time when the Lord will avenge their blood. Why? Because that will be the time when their bodies will be redeemed, they look forward with great anxiety to the time when they shall be again identified with the fleshly tabernacle with which they were known and distinguished while on the earth—hence this prayer.

Here we find another and further existence for the spirits of men who exist in heaven, who are capable of thinking, of using language, of understanding the future, and of anticipating that which was to come. Now, if they could exist after they leave this tabernacle, while the tabernacle lies moldering in the dust, why not exist before the tabernacle had any existence? Was it not just as easy for an existence to be given to spiritual personages before they took possession of bodies as it is for them to exist after the body decays? Yes, and these are our views, founded upon new revelations; not the views of uninspired men, but founded upon direct revelation from God.

Where did we exist before we came here? With God. Where does he exist? In the place John denominated heaven. What do we understand heaven to be? . . . [It is] a tangible world, a heaven that is perfect, a heaven with materials that have been organized and put together, sanctified and glorified as the residence and world where God resides. Born there? Yes, we were born there. Even our great Redeemer, whose death and sufferings we are this afternoon celebrating, was born up in yonder world before he was born of the Virgin Mary. Have you not read, in the New Testament, that Jesus Christ was the firstborn of every creature? From this reading it would seem that he was the oldest of the whole human family, that is, so far as his birth in the spirit world is concerned. How long ago since that birth took place is not revealed; it might have been unnumbered millions of years for aught we know. But we do know that he was born and was the oldest of the family of spirits.

Have you not also read in the New Testament that he is called our elder brother? Does this refer to the birth of the body of flesh and bones? By no means, for there were hundreds of millions who were born upon our earth before the body of flesh and bones was born whom we call Jesus. How is it, then, that he is our elder brother? We must go back to the previous birth, before the foundation of this earth; we have to go back to past ages, to the period when he was begotten of the Father among the great family of spirits.

He became, by his birthright, the great Creator. God, through him, created not only this little world, this speck of creation, but by him the worlds were made and created. How many we know not, for it has not been revealed. Suffice it to say, a great many worlds were created by him. Why by him? Because he had the birthright, he being the oldest of his father's family, and this birthright entitles him, not only to create worlds, but to become the redeemer of those worlds, not only the redeemer of the inhabitants of this our earth, but of all the others whom he created by the will and power of his Father. . . .

. . . You and I were present when this world was created and made—you and I then understood the nature of its creation, and I have no doubt that we rejoiced and sang about it. Indeed, the Lord put a very curious question to the Patriarch Job, *apropos* of this. He said to him, "Where wast thou when I laid the foundation of the earth? Where wast thou, when the morning stars sang together, and all the sons of God shouted for joy?" . . .

But now this carries us back still further, and invites us to ascertain a little in relation to his Father. A great many have supposed that God the Eternal Father, whom we worship in connection with his Son, Jesus Christ, was always a self-existing, eternal being from all eternity, that he had no beginning as a personage. But in order to illustrate this, let us inquire, What is our destiny? If we are now the sons and daughters of God, what will be our future destiny? The Apostle Paul, in speaking of man as a resurrected being, says, "Who (Jesus) shall change our vile body, that it might be fashioned like unto his glorious body," which harmonizes with what John says, "It doth not yet appear what we shall be, but we know that when he shall appear we shall be like him." Our bodies will be glorified in the same manner as his body is; then we shall be truly in his image and likeness, for as he is immortal, having a body of flesh and bones, so we will be immortal, possessing bodies of flesh and bones.

Will we ever become Gods? Let me refer you to the answer of the Savior to the Jews when accused of blasphemy because he called himself the Son of God. Says he, "Is it not written in your law, I said, Ye are gods? If he called them gods, unto whom the word of God came, and the Scriptures cannot be broken." This clearly proves to all Bible believers that in this world, in our imperfect state, being the children of God, we are destined, if we keep his commandments, to grow in intelligence until we finally become like God our Father. By living according to every word which proceeds from the mouth of God, we shall attain to his likeness, the same as our children grow up and become like their parents; and, as children through diligence attain to the wisdom and knowledge of their parents, so may we attain to the knowledge of our Heavenly Parents, and if they be obedient to this commandment they will not only be called the sons of God, but be gods. . . .

Says one, to carry it out still further, "If we become gods and are glorified like unto him, our bodies fashioned like unto his most glorious body, may not he have passed through a mortal ordeal as we mortals are now doing? Why not? If it is necessary for us to obtain experience through the things that are presented before us in this life, why not those beings, who are already exalted and become gods, obtain their experience in the same way? We would find, were we to carry this subject from world to world, from our world to another, even to the endless ages of eternity, that there never was a time but what there was a Father and Son. In other words, when you entertain that which is endless, you exclude the idea of a first being, a first world; the moment you admit of a first, you limit the idea of endless. The chain itself is endless, but each link had its beginning.

Says one, "This is incomprehensible." It may be so in some respects. We can admit, though, that duration is endless, for it is impossible for man to conceive of a limit of it. If duration is endless, there can never be a first minute, a first hour, or first period; endless duration in the past is made up of a continuation of endless successive moments—it had no beginning. Precisely so with regard to this endless succession of personages; there never will be a time when fathers, and sons, and worlds will not exist; neither was there ever a period through all the past ages of duration, but what there was a world, and a Father and Son, a redemption and exaltation to the fullness and power of the Godhead. . . .

Before the earth was rolled into existence we were his sons and daughters. Those of his children who prove themselves during this probation worthy of exaltation in his presence, will beget other children, and, precisely according to the same principle, they too will become fathers of spirits, as he is the Father of our spirits; and thus the works of God are one eternal round—creation, glorification, and exaltation in the celestial kingdom. . . .

How very plain it is when we once learn about our future heaven. We do not have to pray . . . for the Lord to take us to a land beyond time and space, the Saints' secure abode. How inconsistent to look for a heaven beyond space! The heaven of the Saints is something we can look forward to in the confident hope of realizing our inheritances and enjoying them forever, when the earth becomes sanctified and made new. And there, as here, we will spread forth and multiply our children. How long? For eternity. What, resurrected Saints have children? Yes, the same as our God, who is the Father of our spirits; so you, if you are faithful to the end, will become fathers to your sons and daughters, which will be as innumerable as the sands upon the sea shore; they will be your children, and you will be their heavenly fathers, the same as our Heavenly Father is Father to us, and they will belong to your kingdoms through all the vast ages of eternity, the same as we will belong to our Father's kingdom.

"He that receiveth my Father," says the Savior, "receiveth my Father's kingdom, wherefore all that my Father hath shall be given to him." It is a kind of joint stock inheritance, we are to become joint heirs with Jesus Christ to all the inheritances and to all the worlds that are made. We shall have the power of locomotion; and like Jesus, after his resurrection, we shall be able to mount up and pass from one world to another. We shall not be confined to our native earth. There are many worlds inhabited by people who are glorified, for heaven is not one place, but many; heaven is not one world but many. "In my Father's house are many mansions." In other words—In my Father's house there are many worlds, which in their turn will be made glorified heavens, the inheritances of the redeemed from all the worlds who, having been prepared through similar experience to our own, will inhabit them; and each one in its turn will be exalted through the revelations and laws of the Most High God, and they will continue to multiply their offspring through all eternity, and new worlds will be made for their progeny. Amen.

Journal of Discourses, 18:286.

H O M E

~❧ ❧~

LOVE OF MOTHER AND FATHER

JOSEPH F. SMITH

When the *Improvement Era* printed this excerpt in 1910 from a talk by President Joseph F. Smith, it included this explanatory note: "The Granite stake of Zion has set aside Tuesday evening of each week for a 'Home Evening.' Every family in the stake is asked to be at home, and the time is to be spent for the use and benefit of the home. The parents are to teach their children the gospel, there are to be songs, hymns, music, scripture readings, instructions, games, refreshments and counsel—a getting nearer together, in the family circle. The movement was started by a large meeting of parents in the stake tabernacle recently. At this meeting President Joseph F. Smith delivered a stirring sermon on 'Family Government,' and from his remarks on this occasion are selected these beautiful and instructive sentiments."

The poignancy of President Smith's feelings about his mother are better understood in the context of his personal history. He was only five years old when his father, Hyrum, was martyred, and his mother, Mary Fielding Smith, one of the stalwarts among the women during the early days of the Restoration, died eight years later when Joseph was not quite fourteen years old.

I learned in my childhood, as most children, probably, have learned, more or less at least, that no love in all the world can equal the love of a true mother.

I did not think in those days and still I am at a loss to know how it would be possible for anyone to love her children more truly than did my mother. I have felt sometimes how could even the Father love his children more than my mother loved her children? It was life to me; it was strength; it was encouragement; it was love that begot love or *likeness* in myself. I knew she loved me with all her heart. She loved her children with all her soul. She would toil and labor and sacrifice herself day and night, for the temporal comforts and blessings that she could meagerly give, through the results of her own labors, to her children. There was no sacrifice of self—of her own time, of her leisure, or pleasure, or opportunities for rest—that was considered for a moment, when it came in comparison with her duty and her love to her children.

When I was fifteen years of age, and called to go to a foreign country to preach the gospel—or to learn how, and to learn it for myself—the strongest anchor that was fixed in my life, and that helped to hold my ambition and my desire steady, to bring me upon a level and keep me straight, was that love which I knew she had for me, who bore me into the world.

Only a little boy, not matured at all in judgment, without the advantage of education, thrown in the midst of the greatest allurements and temptations that it was possible for any boy or any man to be subjected to—and yet, whenever those temptations became most alluring and most tempting to me, the first thought that rose in my soul was this: "Remember the love of your mother. Remember how she strove for your welfare. Remember how willing she was to sacrifice her life for your good. Remember what she taught you in your childhood, and how she insisted upon your reading the New Testament—the only book, except a few little school books, that we had in the family, or that was within reach of us at that time." This feeling toward my mother became a defense, a barrier between me and temptation, so that I could turn aside from temptation and sin by the help of the Lord and the love begotten in my soul, toward her whom I knew loved me more than anybody else in all the world, and more than any other living being could love me.

A wife may love her husband, but it is different to that of the love of mother to her child. The true mother, the mother who has the fear of God and the love of truth in her soul, would never hide from danger or evil and leave her child exposed to it. But as natural as it is for the sparks to fly upward, as natural as it is to breathe the breath of life, if there were danger coming to her child, she would step between the child and that danger; she would defend her child to the uttermost. Her life would be nothing in the balance, in comparison with the life of her child. That is the love of true motherhood—for children.

Her love for her husband would be different, for if danger should come to him, as natural as it would be for her to step between her child and danger, instead her disposition would be to step behind her husband for protection; and that is the difference between the love of mother for children and the love of wife for husband—there is a great difference between the two. I have learned to place a high estimate upon the love of mother. I have often said, and will repeat it, that the love of a true mother comes nearer being like the love of God than any other kind of love.

The father may love his children, too; and next to the love that the mother feels for her child, unquestionably and rightfully, too, comes the love that the father feels for his child. But . . . the love of the father is of a different character, or degree, to the love of the mother for her child, illustrated by the fact he [a previous speaker] related here of having the privilege of working with his boy, having him in his presence, becoming more intimate with him, learning his characteristics more clearly; becoming more familiar and more closely related to him; the result of which was that his love for his boy increased, and the love of the boy increased for his father, for the same reason, merely because of that closer association. So the child learns to love its mother best, as a rule, when the mother is good, wise, prudent, and intelligent; because the child is with her more, they are more familiar with each other and understand each other better.

Now, this is the thought that I desire to express: Fathers, if you wish your children to be taught in the principles of the gospel, if you wish them to love the truth and understand it, if you wish them to be obedient to and united with you, love them! And prove to them that you do love them, by your every word or act to them. For your own sake, for the love that should exist between you and your boys—however wayward they might be, or one or the other might be, when you speak or talk to them, do it not in anger; do it not harshly, in a condemning spirit. Speak to them kindly: get down and weep with them, if necessary, and get them to shed tears with you if possible. Soften their hearts; get them to feel tenderly towards you. Use no lash and no violence, but argue, or rather reason—approach them with reason, with persuasion and love unfeigned.

With these means, if you cannot gain your boys and your girls, they will prove to be reprobate to you; and there will be no means left in the world by which you can win them to yourselves. But, get them to feel as you feel, have interest in the things in which you take interest, to love the gospel as you love it, to love one another as you love them; to love their parents as the parents love the children. You can't do it any other way. You can't do it by unkindness; you cannot do it by driving—our children are like we are: we couldn't be driven; we can't be driven now. We are like some other animals that we know of in the world: You can coax them; you can lead them, by holding out inducements to them and by speaking kindly to them, but you can't drive them; they won't be driven. *We* won't be driven. Men are not in the habit of being driven; they are not made that way.

That is not the way that God intended, in the beginning, to

deal with his children—by force. It is all free love, free grace. The poet expressed it in these words:

> Know this that every soul is free,
> To choose his course and what he'll be;
> For this eternal truth is given,
> That God will force no man to heaven.

You can't force your boys, nor your girls into heaven. You may force them to hell—by using harsh means in the efforts to make them good, when you yourselves are not as good as you should be. The man that will be angry at his boy, and try to correct him while he is in anger, is in the greatest fault; he is more to be pitied and more to be condemned than the child who has done wrong. You can only correct your children in love, in kindness—by love unfeigned, by persuasion and reason.

When I was a child, sometimes a wayward, disobedient little boy—not that I was wilfully disobedient, but I would forget what I ought to do; I would go off with playful boys and be absent when I should have been at home, and I would forget to do things I was asked to do. Then I would go home, feel guilty, know that I was guilty, that I had neglected my duty and that I deserved punishment.

On one occasion I had done something that was not just right, and my mother said to me: "Now, Joseph, if you do that again I shall have to whip you." Well, time went on, and by and by I forgot it, and I did something similar again; and this is the one thing that I admired more, perhaps, than any secondary thing in her; it was that when she made a promise she kept it. She never made a promise, that I know of, that she did not keep.

Well, I was called to account. She said: "Now, I told you. You knew that if you did this I would have to whip you, for I said I would. I must do it. I do not want to do it. It hurts me worse than it does you, but I must whip you."

Well, she had a little rawhide, already there, and while she was talking or reasoning with me, showing me how much I deserved it and how painful it was to her to inflict the punishment I deserved—I had only one thought and that was: "For goodness sake, whip me; do not reason with me"; for I felt the lash of her just criticism and admonition a thousand fold worse than I did the switch. I felt as if, when she laid the lash on me, I had at least partly paid my debt and had answered for my wrong doing. Her reasoning cut me down into the quick; it made me feel sorry to the very core.

I could have endured a hundred lashes with the rawhide better than I could endure a ten-minute talk in which I felt and was made to feel that the punishment inflicted upon me was painful to her that I loved—punishment upon my own mother!

(During the time the President was relating these incidents, he spoke with great feeling, and at this point was obliged to stop his discourse for a time, to calm his feelings; then he continued:)

You must excuse me. There are two divine personages that I can scarcely think or talk about without it softens my spirit and brings me down to the similitude of a little child; and those two beings are my mother and my Redeemer! My Redeemer, the Savior of my soul, my Redeemer from sin—Jesus of Nazareth, the Son of the living God, he who restored the fulness of his gospel and the plan of life and salvation, through the Prophet Joseph Smith, in the dispensation in which we live. I cannot read the New Testament about the Lord but it softens my soul. When I think of him and of the humiliation that he passed through, the death that he suffered for the redemption of man, I am captured and captivated, and I can't help myself. I thank the Lord that this is so.

Improvement Era, January 1910, 276–80.

~❦ ❧~

HARMONY IN THE HOME

DAVID O. McKAY

"Too many couples," said President David O. McKay, "have come to the altar of marriage looking upon the marriage ceremony as the end of courtship instead of the beginning of an eternal courtship. Let us not forget that during the burdens of home life—and they come—that tender words of appreciation, courteous acts are even more appreciated than during those sweet days and months of courtship."

In this April 1956 general conference talk, President McKay—well known for his lifelong courtship of Emma, his eternal companion—outlined characteristics of loyalty and integrity that lead to the building of a happy marriage and a harmonious home.

M y beloved brethren and sisters: If you knew the weight of the responsibility of this moment, you would gladly answer the prayer of my heart—that I might have your united support and the inspiration of the Lord. I know what I should like to say and will try to say it, but it is a question whether I can get that message over to the thousands who are listening as I should like to give it, and, I hope, as the Lord would have it given.

"Verily I say unto you, . . . [that] marriage is ordained of God unto man.

"Wherefore, it is lawful that he should have one wife, and they twain shall be one flesh, and all this that the earth might answer the end of its creation." (D&C 49:15–16.)

That passage from the Doctrine and Covenants indicates the

message I have in mind to give this morning—some helpful hints for happy homes. . . .

An Appeal for Stability and Harmony in the Home

. . . I am not so sure whether we are maintaining the high standards required of us in our homes. I feel constrained, therefore, . . . to make an appeal for more stability, more harmony and happiness in home life. It has been truly said that "the strength of a nation, especially of a republican nation, is in the intelligent, well-ordered homes of the people." In no other group in the world should there be more contented, more happy homes than in The Church of Jesus Christ of Latter-day Saints.

Just this month there appeared in a leading magazine the encouraging statement that American homes and family life are steadily strengthening. According to that article, the total population of our country has doubled since 1900. The number of families has tripled. This growth in family life is shown by the rapid increase in home ownership. One hundred twenty percent more families owned their own homes in 1955 than in 1940. There are sixty-seven percent more children under five years of age now than in 1940, that is in the country at large. There are sixty-one percent more children in group age five to nine years.

Loyalty As a Contributing Factor

Recently our attention has been called to conditions that seem to justify our admonishing the membership of the Church to keep their homes exemplary before the world.

To the young people of the Church, particularly, I should like to say first that a happy home begins not at the marriage altar, but during the brilliant, fiery days of youth. The first contributing factor to a happy home is the sublime virtue of loyalty, one of the noblest attributes of the human soul. Loyalty means being faithful and true. It means fidelity to parents, fidelity to duty, fidelity to a cause or principle, fidelity to love. Disloyalty to parents during teen age is often a source of sorrow and sometimes tragedy in married life.

I have received several letters this last month from young folk—two of them in their teens—irked because of what they consider interference of parents. Young people in all the Church and all the nation should understand that both the Church and the state hold parents responsible for the conduct and protection of their children. The Church, you will recall, is very explicit in that. "Inasmuch as parents have children in Zion, or in any of her stakes which are organized, that teach them not to understand the doctrine of repentance, faith in Christ the Son of the Living God, and of baptism and the gift of the Holy Ghost by the laying on of the hands, when eight years old, the sin be upon the heads of the parents. For this shall be a law unto the inhabitants of Zion, or in any of her stakes which are organized." (D&C 68:25–26.)

That is explicit, and parents, that is your responsibility.

Some of you would be surprised to know that the statute of the state requires explicitly that not only parents, but also any guardian who has charge of a child eighteen or under is held responsible for the protection of that child and for his moral teachings. Any guardian or parent that will do anything to injure the morals of the child is guilty of a misdemeanor and subject to imprisonment of not more, if I remember rightly, than six months, and a fine of not less than three hundred dollars, or both.

So, girls and boys, your parents, not only because of their love, but also by command of the Lord and by legislative enactment of the state, are compelled to watch over you and guide you. And parents, once again, that is your responsibility. The effect of this guardianship will be shown by illustration.

A New York City judge not long ago wrote to the *New York Times*, saying that in seventeen years that he had on the bench not one Chinese-American teenager had been brought before him on a juvenile delinquency charge. The judge queried his colleagues, and they agreed that not one of the city's estimated 10,000 Chinese-American teenagers, to their knowledge (not one), had ever been hailed into court on a charge of depredation, narcotics, speeding, burglary, vandalism, stickup, purse snatching, or mugging accusations.

A check with San Francisco, where there is a large colony of Chinese-Americans, tells the same story.

P. H. Chang, Chinese Consul-General in New York City, was asked to comment on that. He said, "I have heard this story many times from many judges. I'll tell you why I think this is so. Filial piety is a cardinal virtue my people have brought over from the China that was once free. A Chinese child, no matter where he lives, is brought up to recognize that he cannot shame his parents. Before a Chinese child makes a move, he stops to think what the reaction of his parents will be. Will they be proud or will they be ashamed? Above all other things, the Chinese teenager is anxious to please his parents.

"Most Chinese-Americans, no matter how wealthy or poor, maintain a strict family style home. Mealtime is a ceremonious affair which must be attended by every member of the family. Schooling, reverence for religion, and decorum plus reverence for the elders, are the prime movers in developing the child from infancy."

And the paper says, "The amazing record of the Chinese-American youngster shows that it is in the home that the cure for juvenile delinquency will be found, and in no other place." (From an editorial in the *Saturday Evening Post*, reprinted in the *Reader's Digest*, July 1955.)

So, young people, loyalty to parents, if not a direct contributing factor to a happy home, is at least a safeguard against hastily assuming and lightly esteeming the duties and responsibilities of marriage.

Loyalty to Self

Next to loyalty to parents, I should like to urge loyalty to self. Remember, if you would be happy, if you reach the goal of success in the distant future, your first duty is to be loyal to the best that is in you, not to the basest.

There is a saying in the Bible that "every idle word that men shall speak, they shall give account thereof in the day of judgment." (Matthew 12:36.) Psychology assures us that "We are spinning our own fates, good or evil, and never to be undone. Every smallest stroke of virtue or of vice leaves its never-so-little scar. The drunken Rip Van Winkle, in Jefferson's play, excuses himself for every fresh dereliction by saying, 'I won't count this time.'

"Well!" continues James, the psychologist, "he may not count it, and a kind Heaven may not count it; but it is being counted nonetheless. Down among his nerve cells and fibers the molecules are counting it, registering and storing it up to be used against him when the next temptation comes. Nothing we ever do is, in strict scientific literalness, wiped out. Of course, this has its good side as well as its bad one. As we become permanent drunkards by so many separate drinks, so we become saints in the moral sphere, and authorities and experts in the practical and scientific spheres, by so many separate acts and hours of work. Let no youth have any anxiety about the upshot of his education, whatever the line of it may be. If he keeps faithfully busy each hour of the working day, he may safely leave the final result to itself. He can with perfect certainty count on waking up some fine morning, to find himself one of the competent ones of his generation, in whatever pursuit he may have singled out. Silently, between all the details of his business, the *power of judging* in all that class of matter will have built itself up within him as a possession that will never pass away. Young people should know this truth in advance. The ignorance of it has probably engendered more discouragement and faint-heartedness in youth embarking on arduous careers than all other causes put together." (*Psychology*, William James, Henry Holt, 1892, 150.)

A good ideal for youth to build a happy home is this: Keep true to the best and never let an hour of indulgence scar your life for eternity.

Loyalty to Your Future Companion

Next under that heading of loyalty, I urge *loyalty to your future companion*. When harmony, mutual consideration, and trust pass out of the home, hell enters in. A memory of a simple indulgence in youth sometimes opens hell's door. Girls, choose a husband who has respect for womanhood! Young man, choose a girl who, in her teens, has virtue and strength enough to keep herself true to her future husband! Down the road of indulgence are too many good young girls, seeking vainly for happiness in the by-ways where people grovel but do not aspire. As a result their search for happiness is in vain. They grasp at what seems substance to find only ashes.

If you would have a happy marriage, keep your reputation as well as your character unsullied.

It is a common saying throughout the world that young men may sow their wild oats, but young women should be chaperoned. In general, this is pretty well carried out, but in the Church we have but one single standard, and it is just as important for young men to keep themselves chaste as it is for young women. No matter what the opportunity, no matter what the temptation, let the young man know that to find happiness he must hold sacred his true manhood. Marriage is a failure when manhood is a failure. Let him know that to gain moral strength he must learn to resist temptation, learn to say with Christ, "Get thee hence, Satan: for it is written, Thou shalt worship the Lord thy God, and him only shalt thou serve." (Matthew 4:10.) Then he is happy; there is peace instead of turbulency in his soul.

Continued Courtship

Next to loyalty as contributive to a happy home, I should like to urge *continued courtship*, and apply this to grown people. Too many couples have come to the altar of marriage looking upon the marriage ceremony as the end of courtship instead of the beginning of an eternal courtship. Let us not forget that during the burdens of home life—and they come—that tender words of appreciation, courteous acts are even more appreciated than during those sweet days and months of courtship. It is after the ceremony and during the trials that daily arise in the home that a word of "thank you," or "pardon me, if you please," on the part of husband or wife contributes to that love which brought you to the altar.

It is well to keep in mind that love can be starved to death as literally as the body that receives no sustenance. Love feeds upon kindness and courtesy. It is significant that the first sentence of what is now known throughout the Christian world as the Psalm of Love, is, "Love suffereth long, and is kind." The wedding ring gives no man the right to be cruel or inconsiderate, and no woman the right to be slovenly, cross, or disagreeable.

Self-Control

The next contributing factor to your happy marriage I would name is *self-control*. Little things happen that annoy you, and you speak quickly, sharply, loudly, and wound the other's heart. I know of no virtue that helps to contribute to the happiness and peace of the home more than that great quality of self-control in speech. Refrain from saying the sharp word that comes to your mind at once if you are wounded or if you see something in the other which offends you. It is said that during courtship we should keep our eyes wide open, but after marriage keep them half-shut.

What I mean may be illustrated by a young woman who said to her husband, "I know that my cooking isn't good; I hate it as much as you do, but do you find me sitting around griping about it?" This griping after marriage is what makes it unpleasant. I recall the words of Will Carleton:

"Words"
Boys flying kites haul in their white-winged birds—
You can't do that when you're flying words. . . .
Thoughts unexpressed may sometimes fall back dead,
But God himself can't kill them when they're said.

Children in the Home

Marriage offers an opportunity to share in the love and care of children, and that is the true purpose of marriage. One writer truly says: "Without children, or without believing that children are important, marriage is incomplete and unfulfilled. Children take time, trouble, and more patience than we usually have. They interfere with freedom, good times, and luxury, but children are the real purpose and reason behind marriage. If we do not put the proper value on parenthood, we are not emotionally or socially ready for marriage.

"Marriage is a relationship that cannot survive selfishness, impatience, domineering, inequality, and lack of respect. Marriage is a relationship that thrives on acceptance, equality, sharing, giving, helping, doing one's part, learning together, enjoying humor," and a home is full of humor with children.

The more you keep in company with your wife, the happier you are. Business takes you away from home. She is there alone. Do not let companionship with other women divide your affection, and that applies to woman as well as to man. At one time I thought that it did not; that man was wholly to blame for the unrest, the disagreements and sorrows that are occurring too frequently, but I have had to modify my opinion. Companionship is the means of perpetuating that love which brought about your union.

In conclusion, for the proper solution of the great problems of marriage we may turn with safety to Jesus, our Guide. He declared, as I read in the beginning, that marriage is ordained of God and that only under the most exceptional conditions should it be set aside. In the teachings of The Church of Jesus Christ, the family assumes supreme importance in the development of the individual and of society. "Happy and thrice happy are they who enjoy an uninterrupted union, and whose love, unbroken by any complaints, shall not dissolve until the last day."

It will not dissolve when sealed by the authority of the Holy Priesthood throughout all eternity. The marriage ceremony, when thus sealed, produces happiness and joy unsurpassed by any other experience in the world. "What therefore God hath joined together, let not man put asunder."

> Home's not merely four square walls,
> Though with pictures hung and gilded;
> Home is where Affection calls,
> Filled with shrines the Heart has builded!
> Home's not merely roof and room—
> It needs something to endear it;
> Home is where the heart can bloom,
> Where there's some kind [heart] to cheer it!
> What is home with none to meet,
> None to welcome, none to greet us?
> Home is sweet—and only sweet—
> Where there's one we love to meet us.
>
> Charles Swain

To the Church, not only to young people, but also to married people, I plead this morning for more contented homes brought about through love, faithfulness, loyalty, self-control, and obedience to the principles of marriage as set for us by revelation to the members of the restored Church of Jesus Christ.

May God help us to be exemplary to the world in this respect, I pray in the name of Jesus Christ. Amen.

Conference Report, April 1956, 4–9.

H U M I L I T Y

~⚜~

WHAT IS TRUE GREATNESS?

HOWARD W. HUNTER

"I am confident that there are many great, unnoticed, and forgotten heroes among us," said Elder Howard W. Hunter in this inspiring address. "I am speaking of those of you who quietly and consistently do the things you ought to do." This is an edited version of a talk delivered at Brigham Young University on February 10, 1987.

Many Latter-day Saints are happy and enjoying the opportunities life offers. Yet I am concerned that some among us are unhappy. Some of us feel that we are falling short of our expected ideals. I have particular concern for those who have lived righteously but think—because they haven't achieved in the world or in the Church what others have achieved—that they have failed. Each of us desires to achieve a measure of greatness in this life. And why shouldn't we? As someone once noted, there is within each of us a giant struggling with celestial homesickness. (See Hebrews 11:13–16; D&C 45:11–14.)

Realizing who we are and what we may become assures us that with God nothing is really impossible. From the time we learn that Jesus wants us for a Sunbeam through the time we learn more fully the basic principles of the gospel, we are taught to strive for perfection. It is not new to us, then, to talk of the importance of achievement. The difficulty arises when inflated expectations of the world alter the definition of greatness.

What is true greatness? What is it that makes a person great?

We live in a world that seems to worship its own kind of greatness and to produce its own kind of heroes. A recent survey of young people ages eighteen through twenty-four revealed that today's youth prefer the "strong, go-it-alone, conquer-against-all-odds" individuals and that they clearly seek to pattern their lives after the glamorous and "boundlessly rich." During the 1950s, heroes included Winston Churchill, Albert Schweitzer, President Harry Truman, Queen Elizabeth, and Helen Keller—the blind and deaf writer-lecturer. These were figures who either helped shape history or were noted for their inspiring lives. Today, many of the top ten heroes are movie stars and other entertainers, which suggests something of a shift in our attitudes. (See *U.S. News & World Report,* April 22, 1985, 44–48.)

It's true that most of the world's heroes don't last very long in the public mind; but, nevertheless, there is never a lack of champions and great achievers. We hear almost daily of athletes breaking records; scientists inventing marvelous new devices, machines, and processes; and doctors saving lives in new ways. We are constantly being exposed to exceptionally gifted musicians and entertainers and to unusually talented artists, architects, and builders. Magazines, billboards, and television commercials bombard us with pictures of individuals with perfect teeth and flawless features, wearing stylish clothes and doing whatever it is that "successful" people do.

Because we are being constantly exposed to the world's definition of *greatness,* it is understandable that we might make comparisons between what we are and what others are—or seem to be—and also between what we have and what others have. Although it is true that making comparisons can be beneficial and may motivate us to accomplish much good and to improve our lives, we often allow unfair and improper comparisons to destroy our happiness when they cause us to feel unfulfilled or inadequate or unsuccessful. Sometimes, because of these feelings, we are led into error and dwell on our failures while ignoring aspects of our lives that may contain elements of true greatness.

In 1905, President Joseph F. Smith made this most profound statement about true greatness:

"Those things which we call extraordinary, remarkable, or unusual may make history, but they do not make real life.

"After all, to do well those things which God ordained to be the common lot of all mankind, is the truest greatness. To be a successful father or a successful mother is greater than to be a successful general or a successful statesman." (*Juvenile Instructor,* December 15, 1905, 752.)

This statement raises a query: What are the things God has ordained to be "the common lot of all mankind"? Surely they include the things that must be done in order to be a good father or a good mother, a good son or a good daughter, a good student or a good roommate or a good neighbor.

Pablo Casals, the great cellist, spent the morning on the day he died—at the age of ninety-five—practicing scales on his cello. Giving consistent effort in the little things in day-to-day life leads to true greatness. Specifically, it is the thousands of little deeds and tasks of service and sacrifice that constitute the giving, or losing, of one's life for others and for the Lord. They include gaining a knowledge of our Father in Heaven and the gospel. They also include bringing others into the faith and fellowship of his kingdom. These things do not usually receive the attention or the adulation of the world.

Joseph Smith is not generally remembered as a general, mayor, architect, editor, or presidential candidate. We remember him as the prophet of the Restoration, a man committed to the love of God and the furthering of His work. The Prophet Joseph was an everyday Christian. He was concerned about the small things, the daily tasks of service and caring for others. As a thirteen-year-old boy, Lyman O. Littlefield accompanied the camp of Zion, which went up to Missouri. He later narrated this incident of a small yet personally significant act of service in the life of the Prophet:

"The journey was extremely toilsome for all, and the physical suffering, coupled with the knowledge of the persecutions endured by our brethren whom we were traveling to succor, caused me to lapse one day into a state of melancholy. As the camp was making ready to depart I sat tired and brooding by the roadside. The Prophet was the busiest man of the camp; and yet when he saw me, he turned from the great press of other duties to say a word of comfort to a child. Placing his hand upon my head, he said, 'Is there no place for you, my boy? If not, we must make one.' This circumstance made an impression upon my mind which long lapse of time and cares of riper years have not effaced." (In George Q. Cannon, *Life of Joseph Smith the Prophet* [Salt Lake City: Deseret Book, 1986], 344.)

On another occasion, when Governor Carlin of Illinois sent Sheriff Thomas King of Adams County and several others as a posse to apprehend the Prophet and deliver him to the emissaries of Governor Boggs of Missouri, Sheriff King became deathly ill. At Nauvoo the Prophet took the sheriff to his home and nursed him like a brother for four days. (Ibid., 372.) Small, kind, and yet significant acts of service were not occasional for the Prophet.

Writing about the opening of the store in Nauvoo, Elder George Q. Cannon recorded:

"The Prophet himself did not hesitate to engage in mercantile and industrial pursuits; the gospel which he preached was one of temporal salvation as well as spiritual exaltation; and he was willing to perform his share of the practical labor. This he did with no thought of personal gain." (Ibid., 385.)

And in a letter, the Prophet wrote:

"The store has been filled to overflowing and I have stood behind the counter all day, distributing goods as steadily as any clerk you ever saw, to oblige those who were compelled to go without their Christmas and New Year's dinners for the want of a little sugar, molasses, raisins, etc.; and to please myself also, for I love to wait upon the Saints and to be a servant to all, hoping that I may be exalted in the due time of the Lord." (Ibid., 386.)

About this scene, George Q. Cannon commented:

"What a picture is presented here! A man chosen by the Lord to lay the foundation of His Church and to be its Prophet and President, takes joy and pride in waiting upon his brethren and sisters like a servant. The self-elected ministers of Christ in the world are forever jealous of their dignity and fearful of showing disrespect to their cloth; but Joseph never saw the day when he did not feel that he was serving God and obtaining favor in the sight of Jesus Christ by showing kindness and attention 'even unto the least of these.'" (Ibid., 386.)

To be a successful elders quorum secretary or Relief Society teacher or loving neighbor or listening friend is much of what true greatness is all about. To do one's best in the face of the commonplace struggles of life—and possibly in the face of failure—and to continue to endure and to persevere in the ongoing difficulties of life when those struggles and tasks contribute to others' progress and happiness and one's own eternal salvation—this is true greatness.

We all want to achieve a measure of greatness in this life. Many have already achieved great things; others are striving to achieve greatness. Let me encourage you to achieve and, at the same time, to remember who you are. Don't let the illusion of fleeting worldly greatness overcome you. Many people are losing their souls to such temptations. Your good name is not worth selling—for any price. True greatness is to remain true—"True to the faith that our parents have cherished, True to the truth for which martyrs have perished." (*Hymns*, no. 254.)

I am confident that there are many great, unnoticed, and forgotten heroes among us. I am speaking of those of you who quietly and consistently do the things you ought to do. I am talking about those who are always there and always willing. I am referring to the uncommon valor of the mother who, hour after hour, day and night, stays with and cares for a sick child while her husband is at work or in school. I am including those who volunteer to give blood or to work with the elderly. I am thinking about those of you who faithfully fulfill your priesthood and church responsibilities and of the students who write home regularly to thank their parents for their love and support.

I am also talking about those who instill in others faith and a desire to live the gospel—those who actively work to build and mold the lives of others physically, socially, and spiritually. I am referring to those who are honest and kind and hardworking in their daily tasks, but who are also servants of the Master and shepherds of his sheep.

Now, I do not mean to discount the great accomplishments of the world that have given us so many opportunities and that provide culture and order and excitement in our lives. I am merely suggesting that we try to focus more clearly on the things in life that will be of greatest worth. You will remember that it was the Savior who said, "He that is greatest among you shall be your servant." (Matthew 23:11.)

Each of us has seen individuals become wealthy or successful almost instantaneously—almost overnight. But I believe that even though this kind of success may come to some without prolonged struggle, there is no such thing as instant greatness. The achievement of true greatness is a long-term process. It may involve occasional setbacks. The end result may not always be clearly visible, but it seems that it always requires regular, consistent, small, and sometimes ordinary and mundane steps over a long period of time. We should remember that it was the Lord who said, "Out of small things proceedeth that which is great." (D&C 64:33.)

True greatness is never a result of a chance occurrence or a

one-time effort or achievement. Greatness requires the development of character. It requires a multitude of correct decisions in
the everyday choices between good and evil that Elder Boyd K.
Packer spoke about when he said, "Over the years these little
choices will be bundled together and show clearly what we value."
(*Ensign*, November 1980, 21.) Those choices will also show clearly
what we are.

As we evaluate our lives, it is important that we look not only
at our accomplishments but also at the conditions under which we
have labored. We are each different and unique; we have each had
different starting points in the race of life; we each have a unique
mixture of talents and skills; we each have our own set of challenges and constraints with which to contend. Therefore, our judgment of ourselves and our achievements should not merely include
the size or magnitude and number of our accomplishments; it
should also include the conditions that have existed and the effect
that our efforts have had on others.

It is this last aspect of our self-evaluation—the effect of our
lives on the lives of others—that will help us to understand why
some of the common, ordinary work of life should be valued so
highly. Frequently it is the commonplace tasks we perform that
have the greatest positive effect on the lives of others, as compared
with the things that the world so often relates to greatness.

It appears to me that the kind of greatness our Father in
Heaven would have us pursue is within the grasp of all who are
within the gospel net. We have an unlimited number of opportunities to do the many simple and minor things that will ultimately
make us great. To those who have devoted their lives to service
and sacrifice for their families, for others, and for the Lord, the best
counsel I can give is simply to do more of the same.

To those who are furthering the work of the Lord in so many
quiet but significant ways, to those who are the salt of the earth
and the strength of the world and the backbone of each nation—

to you we would simply express our admiration. If you endure to the end, and if you are valiant in the testimony of Jesus, you will achieve true greatness and will one day live in the presence of our Father in Heaven.

As President Joseph F. Smith has said, "Let us not be trying to substitute an artificial life for the true one." (*Juvenile Instructor*, December 15, 1905, 753.) Let us remember that doing the things that have been ordained by God to be important and needful and necessary, even though the world may view them as unimportant and insignificant, will eventually lead to true greatness.

We should strive to remember the words of the Apostle Paul, especially if we are unhappy with our lives and feeling that we have not achieved some form of greatness. He wrote:

"For our light affliction, which is but for a moment, worketh for us a far more exceeding and eternal weight of glory;

"While we look not at the things which are seen, but at the things which are not seen: for the things which are seen are temporal; but the things which are not seen are eternal." (2 Corinthians 4:17–18.)

The small things are significant. We remember not the amount offered by the Pharisee but the widow's mite, not the power and strength of the Philistine army but the courage and conviction of David.

May we never be discouraged in doing those daily tasks which God has ordained to be "the common lot of man."

That We Might Have Joy, 103–10.

JESUS CHRIST

THE DIVINITY OF JESUS CHRIST

ORSON F. WHITNEY

This address was delivered at the Sunday evening session of the Mutual Improvement Association Jubilee Conference on June 7, 1925. At the time, Elder Orson F. Whitney was an Apostle. In this address, Elder Whitney tells the well-known story of a dream he had, while serving as a young missionary, of the Savior's suffering in Gethsemane. After having viewed the moving scene, Elder Whitney dreamed that he approached the Savior and begged to go with him. "I shall never forget the kind and gentle manner in which he stooped and raised me up and embraced me. It was so vivid, so real, that I felt the very warmth of his bosom against which I rested. Then he said: 'No, my son; these have finished their work, and they may go with me, but you must stay and finish yours.' Still I clung to him. Gazing up into his face—for he was taller than I—I besought him most earnestly: 'Well, promise me that I will come to you at the last.' He smiled sweetly and tenderly and replied: 'That will depend entirely upon yourself.' I awoke with a sob in my throat, and it was morning."

At a time when many religious thinkers were challenging the divinity of Jesus Christ and questioning the reality of biblical accounts of his life, Elder Whitney found great comfort in the solidity and strength of gospel teachings and in his own personal testimony, conveyed to him by the power of the Holy Ghost.

An American newspaper of recent date has a communicated article from which I take the following:

"Columbus, Ohio, May 19, 1925—The General Assembly of the Presbyterian Church, which for the purpose of Church government corresponds to the Congress of the United States, is likely to decide within the next week whether a minister may still remain a minister if he answers: 'I don't know,' or 'I don't believe so,' when asked whether Jesus Christ really raised the dead, walked on water and was born of a virgin mother. . . .

"The Presbyterian Church will face its problem with two determined groups standing militant on either side of the question and a third group in the middle.

"The fundamentalists, who accept the Bible as the Divine word, hold that Jesus, to be God, must be omnipotent, capable of any miracle, . . . the all-powerful God of the universe.

"The modernists, or religious radicals of the clergy, who have been most conspicuous in New York, do not assert that Jesus Christ was no miracle worker. They do not claim that he would be unable, if so minded, to perform a modern miracle. They simply aren't convinced that he was or could.

"The fundamentalists want the dissenters to accept the Presbyterian religion as it is, or get out of the Presbyterian clergy. The modernists, regarding themselves as advanced thinkers, want the rest to catch up with them. And the element in between, who seem to be divided as to their leanings, want above all a constitutional, judicial trial of the case and abhor the idea of summary action." . . .

At a time when the Divine character and mission of the world's Redeemer are being questioned, even by many professing Christians, it is a cause for congratulation and rejoicing that there is still found "faith on the earth"—faith in Jesus Christ as the very Son of God, as the virgin-born Savior of mankind, as the anointed and foreordained messenger of him who "so loved the world, that he gave his only begotten Son, that whosoever believeth in him should not perish, but have everlasting life." (John 3:16.)

Among those who hold fast to this conviction are the Latter-day Saints, or "Mormons." . . .

How Testimony Comes

Such testimony can come but in one way—God's way, not man's. Books can not give it. Schools can not bestow it. No human power can impart it. It comes, if it comes at all, as a gift of God, by direct and immediate revelation from on high.

Said Jesus to his chief Apostle: "Whom say ye that I am?" Peter answered: "Thou art the Christ, the Son of the living God." Then said Jesus: "Blessed art thou, Simon Bar-jona, for flesh and blood hath not revealed it unto thee, but my Father which is in heaven." (Matthew 16:15–17.)

Such was the basis of Peter's testimony and such is the basis of every real testimony of like character. They all rest upon the same foundation.

Testimony means evidence, and it may consist of divers things, fruits of the gospel's varied gifts. Dreams, visions, prophecies, tongues and their interpretation, healings and other manifestations of the Divine Spirit are all included in the category.

The Surest Evidence

But the greatest and most convincing of all testimonies is the soul's illumination under the kindling and enlightening power of the Holy Ghost—the Comforter, promised by the Savior to his disciples, to abide with them after he had departed, to bring things past to their remembrance and show them things to come, making manifest the things of God, past, present and future.

God's Greatest Gift

By that Spirit and by that alone can men know God and Jesus Christ whom he hath sent—to know whom, and to act consistently with that knowledge, is to lay hold upon eternal life. No greater thing can come to men while in the flesh than the knowledge of how to secure that greatest of all heavenly gifts.

To know God, man must know himself, must know whence he came, why he is here, what is expected of him by the One who sent him here, where he is going when he leaves this mortal life, and what awaits him in the great hereafter. The Holy Spirit is the fountain from which flows this knowledge, the most precious that men can possess. By means of it comes the testimony that Jesus Christ was and is Divine.

The Everlasting Gospel

Such a testimony was had by the patriarchs and prophets of old. They were not without the gospel and its glorious gifts. The Holy Ghost did not make its first appearance upon this planet in the days of Jesus and his Apostles. Men had seen God before that time, and had enjoyed the sweet influence and wonder-working power of his Spirit. Framed in the heavens before this earth was organized, the gospel had been among men in a series of dispensations, long before it was preached by the Apostles in the meridian of time.

Testimony of the Ages

"I know that my Redeemer liveth"—the burden of righteous Job's exultant cry, welling up from the depths of his sorely tried, suffering, yet patient soul—is echoed from ten thousand hearts, yea, ten thousand times ten thousand of the faithful and the just, whose heaven-inspired testimonies have come ringing down the ages, from the days of Adam to the days of Joseph Smith. The Holy Scriptures are replete with testimonies of Christ's divinity, attested by miracles and wonders manifold.

A Life and Death Divine

But even if Christ had wrought no miracle—even if he had not walked upon the water, healed the sick, cast out devils, given sight to the blind, caused the lame to walk, or done anything else that men deem supernatural, was there not that about him which bore unimpeachable testimony to his divinity?

What could be more divine than the life of One who "went about doing good," teaching men to forgive their enemies, to pray for those who persecuted them, and to do unto others as they would that others should do unto them? And did he not set the example of Godlike magnanimity, by craving, while upon the cross in the agonies of death, Heaven's pardon upon his guilty murderers? "Father, forgive them; for they know not what they do." (Luke 23:34.)

What could be more divine than that. Who but a God could offer such a prayer at such a time? "Greater love hath no man than this, that a man lay down his life for his friends." (John 15:13.) But here was One who could lay down his life for his enemies, as well as his friends. No mere man could do that. It took a God to die for all men—foes as well as friends—and that act alone stamps divinity upon the character and mission of Jesus Christ.

The Men Who Knew

The Twelve Apostles were his special witnesses. As such they had to know beyond all question that he was what he claimed to be. It was a new thing that was required of them. They were to vouch for his resurrection—and there had been no resurrection upon this planet until Christ came forth from the grave. He was "the firstfruits of them that slept." (1 Corinthians 15:20.) Those Apostles had to know, not merely believe. They could not go into the world and say: "We believe Jesus has risen from the dead—such is our opinion, our conviction." What impression would that have made upon a sin-hardened generation? No; mere belief would not suffice in their case. They must know, and they did know, for they had seen and heard him, had even been permitted to touch him, that they might be convinced that he was indeed the resurrection and the life. It was their right to possess this knowledge, owing to the unique character of their mission. But the world at large was required to believe what the Apostles testified concerning him.

The Case of Thomas

One of the Twelve was absent when his brethren received their first visitation from the risen Redeemer; and when they said, "We have seen the Lord," he—Thomas—answered: "Except I shall see in his hands the print of the nails, and put my finger into the print of the nails, and thrust my hand into his side, I will not believe." Subsequently the Savior appeared to Thomas, saying: "Behold my hands; and reach hither thy hand, and thrust it into my side: and be not faithless, but believing. . . . My Lord and my God," exclaimed the doubter—and was convinced. (John 20:24–28.)

Thomas has been censured for demanding to see and to feel before he would believe. How much blame attaches to him for doubting, I will not presume to say. But this much seems clear: He had the same right as the rest of the Twelve to a personal appearing of the Lord—the right to come in contact with him of whose resurrection he was required to testify. The others had seen and heard—perhaps had even felt, for Jesus offered them that privilege. Why should not Thomas share in the same experience? What else could completely qualify him as a special witness of the resurrection?

Belief and Knowledge

Sign-seeking is an abomination, indicating an adulterous disposition. It is blessed to believe without seeing, since by the exercise of faith comes spiritual development, one of the great objects of man's earthly existence; while knowledge, by swallowing up faith, prevents its exercise, thus hindering that development. "Knowledge is power"; and all things are to be known in due season. But premature knowledge—knowing at the wrong time—is fatal both to progress and to happiness.

The case of the Apostles was exceptional. They stood in a peculiar position. It was better for them to know—nay, absolutely essential—in order to give the requisite force and power to their tremendous testimony.

Power from on High

And yet, even in their case, something more than the seeing of the eye, than the hearing of the ear, than the touch of the senses, was necessary to enable them to know and to testify of Christ's divinity. Peter knew, before the resurrection, that Jesus was the Christ, the Son of the living God—knew it by divine revelation; and his brethren of the Twelve were entitled to the same knowledge, by the same means of imparting it.

That something besides his appearing to them in a resurrected state was necessary to qualify them for their work is shown by the fact that after that appearing, and after he had commissioned them to go "into all the world, and preach the gospel to every creature," they were commanded by him to tarry at Jerusalem until they were "endued with power from on high." They obeyed, and the power came upon them—"a sound from heaven as of a rushing mighty wind. . . . Cloven tongues like as of fire . . . sat upon each of them. And they were all filled with the Holy Ghost, and began to speak with other tongues, as the Spirit gave them utterance." (Acts 2:2–4.)

That same power the Apostles gave to others, even to all who had faith in Jesus Christ, who had repented of their sins, and had been cleansed by baptism at the hands of those having divine authority to so officiate; to the end that they might receive the Holy Ghost and by continued obedience win life everlasting.

Latter-day Testimony

So much for the days of old. Now as to modern times. Joseph Smith, to whom the Father and the Son revealed themselves in the early decades of the nineteenth century, and through whom the everlasting gospel, with all its ancient gifts and blessings, was restored at the opening of this last and greatest of the gospel dispensations; Joseph Smith, who with Sidney Rigdon saw the Son of God sitting on the right hand of God, and gazed upon the glories of eternity; Joseph Smith, who with Oliver Cowdery beheld Jehovah, even Jesus Christ, standing upon the breastwork of the pulpit in the Kirtland Temple; Joseph, the martyred Prophet, who gave his life to lay the foundations of this work—he left upon record more than one mighty testimony to the divinity of Jesus Christ. And tens of thousands of faithful Saints have rejoiced and are rejoicing in those testimonies, confirmed to them by the all-convincing power of the Holy Ghost.

In the Mission Field

May I add my mite to the mass of evidence upon this all-important theme? Fifty years ago, or something less, I was a young missionary in the State of Pennsylvania. I had been praying for a testimony of the truth, but beyond that had not displayed much zeal in missionary labor. My companion, a veteran in the cause, chided me for my lack of diligence in this direction. "You ought to be studying the books of the Church," said he; "you were sent out to preach the gospel, not to write for the newspapers"—for that was what I was doing at the time.

I knew he was right, but I still kept on, fascinated by the discovery that I could wield a pen, and preferring that to any other occupation except the drama, my early ambition, which I had laid upon the altar when, as a youth of twenty-one, I accepted a call to the mission field.

In Gethsemane

One night I dreamed—if dream it may be called—that I was in the Garden of Gethsemane, a witness of the Savior's agony. I saw him as plainly as I see this congregation. I stood behind a tree in the foreground, where I could see without being seen. Jesus, with Peter, James and John, came through a little wicket gate at my right. Leaving the three Apostles there, after telling them to kneel and pray, he passed over to the other side, where he also knelt and prayed. It was the same prayer with which we are all familiar: "O my Father, if it be possible, let this cup pass from me: nevertheless not as I will, but as thou wilt." (Matthew 26:36–44; Mark 14:32–41; Luke 22:42.)

As he prayed the tears streamed down his face, which was toward me. I was so moved at the sight that I wept also, out of pure sympathy with his great sorrow. My whole heart went out to him, I loved him with all my soul, and longed to be with him as I longed for nothing else.

Presently he arose and walked to where the Apostles were kneeling—fast asleep! He shook them gently, awoke them, and in a tone of tender reproach, untinctured by the least suggestion of anger or scolding, asked them if they could not watch with him one hour. There he was, with the weight of the world's sin upon his shoulders, with the pangs of every man, woman and child shooting through his sensitive soul—and they could not watch with him one poor hour!

Returning to his place, he prayed again, and then went back and found them again sleeping. Again he awoke them, admonished them, and returned and prayed as before. Three times this happened, until I was perfectly familiar with his appearance—face, form and movements. He was of noble stature and of majestic mien—not at all the weak, effeminate being that some painters have portrayed—a very God among men, yet as meek and lowly as a little child.

All at once the circumstance seemed to change, the scene remaining just the same. Instead of before, it was after the crucifixion, and the Savior, with those three Apostles, now stood together in a group at my left. They were about to depart and ascend into Heaven. I could endure it no longer. I ran out from behind the tree, fell at his feet, clasped him around the knees, and begged him to take me with him.

I shall never forget the kind and gentle manner in which he stooped and raised me up and embraced me. It was so vivid, so real, that I felt the very warmth of his bosom against which I rested. Then he said: "No, my son; these have finished their work, and they may go with me, but you must stay and finish yours." Still I clung to him. Gazing up into his face—for he was taller than I—I besought him most earnestly: "Well, promise me that I will come to you at the last." He smiled sweetly and tenderly and replied: "That will depend entirely upon yourself." I awoke with a sob in my throat, and it was morning.

The Moral of the Tale

"That's from God," said my companion (Elder A. M. Musser) when I had related it to him. "I don't need to be told that," was my reply. I saw the moral clearly. I had never thought that I would be an Apostle, or hold any other office in the Church; and it did not occur to me even then. Yet I knew that those sleeping Apostles meant me. I was asleep at my post—as any man is, or any woman, who, having been divinely appointed to do one thing, does another.

President Young's Counsel

But from that hour all was changed—I was a different man. I did not give up writing, for President Brigham Young, having noticed some of my contributions in the home papers, wrote advising me to cultivate what he called my "gift for writing" so that I might use it in future years "for the establishment of truth and righteousness upon the earth." This was his last word of counsel to me. He died the same year, while I was still in the mission field, though laboring then in the State of Ohio. I continued to write, but it was for the Church and Kingdom of God. I held that first and foremost; all else was secondary.

The Speaker's Testimony

Then came the divine illumination, which is greater than all dreams, visions, and other manifestations combined. By the light of God's candle—the gift of the Holy Ghost—I saw what till then I had never seen, I learned what till then I had never known, I loved the Lord as I had never loved him before. My soul was satisfied, my joy was full, for I had a testimony of the truth, and it has remained with me to this day.

I know that my Redeemer liveth. Not even Job knew it better. I have evidence that I can not doubt; and this is why I am found among those who tonight unfurl the slogan for which we stand, possessing and proclaiming an individual testimony of the divinity of Jesus Christ.

Improvement Era, January 1926, 219–26.

❧ ❧

THE SACRAMENTAL COVENANT

MELVIN J. BALLARD

This talk was delivered at a Mutual Improvement Association annual conference, Sunday, June 8, 1919, only five months after Elder Melvin J. Ballard was called to be an Apostle. Elder Ballard based his message on the MIA slogan for that year: "We stand for spiritual growth through attendance at sacrament meetings." This address includes Elder Ballard's memorable and moving analogy wherein he demonstrates what Abraham's sacrifice of Isaac teaches us about the atoning sacrifice of Christ.

The sacred covenant of the sacrament with its attendant blessings, which we repeat as we consecrate the emblems of the broken body and the spilt blood of the Lord, has been especially revealed to the Latter-day Saints by the Lord himself, so that we have the very words of the covenant as they were formulated by our Redeemer, with its promised blessings. I appreciate, I believe, to some extent, the sacredness of the covenant which we, as members of the Church, enter into when we partake of the sacred emblems. I realize that each time we partake of these emblems, we manifest before the Father that we do remember his Son; and by the act of partaking of the bread and the water, we make a solemn covenant that we do take upon us the name of our Redeemer, and that we do, further, make a pledge and an agreement by that act that we will keep his commandments.

The Sacrament a Means of Spiritual Growth

Taking the oath of allegiance to the government of the United States, we make a pledge and an agreement that we honor, uphold, and sustain the laws of the land and will be faithful in defending the rights of our country. We expect to receive blessings in return for keeping that covenant, blessings of life, liberty, and the pursuit of happiness. We make our pledge to the United States government when we are admitted as citizens and when we take office in the government, local or national. We do have, therefore, occasions when each citizen, whether he enters the service of his country as a soldier or engages in any other official duty, renews the covenant and pledge that he made when he became a citizen of the country. So our Father in Heaven has provided that, not only once but frequently, we shall meet together to renew our pledge, our covenant, and our agreement to keep his commandments and to take upon us his name again. I have always looked upon this blessed privilege as the means of spiritual growth, and there is none other quite so fruitful in the achievement of that end as the partaking, worthily, of the sacrament of the Lord's supper.

We eat food to stimulate our physical bodies. Without the partaking of food we would become weak and sickly, and fail physically. It is just as necessary for our spiritual body that we should partake of this sacrament and by it obtain spiritual food for our souls. If we were given our physical food only on stated occasions and at specified places, we would all be on hand. We heard how, during the war [World War I], many communities had to feed the inhabitants by distributing bread tickets or rations of various kinds which were given only by application at certain places. We have seen in our country that the people stood in line to get their sugar rations and other provisions, such as were curtailed and limited during the war, and they were always present, at the appointed time and place. If we really realized and felt the need of spiritual food for growth, we would be present at the appointed place where this may be, and is, administered.

We must come, however, to the sacrament table hungry. If we should repair to a banquet where the finest of earth's providing may be had, without hunger, without appetite, the food would not be tempting, nor do us any good. If we repair to the sacrament table, we must come hungering and thirsting for righteousness, for spiritual growth.

How Can We Have Spiritual Hunger?

How can we have spiritual hunger? Who is there among us that does not wound his spirit by word, thought, or deed, from Sabbath to Sabbath? We do things for which we are sorry and desire to be forgiven, or we have erred against someone and given injury. If there is a feeling in our hearts that we are sorry for what we have done, if there is a feeling in our souls that we would like to be forgiven, then the method to obtain forgiveness is not through rebaptism; it is not to make confession to man, but it is to repent of our sins, to go to those against whom we have sinned or transgressed and obtain their forgiveness and then repair to the sacrament table where, if we have sincerely repented and put ourselves in proper condition, we shall be forgiven, and spiritual healing will come to our souls. It will really enter into our being. You have felt it. I am a witness that there is a spirit attending the administration of the sacrament that warms the soul from head to foot; you feel the wounds of the spirit being healed, and the load being lifted. Comfort and happiness come to the soul that is worthy and truly desirous of partaking of this spiritual food.

Why do we not all come? Why do we not come regularly to the sacrament service and partake of these emblems and perform this highest worship we can give to our Father in the name of his Beloved Son? It is because we do not appreciate it. It is because we do not feel the necessity for this blessing, or it is because, perhaps, we feel ourselves unworthy to partake of these emblems.

Concerning Worthiness to Partake of the Sacrament

There is a feature of this pledge to which I should like to call your attention. Let me quote some scripture, because we not only

desire our boys and girls, our brothers and sisters, to come to the
sacrament table and eat of these emblems, but we want them to
eat worthily, for you have already heard quoted the scripture that if
we eat and drink unworthily, we eat and drink damnation to our
own souls. Here is what the Lord said:

"Previous to their partaking of the sacrament, . . . the members
shall manifest before the church, and also before the elders, by a
godly walk and conversation, that they are worthy of it, that there
may be works and faith agreeable to the holy scriptures—walking
in holiness before the Lord." (D&C 20:68–69.)

Again, I read from Paul's teachings: "Ye cannot drink the cup
of the Lord, and the cup of devils: Ye cannot be partakers of the
Lord's table, and of the table of devils." (1 Corinthians 10:21.)

And still, from another sacred scripture: "Ye shall not suffer
any one knowingly, to partake of my flesh and blood unworthily,
when ye shall minister it;

"For whoso eateth and drinketh my flesh and blood unworthily
eateth and drinketh damnation to his soul; therefore if ye know
that a man is unworthy to eat and drink of my flesh and blood ye
shall forbid him." (3 Nephi 18:28, 29.)

And still another, to the prophet of these latter-days: "If any
have trespassed, let him not partake until he makes reconciliation." (D&C 46:4.)

I suggest that perhaps some of us are ashamed to come to the
sacrament table because we feel unworthy and are afraid lest we
eat and drink of these sacred emblems to our own condemnation.
And so we want every Latter-day Saint to come to the sacrament
table because it is the place for self-investigation, for self-
inspection, where we may learn to rectify our course and to make
right our own lives, bringing ourselves into harmony with the
teachings of the Church and with our brethren and sisters. It is the
place where we become our own judges.

There may be some instances where the elders of the Church

could say, properly, to one who, in transgression, stretches forth his hands to partake of the emblems: "You should not do this until you have made restitution"; but ordinarily we will be our own judges. If we are properly instructed, we know that it is not our privilege to partake of the emblems of the flesh and blood of the Lord in sin, in transgression, or having injured and holding feelings against our brethren and sisters. No man goes away from this Church and becomes an apostate in a week or in a month. It is a slow process. The one thing that would make for the safety of every man and woman would be to appear at the sacrament table every Sabbath day. We would not get very far away in one week—not so far away that, by the process of self-investigation, we could not rectify the wrongs we may have done. If we should refrain from partaking of the sacrament, condemned by ourselves as unworthy to receive these emblems, we could not endure that long, and we would soon, I am sure, have the spirit of repentance. The road to the sacrament table is the path of safety for Latter-day Saints.

I have said that I think we stay away, perhaps because we do not appreciate what a blessing the sacrament is. I wonder if we ever will, in this mortal life, understand the value of the sacred and blessed things the Lord has instituted in this Church for its spiritual growth and welfare, and particularly this one ordinance which is attended by certain promised blessings that no man can give, and that the Lord alone can manifest to his children!

It is written in the scriptures that God so loved the world that he gave his Only Begotten Son to die for the world, that whosoever believes on him, yes, and keeps his commandments, shall be saved. But this sacrament did not cost us very much—freely given are all these glorious privileges, and I am reminded of a statement by one of our great writers, running something like this:

> At the devil's booth are all things sold.
> Each ounce of dross costs its ounce of gold.
> (J. R. Lowell, "Vision of Sir Launfal.")

It is heaven alone that is given away. It is only God that may be had for the asking. While we give nothing, perhaps, for this atonement and this sacrifice, nevertheless, it has cost someone something, and I love to contemplate what it cost our Father in Heaven to give us the gift of his Beloved Son, that worthy Son of our Father, who so loved the world that he laid his life down to redeem the world, to save us and to feed us spiritually while we walk in this life, and prepare us to go and dwell with him in the eternal worlds.

Illustrations

I think as I read the story of Abraham's sacrifice of his son Isaac that our Father is trying to tell us what it cost him to give his Son as a gift to the world. You remember the story of how Abraham's son came after long years of waiting and was looked upon by his worthy sire, Abraham, as more precious than all his other possessions; yet, in the midst of his rejoicing, Abraham was told to take this only son and offer him as a sacrifice to the Lord. He responded. Can you feel what was in the heart of Abraham on that occasion? You love your son just as Abraham did; perhaps not quite so much, because of the peculiar circumstances, but what do you think was in his heart when he started away from Mother Sarah, and they bade her goodbye? What do you think was in his heart when he saw Isaac bidding farewell to his mother to take that three days' journey to the appointed place where the sacrifice was to be made? I imagine it was about all Father Abraham could do to keep from showing his great grief and sorrow at that parting, but he and his son trudged along three days toward the appointed place, Isaac carrying the fagots that were to consume the sacrifice. The two travelers rested, finally, at the mountainside, and the men who had accompanied them were told to remain while Abraham and his son started up the hill.

The boy then said to his father: "Why, Father, we have the

fagots; we have the fire to burn the sacrifice; but where is the sacrifice?"

It must have pierced the heart of Father Abraham to hear the trusting and confiding son say: "You have forgotten the sacrifice." Looking at the youth, his son of promise, the poor father could only say: "The Lord will provide."

They ascended the mountain, gathered the stones together, and placed the fagots upon them. Then Isaac was bound, hand and foot, kneeling upon the altar. I presume Abraham, like a true father, must have given his son his farewell kiss, his blessing, his love, and his soul must have been drawn out in that hour of agony toward his son who was to die by the hand of his own father. Every step proceeded until the cold steel was drawn, and the hand raised that was to strike the blow to let out the life's blood when the angel of the Lord said: "It is enough."

The Agony of Christ

Our Father in Heaven went through all that and more, for in his case the hand was not stayed. He loved his Son, Jesus Christ, better than Abraham ever loved Isaac, for our Father had with him his Son, our Redeemer, in the eternal worlds, faithful and true for ages, standing in a place of trust and honor, and the Father loved him dearly, and yet he allowed this well-beloved Son to descend from his place of glory and honor, where millions did him homage, down to the earth, a condescension that is not within the power of man to conceive. He came to receive the insult, the abuse, and the crown of thorns. God heard the cry of his Son in that moment of great grief and agony, in the garden when, it is said, the pores of his body opened and drops of blood stood upon him, and he cried out: "Father, if thou be willing, remove this cup from me."

I ask you, what father and mother could stand by and listen to the cry of their children in distress, in this world, and not render aid and assistance? I have heard of mothers throwing themselves into raging streams when they could not swim a stroke to save their drowning children, rushing into burning buildings to rescue those whom they loved.

We cannot stand by and listen to those cries without its touching our hearts. The Lord has not given us the power to save our own. He has given us faith, and we submit to the inevitable, but he had the power to save, and he loved his Son, and he could have saved him. He might have rescued him from the insult of the crowds. He might have rescued him when the crown of thorns was placed upon his head. He might have rescued him when the Son, hanging between the two thieves, was mocked with, "Save thyself, and come down from the cross. He saved others; himself he cannot save." He listened to all this. He saw that Son condemned; he saw him drag the cross through the streets of Jerusalem and faint under its load. He saw that Son finally upon Calvary; he saw his body stretched out upon the wooden cross; he saw the cruel nails driven through hands and feet, and the blows that broke the skin, tore the flesh, and let out the life's blood of his Son. He looked upon that.

In the case of our Father, the knife was not stayed, but it fell, and the life's blood of his Beloved Son went out. His Father looked on with great grief and agony over his Beloved Son, until there seems to have come a moment when even our Savior cried out in despair: "My God, my God, why hast thou forsaken me?"

God's Love for Us

In that hour I think I can see our dear Father behind the veil looking upon these dying struggles until even he could not endure it any longer; and, like the mother who bids farewell to her dying child, has to be taken out of the room, so as not to look upon the last struggles, so he bowed his head, and hid in some part of his universe, his great heart almost breaking for the love that he had for his Son. Oh, in that moment when he might have saved his Son, I thank him and praise him that he did not fail us, for he had not only the love of his Son in mind, but he also had love for us. I rejoice that he did not interfere, and that his love for us made it possible for him to endure to look upon the sufferings of his Son and give him finally to us, our Savior and our Redeemer. Without him, without his sacrifice, we would have remained, and we would never have come glorified into his presence. And so this is what it cost, in part, for our Father in Heaven to give the gift of his Son unto men.

Appreciation of His Gift and Love

How do I appreciate the gift? If I only knew what it cost our Father to give his Son, if I only knew how essential it was that I should have that Son and that I should receive the spiritual life that comes from that Son, I am sure I would always be present at the sacrament table to do honor to the gift that has come unto us, for I realize that the Father has said that he, the Lord, our God, is a jealous God—jealous lest we should ignore and forget and slight his greatest gift unto us.

Need of the Sacrament for Spiritual Growth

I know that no man or woman shall ever come to stand in the presence of our Father in Heaven, or be associated with the Lord Jesus Christ, who does not grow spiritually. Without spiritual growth we shall not be prepared to enter into the divine presence. I need the sacrament. I need to renew my covenant every week. I need the blessing that comes with and through it. I know that what I am talking about is true. I bear witness to you that I know that the Lord lives. I know that he has made this sacrifice and this atonement. He has given me a foretaste of these things.

A Wonderful Experience and Testimony

I recall an experience which I had two years ago, bearing witness to my soul of the reality of his death, of his crucifixion, and his resurrection, that I shall never forget. I bear it to you tonight, to you, young boys and girls; not with a spirit to glory over it, but

with a grateful heart and with thanksgiving in my soul. I know
that he lives, and I know that through him men must find their
salvation, and that we cannot ignore this blessed offering that he
has given us as the means of our spiritual growth to prepare us to
come to him and be justified.

Away on the Fort Peck Reservation where I was doing missionary work with some of our brethren, laboring among the
Indians, seeking the Lord for light to decide certain matters pertaining to our work there, and receiving a witness from him that
we were doing things according to his will, I found myself one
evening in the dreams of the night in that sacred building, the
temple. After a season of prayer and rejoicing I was informed that
I should have the privilege of entering into one of those rooms, to
meet a glorious Personage, and, as I entered the door, I saw, seated
on a raised platform, the most glorious Being my eyes have ever
beheld or that I ever conceived existed in all the eternal worlds.
As I approached to be introduced, he arose and stepped towards
me with extended arms, and he smiled as he softly spoke my name.
If I shall live to be a million years old, I shall never forget that
smile. He took me into his arms and kissed me, pressed me to his
bosom, and blessed me, until the marrow of my bones seemed to
melt! When he had finished, I fell at his feet, and, as I bathed
them with my tears and kisses, I saw the prints of the nails in the
feet of the Redeemer of the world. The feeling that I had in the
presence of him who hath all things in his hands, to have his love,
his affection, and his blessing was such that if I ever can receive
that of which I had but a foretaste, I would give all that I am, all
that I ever hope to be, to feel what I then felt!

Admonition and Conclusion

Go to the sacrament table. Ah, that is a blessed privilege that
I now rejoice in, and I would be ashamed, I know, as I felt then, to
stand in his presence and try to offer any apology or any excuse for
not having kept his commandments and honored him by bearing

witness, before the Father and before men, that I believe in him, and that I take upon me his blessed Name, and that I live by and through him spiritually.

If we can only bring our boys and girls to feel the need of this thing, they will be at sacrament meeting, and we will be there. I see Jesus not now upon the cross. I do not see his brow pierced with thorns nor his hands torn with the nails, but I see him smiling, with extended arms, saying to us all: "Come unto me!"

Let us go unto him in his appointed hour. Let us take our children with us, and through our faithfulness find all the blessings attendant upon this sacred observance of this holy ordinance— ours in time and in eternity. This I pray, in the name of Jesus Christ. Amen.

Improvement Era, October 1919, 1025–32.

The Purifying Power of Gethsemane

Bruce R. McConkie

Elder Bruce R. McConkie gave this, his last public address, in the Saturday morning session of general conference, April 6, 1985. At the time, he was in the last stages of his battle against cancer. Just thirteen days later, on April 19, he passed away. In retrospect, his closing comments now seem especially moving: "I am one of his witnesses, and in a coming day I shall feel the nail marks in his hands and in his feet and shall wet his feet with my tears. But I shall not know any better then than I know now that he is God's Almighty Son, that he is our Savior and Redeemer, and that salvation comes in and through his atoning blood and in no other way."

I feel, and the Spirit seems to accord, that the most important doctrine I can declare, and the most powerful testimony I can bear, is of the atoning sacrifice of the Lord Jesus Christ.

His atonement is the most transcendent event that ever has or ever will occur from Creation's dawn through all the ages of a never-ending eternity.

It is the supreme act of goodness and grace that only a god could perform. Through it, all of the terms and conditions of the Father's eternal plan of salvation became operative.

Through it are brought to pass the immortality and eternal life of man. Through it, all men are saved from death, hell, the devil, and endless torment.

And through it, all who believe and obey the glorious gospel of God, all who are true and faithful and overcome the world, all who suffer for Christ and his word, all who are chastened and scourged in the Cause of him whose we are—all shall become as their Maker and sit with him on his throne and reign with him forever in everlasting glory.

In speaking of these wondrous things I shall use my own words, though you may think they are the words of scripture, words spoken by other Apostles and prophets.

True it is they were first proclaimed by others, but they are now mine, for the Holy Spirit of God has borne witness to me that they are true, and it is now as though the Lord had revealed them to me in the first instance. I have thereby heard his voice and know his word.

Two thousand years ago, outside Jerusalem's walls, there was a pleasant garden spot, Gethsemane by name, where Jesus and his intimate friends were wont to retire for pondering and prayer.

There Jesus taught his disciples the doctrines of the kingdom, and all of them communed with Him who is the Father of us all, in whose ministry they were engaged, and on whose errand they served.

This sacred spot, like Eden where Adam dwelt, like Sinai from whence Jehovah gave his laws, like Calvary where the Son of God gave his life a ransom for many, this holy ground is where the Sinless Son of the Everlasting Father took upon himself the sins of all men on condition of repentance.

We do not know, we cannot tell, no mortal mind can conceive, the full import of what Christ did in Gethsemane.

We know he sweat great gouts of blood from every pore as he drained the dregs of that bitter cup his Father had given him.

We know he suffered, both body and spirit, more than it is possible for man to suffer, except it be unto death.

We know that in some way, incomprehensible to us, his suffering satisfied the demands of justice, ransomed penitent souls from the pains and penalties of sin, and made mercy available to those who believe in his holy name.

We know that he lay prostrate upon the ground as the pains and agonies of an infinite burden caused him to tremble and would that he might not drink the bitter cup.

We know that an angel came from the courts of glory to strengthen him in his ordeal, and we suppose it was mighty Michael, who foremost fell that mortal man might be.

As near as we can judge, these infinite agonies—this suffering beyond compare—continued for some three or four hours.

After this—his body then wrenched and drained of strength—he confronted Judas and the other incarnate devils, some from the very Sanhedrin itself; and he was led away with a rope around his neck, as a common criminal, to be judged by the arch-criminals who as Jews sat in Aaron's seat and who as Romans wielded Caesar's power.

They took him to Annas, to Caiaphas, to Pilate, to Herod, and back to Pilate. He was accused, cursed, and smitten. Their foul saliva ran down his face as vicious blows further weakened his pain-engulfed body.

With reeds of wrath they rained blows upon his back. Blood ran down his face as a crown of thorns pierced his trembling brow.

But above it all he was scourged, scourged with forty stripes save one, scourged with a multithonged whip into whose leather strands sharp bones and cutting metals were woven.

Many died from scourging alone, but he rose from the sufferings of the scourge that he might die an ignominious death upon the cruel cross of Calvary.

Then he carried his own cross until he collapsed from the weight and pain and mounting agony of it all.

Finally, on a hill called Calvary—again, it was outside Jerusalem's walls—while helpless disciples looked on and felt the agonies of near death in their own bodies, the Roman soldiers laid him upon the cross.

With great mallets they drove spikes of iron through his feet and hands and wrists. Truly he was wounded for our transgressions and bruised for our iniquities.

Then the cross was raised that all might see and gape and curse and deride. This they did, with evil venom, for three hours from 9 A.M. to noon.

Then the heavens grew black. Darkness covered the land for the space of three hours, as it did among the Nephites. There was a mighty storm, as though the very God of Nature was in agony.

And truly he was, for while he was hanging on the cross for another three hours, from noon to 3 P.M., all the infinite agonies and merciless pains of Gethsemane recurred.

And, finally, when the atoning agonies had taken their toll—when the victory had been won, when the Son of God had fulfilled the will of his Father in all things—then he said, "It is finished" (John 19:30), and he voluntarily gave up the ghost.

As the peace and comfort of a merciful death freed him from the pains and sorrows of mortality, he entered the paradise of God.

When he had made his soul an offering for sin, he was prepared to see his seed, according to the messianic word.

These, consisting of all the holy prophets and faithful Saints from ages past; these, comprising all who had taken upon them his name, and who, being spiritually begotten by him, had become his sons and his daughters, even as it is with us; all these were assembled in the spirit world, there to see his face and hear his voice.

After some thirty-eight or forty hours—three days as the Jews measured time—our Blessed Lord came to the Arimathaean's tomb, where his partially embalmed body had been placed by Nicodemus and Joseph of Arimathaea.

Then, in a way incomprehensible to us, he took up that body

which had not yet seen corruption and arose in that glorious immortality which made him like his resurrected Father.

He then received all power in heaven and on earth, obtained eternal exaltation, appeared unto Mary Magdalene and many others, and ascended into heaven, there to sit down on the right hand of God the Father Almighty and to reign forever in eternal glory.

His rising from death on the third day crowned the Atonement. Again, in some way incomprehensible to us, the effects of his resurrection pass upon all men so that all shall rise from the grave.

As Adam brought death, so Christ brought life; as Adam is the father of mortality, so Christ is the father of immortality.

And without both, mortality and immortality, man cannot work out his salvation and ascend to those heights beyond the skies where gods and angels dwell forever in eternal glory.

Now, the atonement of Christ is the most basic and fundamental doctrine of the gospel, and it is the least understood of all our revealed truths.

Many of us have a superficial knowledge and rely upon the Lord and his goodness to see us through the trials and perils of life.

But if we are to have faith like Enoch and Elijah we must believe what they believed, know what they knew, and live as they lived.

May I invite you to join with me in gaining a sound and sure knowledge of the Atonement.

We must cast aside the philosophies of men and the wisdom of the wise and hearken to that Spirit which is given to us to guide us into all truth.

We must search the scriptures, accepting them as the mind and will and voice of the Lord and the very power of God unto salvation.

As we read, ponder, and pray, there will come into our minds a view of the three gardens of God—the Garden of Eden, the Garden of Gethsemane, and the Garden of the Empty Tomb where Jesus appeared to Mary Magdalene.

In Eden we will see all things created in a paradisiacal state—without death, without procreation, without probationary experiences. We will come to know that such a creation, now unknown to man, was the only way to provide for the Fall. We will then see Adam and Eve, the first man and the first woman, step down from their state of immortal and paradisiacal glory to become the first mortal flesh on earth.

Mortality, including as it does procreation and death, will enter the world. And because of transgression a probationary estate of trial and testing will begin.

Then in Gethsemane we will see the Son of God ransom man from the temporal and spiritual death that came to us because of the Fall.

And finally, before an empty tomb, we will come to know that Christ our Lord has burst the bands of death and stands forever triumphant over the grave.

Thus, Creation is father to the Fall; and by the Fall came mortality and death; and by Christ came immortality and eternal life.

If there had been no fall of Adam, by which cometh death, there could have been no atonement of Christ, by which cometh life.

And now, as pertaining to this perfect atonement, wrought by the shedding of the blood of God—I testify that it took place in Gethsemane and at Golgotha, and as pertaining to Jesus Christ, I testify that he is the Son of the Living God and was crucified for the sins of the world. He is our Lord, our God, and our King. This I know of myself independent of any other person.

I am one of his witnesses, and in a coming day I shall feel the nail marks in his hands and in his feet and shall wet his feet with my tears.

But I shall not know any better then than I know now that he is God's Almighty Son, that he is our Savior and Redeemer, and that salvation comes in and through his atoning blood and in no other way.

God grant that all of us may walk in the light as God our Father is in the light so that, according to the promises, the blood of Jesus Christ his Son will cleanse us from all sin.

In the name of the Lord Jesus Christ, amen.

Ensign, May 1985, 9–11.

GOSPEL OF JESUS CHRIST

THE FULNESS OF THE GOSPEL

JAMES E. TALMAGE

In this powerful 1918 conference discourse, Elder James E. Talmage notes, "We have learned the solemn truth that the gospel is greater than any book, greater than the Bible, indispensable though that volume is; greater than the Book of Mormon, great as is the mission of that Scripture, brought to the world in these latter days by the power and inspiration of God; greater than our current volume of modern revelation, for there is more to come. More is included in the gospel than all Scripture thus far written; and the living oracles are established in the Church to give unto the people from time to time the mind and the will of God in addition to what has been placed upon record with relation to the ages past."

Verily these are the last days, the days seen by seers, predicted by prophets, proclaimed by revelators throughout the ages, and affirmed by the representatives of God in this current dispensation. In these days events develop rapidly. As on the mimic stage action increases, and in the working out of the plot and plan developments occur with bewildering rapidity as the finale approaches, so in the great drama of God on the stage of the world, the purpose of the great Master is being made plain through the portentous events of the current day. By the "last days" we do not mean the end of time. Such a concept indeed is impossible to the human mind. Duration is of necessity eternal, just as space is unbounded. So with respect to the gospel of Christ and its effects; this gospel is eternal and its extent unbounded.

Bible students recognize that Israel lived under the law, and that Christ brought the gospel which superseded the law, and they have drawn a wholly incorrect inference, namely, that the law is in fact older than the gospel. Be it known that the gospel, so far as this earth and its inhabitants are concerned, dates from Adam. Unto him was taught the necessity of faith in the Lord Jesus Christ, not merely mental belief, but abiding, impelling, living faith, the necessity of repentance, the indispensability of baptism in water by immersion for the remission of sins, the indispensability of the bestowal of the Holy Ghost. These principles and ordinances were taught unto Adam, administered unto him, and by him were taught and administered to others. So was it also with Enoch, with Noah, with Abraham, with Moses, and with the hosts of God's righteous servants in the early dispensations, who in many instances laid down their lives in defense of the principles which they promulgated.

No, the gospel did not begin upon earth in the meridian of time. There had been gospel dispensations before, and there had been widespread apostasies from the truths declared in those several dispensations. The great apostasy following the apostolic ministry was not the first. There was an apostasy in the days of Noah, and the people suffered therefrom in their disembodied state, until in the Lord's due time He went unto them and offered the principles of the gospel by which they could in a measure make amends.

One of the inherent weaknesses of the human mind is that of reaching after completeness. We like to feel that we can begin and end a subject of study. We are like those thoughtless students in school who seem to think that all that is known about the subject is to be found within the covers of their text book; and a reprehensible but still somewhat popular custom prevails in some of the colleges on the part of the classes who finish the study of some book, to hold a cremation ceremony and burn up the texts as evidence that they have no further use for them; they think they know the whole thing.

We have learned the solemn truth that the gospel is greater than any book, greater than the Bible, indispensable though that volume is; greater than the Book of Mormon, great as is the mission of that Scripture, brought to the world in these latter days by the power and inspiration of God; greater than our current volume of modern revelation, for there is more to come. More is included in the gospel than all Scripture thus far written; and the living oracles are established in the Church to give unto the people from time to time the mind and the will of God in addition to what has been placed upon record with relation to the ages past. We have yet to find the first discrepancy, the first instance of inconsistency, of lack of harmony between the Scriptures that are given unto the people by those who speak in the name and by the power of the living God, and those words that are written of similar ministry in by-gone times.

What, some may ask, are we not told that we have the fulness of the gospel? Verily so. When Moroni came to announce to Joseph Smith the existence of the record from which Joseph was afterwards to translate, by the gift and power of God, the volume known to us as the Book of Mormon, Moroni declared unto him that that book contained the fulness of the everlasting gospel, as made known unto the people in their age; but "fulness" is relative, even as perfection is.

Many have stumbled over that admonition of Christ, "Be ye perfect even as your Father which is in heaven is perfect." Men have asked: How can that be? We are not like Him; we are still mortal, with all our frailties. Even those who believe in the eternal progression of man so reason, so argue, and they would make out that Christ uttered fable and fiction; for to so admonish in the face of impossibility would be nothing less. But Christ told the people in that day, and He has repeated the admonition and injunction unto us: Be perfect in the sense in which your Father in Heaven is perfect.

What man calls "perfection" is after all comparative. Plainly a man in mortality cannot be perfect in power nor in influence nor in righteousness, in all details in the sense in which God the Father and His Son Jesus Christ are perfect. Both of Them are resurrected men, both of Them have passed through conditions strictly analogous to those of mortality through which we are passing, both of whom have died, both of whom have been resurrected, both of whom are glorified, supremely so. In the sense in which They are perfect you and I cannot aspire to be so here in the flesh. But we can be perfect if we will in our sphere, as They are perfect in Their sphere; and perfection in the lesser is the greatest possible preparation for perfection in the greater.

So with respect to the fulness of the gospel. That expression is relative. Unto the Nephites was given a fulness of the gospel as it applied to them, embracing and embodying the fundamental principles and ordinances and blessings arising therefrom, uncounted and innumerable; but nevertheless, there is much more in the gospel, in its possibilities, in the blessings which it holds in store, that shall yet be made known unto man. We recognize the varied offices in the priesthood, and we know something of the functions connected with each, but there are functions of which we have not yet learned, but of which we shall learn hereafter. The powers and functions of the Holy Priesthood, as manifested in mortality today, are but as the foothills compared with the towering peaks beyond. The priesthood is eternal, and, therefore when it is conferred carries with it the possibilities of this endless progression, development and expansion. When shall we have more? God grant that we receive it not until we are well prepared for it, for many of us have not yet learned to live up to what we have received, and if we receive and reject, we bring ourselves under condemnation.

I have met here and there a disgruntled one, one who is saying: Why don't we receive further revelation from God today? We are receiving it day by day. I speak of what I know when I say unto you, if ever the Church of Christ was led by a prophet enjoying communion with God, inspiration from the source of divine revelation, from heaven direct—and none of us can doubt such leadership in the past—this day witnesses that condition. I testify unto you that the man who stands at the head of this Church is the mouthpiece of God unto His people, and if we fail to heed his words, his admonitions, his instructions given unto us as they have been, and are, in love and nevertheless with firmness and with no uncertainty of tone, we bring ourselves under condemnation.

We recognize in the events of the present day the very conditions that were foreseen and foretold. Do you not remember how anxious and eager the eleven apostles were of old to win from Christ some definite expression as to when He would come? Before His crucifixion, before His betrayal, the Twelve seemed to be equally concerned, whatever may have been the personal condition of the mind of Judas, and they asked Him: "When shall these things be, and what shall be the sign of thy coming?" The Lord warned them against men who would set dates, and that warning has never been abrogated, but, on the contrary, has been repeated and emphasized. I say unto you, beware of the men who undertake to set the year and the day in which the Christ shall come, for that has not been revealed unto man. Nevertheless, Christ did give certain signs and conditions which would indicate the imminence of His coming, and one of the most remarkable was this: He told of wars; He told of the awful tragedies that should come upon the earth, and, with respect to all these, He said "the end is not yet." Then having explained further He said: "And this gospel of the kingdom shall be preached in all the world for a witness unto all nations; and then shall the end come."

This Church has been preaching that gospel. It has not yet completed its commission. It was so engaged most earnestly, and is engaged most devoutly to the extent, I believe, of its means, condition, and attendant circumstances. Before the outbreak of this great conflict it maintained a standing army of approximately two thousand, a very small army compared with the needs, but approximately two thousand men in the world, crying repentance, warning the people of the calamities that were to come, crying: "Come out of her, that ye partake not of her plagues." Many heard and believed and are here. Many heard and scoffed, and have remained. Now, not all the good were taken, and not all who were left are bad: but there were those who had faith enough to lay hold on the blessing placed within their reach, and to come out into this land of relative safety, and of great blessing, the land in which the Lord has spoken and from which has gone out the word of God unto the nations.

I would have the Latter-day Saints consider the fact that of all peoples on the face of the earth we are peculiarly interested in the outcome of this struggle. Therefore we have a sound foundation in this for our patriotism, for our sacrifice, for our efforts in behalf of this government, for our unqualified allegiance to the Constitution of the United States, which is veritably the scripture of the nation; for upon this Church has been laid the commission to preach the gospel in every nation as a witness. How can we do this when the doors of the nations are barred and bolted? To discharge this commission we must have freedom; there must be freedom of speech, freedom of the press, and above all, freedom of conscience, ever remembering that freedom means real liberty in righteousness, and not license to do wrong. Therefore we Latter-day Saints are praying, and not only in words but in deeds, that victory may attend the arms that have been taken up in the vindication of the rights of men, that we may have access to the nations, that we may lay before them the saving principles of the gospel of Jesus Christ, and thus discharge the high commission that has been placed upon us.

This gospel is broad enough, and deep enough, and of such towering heights as to surpass the powers of the greatest mind to comprehend, and yet so simple in its fundamentals as to satisfy the honest inquiry of the child. We speak of faith, repentance, baptism, and the laying on of hands, as the first principles and ordinances of the gospel. We have gone so far as to number them—the first, the second, the third and fourth principles, and the first and the second ordinances. Are there others? Verily, verily, yes. What, a fifth? Yes, and a sixth, and a seventh, aye, and a tenth, and a hundredth and a thousandth. There is no end to the principles of truth embodied in the gospel of Jesus Christ, and yet each one is dependent upon the fundamentals, and each one grows out of those that have been given before.

May the Lord open our minds and expand our souls, and give us the desire to live up to what we have, that we may receive the more; for "We believe all that God has revealed, all that He does now reveal, and we believe that He will yet reveal many great and important things pertaining to the kingdom of God." Be we ready, in the name of Jesus Christ. Amen.

Conference Report, April 1918, 159–63.

LOVE

❧ ❦

CHARITY AND FORGIVENESS

HEBER J. GRANT

President Heber J. Grant gave this address two years after he became president of the Church in November 1918. He began his talk by saying, "I am grateful beyond expression for the rich outpourings of the Spirit of the Lord during our conferences that we have held since it fell to my lot to preside over the Church. . . . When I thought of the wonderful blessings of the Lord in the past at our general conferences, . . . I desired with all my heart that there should be no falling off in the inspiration of the Lord to those who might address us, and earnestly supplicated him to this effect. And I am indeed grateful for the blessings that we have enjoyed, and I pray that that same blessing, that same rich outpouring of his Spirit may be given to all who shall speak to us during the sessions of this conference."

In section 64:8–13 [of the] Doctrine and Covenants, we find the following:

My disciples, in days of old, sought occasion against one another, and forgave not one another in their hearts, and for this evil they were afflicted, and sorely chastened:

Wherefore I say unto you, that ye ought to forgive one another, for he that forgiveth not his brother his trespasses, standeth condemned before the Lord, for there remaineth in him the greater sin.

I, the Lord, will forgive whom I will forgive, but of you it is required to forgive all men;

And ye ought to say in your hearts, let God judge between me and thee, and reward thee according to thy deeds.

And he that repenteth not of his sins, and confesseth them not, then ye shall bring him before the Church, and do with him as the Scripture saith unto you, either by commandment or by revelation.

And this ye shall do that God may be glorified, not because ye forgive not, having not compassion, but that ye may be justified in the eyes of the law, that ye may not offend him who is your Lawgiver.

And in section 121:45, 46, we read:

Let thy bowels also be full of charity towards all men, and to the household of faith, and let virtue garnish thy thoughts unceasingly, then shall thy confidence wax strong in the presence of God, and the doctrine of the Priesthood shall distill upon thy soul as the dews from heaven.

The Holy Ghost shall be thy constant companion, and thy sceptre an unchanging sceptre of righteousness and truth, and thy dominion shall be an everlasting dominion, and without compulsory means it shall flow unto thee for ever and ever.

Illustration from Personal Experience

I have a very wonderful respect and regard for this quotation from . . . the Doctrine and Covenants. Some years ago a prominent man was excommunicated from the Church. He, years later, pleaded for baptism. President John Taylor referred the question of his baptism to the apostles, stating that if they unanimously consented to his baptism, he could be baptized, but that if there was one dissenting vote, he should not be admitted into the Church. As I remember the vote, it was five for baptism and seven against. A year or so later the question came up again and it was eight for baptism and four against. Later it came up again and it was ten for baptism and two against. Finally all of the Council of the Apostles, with the exception of your humble servant, consented that this man be baptized and I was then next to the junior member of the quorum. Later I was in the office of the president and he said:

"Heber, I understand that eleven of the apostles have consented to the baptism of Brother So and So," naming the man, "and that you alone are standing out. How will you feel when you get on the other side and you find that this man has pleaded for baptism and you find that you have perhaps kept him out from entering in with those who have repented of their sins and received some reward?"

I said, "President John Taylor, I can look the Lord squarely in the eye, if he asks me that question, and tell him that I did that which I thought was for the best good of the kingdom. When a man holding the holy Priesthood of God goes forth to proclaim the gospel of the Lord Jesus Christ, to call the wicked to repentance, goes to proclaim that God lives, that Jesus is the Christ, that Joseph Smith was a prophet of God, and that the gospel has been restored again to the earth, and that man in the mission home of the Church of Christ commits adultery, I can tell the Lord that he had disgraced this Church enough, and that I did not propose to let any such a man come back into the Church."

"Well," said President Taylor, "my boy, that is all right, stay with your convictions, stay right with them."

I said, "President Taylor, your letter said you wanted each one of the apostles to vote the convictions of his heart. If you desire me to surrender the convictions of my heart, I will gladly do it; I will gladly vote for this man to come back, but while I live I never expect to consent, if it is left to my judgment. That man was accused before the apostles several years ago and he stood up and lied and claimed that he was innocent, and the Lord gave to me a testimony that he lied, but I could not condemn him because of that. I got down on my knees that night and prayed God to give me the strength not to expose that man, seeing that he had lied but that we had no evidence, except only the testimony of the girl that he had seduced. And I prayed the Lord that some day additional testimony might come, and it did come, and we then excommunicated him. And when a man can lie to the apostles, and when he can be guilty while proclaiming repentance of sin, I think this Church has been disgraced enough without ever letting him come back into the Church."

"Well," repeated President Taylor, "my boy, don't you vote as long as you live, while you hold those ideas, stay right with them."

A Change of Heart—The Spirit of Forgiveness

I left the president's office. I went home. My lunch was not ready. I was reading the Doctrine and Covenants through for the third or fourth time systematically, and I had my bookmark in it, but as I picked it up, instead of opening where the bookmark was, it opened to:

"I, the Lord, will forgive whom I will forgive, but of you it is required to forgive all men; but he that forgiveth not his brother standeth condemned before the Lord."

And I closed the book and said: "If the devil applies for baptism, and claims that he has repented, I will baptize him." After lunch I returned to the office of President Taylor and I said, "President Taylor, I have had a change of heart. One hour ago I said, never while I live, did I expect to ever consent that Brother So and So should be baptized, but I have come to tell you he can be baptized, so far as I am concerned."

President Taylor had a habit, when he was particularly pleased, of sitting up and laughing and shaking his whole body, and he laughed and said, "My boy, the change is very sudden, very sudden. I want to ask you a question. How did you feel when you left here an hour ago? Did you feel like you wanted to hit that man right squarely between the eyes and knock him down?"

I said, "That is just the way I felt."

He said, "How do you feel now?"

"Well, to tell you the truth, President Taylor, I hope the Lord will forgive the sinner."

He said, "You feel happy, don't you, in comparison. You had the spirit of anger, you had the spirit of bitterness in your heart toward that man, because of his sin and because of the disgrace he had brought upon the Church. And now you have the spirit of forgiveness and you really feel happy, don't you?"

And I said, "Yes I do; I felt mean and hateful and now I feel happy."

And he said: "Do you know why I wrote that letter?"

I said: "No, sir."

"Well I wrote it, just so you and some of the younger members of the apostles would learn the lesson that forgiveness is in advance of justice, where there is repentance, and that to have in your heart the spirit of forgiveness and to eliminate from your hearts the spirit of hatred and bitterness, brings peace and joy; that the gospel of Jesus Christ brings joy, peace and happiness to every soul that lives it and follows its teachings."

Love and Forgiveness

And so he went on. I cannot remember all of the teachings, but he continued in this way, telling me that he could never have given me that experience, that he could not give to me a testimony of the gospel; that I must receive that testimony for myself; that I must have the right spirit come into my heart and feel it—the spirit of forgiveness, the spirit of long-suffering and charity—before there would any good come to me as an individual; that by simply surrendering my will to his, and voting to baptize this man, I would never have learned the lesson that the spirit of joy and peace comes in the hour of forgiveness, and when our hearts are full of charity and long-suffering to those who have made mistakes. From that day to this I have remembered those teachings.

The Prophet of the Lord said:

My boy, never forget that when you are in the line of

your duty your heart will be full of love and forgiveness, even for the repentant sinner, and that when you get out of that straight line of duty and have the determination that what you think is justice and what you think is equity and right should prevail, you ofttimes are anything but happy. You can know the difference between the Spirit of the Lord and the spirit of the adversary, when you find that you are happy and contented, that you love your fellows, that you are anxious for their welfare; and you can tell that you do not have that spirit when you are full of animosity and feel that you would like to knock somebody down.

I am reminded of one of the finest chapters in all the Bible (1 Corinthians 13):

Though I speak with the tongues of men and of angels, and have not charity, I am become as sounding brass, or a tinkling cymbal.

And though I have the gift of prophecy, and understand all mysteries, and all knowledge; and though I have all faith, so that I could remove mountains, and have not charity, I am nothing.

And though I bestow all my goods to feed the poor, and though I give my body to be burned, and have not charity, it profiteth me nothing.

Charity, suffereth long, and is kind; charity envieth not; charity vaunteth not itself, is not puffed up,

Doth not behave itself unseemly, seeketh not her own, is not easily provoked, thinketh no evil;

Rejoiceth not in iniquity, but rejoiceth in the truth:

Beareth all things, believeth all things, hopeth all things, endureth all things.

Charity never faileth; but whether there be prophecies, they shall fail; whether there be tongues, they shall cease; whether there be knowledge, it shall vanish away.

For we know in part, and we prophesy in part.

But when that which is perfect is come, then that which is in part shall be done away.

When I was a child, I spake as a child, I understood as a

child, I thought as a child; but when I became a man, I put
away childish things.

For now we see through a glass, darkly; but then face to
face; now I know in part; but then shall I know even as also I
am known.

And now abideth faith, hope, charity, these three; but
the greatest of these is charity.

Many people imagine that charity is giving a dollar to somebody; but real, genuine charity is giving love and sympathy, and
that is the kind of charity that the apostle had reference to in this
thirteenth chapter of First Corinthians.

I remember that after that teaching given to me as a young
man, as a boy, almost, by the President of the Church, I read this
chapter about once a week for quite a while, then once a month
for several months. I thought I needed it in my business, so to
speak; that it was one of the things that were necessary for my
advancement.

I remember that a year ago, here at the conference, I read a
very splendid and wonderful song, the half of the first verse of
which reads as follows:

> Let each man learn to know himself,
> To gain that knowledge let him labor,
> Improve those failings in himself
> That he condemns so in his neighbor.

The whole poem was published in the conference pamphlet.
I quoted it some weeks ago, and was asked where one could get
a copy, and again last Sunday, when I told some people that they
could read it in next Saturday night's *News*. So I shall not take
up your time by quoting the whole poem. I also quoted the four
short verses from our hymn on page 66, a part of which reads as
follows:

> Should you feel inclined to censure
> Faults you may in others view,

> Ask your own heart, ere you venture,
> If that has not failings too.

I had not the slightest idea when I quoted these poems, that I would desire to quote from them again today; but in view of the condemnation and the spirit, almost, of animosity, and hate that seems to be manifested by some people among the Latter-day Saints, at the present time, regarding business and political affairs, I desire to emphasize, with all the power of my being, the last verse of that little hymn . . . :

> Do not form opinions blindly,
> Hastiness to trouble tends,
> Those of whom we thought unkindly
> Oft become our warmest friends. . . .

I desire to repeat the last verse of that excellent hymn, which I learned thirty-five or forty years ago, when Francis M. Lyman first sang it for me. I wrote it that very night, and learned it the next day. I would like every Latter-day Saint to apply the teachings of this splendid verse in his or her life, and if we do that I believe we will grow in love and charity; that the spirit of peace and happiness, that President Taylor promised me when I entertained the feeling of determination to keep a man out of the Church, and the spirit of joy and peace which came to me, after the change of heart, will come to Latter-day Saints:

> And in self-judgment, if you find
> Your deeds to others are superior,
> To you has Providence been kind,
> As you should be to those inferior.

> Example sheds a genial ray
> Of light, which men are apt to borrow,
> So first improve yourself today
> And then improve your friends tomorrow. . . .

Keep the Commandments of God

I beg every Latter-day Saint to cultivate the spirit of charity, of long-suffering, and brotherly love. I say to all Latter-day Saints: Keep the commandments of God. That is my keynote speech, just those few words: Keep the commandments of God. Read the psalm that tells you not to fret your soul about the sinner. It is a magnificent psalm to read. . . . Keep the commandments of the Lord. Be honest with God. Never fail to pay an honest tithing to the Lord, on every dollar that comes into your hands. "Oh, but," says one, "the Church does not need it." You are right; you are correct. The Church does not need it, but the man who has made covenant with the living God to keep his commandments, and then does not keep them, he needs it. A man who is not honest with the Lord should repent and be honest with the Lord, and then the windows of heaven shall open and God will pour down upon the heads of the Latter-day Saints blessings, if they are financially honest with the Lord. Observe the Word of Wisdom. Never indulge in those things that the Lord God Almighty, the Creator of heaven and earth, has told us are not good for man.

Conclusion

. . . I rejoice, above all things, in a knowledge that God lives, that Jesus is the Christ, that Joseph Smith is a prophet of the true and living God; that the gospel of Jesus Christ, the plan of life and salvation, has been restored to the earth. I rejoice that you and I have a knowledge of that gospel; and oh, may God help us to live it; may he fill our hearts with charity, with love, with forgiveness, with the desire to serve him, and may we in very deed be Latter-day Saints, is my prayer and desire, and I ask it in the name of Jesus Christ. Amen.

Conference Report, October 1920, 1–11.

~⚜ ⚜~

LOVE IN ACTION

RICHARD L. EVANS

At a time when the followers of the adversary were beginning to promote counterfeits of love, proclaiming promiscuous
sex as "free love," Elder Richard L. Evans, as one of the Lord's
Apostles, plainly proclaimed the truth about God's love for us,
our love for him, and the quality of our love for others. "Anyone
who would induce someone to do that which it is unworthy to
do, or to take advantage, or rob someone of virtue," he said in
this April 1966 conference address, "really doesn't love the person he professes to love."

One of the most quoted New Testament texts is this from
John: "For God so loved the world, that he gave his only
begotten Son, that whosoever believeth in him should
not perish, but have everlasting life." (John 3:16.)

The love of God so simply stated is comfortingly familiar, and
what he did with that love is the evidence of it: He sent his Only
Begotten Son that whoso believes in him should have everlasting
life.

Love Is Expressed by Action

Suppose God had loved the world in a passive way? Suppose
he hadn't sent his Son? Suppose he hadn't given us his gospel?
Suppose he hadn't set out to save mankind or redeem us from
death? Suppose he had let his children drift without plan or purpose or counsel or commandments? Would that have been love?

The point I hope to make, for a particular purpose, is the evidence, the proof, the test of love.

An editorial recently read in a medical magazine had an intriguing title: "Love Is a Verb." And from this the writer turned his attention to the importance of doing, of proving, of performing. The proof of any principle is what it does, and the proof of any person is what he does—how he acts, what he becomes—not simply what he says.

"Love Is a Verb"

We might paraphrase and say that service is a verb, that life is a verb; for it is in doing, in living, in learning, and not just in words that we perform our purpose. No one really proves himself or his principles in neutrality or indifference or inaction. No one proves himself by merely thinking or simply sitting.

The writer of the article referred to above said that in some primitive languages, with their fewness of words, the description of the movement of game, for example, is described simply by one word: *running*. Perhaps we could say much more with fewer words by simply indicating the action: *living, doing*. " . . . when a noun replaces a verb there is a disadvantage . . ." because a noun is static, and life is movement. Some people "assign an intrinsic value to 'things' like purity and gratitude. . . . They take credit for possessing nominal virtues. Or they punish themselves for having vices, . . . [but] we communicate with others in verbs. . . . Gratitude has not even been born until it has been actually conveyed in word or deed. . . ."

The same could be said for sanity, said this same physician. It "is not structural but functional. It is not something one has or is. It is a measure of what one does." (William B. McGrath, M.D., in *Medicine at Work*, February 1966.) If we do sane things, we are sane. If we don't do sane things, we are not sane.

Actions Speak Louder than Words

Actions do speak louder than words.

As to a young person who was speculating upon whether or not she loved someone, there is the reminder that love is not simply a noun and not simply a sentimental feeling. The proof of love is what one is willing to do for the loved one. The proof of love is how one behaves.

Dr. John A. Widtsoe turned his attention to this subject at times: "The full and essential nature of love we may not understand," he said, "but there are tests by which it may be recognized."

Love and Truth

"Love is always founded in truth. . . . Lies and deceit, or any other violation of the moral law, are proofs of love's absence. Love perishes in the midst of untruth. . . . Thus, the lover who falsifies to his loved one, or offers her any act contrary to truth, does not really love her."

Love Does Not Injure

"Further, love does not offend or hurt or injure the loved one. By that test any human venture, past and present, may be measured for its real value. Cruelty is as absent from love . . . as truth is from untruth."

Love Is a Positive Force

" . . . love is a positive, active force. It helps the loved one. If there is need, love tries to supply it. If there is weakness, love supplants it with strength. . . . Love that does not help is a faked or transient love."

Love Gives

"Good as these tests are, there is a greater one. True love sacrifices for the loved one. . . . That is the final test. Christ gave of Himself, gave His life, for us, and thereby proclaimed the reality of his love for his mortal brethren and sisters. The mother gives of her own flesh and blood, and jeopardizes her very life, for her child. In family relationships there must be mutual sacrifices among husband, wife, and children, else true love is not there." (Dr. John A. Widtsoe, *An Understandable Religion*, ch. 8.)

Love Is Honest

Thus, anyone who would induce someone to do that which it is unworthy to do, or to take advantage, or rob someone of virtue, or embarrass, or hurt, really doesn't love the person he professes to love. What he feels under such circumstances is something less than love. The proving is in the doing.

Virtues Are Positive Forces

And so it is with all the virtues. Either we live pure lives or we don't. Either we think pure thoughts or we don't. Purity isn't simply a noun. It is a verb. It is the living of a certain kind of life. It is the thinking of certain kinds of thoughts. Its proof is in keeping the commandments.

Goodness is not theory, it is fact.

We may think of tithing as a principle and discuss it and approve it, but if we are really convinced and converted, we will pay our tithing.

We may think well of the missionary system, but it works only because some leave home and sacrifice and serve sincerely—not merely because it is a good organization or idea.

We may think and talk of chastity as a virtue, but if we are converted and convinced, we will live chaste lives.

If we love our children we won't neglect them or let them run loose. If we love our children we won't leave them ignorant of the law, or of the commandments, or ignorant of how to behave, or unacquainted with sound habits of work, or ignorant of courtesy and acceptable conduct.

If we love our children we will urge them to prepare as fully as they can for life, persuade them to acquire all the training and education possible. If we love our children we will keep as close to them as possible and do our utmost to keep them free from sin and from anything that would clutter or scar their lives.

As parents there is no greater obligation that is ours—and neglect is not the evidence of love. Part of love is doing our duty in love and loyalty, "by persuasion, by long-suffering, by gentleness and meekness, and by love unfeigned;

"By kindness, and pure knowledge. . . ." (D&C 121:41, 42.)

Jesus said: " . . . lovest thou me? . . . Feed my sheep." (John 21:16.)

Elsewhere it is written: "If ye love me, keep my commandments." (John 14:15.)

Doers of the Word

Abstract qualities of character don't mean much in the abstract. It is how we live, how we serve, how we teach our children, what we do from day to day that both indicate what we are and determine what we are; and all the theory and all the speculation, all the quoting of scripture, all the searching of the mysteries, and all the splitting of hairs, and all the knowledge of the letter of the law don't in the final and saving sense amount to very much unless we live the gospel, unless we keep the commandments, unless we prove the principles, unless we live lives of effectiveness, sincerity, and service.

The Best Evidence

Sometimes we hear someone say, "My life is my own. I am going to do with it as I please." But no one's life is his own. Too much of others has gone into the making of all of us.

We cannot hurt ourselves without hurting others. A sorrow, an illness, a disgrace, an accident, trouble, or difficulty of any kind—any loss to loved ones is a loss to family and friends. We are too much a part of one another for this not to be so.

If we love our parents, wouldn't the evidence of it be to do something about it: to be grateful, to help to care for them in their need, to honor them by being honorable, to take them into our confidence—not to worry them?

The best evidence of love for parents would be active evidence

of kindness, consideration, appreciation, respect for their teachings and counsel.

The best evidence of love of country would be not what we
say—or say we feel—but serving it, keeping the laws, preserving
its principles.

The best evidence of love for our Father in Heaven would be
living lives of honor and reverence; not taking his name in vain;
living useful, righteous lives; and keeping his commandments.

As to those who say they love the Church—the best evidence
of that love would be serving, doing, giving of ourselves, living its
standards, keeping the commandments.

God help us to be members not of record only, but members
who place doing and serving and living the requirements of the
gospel above our comfort or convenience.

"Not every one that saith unto me, Lord, Lord, shall enter into
the kingdom of heaven; but he that doeth the will of my Father
which is in heaven." (Matthew 7:21.)

It is important to believe; it is important to be; but it is also
important to do.

Conviction Expressed by Conduct

Even the devil believes. (See James 2:19.) "Conviction is
worthless unless it is converted into conduct." (Thomas Carlyle.)

Thank God for the gospel, for the personal and literal reality
of him who made us in his own image, for his Son our Savior, and
for the blessed plan of everlasting life with our loved ones.

Thank God for his patience, for his understanding, for his
comfort, for his commandments, for it would be a disillusioning
life to be running loose without knowing what was expected of
us—or why. Thank God that he sent his Only Begotten Son to
show us the way, to redeem us from death, to lead us to everlasting
life.

With you, I offer gratitude and a pledge to do my best to
demonstrate love for our Lord and Savior and his Father who gave

us life by living the kind of lives that they would have us live, and leave my witness with you of the truth of that which gathers us here together, in the name of our Lord and Savior, Jesus Christ. Amen.

Conference Report, April 1966, 88–90.

MISSIONARY WORK

WHEN THE WORLD
WILL BE CONVERTED

SPENCER W. KIMBALL

This address was delivered at a Regional Representatives Seminar on April 4, 1974, after Spencer W. Kimball had been president of the Church only a few months. In this electrifying talk, he outlined his vision of the work of the Church and its members, asking that we "lengthen our stride" and "enlarge our vision." Even though the numbers and statistics in this address are now outdated, the principles are timeless.

My beloved brethren and sisters, this is a momentous time. I am sure that you know how weak I feel in this place that Brother [Harold B.] Lee had filled so admirably. No one expected what has happened less than I. I felt absolutely certain that I would die, when my time came, as president of the Twelve. I had no idea that this could ever happen. But since it has happened there is only one thing for us to do and that is to move forward and that is our purpose today.

I said at President Lee's funeral that no one had prayed harder than Sister Kimball and I for his restoration when he was ill and for his continuation while he was well. He was such an admirable leader, and so I approach this new responsibility with fear and trembling.

Now, all of you have much to do with the missionary work of

the Church in stakes or missions. May I now discuss with you some of the things which have been uppermost in my mind.

Every area of the Church must properly feel that its work is of greatest value, but let me quote the Lord in a revelation to the Prophet Joseph Smith:

"And if it so be that you should labor all your days in crying repentance unto this people, and bring, save it be one soul unto me, how great shall be your joy with him in the kingdom of my Father!" (D&C 18:15.)

If there were no converts, the Church would shrivel and die on the vine. But perhaps the greatest reason for missionary work is to give the world its chance to hear and accept the gospel. The scriptures are replete with commands and promises and calls and rewards for teaching the gospel. I use the word *command* deliberately for it seems to be an insistent directive from which we, singly and collectively, cannot escape.

I ask you, what did he mean when the Lord took his Twelve Apostles to the top of the Mount of Olives and said:

" . . . And ye shall be witnesses unto me both in Jerusalem, and in all Judea, and in Samaria, and unto the uttermost part of the earth." (Acts 1:8.)

These were his last words on earth before he went to his heavenly home.

What is the significance of the phrase "uttermost part of the earth"? He had already covered the area known to the apostles. Was it the people in Judea? Or those in Samaria? Or the few millions in the Near East? Where were the "uttermost parts of the earth"? Did he mean the millions in what is now America? Did he include the hundreds of thousands, or even millions, in Greece, Italy, around the Mediterranean, the inhabitants of central Europe? What did he mean? Or did he mean all the living people of all the world and those spirits assigned to this world to come in centuries ahead? Have we underestimated his language or its meaning? How can we be satisfied with 100,000 converts out of nearly four billion people in the world who need the gospel?

After his crucifixion the eleven apostles assembled on a mountain in Galilee and the Savior came to them and said:

" . . . All power is given unto me in heaven and in earth.

"Go ye therefore, and teach all nations, baptizing them in the name of the Father, and of the Son, and of the Holy Ghost:"

(He said "all nations.")

"Teaching them to observe all things whatsoever I have commanded you: and, lo, I am with you alway, even unto the end of the world. Amen." (Matthew 28:18–20.)

Again the word *power* and the word *command* and the promise of continual support.

In 1830 when the Lord sent Parley P. Pratt, Oliver Cowdery, Peter Whitmer, and Ziba Peterson to the Lamanites he added:

" . . . I myself will go with them and be in their midst; and I am their advocate with the Father, and nothing shall prevail against them." (D&C 32:3.)

Did he mean all the nations then extant? And then he said,

" . . . And, lo, I am with you alway, even unto the end of the world. . . ." (Matthew 28:20.)

Do you think he included all the nations that would be organized up until that time? And as he commanded them to go forth, do you think he wondered if it could be done? He reassured us. He had the power. He said, "All power is given me in heaven and in earth . . . and I am with you alway."

Again as Mark records the events after the resurrection, he upbraided those who had some doubts about his resurrection; then commanded them:

" . . . Go ye into all the world, and preach the gospel to every creature." (Mark 16:15.)

And this was just before the ascension. Do you think he meant Egypt and Palestine and Greece? Do you think he included the world of A.D. 33 or the world of 1970, 1980, 1990? What was included in his phrase "all the world" and what did he mean by "every creature"?

And Luke records the event—

" . . . That repentance and remission of sins should be preached . . . among all nations, beginning at Jerusalem." (Luke 24:47.)

Again, his last command. Surely there is significance in these words! There was a universal need and there must be universal coverage.

As I remember the world as Moses saw it—it was a big world.

" . . . And Moses beheld the world and the ends thereof, and all the children of men which are, and which were created. . . ." (Moses 1:8.)

I am constrained to believe that at that time the Lord knew the bounds of the habitations of man and the areas that would be settled and already knew his people who would possess this world.

Still impressing Moses with the magnitude of his works and glory, the Lord showed him more.

" . . . Moses cast his eyes and beheld the earth, yea, even all of it; and there was not a particle of it which he did not behold, discerning it by the spirit of God.

" . . . And their numbers were great, even numberless as the sand upon the sea shore.

"And he beheld many lands; and each land was called earth, and there were inhabitants on the face thereof." (Moses 1:27–29.)

Remember also that Enoch, the prophet, beheld the spirits that God had created. (See Moses 6:36.) These prophets visualized the numerous spirits and all the creations. It seems to me that the Lord chose his words when he said "every nation," "every land," "uttermost bounds of the earth," "every tongue," "every people," "every soul," "all the world," "many lands."

Surely there is significance in these words!

Certainly his sheep were not limited to the thousands about

him and with whom he rubbed shoulders each day. A universal family! A universal command!

My brethren, I wonder if we are doing all we can. Are we complacent in our approach to teaching all the world? We have been proselyting now 144 years. Are we prepared to lengthen our stride? To enlarge our vision?

Remember, our ally is our God. He is our commander. He made the plans. He gave the commandment. Remember what we have quoted thousands of times as told by Nephi:

"And it came to pass that I, Nephi, said unto my father: I will go and do the things which the Lord hath commanded, for I know that the Lord giveth no commandments unto the children of men, save he shall prepare a way for them that they may accomplish the thing which he commandeth them." (1 Nephi 3:7.)

And as I read the scripture I think of the numerous nations that are still untouched. I know they have curtains, like iron curtains and bamboo curtains. I know how difficult it is because we have made some efforts. Surely the Lord knew what he was doing when he commanded. And like Nephi we can say:

"For the fulness of mine intent is that I may persuade men to come unto the God of Abraham, and the God of Isaac, and the God of Jacob, and be saved." (1 Nephi 6:4.)

And certainly the command to the original apostles of this dispensation followed the command of the others of earlier years, and you Twelve have that same command.

The 112th section of the Doctrine and Covenants was addressed to Thomas B. Marsh, the President of the Twelve in 1837, and concerns the Twelve Apostles. The keys of the kingdom were given to the Presidency and the Twelve. Apparently President Marsh had been praying for his brethren and the Lord listened:

" . . . Thine alms have come up as a memorial before me, in behalf of those, thy brethren, who were chosen to bear testimony of my name and to send it abroad among all nations, kindreds, tongues, and people. . . ." (D&C 112:1.)

Further:

" . . . Thou shalt bear record of my name, not only unto the Gentiles, but also unto the Jews; and thou shalt send forth my word unto the ends of the earth." (D&C 112:4.)

He was commanded:

" . . . Let not the inhabitants of the earth slumber, because of thy speech.

" . . . Thy path lieth among the mountains, and among many nations." (D&C 112:5, 7.)

You, the Twelve, today inherited that command.

My brethren, why did the Lord continue to repeat and repeat these phrases if he did not have meaning for them? To President Thomas B. Marsh, and to you, the Twelve, the Lord said:

" . . . I have chosen [you] to hold the keys of my kingdom . . . abroad among all nations—

"That thou mayest be my servant to unlock the door of the kingdom in all places. . . ." (D&C 112:16–17.)

I introduced to you Brother David Kennedy. I have a vision that probably Brother Kennedy and others may assist the Twelve in finding the keys that have apparently been lost to many nations wherein we can open those worlds.

As to Brother Marsh, the promise came to you and me regarding the opening of the doors:

"Wherefore, whithersoever they shall send you, go ye, and I will be with you; and in whatsoever place ye shall proclaim my name an effectual door shall be opened unto you. . . ." (D&C 112:19.)

When I read Church history, I am amazed at the boldness of the early brethren as they went out into the world. They seemed to find a way. Even in persecution and hardship, they went and opened doors which evidently have been allowed to sag on their hinges and many of them to close. I remember that these fearless men were teaching the gospel in Indian lands before the Church was even fully organized. As early as 1837 the Twelve were in England fighting Satan, in Tahiti in 1844, Australia in 1851, Iceland 1853, Italy 1850, and also in Switzerland, Germany, Tonga, Turkey, Mexico, Japan, Czechoslovakia, China, Samoa, New Zealand, South America, France, and Hawaii in 1850. When you look at the progress we have made in some countries, with no progress in many of their nearby countries, it makes us wonder. Much of this early proselyting was done while the leaders were climbing the Rockies and planting the sod and starting their homes. It is faith and super faith.

These men of valor began to walk the earth with dignity and honor, with mantles on their shoulders and keys in their hands and love in their hearts.

To the Twelve the Lord said,

"You have a work to do that no other men can do. . . . There will be times when nothing but the angels of God can deliver you out of their hands. . . ." (*History of the Church,* 2:178.)

Now let me speak of the expansion which I think is necessary and, may I add, which I think is possible. The Lord said again:

" . . . All power is given unto me in heaven and in earth." (Matthew 28:18.)

The Lord gave to Thomas B. Marsh and Joseph and Sidney and Hyrum power "to hold the keys" of the kingdom and that they would be the servants who could "unlock the door of the kingdom." (See D&C 112:16–17.)

To those intrepid leaders the command came:

" . . . And in whatsoever place ye shall proclaim my name an effectual door shall be opened unto you, that they may receive my word." (D&C 112:19.)

The Twelve have the keys and those they send have the command to open doors. Today we are blessed with many strong, trained men, in government, in foreign service, and with much prestige and "know-how." Perhaps we can bring to our call men like these who can make new contacts with emperors and kings and rulers and magistrates.

Somehow I believe the Lord meant what he said through the centuries.

Again to the apostles through their president, Thomas B. Marsh:

"Contend thou, therefore, morning by morning; and day after day let thy warning voice go forth; and when night cometh let not the inhabitants of the earth slumber, because of thy speech." (D&C 112:5.)

"For verily the voice of the Lord is unto all men, and there is none to escape; and there is no eye that shall not see, neither ear that shall not hear, neither heart that shall not be penetrated.

"And the voice of warning shall be unto all people, by the mouths of my disciples, whom I have chosen in these last days." (D&C 1:2, 4.)

Somehow, brethren, I feel that when we have done all in our power that the Lord will find a way to open doors. That is my faith.

"Is any thing too hard for the Lord?" he asked, when Sarah laughed when she was told that she would have a son. When she heard this in the tent door, she knew that both Abraham at one hundred years and she at ninety years were past the age of reproduction. She could not bear children. She knew that, as well as it has been known that we could not open doors to many nations.

"And the Lord said unto Abraham, Wherefore did Sarah laugh. . . .

"Is any thing too hard for the Lord? At the time appointed I will return unto thee, according to the time of life, and Sarah shall have a son." (Genesis 18:13–14.)

Brethren, Sarah did have a son, from Abraham, the father of nations.

"Therefore sprang there even of one, and him as good as dead [and that was Abraham, one hundred years old], so many as the stars of the sky in multitude, and as the sand which is by the sea shore innumerable." (Hebrews 11:12.)

Is anything too hard for the Lord?

Also to Jeremiah he had said:

"Behold, I am the Lord, the God of all flesh: is there any thing too hard for me?" (Jeremiah 32:27.)

If he commands, certainly he can fulfill.

We remember the exodus of the children of Israel crossing the uncrossable Red Sea.

We remember Cyrus diverting a river and taking the impregnable city of Babylon.

We remember the Lehites getting to the promised land.

We remember the Revolutionary War and the power of God that gave us triumph.

I believe the Lord can do anything he sets his mind to do.

But I can see no good reason why the Lord would open doors that we are not prepared to enter. Why should he break down the Iron Curtain or the Bamboo Curtain or any other curtain if we are still unprepared to enter?

I believe we have men who could help the apostles to open these doors—statesmen, able and trustworthy—but, when we are ready for them.

Today we have 17,600 missionaries. We can send more. Many more! Eight thousand, nine hundred went through the mission home in 1973.

I believe it was John Taylor who said, "God will hold us responsible to the people we might have saved, had we done our duty."

When I ask for more missionaries, I am not asking for more testimony-barren or unworthy missionaries. I am asking that we start earlier and train our missionaries better in every branch and every ward in the world. That is another challenge—that the young people will understand that it is a great privilege to go on a mission and that they must be physically well, mentally well, spiritually well, and that "the Lord cannot look upon sin with the least degree of allowance."

I am asking for missionaries who have been carefully indoctrinated and trained through the family and the organizations of the Church, and who come to the mission with a great desire. I am asking for better interviews, more searching interviews, more sympathetic and understanding interviews, but especially that we train prospective missionaries much better, much earlier, much longer, so that each anticipates his mission with great joy.

Not that I had much influence on it, but when I came into the Council of the Twelve in 1943 there were less than one million members; today there are 3,353,000. We then had 146 stakes and about 40 missions, and we now have 633 stakes and 107 missions. We have grown from 937,000 in 1943 to 1,116,000 in 1959, and 3,300,000 in 1973. That means approximately a 19 percent increase in the 16 years between 1943 and 1959 and approximately a 196 percent increase from 1959 to 1974. This is phenomenal growth.

It may be of interest to you brethren, some of you, to know that of the 17,564 missionaries, as of last week, 9,560 are teaching the gospel in English, which is about 55 percent of all the missionaries, and these are in the United States, Canada, Great Britain, Australia, New Zealand, and the Philippines. About 8,000 missionaries are learning languages in the language training missions. These 45 percent are training in the three language schools—about 17 percent or 3,000 in Spanish, about 1,000 in German, about 1,000 in Japanese, about 400 in French, and about 600 in Portuguese, and substantial numbers in Danish, Finnish, Dutch, Norwegian, Swedish, Chinese, Italian, Korean, Thai, Samoan, Afrikaans, and Navajo.

It is interesting to me that some statistician told us that in 33 A.D. when the Savior himself was stressing so strongly "every nation, kindred, tongue, and people" that there were on the earth possibly a quarter billion people (250,000,000).

Eighteen hundred years later, when the command came through Joseph Smith to proselyte the world, our experts estimated that there were one billion people (1,000,000,000), or about four times as many as in the meridian of time. And now as we renew the injunction to cover the earth with the gospel, it is estimated that there are probably almost three and a half billion (3,400,000,000).

The question is frequently asked: Should every young man fill a mission? And the answer has been given by the Lord. It is "Yes." Every young man should fill a mission. He said:

"Send forth the elders of my church unto the nations which are afar off [He said elders—we have been talking about elders]; unto the islands of the sea; send forth unto foreign lands; call upon all nations, first upon the Gentiles, and then upon the Jews." (D&C 133:8.)

He did not limit it.

The answer is "yes." Every man should also pay his tithing. Every man should observe the Sabbath. Every man should attend his meetings. Every man should marry in the temple and properly train his children, and do many other mighty works. Of course he should. He does not always do it.

We realize that while all men definitely should, all men are not prepared to teach the gospel abroad. Far too many young men arrive at the missionary age quite unprepared to go on a mission, and of course they should not be sent. But they should all be prepared. There are a few physically unfit to do missionary service, but Paul also had a thorn in his side. There are far too many unfit emotionally and mentally and morally, because they have not kept their lives clean and in harmony with the spirit of missionary work. They should have been prepared. Should! But since they have broken the laws, they may have to be deprived, and thereon hangs one of our greatest challenges: to keep these young boys worthy. Yes, we would say, every able worthy man should shoulder the cross. What an army we should have teaching Christ and him crucified! Yes, they should be prepared, usually with saved funds for their missions, and always with a happy heart to serve.

The Lord says:

"And that every man"—(Did you catch the words, "every man"?)—"should take righteousness in his hands and faithfulness upon his loins, and lift a warning voice unto the inhabitants of the earth: and declare both by word and by flight that desolation shall come upon the wicked." (D&C 63:37.)

Note that he said *every man;* but we must find a way to have every man prepared.

Now, how can we do this? We see that there are these elements to be considered: the breaking down of resistance of the nations of the world to receive our missionaries; a greatly increased missionary force (greatly, I emphasize); a better trained missionary army; and better and additional methods and approaches.

Now here we will consider each one in its turn. We need to *enlarge our field of operation.* We will need to make a full, prayerful study of the nations of the world which do not have the gospel at this time, and then bring into play our strongest and most able men to assist the Twelve to move out into the world and to open the doors of every nation as fast as it is ready. I believe we have many men in the Church who can be helpful to us, who are naturally gifted diplomats. I believe we should bring them to our aid and as stated before, I have faith that the Lord will open doors when we have done everything in our power.

Second, I have already discussed and will discuss a little further, an enlarged army of missionaries.

Third, I believe that the Lord is anxious to put into our hands inventions of which we laymen have hardly had a glimpse.

The Prophet Joseph Smith declared: "The truth of God will go forth boldly, till it has penetrated every continent, and sounded in every ear, till the purposes of God shall be accomplished."

A significant revelation states: "For, verily, the sound must go forth from this place into all the world, and unto the uttermost parts of the earth—the gospel must be preached unto every creature. . . ." (D&C 58:64.)

I am confident that the only way we can reach most of these millions of our Father's children is through the spoken word over the airwaves, since so many are illiterate. We have proved the ability of our young men to learn other languages.

President David O. McKay, speaking in the October 1966 conference of the Church, said of the scientific discoveries of recent years which will make possible the preaching of the gospel to every kindred, tongue, and people: "They stagger the imagination."

And further: " . . . discoveries latent with such potent power, either for the blessing or the destruction of human beings as to make men's responsibility in controlling them the most gigantic ever placed in human hands. . . . This age is fraught with limitless perils, as well as untold possibilities."

King Benjamin, that humble but mighty servant of the Lord, called together all the people in the land of Zarahemla, and the multitude was so great that King Benjamin " . . . caused a tower to be erected, that thereby his people might hear the words which he should speak unto them." (Mosiah 2:7.)

Our Father in Heaven has now provided us mighty towers—radio and television towers with possibilities beyond comprehension—to help fulfill the words of the Lord that "the sound must go forth from this place unto all the world."

Even though there are millions of people throughout the world who cannot read or write, there is a chance to reach them through radio and television. The modern transistor radio can be mass produced by the thousands in a size that is small and inexpensive. We can preach the gospel to eager ears and hearts. These should be carried by people in the marketplaces of South America, on the steppes of Russia, the vast mountains and plains of China, the subcontinent of India, and the desert sands of Arabia and Egypt. Some authorities claim that this tiny miracle will be recorded by future historians as an event even greater than the invention of the printing press. The transistor is an eloquent answer to the illiteracy and ignorance which reign supremely over the earth. The spoken voice will reach millions of hearers who can listen through a $3 or $4 transistor but could not read even an elementary treatise.

There are over seven thousand AM and FM radio stations in the United States, with thousands more in other parts of the world. There are innumerable opportunities for us to use these stations overseas, if we only prepare the message in the native languages.

Also, missionaries could be supplied with small portable cassette tape players and go into the homes with prepared messages to humble family groups all around the globe. Millions of people are anxious and willing to learn, if only they can hear the "sound" in their own language and in a manner that they can grasp and understand.

Just think what can be accomplished when we broadcast our message in many languages over numerous radio stations, large and small, around the world, and millions of good people listening on their transistors are being indoctrinated with the truth.

The Lord has blessed the world with many Early Bird satellites. They are stationed high in the heavens, relaying broadcast signals back to almost every corner of the earth's surface. Today there are sixty-seven earth-receiving stations operating in fifty countries of the world. Certainly these satellites are only the genesis of what is in store for the future of worldwide broadcasting.

With the Lord providing these miracles of communication, and with the increased efforts and devotion of our missionaries and all of us, and all others who are "sent," surely the divine injunction will come to pass: "For, verily, the sound must go forth from this place into all the world, and unto the uttermost parts of the earth—the gospel must be preached unto every creature. . . ." (D&C 58:64.) And we must find a way.

We are happy with the people of Hong Kong, but according to our records only one thousand, or less than 1 percent of the people, have accepted the gospel.

We have a stake in South Korea and a mission there, with about 7,500 members. What must be done to reach the other 37 million? There must be a way, for the Lord does not talk in riddles. He must have anticipated that something could be done so that his word might be fulfilled.

The millions of people in the Philippines would receive the gospel in large numbers if it were properly presented to them. We have two missions and a stake there. We should use their own young men as missionaries and then every facility that is available to bring them to a knowledge of the true church.

There are 14 million people in Taiwan, 2 million in Singapore, 119 million in Indonesia, 31 million in Korea, 40 million in Thailand, and 103 million in Japan, and all these 300 million people are sons and daughters of God and have a right to hear the gospel, and we have not only the right to give it to them but the obligation to do so.

We mention Australia with its over 13 million people, and we have been doing missionary work there since 1851. Now, after 123 years, we still have only 29,000 members, for which we are grateful, with 13 million yet to touch, and for 123 years we have been sending missionaries from this land to that land and today have more than 600 missionaries in Australia. Of this 600-plus missionaries, only a relatively small handful, about 5.5 percent, are Australians. Where have we failed to help these good people to see their duty in this pivotal matter?

In Mexico we have around 54 million people with about 92,000 members. We have 489 full-time missionaries now serving in that country, only 122 of which are native Mexicans. We have had some difficulty getting missionaries from the United States into Mexico or we would have far more. There has been a limitation of about 360 American missionaries that could get visas. We are unable to send a new elder from the United States until another elder is released and has surrendered his visa. In addition to this problem, the cost of placing missionaries in Mexico has greatly increased, and so for both these reasons there is ample argument that Mexico, with its nine stakes and five missions, should furnish its own missionaries, or the equivalent.

Suppose that South Korea with its 37 million people and its 7,500 members were to take care of its own proselyting needs and thus release to go into North Korea and possibly to Russia the hundreds who now go from the states to Korea.

If Japan could furnish its own one thousand missionaries and then eventually ten thousand more for Mongolia and China, if Taiwan could furnish its own needed missionaries plus five hundred for China and Vietnam and Cambodia, then we would begin to fulfill the vision. Suppose that Hong Kong could furnish its needed missionaries and another thousand to go to both of the Chinas; suppose the Philippines could fill its own needs and then provide an additional thousand for the limitless islands of southeast Asia; suppose the South Seas and the islands therein and the New Zealanders and the Australians could furnish their own and another several thousand for the numerous islands of south Asia and for Vietnam, Cambodia, Thailand, Burma, Bangladesh, and India.

With this movement of missionaries who would be traveling north and west, the lands of the world could begin to be covered with the gospel as the lowlands of the world are covered with the oceans.

Now in another part of the world, suppose that Mexico and Central America provided far more missionaries than they needed themselves and the people of South America had reached the point where they could export numerous fine missionaries and then suppose that the United States and Canada awakened to their real responsibility, sending thousands of missionaries to join them, going east and north so that Iceland, Scandinavia, southern Europe, Germany, and Europe could be covered.

Great Britain, with seven missions and fourteen stakes now but numerous others later, should join that army and all together the army of the west would move across western Europe and central Europe and Arab lands, and in a great pincer movement join their efforts with the missionary army from the east to bring the gospel to millions in China and India and other populous countries of the world. . . .

May we emphasize again that numbers are incidental and secondary to our main purpose, which is the same as that of our Heavenly Father—to bring to every soul the gospel which can open the doors to eternal life for man. Our objective is not for power or domain, but totally spiritual. And to every nation and people which opens its borders to the gospel will come unbelievable blessings.

It must be realized, too, that the directions of the assignments are, as indicated by the arrows, merely suggestive. The individual assignments could be merely an expansion of the present-day coverage. The missionaries would be sent where the most good could be accomplished. . . . The sharing of the gospel often requires us to cross language and cultural barriers and the arrows you see on the screen are representative of what needs to happen and will not, in every case, represent a perfect match of which country could best supply the missionaries to preach the gospel in another country. The basic point is, where the land masses of the world are, there, also, are the population masses to whom we must bring the gospel of Jesus Christ.

This would be difficult. It would take some time. Sometimes it might seem impossible but again remember the little stone cut out of the mountain without hands which was destined to roll forth and fill the whole earth. It has gone a long way but it must go farther.

Using all the latest inventions and equipment and paraphernalia already developed and that which will follow, can you see that perhaps the day may come when the world will be converted and covered?

If we do all we can, and I accept my own part of that responsibility, I am sure the Lord will bring more discoveries to our use. He will bring a change of heart into kings and magistrates and emperors, or he will divert rivers or open seas or find ways to touch hearts. He will open the gates and make possible the proselyting. Of that, I have great faith.

Now, we have the promise from the Lord that the evil one will never be able to frustrate totally the work that he has commanded us to do.

"This kingdom will continue to increase and to grow, to spread and to prosper more and more. Every time its enemies undertake to overthrow it, it will become more extensive and powerful; instead of decreasing it will continue to increase; it will spread the more, become more wonderful and conspicuous to the nations, until it fills the whole earth." (President Brigham Young, April conference, 1852.)

Further, Brigham Young wrote:

"We believe, as the time draws near, the Lord will hasten his work, and nations will soon be gathered into the fold of Christ.

"The work urges and is becoming very much enlarged and

extended, and requires a commensurate accumulation of men and means, and expansion of mind and energy, ability and perseverance. The Lord, our God, is our strength, and under this accumulation and weight of care and business, has hitherto given in grace and strength, according to our day and generation, has sustained us in every time of need and preserved and delivered us from the hands of our enemies. Blessed forever be his holy name; great and wondrous are his ways. Let all nations give heed to his servants, for they are preparing the way for his coming; yea, when he shall come in power and great glory, to take unto himself a kingdom, prepared and made ready in the due time of the Lord; for this is the Lord's work; woe be unto him who putteth forth his hand, his influence, his energies, or any of his powers to oppose it." (From a letter written by President Brigham Young to Elder Samuel W. Richards, who was presiding over the European Mission. The date of the letter is October 29, 1852. It is found in the *Millennial Star*, 15:106–7.)

You are acquainted with the statement of the Prophet Joseph Smith in the Wentworth Letters written March 1, 1842. (*History of the Church*, 4:536.) I am sure the Prophet Joseph looked ahead and saw many problems with national animosities and fears with war and commotions and jealousies, and I am sure that he saw all these things would happen and yet in spite of everything he said with great boldness and assurance:

"No unhallowed hand can stop the work from progressing; persecutions may rage, mobs may combine, armies may assemble, calumny may defame, but the truth of God will go forth boldly, nobly and independent, till it has penetrated every continent; visited every clime, swept every country and sounded in every ear; till the purposes of God shall be accomplished, and the great Jehovah shall say the work is done."

The immensity of the work before us is emphasized as we consider the population of the world as it approaches the four billion mark.

I am under no delusion, brethren, to think that this will be an easy matter without strain or that it can be done overnight, but I do have this faith that we can move forward and expand much faster than we now are.

As I see this almost impossible demand, I believe that you brethren, our representatives, can immediately accept the challenge and in your stakes and missions explain to the people how they must increase their missionaries, how they can finance their missionaries, how they can indoctrinate and train these additional missionaries, and how, through all the agencies of the Church, they can move ahead. Here is where you come in.

A year ago now I was in Japan and Korea, and as I saw the many handsome young men joining the Church and giving leadership to its organizations, I seemed to envision a great movement when there would be thousands of local men prepared and anxious and strong to go abroad. As I have been in Mexico since that time, I seemed to envision again Mexican youth and Latins from Central and South America in great numbers qualifying themselves for missionary service within their own country and then finally in other lands until the army of the Lord's missionaries would cover the earth as the waters cover the mighty deep.

I have stated the problem. I believe there is a solution. I think that if we are all of one mind and one heart and one purpose that we can move forward and change the image which seems to be that "We are doing pretty well. Let's not 'rock the boat.'"

In all the countries I have ever visited I have found many intelligent and qualified people who give leadership in their countries, and I also remember numerous people from deprived countries enjoying benefits from the gospel.

In our stake missionary work at home we have hardly scratched the surface.

Brother T. Bowring Woodbury told us of ninety-three cooperating families in one Utah stake who were working with ninety-three non- or part-member families. Clifford Johnson told us of bringing five of twenty-six nonmembers into the Church in a few months.

It can be done.

We can change the image and approach the ideals set out by President McKay, "Every member a missionary." That was inspired!

I know this message is not new, and we have talked about it before, but I believe the time has come when we must shoulder arms. I think we must change our sights and raise our goals.

When we have increased the missionaries from the organized areas of the Church to a number close to their potential, that is, every able and worthy boy in the Church on a mission; when every stake and mission abroad is furnishing enough missionaries for that country; when we have used our qualified men to help the apostles to open these new fields of labor; when we have used the satellite and related discoveries to their greatest potential and all of the media—the papers, magazines, television, radio—all in their greatest power; when we have organized numerous other stakes which will be springboards; when we have recovered from inactivity the numerous young men who are now unordained and unmissioned and unmarried; then, and not until then, shall we approach the insistence of our Lord and Master to go into all the world and preach the gospel to every creature.

Brethren, I am positive that the blessings of the Lord will attend every country which opens its gates to the gospel of Christ. Their blessings will flow in education, and culture, and faith, and love, like Enoch's city of Zion, which was translated, and also will become like the two hundred years of peaceful habitation in this country in Nephite days. There will come prosperity to the nations, comfort and luxuries to the people, joy and peace to all recipients, and eternal life to those who accept and magnify it.

Someone gave us this:

> To walk with God, no strength is lost.
> Walk on.

> To talk with God, no breath is lost.
> Talk on.
> To wait on God, no time is lost.
> Wait on.

I pray the blessings of the Lord will be upon us as we approach our great responsibilities, in the name of the Lord, Jesus Christ. Amen.

Ensign, October 1974, 3–14.

‑‑❦ ❧‑‑

MISSIONARY EXPERIENCES

LEGRAND RICHARDS

Missionary work was one of the favorite themes of Elder LeGrand Richards. He served in four different missions (twice in the Netherlands, in the Eastern States Mission, and in the Southern States Mission), presiding over two of them. The author of *A Marvelous Work and a Wonder*, Elder Richards came from a long line of Church leaders; his father and his grandfather both served as presidents of the Quorum of the Twelve Apostles. When he delivered this devotional address in the Marriott Center at Brigham Young University on October 20, 1981, Elder Richards was both the oldest living General Authority (ninety-five) and the one who had been serving the longest (forty-three years).

I'm very happy to greet all of you wonderful students here this morning and your leaders, and I understand that you have a group of missionaries here, as you did a year ago when I spoke at a devotional; so being a missionary, I decided, when I was trying to decide what to speak about this morning, to tell you some of my missionary experiences. I think that you'll get more out of that than if I tried to discuss any particular subject or principle of the gospel. If you don't think I could, read the books I've written, and you'll know that I could.

First, I started way back in 1905 when I went on my first mission to Holland. My cousin and I rode together until we reached Liverpool, then he was sent up into Norway, the Land of the Midnight Sun, and I was sent into Holland. After we had been in the mission field a few months, I received a letter from him calling me by name, and he said, "I met a man the other day who knows more about religion than I've ever dreamed of knowing, and I told him if he had something better than I had, I'd join his church."

So I wrote him back and called him by name, and I said, "If he has something better than you have, you *ought* to join his church, but does he have something better than a personal visitation to this earth after centuries of darkness by God the Eternal Father and his Son Jesus Christ to usher in the dispensation of the fulness of times and to reveal the real personalities of God and his Son Jesus Christ? Does he have something better than the coming of Moroni with the plates from which the Book of Mormon was translated, which gives us the history of God's dealings with his prophets in this land of America over a period of a thousand years? Does he have something better than the coming back to this earth of John the Baptist, who was beheaded for his testimony of Jesus, to restore the Aaronic Priesthood, the power to baptize by immersion for the remission of sins? Does he have something better than the coming of Peter, James, and John, who were upon the Mount of Transfiguration with the Savior and returned to this earth to restore the holy priesthood, the power of the apostleship, the power to organize the church and kingdom of God upon the earth? Does he have something better than the coming of Moses with the keys of the gathering of latter-day Israel? Does he have something better than the coming of Elijah the prophet, of whose coming Malachi testified that before the coming of the great and dreadful day of the Lord, the Lord would send Elijah the prophet to turn the hearts of the fathers to the children and the hearts of the children to the fathers, lest he come and smite the whole earth with a curse? Now that's an important mission." I said, "If he has something better than that, you ought to join his church."

I tell the missionaries that if you learn how to tell our story, you never need to argue with anybody. You tell them things they've never heard of, and you prove them to them out of the Lord's holy scriptures.

When I was president of the Southern States Mission, I preached a sermon down in Quitman, Georgia, on the eternal duration of the marriage covenant and the family unit. I quoted from Rulon Howell's book *Do Men Believe What Their Churches Prescribe?* Along one side he has the names of all of the important subjects and across the top the names of various large churches of the world. I read from that book. Not one of the major churches believed in the eternal duration of the marriage covenant and the family unit. As the meeting closed, I stood at the door shaking hands with the people who were there. A man came up and introduced himself as a Baptist minister, and I said, "Did I misquote you here tonight?"

"No, Mr. Richards," he said. "It's like you say; we don't all believe all the things that our churches teach."

I said, "You don't believe them either. Why don't you go back and teach your people the truth. They'll take it from you, and they're not ready to take it from the Mormon elders yet."

He said, "I'll see you again."

I didn't see him for about four months until I went back to that branch. My coming was announced in the newspaper, and as I walked to that little church, there stood that Baptist minister. As we shook hands, I said, "I'd certainly be interested to know what you thought of my talk the last time I was here."

He said, "Mr. Richards, I've been thinking about it ever since. I believe every word you said, only I'd like to have heard the rest of it." Now you know we never get talked out when we get talking about the principles of the gospel. There was a man occupying a pulpit in the Baptist Church who believed every word I'd said, and yet he couldn't preach it to his people.

In the Book of Mormon we read about when Lehi was in the

desert. He told his son Joseph that the Lord had promised Joseph who was sold into Egypt that in the latter days he would raise up a prophet from his loins whose name would be Joseph and whose father's name would be Joseph. (Now obviously that was Joseph Smith.) The Lord said about him: "[That prophet shall] bring forth my word." (2 Nephi 3:11.)

The Prophet Joseph brought us the Book of Mormon, the Doctrine and Covenants, the Pearl of Great Price, and many other writings. He has given us more revealed truth than any other prophet who has ever lived upon the face of the earth as far as our records are concerned. That was written in the Book of Mormon before this Church was ever organized.

Then [the Lord] said, "Not to the bringing forth my word only . . . but to the convincing them of my word, which shall have already gone forth among them." (2 Nephi 3:11.)

What did he mean by that? That in this world, where there are hundreds of different churches preaching men's interpretation of the scriptures, the Lord would give this new prophet an understanding of the scriptures to reveal them in the spirit in which they were written. Then he said: "For the thing, which the Lord shall bring forth by his hand, by the power of the Lord shall bring my people unto salvation." (2 Nephi 3:15.)

Why? Because this prophet would be clothed upon by the holy priesthood, the power to administer the saving ordinances of the gospel.

Then the Lord adds: "And I will make him great in mine eyes; for he shall do my work." (2 Nephi 3:8.)

Whatever the world may think of this prophet of this dispensation, there's the testimony of the Lord that he shall be great in his eyes.

Now, referring to the statement about "convincing them of my word which shall have already gone forth among them," I want to tell you of a little experience I had when I was in Holland. I had an invitation from some businessmen to attend one of their Bible classes. They met every week in one of the homes. We met that week in the home of a prominent furniture dealer. There were about 20 men there, and the only woman was the daughter of the man of the house. They gave me an hour and a half to discuss universal salvation, which includes our doctrine of preaching the gospel in the eternal worlds to the spirits that were disobedient here upon the earth and the doctrine of baptism of the living for the dead. So after I had discussed that matter, I just gave them chapter and verse and let them read it in their own copies of the Bible. I figured that they would believe it more if they read it in their Bible; otherwise, they would think that I had a different Bible. When I was through, I laid my Bible on the table and folded my arms and waited for a comment.

The first comment came from the daughter of the man of the house. She said, "Father, I just can't understand it. I have never attended one of these Bible classes in my life when you haven't had the last word to say on everything, and tonight you haven't said a word."

He shook his head and said, "My daughter, there isn't anything to say. This man has been teaching us things we have never heard of, and he's been teaching them to us out of our own Bible." That's what the Lord meant when he said that the prophet of this dispensation would not only bring forth his words, but would convince people of his words that had already gone forth among them.

Along that line, some years ago the congregational and evangelical churches of these western states—California, Oregon, Washington, Idaho, Utah, and Nevada—were holding a conference of their leaders and ministers in Salt Lake. The leader of the group wrote a letter to President McKay and asked him if he would send one of the General Authorities of the Church to attend the morning session of their conference and tell them the story of Mormonism, to be their guest for lunch, and to remain for an hour and a half in the afternoon and let them ask questions. I got the assignment, and I don't mind telling you that I was happy to get it. I tell the missionaries you'll never need to argue with anybody if you learn how to tell our story and you keep the lead. So when I arrived I said, "Do you want it just the way we got our Church and what we believe?"

The man in charge said, "That's just what we want."

Some of them wanted to get away on earlier planes to the Northwest, so they set the luncheon back half an hour so that they could give me two and a half hours in that morning meeting. I presented our message to them just about the same way that I have presented it in *A Marvelous Work and a Wonder,* which many of you have read, showing what we got by revelation rather than by reformation. The churches of this world have not been able to agree because they have not understood the scriptures as they have tried to interpret them; and no two of them can agree, so that has brought into the world many churches. But we have a gospel that has come directly from heaven. When I wrote *A Marvelous Work and a Wonder,* I predicated it on the thought that we are the only Christian church in the world that didn't get our religion out of the Bible; we got it by revelation from heaven; then we use the Bible to prove that what we have is what we should have.

After I had presented what we got by revelation (and I've already referred to a little of that when I told you about my cousin who was in Norway), I said, "While I was the presiding bishop of the Church, we directed the building program of the Church. We had the plans prepared for the Los Angeles Temple. One day we showed those plans to the First Presidency. We had 84 pages about 4 feet long and 2½ feet wide. We didn't have the electric plans or the plumbing plans complete, and yet there was that temple built spiritually, and there was not a hole in the ground. You could take those plans and go all over this world and try to fit them to every building in the world, but there's only one building they would fit, and that's the Mormon temple in Los Angeles. Of course, you could find buildings that have material in them like the material in that temple, such as lumber, cement, tiling, electrical wiring, and plumbing, but you can't find any other building in the world that those plans will fit except the Mormon temple in Los Angeles."

Then I held up the Bible and said, "Here's the Lord's blueprint. Isaiah said the Lord had declared the end from the beginning. It's all here when you know how to understand it. Isaiah said, 'The grass withereth, and the flower fadeth, but the word of our God shall stand forever.' (Isaiah 40:8.)

"You could take this, the Lord's blueprint, and try to fit it to every church in this world, but there's only one church that it will fit, and that's The Church of Jesus Christ of Latter-day Saints. Of course, you can find other churches that have some of the same things in them like are in this blueprint, but you can't find any other church that this, the Lord's blueprint, will fit."

Then I said, "Now I'll proceed to illustrate to you what I mean. In Farrar's *Life of Christ,* he said there were two passages in the New Testament for which he could find no excuse. The first was John 10:16, where Jesus said, "Other sheep I have, which are not of this fold: them also I must bring, and they shall hear my voice; and there shall be one fold, and one shepherd."

I said, "Do any of you men know why that's in the Bible?"

No answer.

"Do any of you know any church in the world that does know why it's in the Bible?"

No answer.

"Well, we know all about it." Then I tied it to what I'd told them about the promise of Moses to Joseph who was sold into Egypt of a new land separated from his brethren in the utmost bounds of the everlasting hills, and, describing that land, Moses used the word *precious* five times in just four little verses (see Deuteronomy 33:13–16).

"Do any of you know where the land of Joseph is?"

No answer.

"Do any of you know any church in the world that does know where it is?"

No answer.

"Well, we know all about it," I said. "It's the land of America." And then I led up to where the Lord commanded Ezekiel that the two records should be kept, one of Judah and his followers, the house of Israel, and one of Joseph and his followers, the house of Israel, and in the days of their children—that is in the latter days—when they would say, "Wilt thou not shew us what thou meanest by these? Say unto them, Thus saith the Lord God; Behold, I will take the stick of Joseph, which is in the hand of Ephraim, and the tribes of Israel his fellows, and will put them with him, even with the stick of Judah, and make them one stick, and they shall be one in mine hand." (Ezekiel 37:18–19.)

"Do any of you," I said, "know where that stick or record of Joseph is that the Lord commanded should be written?"

No answer.

"Well, we know all about it; it's the Book of Mormon. And when you get the Book of Mormon, you read about when Jesus visited his people here in the land of America, when he told them that they were the other sheep of whom he spoke to his disciples in Jerusalem. He said never at any time had the Lord commanded him to tell his disciples who the other sheep were, only that he had other sheep that were not of that fold." See how beautifully the scriptures fit together when you understand them?

The second passage that Canon Farrar couldn't understand is 1 Corinthians 15:29, where Paul said: "Else what shall they do which are baptized for the dead, if the dead rise not at all? why are they then baptized for the dead?"

I said, "Do any of you know why that is in the Bible?"

No answer.

"Do any of you know of any church in the world that does know why that's in the Bible?"

No answer.

"Well, we know all about it." Then I told them that Peter said that Jesus was "put to death in the flesh, but quickened by the Spirit: By which also he went and preached unto the spirits in prison; Which sometime were disobedient . . . in the days of Noah, while the ark was a preparing, wherein few, that is, eight souls were saved by water." (1 Peter 3:18–20.)

"Now," I said, "obviously if Jesus preached to them, his gospel was faith, repentance, baptism by immersion for the remission of sins, and the laying on of hands for the gift of the Holy Ghost. And since you can't baptize a spirit in water, the Lord had to give them a vicarious baptism of the living for the dead so that holy and sacred ordinance could be performed for them." I went on to point out that Peter said, "For this cause was the gospel preached also to them that are dead, that they might be judged according to men in the flesh, but live according to God in the spirit." (1 Peter 4:6.)

That helps you to understand what Jesus meant when he said: "The hour is coming, and now is, when the dead shall hear the voice of the Son of God: and they that hear shall live." (John 5:25.)

The world has interpreted that to mean those who are dead in sin, but Jesus amplified it by saying: "Marvel not at this; for the hour is coming, in the which all that are in the grave shall hear his voice." (John 5:28.)

See how beautifully that fits together?

Then I gave those men some more passages concerning the kingdom that God was to set up in the latter days and the heavens that were to receive the Christ until the restitution of all things spoken by the mouths of all the holy prophets since the world began and then the angel that was to bring the gospel in the latter days to be preached to every nation, kindred, tongue, and people; and in each one I would say, "Do you know why these passages are in the scripture as part of the Lord's blueprint? Do you know any church in the world that claims that these things have been fulfilled?" Do you see how beautifully the gospel and all these beautiful fulfillments of the words of the holy prophets fit together?

Toward the close of my remarks, the man in charge said, "Now, Mr. Richards, we've heard it said that you believe that God has a wife. Would you explain that to us?" I think he thought he had me over a barrel or in a corner that I couldn't get out of.

Rather facetiously I said, "Well, I don't see how in the world God could have a son without a wife, do you?" They all began to twitter, and I didn't have any trouble with that question.

Those ministers and church leaders wanted to have an hour and a half to ask questions, and after they had listened to me for two and a half hours, I got that one question from them, and that was the only one. The man in charge said when I left them, "Mr. Richards, this has been one of the most interesting experiences of my entire life." No wonder Isaiah said it would be a marvelous work and a wonder. That's what it is to me, and that's what every missionary ought to make it be to those who are yet in darkness.

Now, I'll tell you a little experience. I had a debate with a minister in Amsterdam when I was on my first mission. One of the Saints invited me to come to her home. She wanted to invite her neighbor in and let me preach the gospel to her. When my companion and I went to that home, the neighbor was there, but she brought her minister with her. Well, we had a little difference of opinion on the discussion of the priesthood, and right there he challenged me for a debate in his church. I was young and had a lot of oomph in me, and I accepted the challenge. We were not advised in those days not to debate.

When we arrived in his church on Saturday night according

to our appointment, that church was full. All of his people were there, and all of our people were there. I didn't know how our people found it out; I didn't tell them. He stood up and said, "Now inasmuch as Mr. Richards is a guest in our church, we'll accord him the privilege of opening the debate. We'll each talk for twenty minutes and continue as long as it is mutually agreeable. Is that satisfactory to you, Mr. Richards?"

I said, "Very much so." I didn't tell him, but I would have given him the shirt off my back for the privilege of opening that debate, and he just handed it to me on a silver platter. I didn't know whether the Lord had anything to do with that or not, but I always thought he did.

I stood up and said, "The last time I talked to my friend here, we had a difference of opinion on the principle of priesthood. I've come here tonight prepared to discuss that subject, but I don't propose to start at that point. If you were going to build a house, you wouldn't try to put the roof on it until you got the foundation in because if a foundation were faulty, it wouldn't do you any good to put the roof on because the house would fall. I propose to open this debate by laying the foundation of the gospel of Jesus Christ, and I choose for my text the sixth chapter of Hebrews where Paul said:

"Leaving the principles of the doctrine of Christ, let us go on unto perfection; not laying again the foundation of repentance from dead works, and of faith toward God, of the doctrine of baptisms, and of laying on of hands, and of resurrection of the dead, and of eternal judgment." (Hebrews 6:1–2.)

I hurried over faith and repentance because I thought they believed them. I spiked down baptism by immersion for the remission of sins until everybody in the audience was giving me approval. Then I came to the laying on of hands for the gift of the Holy Ghost. They didn't believe that. They thought the Holy Ghost came just like the breezes that blow over your head. You remember when the apostles at Jerusalem heard that Samaria had accepted the word of God through the preaching of Philip. They sent Peter and John to them, and when they came, they prayed for these men. They laid their hands upon them, and they received the Holy Ghost. And when Simon the sorcerer saw that the Holy Ghost was conveyed by the laying on of the apostles' hands, he offered them money, saying:

"Give me also this power; that on whomsoever I lay my hands, he may receive the Holy Ghost. But Peter said unto him, Thy money perish with thee, because thou has thought that the gift of God may be purchased with money." (Acts 8:19–20.)

Then I gave another reference or two about the laying on of hands out of the Bible and sat down. "My friend" stood up. He never mentioned a word I'd said. He started on the Mountain Meadows Massacre and the Golden Bible and the fact that Joseph Smith admitted that he'd made many mistakes, and then he turned to me and said, "Now if Mr. Richards will explain these matters, this audience will be most appreciative."

I was on my feet just like that. (My companion said, "How did you think so fast?" and I said, "What have you been praying for all week?") I stood on my feet and said, "In the days of the Savior, his enemies tried to trick him with cunningness and craftiness. I don't suppose there is anybody here today that would like to see us resort to those old tactics. This friend of mine offered me the courtesy of opening this debate as a guest in his church, and now he wants to steal from me the very courtesy that he extended to me, and I don't propose to let him do it. So, my friend, you may have your twenty minutes over again."

He couldn't do it, and I knew he couldn't. His wife stood up in the audience and said, "What Mr. Richards is asking is fair; you ought to answer him." Even then he couldn't do it.

I said to my companion, "Stand up and give me my coat and hat." It was wintertime. I said, "I'm willing to remain here till ten o'clock tomorrow morning, when I have to be in my own church, provided this debate can go forward on the basis that you set up, but if not, I'm going to leave and ask my companion to leave and ask our Saints to leave, and we'll leave it to you to settle with your people what's happened here tonight." He still couldn't do it, so we all walked out on him. I met him on the street time and time again after that, and he always ducked his head so he wouldn't have to speak to me.

Now, brothers and sisters, as you've listened to me this morning, I think you can understand why I tell our missionaries you never need to argue with anybody if you learn how to tell our story, and it's the sweetest story that has been told in this world since the resurrection of the Christ. It is true, and that is my testimony to you. I pray God to help you to do your part to share it with those who are yet in darkness, and I leave you my love and blessings in the name of the Lord Jesus Christ. Amen.

Brigham Young University 1981–82 Fireside and Devotional Speeches, 27–32.

O B E D I E N C E

❧ ❧

THE POTTER AND THE CLAY

HEBER C. KIMBALL

This discourse was delivered in the "Old Tabernacle" in Salt Lake City on April 2, 1854. This tabernacle stood on Temple Square but predated the Tabernacle as we now know it, which was constructed between 1863 and 1867. Heber C. Kimball, then a member of the First Presidency, was a potter by trade, and he frequently referred to the Saints as "clay in the hands of the potter." He drew this figure from the writings of Jeremiah:

"The word which came to Jeremiah from the Lord, saying, Arise, and go down to the potter's house, and there I will cause thee to hear my words. Then I went down to the potter's house, and, behold, he wrought a work on the wheels. And the vessel that he made of clay was marred in the hand of the potter: so he made it again another vessel, as seemed good to the potter to make it. Then the word of the Lord came to me, saying, O house of Israel, cannot I do with you as this potter? saith the Lord. Behold, as the clay is in the potter's hand, so are ye in mine hand, O house of Israel." (Jeremiah 18:1–3.)

———————

To me it would be one of the best and most joyful things in the world, if men and women who call themselves "Mormons," or Latter-day Saints, would live up to their profession, and learn to speak the truth as it is in Jesus Christ, and do His will on the earth, as it is done in heaven.

I ask you, brethren and sisters, if you expect to go into heaven, if you do not do His will on earth as it is done in heaven? Can those persons who pursue a course of carelessness, neglect of duty, and disobedience, when they depart from this life, expect that their spirits will associate with the spirits of the righteous in the spirit world? I do not expect it, and when you depart from this state of existence, you will find it out for yourselves. . . .

That man or woman who will not learn the principle of subjection, and become like clay in the hands of the potter, will be led astray. . . .

The Saints are receiving their endowment, and preparing for that which is in the future; to dwell in the heavens, and sit upon thrones, and reign over kingdoms and dominions, principalities and powers; and as this work progresses, the works of Satan will increase, and he will continue to present one thing after another, following up the work of God, and increasing means of deception, to lead astray such men and women, and take them captive. As the work of God increases in power and extent upon the earth, so will the works of Satan increase. I expect that tribulation will be upon the wicked, and continue from this time until they are swept off from the earth. I just as much expect these things as I do to see the sun rise and set tomorrow.

I would like to see all this people do right, and keep the commandments of God. I would like to see them fulfil their covenants, and live up to their vows and promises, and fulfil their obligations, for they have obligated themselves before God, and before angels, and before earthly witnesses, that they would do this. . . .

Comparing us to clay that is in the hands of the potter, if that clay is passive, I have power as a potter to mold it and make it into a vessel unto honor. Who is to mold these vessels? Is it God Himself in person, or is it His servants, His potters, or journeymen, in company with those He has placed to oversee the work? The great Master Potter dictates His servants, and it is for them to carry out His purposes, and make vessels according to His designs; and when they have done the work, they deliver it up to the Master for His acceptance; and if their works are not good, He does not accept them; the only works He accepts, are those that are prepared according to the design He gave. God will not be trifled with; neither will His servants; their words have got to be fulfilled, and they are the men that are to mold you, and tell you what shape to move in.

I do not know that I can compare it better than by the potter's business. It forms a good comparison. This is the course you must pursue, and I know of no other way that God has prepared for you to become sanctified, and molded, and fashioned, until you become modeled to the likeness of the Son of God, by those who are placed to lead you. This is a lesson *you* have to learn as well as myself.

When I know that I am doing just as I am told by him who is placed to lead this people, I am then a happy man, I am filled with peace, and can go about my business with joy and pleasure; I can lie down and rise again in peace, and be filled with gladness by night and by day. But when I have not done the things that are right, my conscience gnaws upon my feelings. This is the course for me to take. If it is the course for me to take, it is the course for every other Elder in Israel to take—it does not matter who he is, or where he came from; whether he be an American, an Englishman, Irishman, Frenchman or German, Jew or Gentile; to this you have got to bow, and you have got to bow down like the clay in the hands of the potter, that suffers the potter to mold it according to his own pleasure. You have all got to come to this; and if you do not come to it at this time, as sure as the sun ever rose and set, you will be cut from the wheel, and thrown back into the mill.

You have come from the mill, and you have been there grinding. For what purpose? To bring you into a passive condition. You have been gathered from the nations of the earth, from among the kindreds, tongues, and peoples of the world, to the Valley of the Great Salt Lake, to purify and sanctify yourselves, and become like the passive clay in the hands of the potter. Now suppose I subject myself enough, in the hands of the potter, to be shaped according as he was dictated by the Great Master potter that rules over all things in heaven and on earth, he would make me into a vessel of honor.

There are many vessels that are destroyed after they have been molded and shaped. Why? Because they are not contented with the shape the potter has given them, but straightway put themselves into a shape to please themselves; therefore they are beyond understanding what God designs, and they destroy themselves by the power of their own agency, for this is given to every man and woman, to do just as they please. That is all right, and all just. Well, then, you have to go through a great many modellings and shapes, then you have to be glazed and burned; and even in the burning, some vessels crack. What makes them crack? Because they are snappish; they would not crack, if they were not snappish and willful.

If you go to the potteries in Staffordshire, England, where the finest china ware is manufactured, you will see them take the coarsest materials about the pottery, and make a thing in the shape of a half bushel; then put the finest ware in these to secure it from danger in the burning operation. All the fine ware made in Europe and in China is burnt in this kind of vessel. After they are done with, they are cast away—they are vessels of wrath fitted for destruction. So God takes the wicked, and makes them protect the righteous, in the process of sanctifying, and burning, and purifying, and preparing them, and making them fit for the Master's use.

These saggars, as they are called, are compounded of refuse articles that have been cast out; so even they are good for something. The wicked are of use, for they are a rod in the hands of the Almighty to scourge the righteous, and prepare them for their

Master's use, that they may enter into the celestial world, and be crowned with glory in His presence.

Brethren who hold the Priesthood, how do you like to rebel against those who are placed over you in the Priesthood, to rule and guide you in the proper way? You Bishops, or Presiding Elder, Teacher, Deacon, Apostle, or Prophet, how do you appear when you rebel against your head? You look like the woman who rebels against her husband or Lord. It also makes the children as bad as the parents; for if the parents are rebellious against their superiors, the children will be rebellious against their parents. Because the parents do not pursue a proper course, God makes their children a scourge to them.

Parents, if you do not listen to counsel, and walk in the path the Priesthood marks out, the Lord will prepare a scourge for you, if it is in your own family, to chasten you, and bring you to a knowledge of the truth, that you may be humble and penitent, and keep the commandments of God. . . .

Do you expect to have peace and plenty, to continue to thrive, and increase in property, in life, in herds, in flocks, and in the comforts of this life, while you are disobedient to those placed over you? You may for a season, but there is a rod preparing for the rebellious, and the righteous will have to suffer with the guilty. I know that by experience.

I will tell you another thing that I know. While the righteous are taking the rod along with the wicked, and it comes upon them severely, (I have passed through it many times), they have joy, and peace, and consolation, and the Spirit of the Lord God rests mightily upon them, and is round about them, and they say, in the midst of it all, "We are determined, by the help of God, to keep His commandments, and by His help to do the will of our President." For if there is no man on God's footstool that will stand by him, and assist him, I am determined to do all that lies in my power to sustain him while I am upon the earth.

My prayer is, O Lord help me to do Thy will, and walk in the footsteps of my leader; light up my path, and help me to walk so that my feet may never slip, and to keep my tongue from speaking guile; that I may never be left to betray my brethren, who hold the Priesthood of the Son of God; but that I may always honor that Priesthood, magnify it, reverence it, and love it more than I do my life, or my [family]. If I do that, I know the Priesthood will honor me, and exalt me, and bring me back into the presence of God, and also those who listen to my counsel as I listen to the counsel of him whose right it is to dictate me. If brother Brigham should get a revelation containing the will of God concerning His servant Heber, it would be, "Let my servant Heber do all things whatsoever my servant Brigham shall require at his hands, for that is the will of his Father in Heaven." If that is the will of God concerning me, what is the will of God concerning you? It is the same.

Brethren of the Priesthood, let us rise up in the name of Israel's God, and dispense with everything that is not of God, and let us become one, even as the Father and the Son are one. If we take that course we shall triumph over hell, the grave, and over everything else that shall oppose our onward progress in earth, or in hell; there is nothing we need fear. I fear nothing only to grieve my Father who is in heaven, and my brethren who are upon the earth. . . .

Do you suppose I am afraid of the world? No. I have nothing to do with the world, with the devil, with any of his servants, nor with his commandments. All I have to do with is the Saints. I belong to the Kingdom of God, with my family, and with everything I possess on earth or in heaven, it is the Lord's, and I am His servant, and I devote all I have to Him, and to His cause, it is all at the service of this Church and people. . . .

I have not anything but what the Lord has given to me; He has given me my houses and my land. I have built my houses out of the elements that He organized when He organized the earth. My [family], myself, and all I own, belong to the Lord God; and when I lay down this tabernacle of clay, my spirit will return to God who gave it. What can I retain of this world when I have done with it in this mortal state? I do not know of anything I can take with me. I came into the world naked, and I shall go from it taking nothing with me. . . .

If we are united, and the Priesthood is united, and the families of this Church, with their husbands at their head, are united, we stand, and all hell, with the devil at their head, have nothing to do with us; they cannot move us. But if we are divided we fall.

What do you say to our being one, and clinging together? . . . Would we not be a happy company? It is that alone that will make you truly happy; and to be perfectly limber in the hands of the potter like clay. What makes the clay snap? Because it wants its own way; and you cannot be happy unless you submit to the law of God, and to the principles of His government.

When a person is miserable, wretched, and unhappy in himself, put him in what circumstances you please, and he is wretched still. If a person is poor, and composes his mind, and calmly submits to the providences of God, he will feel cheerful and happy in all circumstances, if he continues to keep the commandments of God. But you may fill the house of a dissatisfied person with everything the world can produce, and he will be miserable with all. All heaven could not satisfy discontented persons; they must first be satisfied with themselves, and content in the situation in which they are placed, and learn to acknowledge the hand of God in all things. . . .

May the Lord bless you. Amen.

Journal of Discourses, 2:150–54.

⚜

BLESSINGS OF THE GOSPEL OBTAINED ONLY BY COMPLIANCE TO THE LAW

LORENZO SNOW

This talk, given while Lorenzo Snow was an Apostle and assistant counselor to President Brigham Young, was delivered at general conference in Salt Lake City on April 7, 1879. President Snow explained that the *power* of the gospel enables us to keep the *laws* of the gospel: "When we once get it into our minds that we really have the power within ourselves through the gospel we have received, to conquer our passions, our appetites and in all things submit our will to the will of our Heavenly Father, . . . then the battle may be said to be half won." This talk was republished in the *Ensign* in October 1971.

A nd when Abram was ninety years old and nine, the Lord appeared to Abram, and said unto him, I am the Almighty God; walk before me, and be thou perfect." (Genesis 17:1.)

In connection with this I will quote part of the words of the Savior in his sermon on the Mount, as contained in the last verse of the fifth chapter of Matthew.

"Be ye therefore perfect, even as your Father which is in heaven is perfect." (Matthew 5:48.)

In occupying a short time this morning, I desire an interest in your faith and prayers.

We learn that the Lord appeared to Abraham and made him

very great promises, and that before he was prepared to receive them a certain requirement was made of him, that he should become perfect before the Lord. And the same requirement was made by the Savior of his disciples, that they should become perfect, even as he and his Father in Heaven were perfect. This I conceive to be a subject that concerns the Latter-day Saints; and I wish to offer a few remarks by way of suggestion, for the reflection of those whom it concerns.

The Lord proposes to confer the highest blessings upon the Latter-day Saints; but, like Abraham, we must prepare ourselves for them, and to do this the same law that was given to him of the Lord has been given to us for our observance. We also are required to arrive at a state of perfection before the Lord; and the Lord in this case, the same as in every other, has not made a requirement that cannot be complied with, but on the other hand, He has placed for the use of the Latter-day Saints the means by which they can conform to His holy order.

When the Lord made this requirement of Abraham, He gave him the means by which he could become qualified to obey that law and come up fully to the requirement. He had the privilege of the Holy Spirit, as we are told the Gospel was preached to Abraham, and through that Gospel he could obtain that divine aid which would enable him to understand the things of God, and without it no man could arrive at a state of perfection before the Lord.

So in reference to the Latter-day Saints, they could not possibly come up to such a moral and spiritual standard except through supernatural aid and assistance. Neither do we expect that the Latter-day Saints, at once will or can conform to this law under all circumstances. It requires time; it requires much patience and discipline of the mind and heart in order to obey this commandment. And although we may fail at first in our attempts, yet this should not discourage the Latter-day Saints from endeavoring to exercise a determination to comply with the great requirement.

Abraham, although he might have had faith to walk before the Lord according to this divine law, yet there were times when his faith was sorely tried, but still he was not discouraged because he exercised a determination to comply with the will of God. We may think that we cannot live up to the perfect law, that the work of perfecting ourselves is too difficult. This may be true in part, but the fact still remains that it is a command of the Almighty to us and we cannot ignore it. When we experience trying moments, then is the time for us to avail ourselves of that great privilege of calling upon the Lord for strength and understanding, intelligence and grace by which we can overcome the weakness of the flesh against which we have to make a continual warfare.

Abraham was called to leave his kindred and country. Had he not complied with this requirement, he would not have been approved of the Lord. But he did comply; and while he was leaving his home, he no doubt was living in obedience to this divine law of perfection. Had he failed in this, he certainly could not have obeyed the requirements of the Almighty. And while he was leaving his father's house, while he was subjecting himself to this trial, he was doing that which his own conscience and the Spirit of God justified him in doing, and nobody could have done better, providing he was doing no wrong when he was performing this labor.

When the Latter-day Saints received the Gospel in the nations afar, and when the voice of the Almighty to them was, to leave the lands of their fathers, to leave their kindred as Abraham did, so far as they complied with this requirement, so far they were walking in obedience to this law; and they were as perfect as men could be under the circumstances, and in the sphere in which they were acting, not that they were perfect in knowledge or power, etc.; but in their feelings, in their integrity, motives and determination. And while they were crossing the great deep, providing they did not murmur nor complain, but obeyed the counsels which were given them, and in every way comported themselves in a becoming manner, they were as perfect as God required them to be.

The Lord designs to bring us up into the celestial kingdom. He has made known, through direct revelation, that we are His offspring, begotten in the eternal worlds, that we have come to this earth for the special purpose of preparing ourselves to receive a fullness of our Father's glory when we shall return into his presence. Therefore, we must seek the ability to keep this law, to sanctify our motives, desires, feelings and affections, that they may be pure and holy, and our will in all things be subservient to the will of God, and have no will of our own except to do the will of our Father. Such a man in his sphere is perfect, and commands the blessing of God in all that he does and wherever he goes.

But we are subject to folly, to the weakness of the flesh, and we are more or less ignorant, thereby liable to err. Yes, but that is no reason why we should not feel desirous to comply with this command of God, especially seeing that he has placed within our reach the means of accomplishing this work. This I understand is the meaning of the word perfection, as expressed by our Savior and by the Lord to Abraham. A person may be perfect in regard to some things and not others. A person who obeys the word of wisdom faithfully, is perfect as far as that law is concerned. When we repented of our sins and were baptized for the remission of them, we were perfect as far as that matter was concerned. Now we are told by the Apostle John, that we are "the sons of God, and it doth not yet appear what we shall be: but we know that, when he shall appear, we shall be like him; for we shall see him as he is.

"And every man that hath this hope in him purifieth himself, even as he [Christ] is pure." (1 John 3:2–3.)

The Latter-day Saints expect to arrive at this state of perfection; we expect to become as our Father and God, fit and worthy children to dwell in his presence; we expect that when the Son of

God shall appear, we shall receive our bodies renewed and glorified, and that these vile bodies will be changed and become like unto his glorious body. (See Philippians 3:21.) These are our expectations.

Now let all present put this question to themselves. Are our expectations well founded? In other words, are we seeking to purify ourselves? How can a Latter-day Saint feel justified in himself unless he is seeking to purify himself even as God is pure—unless he is seeking to keep his conscience void of offense before God and man every day of his life. We doubtless, many of us, walk from day to day and from week to week, and from month to month, before God, feeling under no condemnation, comporting ourselves properly, and seeking earnestly and in all meekness for the Spirit of God to dictate our daily course; and yet there may be a certain time or times in our life, when we are greatly tried and perhaps overcome; even if this be so, that is no reason why we should not try again, and that, too, with redoubled energy and determination to accomplish our object.

There was the Apostle Peter, for instance, a man valiant for the truth, and a man who walked before God in a manner that met with his divine approval; he told the Savior on a certain occasion that though all men forsook him he would not. But the Savior, foreseeing what would happen, told him that on that same night, before the cock crowed, he would deny him thrice, and he did so. He proved himself unequal for the trial; but afterwards he gained power, and his mind was disciplined to that extent that such trials could not possibly affect him.

And if we could read in detail the life of Abraham, or the lives of other great and holy men, we would doubtless find that their efforts to be righteous were not always crowned with success. Hence we should not be discouraged if we should be overcome in a weak moment; but, on the contrary, straightway repent of the error or the wrong we may have committed, and as far as possible repair it, and then seek to God for renewed strength to go on and do better.

Abraham could walk perfectly before God day after day when he was leaving his father's house, and he showed evidences of a superior and well-disciplined mind in the course he suggested when his herdsmen quarreled with the herdsmen of his nephew, Lot. There came a time in Abraham's life, however, which must have been very trying; in fact, anything more severe can scarcely be conceived of; that was when the Lord called upon him to offer as a sacrifice his beloved and only son, even him through whom he [Abraham] expected the fulfillment of the great promise made him by the Lord; but through manifesting a proper disposition he was enabled to surmount the trial, and prove his faith and integrity to God. It can hardly be supposed that Abraham inherited such a state of mind from his idolatrous parents; but it is consistent to believe that under the blessing of God he was enabled to acquire it, after going through a similar warfare with the flesh as we are, and doubtless being overcome at times and then overcoming until he was enabled to stand so severe a test.

"Let this mind be in you," says the Apostle Paul, "which was also in Christ Jesus: Who, being in the form of God, thought it not robbery to be equal with God." (Philippians 2:5–6.)

Now every man that has this object before him will purify himself as God is pure, and try to walk perfectly before him. We have our little follies and our weaknesses; we should try to overcome them as fast as possible, and we should inculcate this feeling in the hearts of our children, that the fear of God may grow up with them from their very youth, and that they may learn to comport themselves properly before him under all circumstances. If the husband can live with his wife one day without quarreling or without treating anyone unkindly or without grieving the Spirit of God in any way, that is well so far; he is so far perfect. Then let him try to be the same the next day. But supposing he should fail in this

his next day's attempt? That is no reason why he should not succeed in doing so the third day. If the Apostle Peter had become
discouraged at his manifest failure to maintain the position that he
had taken to stand by the Savior under all circumstances, he would
have lost all; whereas, by repenting and persevering he lost nothing but gained all, leaving us too to profit by his experience.

The Latter-day Saints should cultivate this ambition constantly which was so clearly set forth by the apostles in former
days. We should try to walk each day so that our conscience would
be void of offense before everybody. And God has placed in the
Church certain means by which we can be assisted, namely,
apostles, and prophets, and evangelists, etc., "for the perfecting of
the Saints," etc. And he has also conferred upon us his Holy Spirit
which is an unerring guide, standing, as an angel of God, at our
side, telling us what to do, and affording us strength and succor
when adverse circumstances arise in our way.

We must not allow ourselves to be discouraged whenever we
discover our weakness. We can scarcely find an instance in all the
glorious examples set us by the prophets, ancient or modern,
wherein they permitted the Evil One to discourage them; but on
the other hand they constantly sought to overcome, to win the
prize, and thus prepare themselves for a fulness of glory. The
Prophet Elijah succeeded. He so walked before God that he was
worthy to be translated. And Enoch was found worthy to walk
with God some 300 years, and was at last, with his people, taken
up to heaven.

We are told that in the latter days "there shall be no more
thence an infant of days, nor an old man that hath not filled his
days: for the child shall die an hundred years old." (Isaiah 65:20.)
And in another scripture we are told that the age of the infant
shall be as the age of a tree, and that it shall not die until it shall
be old, and then it shall not slumber in the dust but be changed in
the twinkling of an eye. (See D&C 101:30–31.) But in those days

people must live perfectly before the Lord, for we are told in the same passage "the sinner," instead of being favored, "being an hundred years old, shall be accursed." (Isaiah 65:20.)

When we once get it into our minds that we really have the power within ourselves through the gospel we have received, to conquer our passions, our appetites and in all things submit our will to the will of our Heavenly Father, and, instead of being the means of generating unpleasant feeling in our family circle, and those with whom we are associated, but assisting greatly to create a little heaven upon earth, then the battle may be said to be half won.

One of the chief difficulties that many suffer from is, that we are too apt to forget the great object of life, the motive of our Heavenly Father in sending us here to put on mortality, as well as the holy calling with which we have been called; and hence, instead of rising above the little transitory things of time, we too often allow ourselves to come down to the level of the world without availing ourselves of the divine help which God has instituted, which alone can enable us to overcome them. We are no better than the rest of the world if we do not cultivate the feeling to be perfect, even as our Father in Heaven is perfect.

This was the exhortation of the Savior to the former-day Saints, who were a people of like passions and who were subject to the same temptations as ourselves, and he knew whether the people could conform to it or not; the Lord never has, nor will he require things of his children which it is impossible for them to perform. The Elders of Israel who expect to go forth to preach the gospel of salvation in the midst of a crooked and perverse generation, among a people who are full of evil and corruption, should cultivate this spirit especially. And not only they, but everybody, every young man and woman belonging to this Church who is worthy to be called a Saint should cultivate this desire to live up to this requirement that their consciences may be clear before God. It is a beautiful thing, either in young or old, to have this object in view; it is especially delightful to see our young people take a course that the light and intelligence of God can beam in their countenances, that they may have a correct understanding of life, and be able to live above the follies and vanities of the world and the errors and wickedness of man.

May God bless you, brethren and sisters, and pour out His Holy Spirit upon you, that you may be blessed in all your acts, in your incomings and your outgoings and in the performance of every duty, and be blessed in calling upon the Almighty, that His Spirit may be in you as a well of water springing up to everlasting life, to guide you in His fear through all the scenes of life, is my prayer, in the name of Jesus. Amen.

Journal of Discourses, 20:187–92.

PRIESTHOOD

~❦❧~

PRINCIPLES OF PRIESTHOOD

JOSEPH SMITH

This address was delivered on Monday morning, October 5, 1840, at a general conference of the Church in Nauvoo, Illinois. The speech was written by Joseph Smith but was read by Robert B. Thompson, a personal secretary to the Prophet. Robert Thompson was married to Mercy Fielding, sister of Mary Fielding, and thus was an uncle to President Joseph F. Smith, whose talks are also represented in this volume.

———————

I n order to investigate the subject of the Priesthood, so important to this, as well as every succeeding generation, I shall proceed to trace the subject as far as I possibly can from the Old and New Testaments.

There are two Priesthoods spoken of in the Scriptures, viz., the Melchizedek and the Aaronic or Levitical. Although there are two Priesthoods, yet the Melchizedek Priesthood comprehends the Aaronic or Levitical Priesthood, and is the grand head, and holds the highest authority which pertains to the Priesthood, and the keys of the Kingdom of God in all ages of the world to the latest posterity on the earth, and is the channel through which all knowledge, doctrine, the plan of salvation, and every important matter is revealed from heaven.

Its institution was prior to "the foundation of this earth, or the morning stars sang together, or the Sons of God shouted for joy," and is the highest and holiest Priesthood, and is after the order of the Son of God, and all other Priesthoods are only parts, ramifica-tions, powers and blessings belonging to the same, and are held, controlled, and directed by it. It is the channel through which the Almighty commenced revealing His glory at the beginning of the creation of this earth, and through which He has continued to reveal Himself to the children of men to the present time, and through which He will make known His purposes to the end of time.

Commencing with Adam, who was the first man, who is spo-ken of in Daniel as being the "Ancient of Days," or in other words, the first and oldest of all, the great, grand progenitor of whom it is said in another place he is Michael, because he was the first and father of all, not only by progeny, but the first to hold the spiritual blessings, to whom was made known the plan of ordinances for the salvation of his posterity unto the end, and to whom Christ was first revealed, and through whom Christ has been revealed from heaven, and will continue to be revealed from henceforth. Adam holds the keys of the dispensation of the fullness of times; i.e., the dispensation of all the times have been and will be revealed through him from the beginning to Christ, and from Christ to the end of all the dispensations that are to be revealed. "Having made known unto us the mystery of His will, according to His good pleasure which He hath purposed in Himself: that in the dispen-sation of the fullness of times He might gather together in one all things in Christ, both which are in heaven, and which are on earth; even in him." (Ephesians 1:9–10.)

Now the purpose in Himself in the winding up scene of the last dispensation is that all things pertaining to that dispensation should be conducted precisely in accordance with the preceding dispensations.

And again, God purposed in Himself that there should not be an eternal fullness until every dispensation should be fulfilled and gathered together in one, and that all things whatsoever, that should be gathered together in one in those dispensations unto the same fullness and eternal glory, should be in Christ Jesus; therefore He set the ordinances to be the same forever and ever, and set Adam to watch over them, to reveal them from heaven to man, or to send angels to reveal them. "Are they not all ministering spirits, sent forth to minister for them who shall be heirs of salvation?" (Hebrews 1:14.)

These angels are under the direction of Michael or Adam, who acts under the direction of the Lord. From the above quotation we learn that Paul perfectly understood the purposes of God in relation to His connection with man, and that glorious and perfect order which He established in Himself, whereby He sent forth power, revelations, and glory.

God will not acknowledge that which He has not called, ordained, and chosen. In the beginning God called Adam by His own voice. "And the Lord called unto Adam and said unto him, Where art thou? And he said, I heard thy voice in the garden, and I was afraid because I was naked, and hid myself." (See Genesis 3:9–10.) Adam received commandments and instructions from God: this was the order from the beginning.

That he received revelations, commandments and ordinances at the beginning is beyond the power of controversy; else how did they begin to offer sacrifices to God in an acceptable manner? And if they offered sacrifices they must be authorized by ordination. We read in Genesis (4:4) that Abel brought of the firstlings of the flock and the fat thereof, and the Lord had respect to Abel and to his offering. And, again, "By faith Abel offered unto God a more excellent sacrifice than Cain, by which he obtained witness that he was righteous, God testifying of his gifts; and by it he being dead, yet speaketh." (Hebrews 11:4.) How doth he yet speak? Why he magnified the Priesthood which was conferred upon him, and died a righteous man, and therefore has become an angel of God by receiving his body from the dead, holding still the keys of his dispensation; and was sent down from heaven unto Paul to minister consoling words, and to commit unto him a knowledge of the mysteries of godliness.

And if this was not the case, I would ask, how did Paul know so much about Abel, and why should he talk about his speaking after he was dead? Hence, that he spoke after he was dead must be by being sent down out of heaven to administer.

This, then, is the nature of the Priesthood; every man holding the Presidency of his dispensation, and one man holding the Presidency of them all, even Adam: and Adam receiving his Presidency and authority from the Lord, but cannot receive a fullness until Christ shall present the Kingdom to the Father, which shall be at the end of the last dispensation.

The power, glory and blessings of the Priesthood could not continue with those who received ordination only as their righteousness continued; for Cain also being authorized to offer sacrifice, but not offering it in righteousness, was cursed. It signifies, then, that the ordinances must be kept in the very way God has appointed; otherwise their Priesthood will prove a cursing instead of a blessing.

If Cain had fulfilled the law of righteousness as did Enoch, he could have walked with God all the days of his life, and never failed of a blessing. "And Enoch walked with God after he begat Methuselah 300 years, and begat sons and daughters, and all the days of Enoch were 365 years; and Enoch walked with God, and he was not, for God took him." (Genesis 5:22.) Now this Enoch God reserved unto Himself, that he should not die at that time, and appointed unto him a ministry unto terrestrial bodies, of whom there has been but little revealed. He is reserved also unto the Presidency of a dispensation, and more shall he said of him and terrestrial bodies in another treatise. He is a ministering angel, to minister to those who shall be heirs of salvation and appeared unto Jude as Abel did unto Paul; therefore Jude spoke of him (Jude

1:14–15.) And Enoch, the seventh from Adam, revealed these sayings: "Behold, the Lord cometh with ten thousands of His saints."

Paul was also acquainted with this character, and received instructions from him. "By faith Enoch was translated, that he should not see death, and was not found, because God had translated him; for before his translation he had this testimony, that he pleased God; but without faith, it is impossible to please Him, for he that cometh to God must believe that He is, and that he is a revealer to those who diligently seek him." (Hebrews 11:5–6.)

Now the doctrine of translation is a power which belongs to this Priesthood. There are many things which belong to the powers of the Priesthood and the keys thereof that have been kept hid from before the foundation of the world; they are hid from the wise and prudent to be revealed in the last times.

Many have supposed that the doctrine of translation was a doctrine whereby men were taken immediately into the presence of God, and into an eternal fullness, but this is a mistaken idea. Their place of habitation is that of the terrestrial order, and a place prepared for such characters He held in reserve to be ministering angels unto many planets, and who as yet have not entered into so great a fullness as those who are resurrected from the dead. "Others were tortured, not accepting deliverance, that they might obtain a better resurrection." (See Hebrews 11:35.)

Now it was evident that there was a better resurrection, or else God would not have revealed it unto Paul. Wherein then, can it be said a better resurrection? This distinction is made between the doctrine of the actual resurrection and translation: translation obtains deliverance from the tortures and sufferings of the body, but their existence will prolong as to the labors and toils of the ministry, before they can enter into so great a rest and glory.

On the other hand, those who were tortured, not accepting deliverance, received an immediate rest from their labors. "And I heard a voice from heaven, saying, Blessed are the dead who die in the Lord, for from henceforth they do rest from their labors and their works do follow them." (See Revelation 14:13.)

They rest from their labors for a long time, and yet their work is held in reserve for them, that they are permitted to do the same work, after they receive a resurrection for their bodies. But we shall leave this subject and the subject of the terrestrial bodies for another time, in order to treat upon them more fully.

The next great, grand Patriarch [after Enoch] who held the keys of the Priesthood was Lamech. "And Lamech lived one hundred and eighty-two years and begat a son, and he called his name Noah, saying, this same shall comfort us concerning our work and the toil of our hands because of the ground which the Lord has cursed." (See Genesis 5:28–29.) The Priesthood continued from Lamech to Noah: "And God said unto Noah, The end of all flesh is before me, for the earth is filled with violence through them, and behold I will destroy them with the earth." (Genesis 6:13.)

Thus we behold the keys of this Priesthood consisted in obtaining the voice of Jehovah, that He talked with him [Noah] in a familiar and friendly manner, that He continued to him the keys, the covenants, the power and the glory, with which he blessed Adam at the beginning; and the offering of sacrifice, which also shall be continued at the last time; for all the ordinances and duties that ever have been required by the Priesthood, under the directions and commandments of the Almighty in any of the dispensations, shall all be had in the last dispensation, therefore all things had under the authority of the Priesthood at any former period, shall be had again, bringing to pass the restoration spoken of by the mouth of all the Holy Prophets; then shall the sons of Levi offer an acceptable offering to the Lord. "And he shall sit as a refiner and purifier of silver: and he shall purify the sons of Levi, and purge them as gold and silver, that they may offer unto the Lord." (See Malachi 3:3.)

It will be necessary here to make a few observations on the

doctrine set forth in the above quotation, and it is generally supposed that sacrifice was entirely done away when the Great
Sacrifice [i.e., the sacrifice of the Lord Jesus] was offered up, and
that there will be no necessity for the ordinance of sacrifice in [the]
future; but those who assert this are certainly not acquainted with
the duties, privileges and authority of the priesthood, or with the
Prophets.

The offering of sacrifice has ever been connected and forms a
part of the duties of the Priesthood. It began with the Priesthood,
and will be continued until after the coming of Christ, from generation to generation. We frequently have mention made of the
offering of sacrifice by the servants of the Most High in ancient
days, prior to the law of Moses; which ordinances will be continued when the Priesthood is restored with all its authority, power
and blessings.

Elijah was the last Prophet that held the keys of the
Priesthood, and who will, before the last dispensation, restore the
authority and deliver the keys of the Priesthood, in order that all
the ordinances may be attended to in righteousness. It is true that
the Savior had authority and power to bestow this blessing; but the
sons of Levi were too prejudiced. "And I will send Elijah the
Prophet before the great and terrible day of the Lord," etc., etc.
Why send Elijah? Because he holds the keys of the authority to
administer in all the ordinances of the Priesthood; and without the
authority is given, the ordinances could not be administered in
righteousness.

It is a very prevalent opinion that the sacrifices which were
offered were entirely consumed. This was not the case; if you read
Leviticus, second chapter, second and third verses, you will observe
that the priests took a part as a memorial and offered it up before
the Lord, while the remainder was kept for the maintenance of the
priests; so that the offerings and sacrifices are not all consumed

upon the altar—but the blood is sprinkled, and the fat and certain other portions are consumed.

These sacrifices, as well as every ordinance belonging to the Priesthood, will, when the Temple of the Lord shall be built, and the sons of Levi be purified, be fully restored and attended to in all their powers, ramifications, and blessings. This ever did and ever will exist when the powers of the Melchizedek Priesthood are sufficiently manifest; else how can the restitution of all things spoken of by the Holy Prophets be brought to pass? It is not to be understood that the law of Moses will be established again with all its rites and variety of ceremonies; this has never been spoken of by the Prophets; but those things which existed prior to Moses' day, namely, sacrifice, will be continued.

It may be asked by some, what necessity for sacrifice, since the Great Sacrifice was offered? In answer to which, if repentance, baptism, and faith existed prior to the days of Christ, what necessity for them since that time? The Priesthood has descended in a regular line from father to son, through their succeeding generations.

History of the Church, 4:207–12.

RESURRECTION

～❦ ❦～

OUR INDESTRUCTIBLE,
IMMORTAL IDENTITY

JOSEPH F. SMITH

This comforting message was given at the funeral of Rachel
Ridgeway Ivins Grant, who died at age eighty-seven on January
27, 1909. Sister Grant, the mother of Heber J. Grant, had been
married to Jedediah M. Grant of the First Presidency from
November 1855 until his death in December of the following
year. At the time of Jedediah's death, Heber was only nine days
old. Sister Grant remained a widow from 1856 until her death
in 1909. For thirty-five of those years she served faithfully as
president of her ward Relief Society; for the last forty years of
her life she was almost completely deaf. "She bore it all, however, with that great patience and calmness so characteristic of
her noble life," the *Improvement Era* recorded. "[She was a] true
soldier of the cause and [a] choice jewel of God." (June 1909,
585–86.)

I trust that I may be able to control my feelings and that I may say
just a few words in connection with the many most pleasing and
excellent things that have been said. I have felt especially and
rather peculiarly touched since hearing of the sickness and death of
Aunt Rachel Grant; not that the result of her sickness is anything
extraordinary or unusual at her period of life, but because memories
of the past are brought up, memories of relationships that have made
her rather more to me than a mere sister or friend. Her life's history,

altogether, may not be publicly known, and it is not my purpose to say anything especially of that, more than that the relationships and ties that have been formed here under the bond of the new and everlasting covenant are most sacred things of which the Lord himself will take cognizance and will adjust in the great future, according to his own wisdom and principles of righteousness.

I have learned to look upon Aunt Rachel as very near to me, from the days of my childhood. . . . Hers was a life exceptionally grand and pure and lovely. She was not only lovely in her appearance, and in her earthly being, but she was lovely in her spirit, her faith, her love of God, and in her integrity to the truth that she received in her youth. In heart and soul she has been true to these things all her life.

What a glorious thing it is to know and be true to that which has been revealed in these latter times through the instrumentality of the Prophet Joseph Smith. It was revealed anciently by the Savior himself, and he exemplified that glorious principle of which I wish to say a few words, and which has been renewed and emphasized more especially in these latter-days through Joseph Smith—I refer to our identity, our indestructible, immortal identity. As in Christ we have the example, he was born of woman, he lived, he died, and he lived again in his own person and being, bearing even the marks of the wounds in his flesh, after his resurrection from the dead—so also a testimony has been given to you in latter days through the Prophet Joseph Smith and others who have been blest with knowledge that the same individual being still lives and will always live. Jesus is possessed of immortality, and eternal life; and in evidence of his existence and his immortality, and in evidence of the great and glorious truths of the gospel which he taught, the death which he died, and the resurrection that he wrought from the dead, he has revealed himself and borne his own record and testimony to those who have lived and still live in this day and age.

What a glorious thought it is, to me at least, and it must be to all who have conceived of the truth or received it in their hearts, that those from whom we have to part here, we will meet again and see as they are. We will meet the same identical being that we associated with here in the flesh—not some other soul, some other being, or the same being in some other form, but the same identity and the same form and likeness, the same person we knew and were associated with in our mortal existence, even to the wounds in the flesh. Not that a person will always be marred by scars, wounds, deformities, defects or infirmities, for these will be removed in their course, in their proper time, according to the merciful providence of God. Deformity will be removed; defects will be eliminated, and men and women shall attain to the perfection of their spirits, to the perfection that God designed in the beginning.

It is his purpose that men and women, his children, born to become heirs of God, and joint heirs with Jesus Christ, shall be made perfect, physically as well as spiritually, through obedience to the law by which he has provided the means that perfection shall come to all his children. Therefore, I look for the time when our dear Brother William C. Staines, whom we all knew so well, and with whom we were familiar for years—I was familiar with him all my life, just as I was familiar with Aunt Rachel here all my life, and do not remember the time when I did not know her— I look for the time, I say, when Brother Staines will be restored. He will not remain the crippled and deformed William C. Staines that we knew, but he will be restored to his perfect frame—every limb, every joint, every part of his physical being will be restored to its perfect frame. This is the law and the word of God to us, as it is contained in the revelations that have come to us, through the Prophet Joseph Smith.

The point in my mind which I desire to speak of particularly is this: When we shall have the privilege to meet our mother, our aunt, our sister, this noble woman whose mortal remains lie here now, but whose immortal spirit has ascended to God from whence it came, when that spirit shall return to take up this tabernacle again, she will be Aunt Rachel in her perfection. She will not always remain just as she will appear when she is restored again to life, but she will go on to perfection. Under that law of restoration that God has provided, she will regain her perfection, the perfection of her youth, the perfection of her glory and of her being, until her resurrected body shall assume the exact stature of the spirit that possessed it here in its perfection, and thus we shall see the glorified, redeemed, exalted, perfected Aunt Rachel, mother, sister, saint and daughter of the living God, her identity being unchanged, as a child may grow to manhood or womanhood and still be the same being.

I want to say to my friends, my brethren and sisters, and to the kindred, that the Lord Almighty has revealed these truths to us in these days. We not only have it in the written word, we have it in the testimony of the Spirit of God in the heart of every soul who has drunk from the fountain of truth and light, and that witness bears record of these words to us.

What else would satisfy us? What else would satisfy the desire of the immortal soul? Would we be satisfied to be imperfect? Would we be satisfied to be decrepit? Would we be satisfied to remain for ever and ever in the form of infirmity incident to age? No!

Would we be satisfied to see the children we bury in their infancy remain as children only, throughout the countless ages of eternity? No! Neither would the spirit that did possess the tabernacles of our children be satisfied to remain in that condition. But we know our child will not be compelled to remain a child in stature always, for it was revealed from God, the fountain of truth, through Joseph Smith the prophet, in this dispensation, that in the resurrection of the dead the child that was buried in its infancy will come up in the form of the child that it was when it was laid down, then it will begin to develop.

From the day of the resurrection, the body will develop until it reaches the full measure of the stature of its spirit, whether it be male or female. If the spirit possessed the intelligence of God and the aspirations of mortal souls, it could not be satisfied with anything less than this.

You will remember we are told that the spirit of Jesus Christ visited one of the ancient prophets and revealed himself to him, and he declared his identity, that he was the same Son of God that was to come in the meridian of time. He said he would appear in the flesh just as he appeared to that prophet. He was not an infant; he was a grown, developed spirit; possessing the form of man and the form of God, the same form as when he came and took upon him a tabernacle and developed it to the full stature of his spirit.

These are truths that have been revealed to us. What for? To give us intelligent hope; to give us intelligent aspiration; to lead us to think, to hope, to labor and accomplish what God has aimed and does aim and design that we should accomplish, not only in this life, but in the life to come.

I rejoice exceedingly that I know and have known nearly all my life such a noble woman. I do not remember the first time that I saw Aunt Rachel, I can't recall it; it seems to me I always knew her, just as I knew my mother in my childhood and all the way through life; and I rejoice exceedingly in this testimony of the Spirit of the Lord that has come to us through revelation in the latter days. Through this testimony I am confident that I shall see Aunt Rachel by and by; and when I go—and I expect to go, perhaps, long before she shall recover this tabernacle—I expect to meet her there. I expect to meet the same individual that I knew here. I expect to be able to recognize her just as I could recognize her tomorrow, if she were living. I believe I will know just exactly whom she is and what she is, and I will remember all I knew about her; and enjoy her association in the spirit as I did in the flesh; because her identity is fixed and indestructible, just as fixed and indestructible as the identity of God the Father and Jesus Christ the Son. They cannot be any other than themselves. They cannot be changed; they are from everlasting to everlasting, eternally the same; so it will be with us. We will progress and develop and grow in wisdom and understanding, but our identity can never change.

We did not spring from spawn. Our spirits were from the beginning, have existed always, and will continue forever. We did not pass through the ordeals of embodiment in the lesser animals in order to reach the perfection to which we have attained in manhood and womanhood, in the image and likeness of God. God was and is our Father, and his children were begotten in the flesh in his own image and likeness, male and female. There may have been times when they did not possess the same intelligence that they possessed at other times. There are periods in the history of the world when men have dwindled into ignorance and barbarism, and then there were other times when they have grown in intelligence, developed in understanding, enlarged in spirit and comprehension, approaching nearer to the condition and likeness of their Father and God, and then losing faith, losing the love of God, losing the light of the Spirit and returning again to semi-barbarism. Then again, they have been restored, by the power and operation of the Spirit of the Lord upon their mind, until they again reached a degree of intelligence.

We have reached a degree of intelligence in our dispensation. Will this same degree of intelligence that now exists throughout the world continue to exist? Yes, if the world continues to abide in the light that has been shed abroad in the world by the Father of light, with whom there is no variableness nor shadow of turning. But let them deny God, let them deny truth, let them depart from righteousness, let them begin again to wallow in wickedness and transgression of the laws of God, and what will be the result? They

will degenerate; they will again recede possibly into absolute barbarism, unless they repent, and the power of God be again restored
to them and they be again lifted up by that light which shines and
is never dim, except to men who shut their hearts and eyes and
ears against it and will not receive it.

I did not expect to enter into any lengthy discourse. I thank
God for my relationship and acquaintance with this noble, good
mother. I expect to be associated with her throughout all the ages
to come, if I can be as faithful as she has been. I desire to be, and
that isn't all—with the help of God, *I intend* to be faithful, as she
has been faithful, that in the end I may be worthy to dwell where
she will dwell, with the Prophet Joseph Smith, with her husband
with whom she was associated here in the flesh, with her son and
her children, from generation to generation. I expect to be associated with them in the mansions that are prepared for the righteous, where God and Christ are, where those shall be who believe
in his name, who receive his work and abide in his law.

Oh! that I could be instrumental in the hands of the Lord in
bringing every loved soul unto him, for there are souls that are still
lacking, whom I love, and if it were possible, how I would love to
be instrumental in the hand of the Lord in bringing those loved
souls to a knowledge of this truth, that they might receive of its
glory, benefits and blessings in this life and in the life to come.
From my childhood, I have always tried to be a savior on Mount
Zion, a savior among men. I have that desire in my heart. I may
not have been very successful in my ambition to accomplish this
work, but I have desired it, and I still desire that I may be instrumental in helping to spread this truth to the earth's remotest
bounds and the testimony of it to the children of men in every
land. I know it is true. It appeals to my judgment, to my desires;
and to the aspirations of my soul. I want my family, I want those
the Lord has given to me; I want them now; I want them forever!

I want to be associated with them forever. I do not want them to change their identity. I do not want them to be somebody else.

This idea of theosophy, that is gaining ground even among so-called Christians, in these latter days, is a fallacy of the deepest kind. It is absolutely repugnant to the very soul of man to think that a civilized, intelligent being might become a dog, a cow, a cat; that he might be transformed into another shape, another kind of being. It is absolutely repulsive, and so opposed to the great truth of God, that has been revealed from the beginning, that he is from the beginning always the same, that he cannot change, and that his children cannot change. They may change from worse to better; they may change from evil to good, from unrighteousness to righteousness, from humanity to immortality, from death to life everlasting. They may progress in the manner in which God has progressed; they may grow and advance, but their identity can never be changed, worlds without end—remember that.

God has revealed these principles, and I know they are true. They assert their truth upon the intelligent mind and soul of man. They embrace or embody that which the Lord has planted in our hearts and souls to desire. . . . They put us in the way of receiving that which we most desire and most love, that which is most necessary and essential to our happiness and exaltation. They take of the things of God and give them to us, and they prepare us for the future, for exaltation and for eternal happiness, a reward which all the souls in the world desire, if they are correct in their lives and thoughts.

It is only the vicious and the truly wicked who do not desire purity; they do not love purity and truth. I do not know whether it is possible for any soul to become so debased as to lose all regard for that which is pure and chaste, good and true and godlike. I believe that there still lingers in the heart of the most vicious and wicked, at times at least, a spark of that divinity that has been planted in the souls of all the sons of God. Men may become so corrupt that they do not have more than mere glimpses of that divine inspiration that strives to lead them toward and to love good; but I do not believe there is a soul in the world that has absolutely lost all conception and admiration of that which is good and pure, when he sees it. It is hard to believe that a human being may become so depraved that he has lost all desire that he might also be good and pure, if it were possible; but many people have abandoned themselves to evil and have come to the conclusion that there is no chance for them.

While there is life there is hope, and while there is repentance there is a chance for forgiveness; and if there is forgiveness, there is a chance for growth and development until we acquire the full knowledge of those principles that will exalt and save us and prepare us to enter into the presence of God the Father, who is the Father of our spirits, and who is the Father, in the flesh, of his Only Begotten Son, Jesus Christ, who joined divine immortality with the mortal, welded the link between God and man, and made it possible for mortal souls, on whom the sentence of death had been placed, to acquire eternal life, through obedience to his laws. Let us, therefore, seek for the truth and walk in the light as Christ is in the light, that we may have fellowship with him, and with each other, that his blood may cleanse us from all sin.

May the Lord comfort my Brother Heber, and I know he will. Brother Heber does not feel that there is any death here. I don't think I could weep for sorrow. I could give way to tears just now, but they would not be tears of sorrow, of mourning or of grief, for this good soul. They would only express the love I have for her; they would only indicate my feelings toward her, for the noble and pure example she set before me and all who have known her. I could weep for joy in the knowledge that I possess that she, in her spirit life and being, is and will be associated with all those who have been endeared to her by the persecutions, the experiences and the trials through which she has had to pass in this world.

With them she is rejoicing today, as one born out of death into life everlasting.

She is not dead; she lives! What greater proof do you want of that fact than to see her lifeless form? Where is she? This is her casket. This is mortal tenement; this is but the clay that enveloped the immortal, living Aunt Rachel, the living spirit. The spirit has fled. Her spirit, the immortal part, has departed from this tabernacle; hence, this tabernacle lies here lifeless and ready to return to mother earth from whence it came, but to be restored again, every element to be recalled and reformed in its perfect frame, when Aunt Rachel will come and take possession of it and inherit it forever, just as Christ came and took up his body that was not suffered to see corruption, and inherited it in its immortal state, never to be separated again; so it will be with her.

God bless you, my brethren and sisters. May he help us to be faithful to the light of truth and walk uprightly in it, is my prayer in the name of Jesus. Amen.

Improvement Era, June 1909, 591–99.

REVELATION

~e %~

HOW TO KNOW THE
THINGS OF GOD

JOHN TAYLOR

Elder John Taylor delivered this address in the Tabernacle in Salt Lake City on May 6, 1870, when he was still a member of the Quorum of the Twelve. Elder Taylor had a philosophical turn of mind, as this talk shows, but he also spoke with understanding and power: "We consider, and always have since this Church was organized, that that part of Scripture that I quoted before is true—namely, 'No man knows the things of God but by the Spirit of God.' We, as Latter-day Saints, understood no correct principle until it was revealed to us."

The Scriptures inform us "that no man knows the things of God, but by the Spirit of God"; and then no man can speak the things of God unless aided by the Spirit of the Lord; and no people can comprehend the things spoken unless inspired and guided by the same Spirit. We need this Spirit continually and so do all mankind, to guide us, to enable us to comprehend the laws of life, to regulate and concentrate our thoughts, to elevate and ennoble our feelings, to give force and vitality to our actions, and to place us in a position before God, before men, and before the holy angels, that will be right, acceptable and proper to all true intelligence, to the angelic host, and to our Heavenly Father. It matters very little what we are engaged in, it is impossible for us to do right without the guidance of the Almighty;

but aided and directed by the Spirit of the Lord, we can act in consonance with the dignity of our high position as immortal beings possessing the holy Priesthood, and participating in the new and everlasting covenant; by the aid of that unerring Spirit we can fulfil the measure of our creation and prepare ourselves for an inheritance in the celestial kingdom of our God.

We are told "that the world by wisdom knows not God"; yet they do comprehend a great many things, and because of the spread of general intelligence and the great progress of science, literature and the arts, they believe they can find out God. Like the framers of Babel's Tower, they seek to penetrate the heavens on natural principles. Like them they are mistaken, as all men have been who have sought to solve the problem of life through the influence of human wisdom. No man ever did understand God on this principle; neither can they by mortal agency alone understand the principles of life and salvation. No man in the present generation comprehends them on this principle; neither will human wisdom enable any man who ever will live to understand them.

It is true that mankind, within a short time, have made great advances in the arts and sciences. During the last half century scientific research has made many wonderful developments; and many things which, before that time, were unknown to the human family, are now quite familiar. There was very little known of the application of the power of steam half a century ago. I remember, very well, the first steamboat and locomotive that were propelled by steam, and riding on the first railway. Before that, locomotion had to depend upon the winds and tides and horse power and a few other agencies. These are now supplanted by what all will acknowledge as a very superior agent—namely, the power of steam.

Electricity, or rather its application, so as to subserve the wants of man, was unknown until a comparatively recent period. I refer now more particularly to the electric telegraph. That has been a means of greatly facilitating the transmission of thought and the spread of intelligence among the human family, and has been a great advantage to the world at large. When we came to this valley, for instance, even so late as that, we had to depend upon ox teams to bring our mails and to convey intelligence from the East, and I have known it to be four, five, and sometimes as long as six months before we knew what President was elected. Now we can have it in fewer minutes; this exhibits a great improvement in such matters.

I can remember the time when we had to plod along at night, nearly in the dark, in our largest cities, the streets being lighted only by dim oil lamps. Now we have gas and various luminous oils, which we have made the earth teem forth by millions of gallons, that are almost equivalent to gas. Daguerreotyping, or as it is more generally called, photography, is another great achievement of the human mind, conferring the power to take likenesses, landscapes and views in a moment, which formerly required days or months, even by the most eminent artists.

In machinery and chemistry, manufactures, and many other scientific developments connected with human life, wonderful advances have been made, and the world seems to have been progressing with great rapidity in the arts and sciences, in regard to manufactures. Some years ago every texture had to be spun by a single thread; now, by the aid of steam and machinery, it is done by thousands and hundreds of thousands. We might go on enumerating many other improvements which have taken place within the past few years; from which it is very evident that the progress of the present generation has far eclipsed that of any preceding it, of which we have any knowledge.

Because of these things it has been supposed by many that the human intellect is capable of grasping everything in this world and the world to come—even eternal things, and many men have got puffed up and vain in their imaginations because of the discoveries they have made and the advancement in science, literature and the arts. They forget "that every good and perfect gift proceeds from God, the Father of light, in whom there is no variableness nor the shadow of a turning." They forget that every particle of wisdom that any man possesses comes from God, and that without Him they would still continue to grope in the dark. They forget that, with all the increase of wisdom and intelligence and the expansion of the human mind, they are in the dark in regard to God, and that no man by wisdom can find Him out. The mystery which enshrouds Him is as high as heaven, as deep as hell and as wide as the universe; and it is unfathomable and incomprehensible by human intelligence, unaided by the inspiration of the Almighty.

There are men, it is true, who profess from the little knowledge they have of earthly things, by a series of deductions, to be able to find out heavenly things, but there is a very material difference between the two. There is a philosophy of the earth and a philosophy of the heavens; the latter can unravel all mysteries pertaining to earth; but the philosophy of the earth cannot enter into the mysteries of the kingdom of God, or the purposes of the Most High. But because of the advancement to which I have alluded, men set themselves up as teachers of things pertaining to spiritual matters, of which they know nothing. But the moment they do that, they exhibit their folly, vanity, imbecility and shortsightedness, for, as I have stated, they never did comprehend the things of God without the Spirit of God, and they never will.

What folly it is, for men with the breath in their nostrils, who are but worms of the earth, existing as it were for a day, and tomorrow are cut down like the grass; or like the moth or butterfly, which flutters around for a brief space and then passes away into everlasting oblivion; I say what folly it is for beings so circumstanced, so weak, imbecile, circumscribed and controlled to set themselves forward, unaided by the Spirit of the Almighty, to fathom the designs of God, to unravel the principles of eternal life, to comprehend the relationship that subsists between God and man and to draw aside the curtain of futurity.

Who is there who has seen God or can comprehend Him, His designs and purposes? No man is capable of fathoming these mysteries. Man, indeed, can comprehend some of the principles which are developed in nature, and only a few of these. But who can grasp the intelligence that dwells in the bosom of Jehovah? Who can unravel His designs and penetrate the unfathomable abyss of the future? Who can tell upon what principle this world was organized or anything about the denizens of those worlds that we see moving around us? It is true that by the science of astronomy nice calculation in regard to the heavenly bodies can be made; but none can tell who put those bodies in motion, how they are controlled, or by what class of people they are inhabited. As the Scriptures say, "What man, by his wisdom, can find out God?" No one can comprehend Him.

We can find ourselves to be a remarkable enigma, both in regard to body and mind—each individual man, woman and child; but who can draw aside the veil and tell how or why we came here, and what awaits us when we lay aside this mortal coil? None can do this, unless God reveals it. There never was a man, neither is there a man now, nor ever will be, that can comprehend these things upon the principle of natural or human philosophy, and nothing short of the philosophy of heaven—the intelligence that flows from God, can unravel these mysteries.

Some men will stultify themselves with the idea that in ages gone and past the human race was in a semi-civilized or barbarous condition, and that any kind of a religion would do for the people in those days; but with the progress of intelligence, the march of intellect, the development of the arts and sciences and the expansion of the human mind, it is necessary that we should have something more elevated, refined and intellectual than that which existed then. To me such notions are perfect foolishness. If I read my Bible aright and believe in it, known unto God were all things from before the foundation of the world, and I do not think that the intelligence of the nineteenth century can enlighten His mind in relation to these matters.

He that framed the body, shall He not know its structure? He that organized the mind, shall not He understand it? Before this world rolled into existence or the morning stars sang together for joy, the great Eloheim comprehended all things pertaining to the world that He organized and the people who should inhabit it; the position that they would occupy and the intelligence that they would possess; their future destiny and the destiny of the world that He then made.

It is vanity, puerility and weakness for men to attempt to gain-say the designs of God, or to boast of their own intelligence. What do they know? Why, they discovered a while ago that there is such a thing as electricity. Who made that electricity? Did man? Did he originate and place it among the nature's forces? Did it proceed from the acumen of man's intelligence and his expansive mind? No, it always existed, and the man who discovered it—a little smarter than his fellows—only found out one of the laws of nature that emanated from and originated with God. It is just so with steam—the properties which render it so useful in subserving man's purposes always existed, but man discovered them; if there had been no God to make these properties, no one could have found them out. It is so with the various gases and their properties, with minerals—their attractions and repulsions—they originated with God; man is incompetent to form anything of the kind.

So we might go on through all man's boasted achievements; they amount to no more than the discovery of some of the active or latent laws of nature, not comprehended by men generally, but discovered by some who consider themselves, and they no doubt are, smarter than their fellows. Where, then, is the boasted intelligence of man?

Science reveals the beauty and harmony of the world material; it unveils to us ten thousand mysteries in the kingdom of nature, and shows that all forms of life through fire and analogous decay are returned again to its bosom. It unfolds to us the mysteries of cloud and rains, dew and frost, growth and decay, and reveals the operation of those silent irresistible forces which give vitality to the world. It reveals to us the more wonderful operations of distant orbs and their relations to the forces of nature.

It also reveals another grand principle, that the laws of nature are immutable and unchangeable as are all the works of God. Those principles and powers and forces have undergone no change since they were first organized, or, if changed, they have returned again to the original elements from which they were derived. All of the properties of nature were as perfect at the creation as now; all the elements of nature possessed the same specific properties, affinities and capacity of combination that they do at present. Trees, shrubs, plants, flowers, birds, beasts, fishes and man were as perfect then as now. God's works are all perfect and governed by eternal laws.

It reminds me of an infant; I can compare it to nothing else. The newborn child is perfectly oblivious to anything and everything around it, although marvelous in its organization and perfect in its structure. By and by it holds up its hand and discovers for the first time that it has a hand. It had it before, but a new light bursts upon the brain of the child, and it discovers it has a hand, and no doubt thinks it is wonderful wise in finding it out, just as some of our philosophers do when they discover the properties of matter.

But God made the child's hand, and it was in existence before its brain was capable of comprehending it. And so were all these things, about the discovery of which men boast so much. God made them and made them perfect. Yet men will boast that they know things independent of God, whereas unless they had been aided by the Spirit of the Lord, and unless the principles had existed they never could have been found out, for no man could have originated them himself. All that man has ever done, with all his boasted intelligence, has been simply to develop or find out a few of the common principles of nature that always have existed, and always will exist, for these things and every principle of nature are eternal.

The Gospel is also eternal. But where is there a man who understands heavenly things? Who can unravel them? Who has been behind the veil and talked with the Gods? Who among the wise men, philosophers, divines, philanthropists, kings, rulers or authorities of the earth can comprehend God or His designs? If we can understand so imperfectly the laws of nature with which we are surrounded, with the privileges of seeing, feeling, comparing and analyzing, what do we know of things beyond our vision, hearing, or comprehension?

We can read, in the history of the past, of the rise and fall of nations, of the downfall of thrones and of the destruction of kingdoms; we can read of wars and rumors of wars. History points out what has transpired in relation to the nations of the earth and to men who have lived upon it, but who can penetrate into the future? Man is an immortal being: he is destined to live in time and throughout all eternity. He possesses not only a body, but a soul that will exist while "life or thought or being lasts, or immortality endures." Who can tell in relation to this future? Who can tell things pertaining to our heavenly existence, or the object God had in view for creating this and other worlds, and the destiny of the human family? No man, except God reveals it to him.

What has been and still is the position of the world in relation to these things? It has been governed by every kind of dogma and theory of religion. "Isms" of every kind have prevailed in turn— polytheism, infidelity, Christianity in its ten thousand forms, and every kind of theory and dogma that the human imagination could invent. Such contrarieties show definitely and positively that men, by wisdom, cannot find out God. . . .

We consider, and always have since this Church was organized, that that part of Scripture that I quoted before is true—namely, "No man knows the things of God but by the Spirit of God." We, as Latter-day Saints, understood no correct principle until it was revealed to us. I did not, nor have I ever met with anybody that did, and I have traveled very extensively over the world that we live in, and have met with all classes and grades of men in different nations. We, as Latter-day Saints, are indebted to the revelations of God, given unto Joseph Smith, for the knowledge of the very first principles of the doctrine of Christ, and he could not have known it unless it had been revealed to him. One thing I did know of myself before I came into this Church, and that is more than a great many know of themselves—namely, that I was a fool, and did not know anything unless God revealed it. It takes a great deal of hammering to get that into some men's minds. The main questions in my mind, when this Gospel came, were, "Is this true?" "Is this from God, or is it not?" "Has God, indeed, spoken as this man says He has?" If He has not, it is all a fiction, a farce and delusion, like the other "isms" that exist in the world; if He has, it is for me to obey, no matter what the consequences may be.

There is one thing that has always been satisfactory to my mind in relation to this Gospel—there has never been one principle revealed, at any time, but what has been instructive and in accordance with the Scriptures, which we consider to be of divine origin. Never one principle but what could be substantiated by the word of God, although we did not know it before, and the world does not know it now. And I may also say that there has never been a principle revealed but what has been strictly philosophical and is in accordance with good, sound common sense; and, furthermore, I will go on beyond that and say that no principle ever will be revealed but what will be in accordance with philosophy, if we can comprehend it. As there is a philosophy of the earth and a philosophy of the heavens, it needs heavenly instruction to comprehend the heavenly things. But, as I said before, "no man knows the things of God, but by the Spirit of God." The Scriptures show unto us how we may obtain that Spirit, which will give us a knowledge for ourselves.

When this Gospel was revealed, it was declared unto us that it was an everlasting Gospel, that there was a Priesthood associated with it, and that that Priesthood was everlasting; so we were presented with an everlasting Priesthood, and with an everlasting Gospel. There was also an everlasting covenant associated with it. We were told how we might obtain a knowledge of this Gospel for ourselves—the promise being that if we would repent of our sins and be baptized in the name of Jesus Christ for the remission of them, by one having authority, we should receive the Holy Ghost. We were also told that that Holy Ghost would place us in communication with God; that it would take of the things of God and show them unto us, and that we should know for a certainty, each of us for ourselves, of the truths that had been proclaimed unto us.

This was the position that we were placed in. We went forward and obeyed it, for we were told that God had revealed Himself from the heavens, that He had restored the Gospel by the means of a holy angel, as referred to by John the Revelator, and that He had restored, by authority direct from heaven, communication between Himself, the heavenly world and His creatures here. We were told that by obedience to that Gospel we should be made the recipients of a Spirit which would bring things past to our remembrance, that would lead us into all truth and show us things to come.

Believing in this message, this vast crowd of people before me today, went forth and bowed in obedience, and they received that Spirit, and they knew and do know that the Gospel they had preached unto them came not in word only, but in power and in the demonstration of the Spirit, and that the Holy Ghost accompanied it. You know, and I know, that when you obeyed this Gospel and had hands laid upon you for the reception of the Holy Ghost, you received it. Who else knows anything about it? Nobody. Do any of these strangers around? No.

Jesus said to Nicodemus, "Except a man is born again, he can not see the kingdom of God." Then what do they know about it? You talk to a blind man about colors, and ask him to tell the difference between red and white, black and blue, and he would tell you perhaps that one was long and the other short, that one was light and the other heavy. He could not describe, nor his sense comprehend it. Jesus said a man could not see the kingdom of God unless he was born of the Spirit. Did he speak the truth? I think he did. And when you were born again of the water and of the Spirit, you saw and you entered into the kingdom of God, and things that you were ignorant of before, you then comprehended.

Many of you felt a good deal like the blind man spoken of in the Scriptures, after he had been healed by our Savior. The Scribes and Pharisees, a learned and very holy body of men—spoke to his father, saying, "Give God the glory, for we know that this man is a sinner." They knew that Jesus was an imposter, a deceiver, a false prophet, a blasphemer, and that he cast out devils through Beelzebub, the prince of devils, and that he was one of the wickedest, meanest curses in existence. "Give God the glory," said they, "for we know this man is a sinner." The father of him who had been healed of his blindness said, "Whether he is a sinner, I know not; but this I do know, that whereas this my son was once blind and now he sees."

Now a great many of you here are very much deluded in the estimation of the philosophers, wise men and priests of the world; but if you do not comprehend the philosophy of the whole matter, one thing you all know—that once you were blind, but now you see. You understood that years ago and you understand it today, and no man can deprive you of that knowledge, or strip you of that information. No man can rob you of that light: it is the gift of God, it emanates from Jehovah, and no man can take it away, or reason or legislate it away; it is an eternal principle, emanating from God, and that is something the worldly-wise and great know nothing about. You who are here today, who have obeyed this Gospel, are witnesses of the truth of which I speak; I am a witness and I bear witness to it.

We are told that Jesus said on a certain occasion to his disciples, "It is necessary that I go away, for if I go not away the Comforter will not come. If I go away I will send you a Comforter, which is the Holy Ghost." What will it do for you? It will lead you into all truth, so that you will see eye to eye and comprehend the purposes of God; you will march in line; you will be under one instructor; you will have one Lord, one faith, one baptism; one God who is in all and through all, will inspire and guide and dictate you; you will not be split up and divided as the sectarians are—every man taking his own course, every man for himself and the devil for the whole; it will not be setting up human intellect above the intelligence and inspiration of the Almighty. Instead of this, all will bow to the dictates of Jehovah; the aspiration of every heart will be, "O, God, thou that rulest in the heavens; O, thou Supreme Governor of the universe, that created all things and controls all things, impart to me a small moiety of Thy wisdom! Inspire me with a little of that intelligence that dwells in Thy bosom! Give me a little of Thy Holy Spirit, that I may comprehend Thee and Thy laws, and walk in obedience to Thy commands!" This will be the feeling of that individual. "O, God, teach me the paths of life and then give power to walk in them!"

Jesus told them they should have the Holy Ghost, the Comforter; the Spirit should bring things past to their remembrance, it should enable them to comprehend something about the world and why it was organized and by whom; why man was placed upon it; what the position of the human family is in relation to the present, past and future; find out what God's dealings had been with the human family in ages gone and past, and His designs in relation to the world. Then it should unfold things to come, it should draw back the curtain of futurity and by the inspiration and intelligence of that Spirit which proceeds from God, it should grasp the future. It should comprehend the destiny of the human family, and by the revelations which God should communicate, make known the life to come in the eternal worlds. This is the kind of thing that the everlasting Gospel communicates, and it is the revelation of God to man. But the world, as I said before, know not the things of God, and they cannot comprehend them.

I have had it asked me by philosophers, "Is this the only way you propose to ameliorate the condition of the human family— faith in the Lord Jesus Christ, baptism for the remission of sins and the laying on of hands for the reception of the Holy Ghost?" Yes, that is God's way of doing it; that is the way He has pointed out.

I remember, on one occasion, being in the city of Paris, and a gentleman came to me to inquire concerning the Gospel. He was associated with a system of socialism, very common in France, called Icarianism. A company of them went to Nauvoo after we left. This gentleman was a philosopher, and the society was trying to carry out its philosophy in France, and they aimed to bring about the Millennium. They never prayed to God; they were going to do it by human intelligence. This gentleman, whose name was Krolikrosky, called upon me, when after a lengthy conversation on the principles of our faith, said he, referring to faith, repentance, baptism and the laying on of hands for the reception of the Holy Ghost, the first principles of our Gospel: "Is this all you propose to ameliorate the condition of the world?"

"Yes."

He answered, "I hope you will succeed, but I am afraid you will not."

"Permit me," I said, "to draw your attention to one or two things. I am a religionist."

"Yes."

"I profess to have had revelation from God; you do not."

"That is so," said he.

"You have sent out to Nauvoo a number of your most intellectual men, well provided with means of every kind and with talent of the first order. Now what is the result? They have gone to a place that we have deserted; they found houses built, gardens and farms enclosed, nothing to do but to take possession of them?"

"Yes."

"They found buildings of all kinds, public and private, in which they could live and congregate?"

"Yes."

"Was there ever a people better situated in regard to testing your natural philosophy? You could not have hit upon a better place. It is a fertile country, on the banks of the most magnificent stream in the United States—the Mississippi. Houses built, gardens made, fields enclosed and cultivated. You have wise men among you—the wisest, the *crème de la crème* of your society, yet with all this and the favorable circumstances under which your people commenced there, what have you done? Every time that I take up a paper of yours the cry from there is, 'Send us means'; 'we want means'; 'we are in difficulty'; 'we want more money.' This is their eternal cry, is it not?"

"Yes."

"Now," said I, "on the other hand, we left our farms, houses, gardens, fields, orchards, and everything we had, except what we took along in the shape of food, seeds, farming utensils, wagons, carts, and we wandered for from ten to fifteen hundred miles, with hand-carts, ox teams and any way we could, and settled, finally, among the red savages of the forest. We had no fields to go to and no houses built; when we went there it was a desert—a howling wilderness, and the natives with which we were surrounded were as savage as the country itself. Now then, what is the result? We have only been there a few years, but what are we doing? We are sending money to bring in our emigration; we are sending hundreds of thousands of dollars, and have expended half a million a year in teams to bring in our poor from the nations. But what of you wise men who know not God, and think you know better than He does, what are you doing—you philosophers, intelligent men and philanthropists, crying out eternally, 'Send us help'? Which is the best?"

Said he, "Mr. Taylor, I have nothing to say."

We care nothing about the opinions of men; let them look upon us as they may. We can say as the old Apostle said, "We are living epistles, known and read of all men." Judge us by our works. Do thieves, renegades, blacklegs and corrupt men accomplish the work done here? Where are your Gentile associations? Here we have a magnificent city called Corinne, instituted by you gentlemen Gentiles here. What a magnificent place it is! It looks as if Tophet has been spewed out to people it with *honorable* American citizens! Yet these men will prate to us about morality, the poor miserable curses! O, shame, if thou hadst any blood in thy body, thou wouldst blush for very shame at the transactions of this world in which we live.

But we believe in God, and you Latter-day Saints, your religion is as true as it was ten, twenty, thirty, or eighteen hundred or six thousand years ago. It has not changed, and I do not think that it will. It is everlasting; it is eternal in its nature and its consequences, and, whether other men know what they are doing or not, we do. If others do not attend to eternity, we do; if others know nothing about God, we do, and we know where we are going and how we are going. God has pointed out to us the path, and we intend to walk in it, in spite of all the powers of earth and hell.

God has taught us the relationship that should exist between us and the eternal worlds. That is a thing that is very much found fault with. He has unveiled the future to us and told us that man is not made for here alone, and then to die and rot and be forgotten, or to sing himself away somewhere beyond the bounds of time and space where nobody ever was nor ever will be. We have been taught something different from that. We are aiming at eternal exaltation, at thrones, principalities and powers in the eternal worlds. Being made in the image of God, male and female, and having had developed to us the laws of this life and the laws of the life to come, we take the privilege of walking according to these laws, despite the ideas and notions of men.

Who is there among the men of the world who know anything about the future? I know how it was with me, and how it was with you, Jew, Gentile, Mormon, everybody. What was it! If you applied to the priesthood of the day to be married, the priest told you he joined you in the holy bonds of matrimony until death. And what then? You had to find out the rest by your own ingenuity. No matter about the future. Is that all man was made for—to live, marry and die—and nothing pertaining to the future? Is man made in the image of God? Is God our Father? Is there a heaven above? Is there an eternity before us, and are we to prepare ourselves for it or not? We take the liberty of following the counsel of Jehovah, revealed to us in relation to it.

What man has a claim upon his wife in eternity? It is true that some of the writers of the yellow-backed literature have a philosophy a little in advance of the priests of the day. Some of them do tell us about eternal unions. They expect to be married here and hereafter. They know nothing about it; still they are in advance of the clergy. They follow the instincts of nature, and nature unperverted looks forward to a reunion. We are not governed by opinion in these matters. God has revealed the principle, and our wives are sealed to us for time and eternity. When we get through with this life we expect to be associated in the next, and therefore we pursue the course that we do, and no power this side of hell, nor there either, can stop it.

Our course is onward. The Lord has revealed to us the pearl of great price. We have sacrificed everything that the world calls good to purchase it; we are in possession and we will not part with it for worlds. We "fear not men, who can kill the body," as Jesus said; and after that there is no more that they can do. We fear God who is able to cast both soul and body into hell. Yea, we fear Him.

We make our covenants, then, for eternity, because the Gospel is an everlasting Gospel. Every truth that ever did exist is everlasting. Man is an eternal being; his body is eternal. It may die and slumber, but it will burst the barriers of the tomb and come forth in the resurrection of the just. I know that some of our wise men, even some among us, profess to think that these things are only folly. However, I look at them differently. I believe the Bible; I believe in the revelations of God and in the manifestations of the Spirit of God. I would rather possess the feeling that Job had when he was afflicted, cast out, oppressed and despoiled, when he lay scraping himself with a potsherd, wallowing in ashes, than the proud and lofty folly that dwells in the heart of the unbeliever and scorner. Said Job, "I know that my Redeemer lives, and that He shall stand in the latter days upon the earth; and though after my skin worms destroy this body, yet in my flesh shall I see God; whom I shall see for myself and mine eyes shall behold, not for another; and though worms destroy this body, yet in my flesh shall I see God." Those were his feelings. This transpired in the "dark ages," when men did not know so much about electricity, locomotives and a few other scientific discoveries, as they do in this enlightened age.

I also read in the sayings of the prophets, given under the

inspiration of the Almighty, that "the dead, small and great, shall rise, and that bone shall be joined to its bone, sinew to sinew, and they became a living army before God." I knew a man, whom many of you knew, who built a tomb for himself in the city of Nauvoo. His name was Joseph Smith, and many of you heard him say what I shall now relate. Said he, "I expect when the time of the resurrection comes to rise up in my tomb *there*, and strike hands with my brethren, with my father and with my mother, and hail the day when we shall burst from the barriers of the tomb and awake to immortal life." Have you never heard him talk thus? I have. Shall we reject from our belief the glorious principles of eternity—the resurrection of the just? Says John, when wrapt in prophetic vision, and clothed upon with the Spirit and power of God and the revelations of Jehovah, "I saw the dead, small and great, stand before God; and the sea gave up the dead which were in it; and death and hell delivered up the dead which were in them, and all nations stood before God."

I want a part in the resurrection. The angel said, "Blessed and holy is he who has part in the first resurrection." I want to have part in the first resurrection. It is that which leads me to hope. It is that hope which buoys me up under difficulties and sustains me while passing through tribulation, for I know as well as Job knew that my "Redeemer lives, and that He shall stand in the latter day upon the earth," and I know that I shall stand upon it with him. I therefore bear this testimony.

Allow me to quote a little Scripture. You know that there is a saying, by one of the Apostles, that Jesus was a priest for ever after the order of Melchizedek; and speaking further of this Melchizedek, the Apostle says he was "without father, without mother, without descent, having neither beginning of days nor end of years." A very singular sort of man, was he not? Did you ever see a man like that? We are told that Jesus was a priest for ever after the order of Melchizedek. Now, there never was a man without father or mother, but this refers to his Priesthood, which was without beginning of days or end of years, and Jesus had the same kind of Priesthood that Melchizedek had.

Now we talk about the everlasting Gospel, and we will go back to some of these dark ages referred to. The Melchizedek Priesthood holds the mysteries of the revelations of God. Wherever that Priesthood exists, there also exists a knowledge of the laws of God; and wherever the Gospel has existed, there has always been revelation; and where there has been no revelation, there never has been the true Gospel. Let us go back to those times. We find that the Gospel was preached unto Abraham, and that Melchizedek was the man to whom Abraham paid tithes, and that Melchizedek blessed him. Paul tells us, "Verily the less is blessed of the better." Now Abraham had the Gospel, and Melchizedek had it, and the law was added because of transgression; and by and by, when Jesus came, he was a priest for ever after the order of Melchizedek, and he restored the Gospel, and consequently revelations, the opening of the heavens and the manifestation of the power of God; and whenever the Gospel has existed, in any age of the world, these same manifestations have existed with it; and whenever these have not been upon the earth, there has been no Gospel. "The Gospel is the power of God unto salvation to every one that believes, for therein is the righteousness of God revealed from faith to faith."

In addition to Melchizedek, the Bible also mentions a man called Moses, and he had the Gospel, for Paul tells us "that he preached it to the children of Israel in the wilderness, but that it profited them nothing, not being mixed with faith." There was another man called Elijah, that we read of in the Bible. He was one of those fanatics who believe in revelation, and he had the Gospel. We come down to the time that Jesus was here on the earth; and on one occasion we read that he was on the mount with three of his disciples, Peter, James and John, and Jesus was transfigured before them. And Peter said, "Master, it is good for us to be here, let us make three tabernacles, one for thee, one for Moses and one for Elias." What? Was Moses, that old fellow who led the children of Israel from Egypt, there? That shows that he had the everlasting Gospel and Priesthood; and having got rid of the affairs of this world, he returned to minister to Jesus when he was on the earth. Was Elias there too? So Peter said. What was he doing there? He died long before, but having held the everlasting Priesthood he lived again, and lives for evermore.

We will go to another man. There are curious things in the Bible, if the people only believed them; but they do not, and that is the trouble. I refer to John, the beloved disciple. We are told that he was banished because he was a fanatic—I was going to say a Mormon—as John did not agree with the enlightenment, philosophy and intelligence that existed then. What did they do with him? They banished him and sent him to the Isle of Patmos; and compelled him to labor among the slaves in the lead mines; he was not fit for civilized society, but they could not deprive him of fellowship.

While there with the Almighty, he was carried away in the Spirit, and that Spirit manifested to him things past, for generations gone; things present—the condition of the churches that then existed; and also things to come—the world with all its myriads of inhabitants down to the winding-up scene. He saw the dead, small and great, stand before God, and the books were opened; and another book was opened, called the Book of Life; and he saw a hundred and forty-four thousand, and a number that no man can number, who sang a new song, and the glories of eternity, and the past, present and future were unveiled before his vision. He saw the new Jerusalem descend from above, and the Zion from above meeting the Zion from below, and they were married and became one. He saw the end of the nations, and of the world. "Cloud-capped towers and gorgeous palaces were dissolved," and everything passed away.

He gazed upon the whole; and a mighty angel stood before

him, and he was about to bow down before him and to worship him; but the angel said, "Stop, do not worship me!"

"Why? Who are you? You are a glorious personage; you are filled with greatness, and surrounded by majesty, glory and power, and the visions of eternity seem to be at your command, for you have unfolded them to me. Will you not let me worship you?"

"No."

"Who are you?"

"I am one of thy fellow-servants, the prophets, who kept the testimony of Jesus, and the word of God, while here upon the earth, and feared God and kept His commandments. Do not worship me, worship God." Said he, "I am one of those old fellows who were buffeted, persecuted and misrepresented just as you are; despised as you are by fools who knew nothing about God or eternity."

Well, now, we believe these things. We believe in a religion that will reach into eternity, that will bring us into connection with God. We believe that God has set up His kingdom on the earth; we believe and know that it will roll forth and spread and extend, that Zion will be built up, that the glory of God will rest upon it; that the arm of Jehovah will be made bare in its defense; that the power of God will be exerted in behalf of His people; that Zion will rise and shine, and that the glory of God will be manifested among His Saints. We know that this kingdom will grow and increase until the kingdoms of this world will become the kingdoms of our God and His Christ, and that He shall rule and reign for ever and ever. And we expect to join in the universal anthem, "Hosanna, hosanna, for the Lord God omnipotent reigneth," and will reign until all enemies are under His feet.

God bless Israel. God bless all His Saints, and let the wrath of God be upon the enemies of Zion from this time henceforth and for ever, in the name of Jesus. Amen.

Journal of Discourses, 13:220–33.

❧ ❦

FOLLOW THE SPIRIT

WILFORD WOODRUFF

This talk was given at the Bear Lake Stake conference in
Paris, Idaho, on Monday, August 10, 1891. President Wilford
Woodruff began his remarks by saying, "I am very pleased indeed
to meet with so many Latter-day Saints in this tabernacle on a
working day, and I hope you will get paid for coming to meeting
today. I have felt amply paid myself for my journey from Salt
Lake City in listening to the instructions which our brethren
have given unto us. I told Brother [George Q.] Cannon this
morning that if, when a young man, I could have attended a
meeting of this kind and heard instructions as we have had
given to us, I should have felt that I was in heaven; I should
have been satisfied that I had received what I had prayed for and
desired from my childhood."

When I was a boy I read in the New Testament concerning Jesus Christ and His gospel, and the gifts and
graces that were then manifested, and I felt that the
principles there taught were the ones that I desired to live to hear
taught. I prayed for this earnestly in my early manhood. I have
read the Bible through a good many times in my life. I have read
the Book of Mormon through a number of times. I have also read
the book of Doctrine and Covenants through a number of times;
and I have felt that God had never given unto us stronger principles and more glorious instructions in any of the revelations of
God than are recorded in the book of Doctrine and Covenants.
They are all by the same author, but to different men, and at

different times. I will read a few verses from the 121st section of the Doctrine and Covenants. This section contains the prayer and prophecy of the Prophet Joseph while he was in Liberty Jail; and the truths embodied therein are among the sublimest that God has ever revealed to man: [reads D&C 121:25–40].

Who can comprehend this grand language? Scarcely any person. The Lord says in this revelation that whether there be one God or many Gods, they shall be revealed; and all kingdoms, thrones, principalities and powers shall be revealed unto those who keep His commandments. Can we comprehend this? Why, there is not an astronomer that can tell us scarcely one thing that is done in Mars, or Venus, or Jupiter, or in any of the planets, aside from the earth. Here are worlds upon worlds—millions of them—and what do we know about them? Our own little planet, upon which we live, is about as much as we can comprehend. Look at the extent of the blessings that are promised us! These blessings and these revelations are worthy of the attention of the Latter-day Saints.

In this revelation it is shown that the Priesthood of which we have been speaking has power. It has power with the heavens; it has power on earth. And as was said this morning, it does not make any difference what portion of that Priesthood a man holds—whether it is a President, an Apostle, a High Priest, a Seventy, an Elder, a Priest, a Teacher or a Deacon—when he goes before God in prayer, with a pure heart, that Priesthood has power with the heavens. If a man magnifies that Priesthood, the blessings of God are with him.

The first sermon that I ever heard in this church was in 1833, by old father Zera Pulsipher, who died in the South after having lived to be considerably over eighty years old. That sermon was what I had prayed for from my childhood. When I heard it I had a testimony for myself that it was true. I received it with every sentiment of my heart. He preached in a school house upon a farm that we owned in Oswego County, New York. He opened the door for any remarks to be made. The house was crowded. The first thing I knew I stood on top of a bench before the people, not knowing what I got up for. But I said to my neighbors and friends, "I want you to be careful what you say as touching these men (there were two of them) and their testimony, for they are servants of God and they have testified unto us the truth—principles that I have been looking for from my childhood." I went forth and was baptized. I was ordained a Teacher. I was always sorry that I was not a Deacon first; for I had a desire to bear the Priesthood in its various degrees, as far as I was worthy.

I had had a desire for years, not only to hear the gospel, but to have the privilege and power of preaching it to my fellow men. I was a miller by trade, and I spent many a midnight hour in the mill calling upon the Lord for light and truth, and praying that I might hear the gospel of Christ and be able to teach it to my fellow men. I rejoiced in it when I did receive it.

I afterwards went with Zion's Camp to Missouri in the spring of 1834, with the Prophet Joseph, his brother Hyrum, and over two hundred of the Saints of God. That was a great mission to me. I was with the Prophet. I had read his revelations. I had read the vision recorded in this Book of Doctrine and Covenants, and it had given me more light and more knowledge with regard to the dealings of God with men than all the revelations I had ever read, in the Bible or anywhere else. I had been taught that there was one heaven and one hell; and everybody that was not sprinkled or baptized, infants and all, would have to go to hell. It made no difference whether the individual had committed no wrong, if he had not been received into the church by sprinkling or baptism, he would have to go to hell with the murderer, with the whoremonger, with the wickedest of men. On the other hand, everybody that was sprinkled would go to heaven. No matter if they had never made a single sacrifice for the gospel of Christ, they would have the same glory as Peter, James and John, who had sacrificed their lives for the gospel's sake. That was the kind of teaching I heard in my boyhood. I did not believe one word of it then; and I don't now. But this vision of which I speak opened my eyes. It showed me the power of God and the righteousness of God in dealing with the human family.

Before I saw Joseph I said I did not care how old he was, or how young he was; I did not care how he looked—whether his hair was long or short; the man that advanced that revelation was a prophet of God. I knew it for myself. I first met Joseph Smith in the streets of Kirtland. He had on an old hat, and a pistol in his hand. Said he, "Brother Woodruff, I've been out shooting at a mark, and I wanted to see if I could hit anything"; and says he, "Have you any objection to it?"

"Not at all," says I; "there is no law against a man shooting at a mark, that I know of."

He invited me to his house. He had a wolf skin, which he wanted me to help him to tan; he wanted it to sit on while driving his wagon team. Now, many might have said, "You are a pretty prophet; shooting a pistol and tanning a wolf skin." Well, we tanned it, and used it while making a journey of a thousand miles. This was my first acquaintance with the Prophet Joseph. And from that day until the present, with all the apostasies that we have had, and with all the difficulties and afflictions we have been called to pass through, I never saw a moment when I had any doubt with regard to this work. I have had no trial about this. While the people were apostatizing on the right hand and the left, and while Apostles were urging me to turn against the Prophet Joseph, it was no temptation to me to doubt this work or to doubt that Joseph Smith was a prophet of God.

As I have said, while holding the office of Teacher, I went to Missouri in Zion's Camp. After arriving in Missouri, having gone through many trials and tribulations, and suffering from cholera, which caused us to lay in the grave fifteen of our brethren, we stayed at brother Lyman Wight's. While at Lyman Wight's, I attended council meetings with the Prophet, with David Whitmer, with Oliver Cowdery and other leading brethren of the Church. David Whitmer was the President of the Stake of Zion. Brother Joseph reproved him very sharply, as well as some of the other brethren, because of their lack in fulfilling the commandments of God and doing their duty.

While at that place I had a great desire in my heart to go and preach the gospel. I went off one Sunday night by myself into a hickory grove, several hundred yards from the settlement, and I asked the Lord to open the door for me that I might go and preach the gospel. I did not want to preach the gospel for any honor I might get on this earth; for I thoroughly understood as far as a man could in my condition, what a preacher would have to pass through. It was not honor, nor wealth, nor gold, nor silver that I desired; but I knew this was the gospel of Christ, revealed to me by the power of God; I knew this was the Church of Christ; I knew Joseph Smith was a prophet of God; and I had a desire that I might preach that gospel to the nations of the earth. I asked the Lord to give me that privilege. The Lord answered that prayer and said I should have my desire granted. I got up rejoicing. I walked about two hundred yards out in the open road, and when I got into the road, there stood Judge Higbee. Says he, "Brother Woodruff, the Lord has revealed to me that it is your duty to be ordained to go and preach the gospel."

Says I, "Has He?"

"Yes."

"Well," says I, "if the Lord wants me to preach the gospel, I am perfectly willing to go and do that."

I did not tell him I had been praying for this. The consequence was, I attended a council at Lyman Wight's, and was called and ordained to the office of a Priest in the Aaronic Priesthood, while other brethren were ordained Elders. I was called by Bishop Partridge to go to the Southern country on a mission. Bishop Partridge asked me a great many questions, and I asked him questions. It was then dangerous for any of our brethren to go through Jackson County. He wanted me to go to Arkansas, and the road led square through Jackson County. I asked him if we should go through there (I had a companion with me—an Elder). Says he, "If you have got faith to do it, you may; I haven't." I thought that was a curious remark from a Bishop.

"Well," says I, "the Lord says we must travel without purse or scrip; shall we do it?"

Says he, "That is the law of God; if you have got faith to do it, you can do it." He said he had hardly got faith to go into Jackson County. However, we started and went through Jackson County. We came near losing our lives, and were saved almost by a miracle. We traveled through Arkansas and other parts.

But I do not want to dwell on these things. I merely wish to say that I went out as a Priest, and my companion as an Elder, and we traveled thousands of miles and had many things manifested to us. I desire to impress upon you the fact that it does not make any difference whether a man is a Priest or an Apostle, if he magnifies his calling. A Priest holds the keys of the ministering of angels. Never in my life, as an Apostle, as a Seventy, or as an Elder, have I ever had more of the protection of the Lord than while holding the office of a Priest. The Lord revealed to me, by visions, by revelations, and by the Holy Spirit, many things that lay before me.

I was once moved upon to go and warn old Father Hakeman, living on Petty-John Creek, Arkansas. He had been in Jackson County during the persecution period. His wife died there. His family consisted of five sons, all over six feet tall. Most of them had been whipped with hickory gads by mobs, and he went south into Arkansas, taking his sons with him. We went a good deal out of our way for the purpose of visiting Father Hakeman. I had a vision the night previous, in which was manifested to me the trouble that lay before us, but that the Lord would deliver us. We arrived at his house on Sunday morning. He was taking breakfast. We had had breakfast at the place where we stayed overnight. I saw a Book of Mormon on his shelf. He did not seem to pay any attention to us or to take any interest in us. I took up the Book of Mormon, and said, "You have a very good book here."

"Yes," said he, "but it is a book that came from the devil."

That opened my eyes. He had been an Elder; he had been in Zion; he had been persecuted there and driven out; but I found that he had apostatized, and he was our enemy. I saw he would do anything he could against us.

We left him and went to Brother Hubbard's and stayed with him three weeks, during which we took our axes and cleared some land for him. I was strongly impressed three times to go up and warn Father Hakeman. At last I did so, according to the commandment of God to me. The third time I met with him, his house seemed to be full of evil spirits, and I was troubled in spirit at the manifestation. When I finished my warning, I left him. He followed me from his house with the intention of killing me. I have no doubt about his intention, for it was shown to me in vision. When he came to where I was, he fell dead at my feet, as if he had been struck with a thunderbolt from heaven.

I was then a Priest, but God defended me and preserved my life. I speak of this because it is a principle that has been manifest in the Church of God in this generation as well as in others. I had the administration of angels while holding the office of a Priest. I had visions and revelations. I traveled thousands of miles. I baptized men, though I could not confirm them because I had not the authority to do it.

I speak of these things to show that a man should not be ashamed of any portion of the Priesthood. Our young men, if they are Deacons, should labor to fulfil that office. If they do that, they may then be called to the office of a Teacher, whose duty it is to teach the people, visit the Saints, and see that there is no evil or iniquity carried on. God has no respect to persons in this Priesthood any further than as they magnify their callings and do their duty.

It may be called egotism for a man to talk about himself; but I have a right to give my experience as you have a right to give yours; and I will give a little of mine to my friends, because I want our young men as well as our old men to understand that the Lord is not trifling with us at all. Brother Cannon has told you that it is the right of all the Latter-day Saints to have revelation. That is true. There is not a man, woman or child who has received the gospel, but has the right to receive revelation for himself or herself, as well as the Presidency of the Church. . . .

. . . What is revelation? It is the inspiration of the Holy Ghost to man. Joseph Smith said to Brother John Taylor in his day: "Brother Taylor, you watch the impression of the Spirit of God; you watch the whisperings of that Spirit to you; you carry them out in your life, and it will become a principle of revelation in you, and you will know and understand this Spirit and power." This is the key, the foundation stone of all revelation. Joseph Smith was full of revelation. He could translate anything given to him of God. He could receive revelation without the Urim and Thummim. Many of the principal revelations contained in the Doctrine and Covenants were received without the use of the Urim and Thummim. They were given to him by the inspiration of Almighty God.

In my own experience I have endeavored to get acquainted with that Spirit and to learn its operations. I have many times had that Spirit manifested to me, and if I had not followed its whisperings to me, I should have been in my grave long ago, with many of my companions. A few incidents I will name.

After I came to these valleys and returned to Winter Quarters, I was sent to Boston by President Young. He wanted me to take my family there and gather all the Saints of God in New England, in Canada, and in the surrounding regions, and stay there until I gathered them all. I was there about two years. While on the road there, I drove my carriage one evening into the yard of Brother Williams. Brother Orson Hyde drove a wagon by the side of mine. I had my wife and children in the carriage. After I turned out my team and had my supper, I went to bed in the carriage. I had not been there but a few minutes when the Spirit said to me, "Get up and move that carriage."

I told my wife I had to get up and move the carriage.

She said, "What for?"

I said, "I don't know." That is all she asked me on such occasions; when I told her I did not know, that was enough.

I got up and moved my carriage four or five rods and put the off fore wheel against the corner of the house. I then looked around me and went to bed. The same Spirit said, "Go and move your animals from that oak tree." They were two hundred yards from where my carriage was. I went and moved my horses and put them in a little hickory grove. I again went to bed. In thirty minutes a whirlwind came up and broke that oak tree off within two feet from the ground. It swept over three or four fences and fell square in that dooryard, near Brother Orson Hyde's wagon, and right where mine had stood. What would have been the consequences if I had not listened to that Spirit? Why, myself and wife and children doubtless would have been killed. That was the still, small voice to me—no earthquake, no thunder, no lightning; but the still, small voice of the Spirit of God. It saved my life. It was the spirit of revelation to me.

When I moved the last company of Saints from the East (there were about one hundred of them), we arrived at Pittsburgh one day at sundown. We did not want to stay there, so I went to the first steamboat that was going to leave. I saw the captain and engaged passage for us on that steamer. I had only just done so when the

Spirit said to me, and that too very strongly, "Don't go aboard that steamer, nor your company." Of course, I went and spoke to the captain and told him I had made up my mind to wait. Well, it started and had only got five miles down the river when it took fire and three hundred persons were burned to death or drowned. If I had not obeyed that Spirit and had gone on that steamer with the rest of the company, you can see what the result would have been.

Well, I have had a good deal of experience in these things in my day. I have learned them so thoroughly that I dare not disobey that Spirit. After one conference, when we had set apart a good many missionaries, I went home quite weary, and I said to myself, I will go and have a rest. Before I got in my house, the Spirit told me to take my team and go to my farm. My wife says, "Where are you going?"

"I am going down to the farm."

"What for?"

"I don't know," says I.

I went down to the farm. I found that the river had broken over and had surrounded my house. The water was two feet deep around my house. My hogs were drowning, and my stables were full. By going there I saved my house and surroundings and stopped up the break.

These may be considered small things; still they show the working of the Spirit. I will now tell you one incident where I did not obey the Spirit of the Lord, and it came pretty near costing me my life. I was over at Randolph one December, visiting. On Monday morning the Spirit said to me, "Take your team and go home." I made up my mind to do it; but some of my friends felt anxious that I should stop, as my visit had been rather short, and I was persuaded to stop. I stayed until Saturday morning; but I felt uneasy. That warning of the Spirit rested upon me to that degree that I felt condemned, and I told my friends that I was going home. I ate an early breakfast that morning, put my horses in my wagon, took some hay and grain, and started for home by way of Wasatch, which was some thirty miles from there. When I got to Woodruff, the Bishop wanted me to stay and hold meeting there on Sunday. "No," says I, "I have already stayed too long by one week."

Well, after I got about three miles from Woodruff, which is fifteen miles from Wasatch, I met with one of the most terrific snowstorms I ever saw in my life. It was not five minutes after it commenced before I could not see the road. I could not guide my horses at all, so I let them go where they pleased. They had been twice over the ground before. I shut down the wagon cover and went to praying. I asked the Lord to forgive me for not obeying His commandments. At eight o'clock my horses carried me into Wasatch, the hubs of the wheels being under the snow. I think they must have got there by inspiration. I stayed there until the Monday night. I made up my mind then that whenever the Lord told me to do anything I would do it.

I speak of this because every man should get the Spirit of God and then follow its dictates. This is revelation. It [doesn't] make any difference what the Spirit tells you to do, it will never tell you to do anything that is wrong. . . . This Priesthood has power on the earth; and when those holding this Priesthood go before the Lord and pray to Him, He will hear them and answer their prayers. This, brethren and sisters, is where our power lies. It is with God, not with man. He has heard us in the past, and we have been preserved and protected until the present time. We still live, notwithstanding all the exertions that have been made for our destruction. We live in these valleys of the mountains, and if we will do our duty we shall live here.

I want our young people and their parents to listen to the counsels that have been given concerning the Sabbath schools, the Mutual Improvement Associations and the Primaries. We are held responsible for the sons and daughters that have been given us. I meet with sons of President Kimball, with sons of President Young, with sons of President Taylor, and with sons of Apostles who have passed away. I rejoice when I meet them. Their fathers helped lay the foundation of this work. They labored to promote the interests and welfare of Zion. I rejoice to see their posterity on the earth. I hope all these young men bear a portion of the Priesthood, and that they will magnify their callings. The eyes of their fathers who dwell in the spirit world are over them. Their bodies are in the tomb; but their spirits are awake. They are mingling with the righteous. And they have an anxiety about the welfare of their children here. I am anxious myself to have the rising generation take hold of this work; and I hope we will not disappoint our Heavenly Father. We should read and study these revelations of God and lay them to heart, and inasmuch as we do this, they will prove of profit unto us.

Brethren and sisters, I am glad to meet with you, and to bear my testimony to you of the gospel of Christ. As I have often said, I have lived to more than the allotted age of man. I have lived while most everybody with whom I was acquainted in Kirtland and Nauvoo has passed to the other side of the veil. I expect to go there myself, the same as the rest of my brethren. But while I live I want to be true and faithful to my God and to the Saints.

One of the greatest blessings of God to me has been the fact that myself and counselors live in the hearts of the Latter-day Saints, and I have felt to be humbled in the dust before the Lord for this. We know that you pray for us. We know that you have respect for us. And we live upon this principle. God has led this Church from the beginning, by prophets and inspired men. He will lead this Church until the scene is wound up. He will neither permit me nor any other man to lead this Church astray. If I turn from the commandments of God and attempt to lead the people astray, the Lord will remove me out of my place, for the Lord has set His hand to lead this people by revelation and by inspired men.

The Lord has "chosen the weak things of the world to con-
found the things which are mighty; . . . and things which are not,
to bring to nought things that are." We feel our weaknesses. I wish
myself that I were a better man than I am. Of course, I have
endeavored to do about the best I could in my weak way. I still
wish to do so. But I am dependent upon the Lord and upon the
prayers of the Saints, the same as my brethren. I pray God to bless
you and me. I pray that He will seal upon the hearts of the Saints
of God the teachings that we have heard during this conference.
This is my prayer in the name of Jesus Christ. Amen.

Millennial Star, 23:627–44.

~☙ ❧~

CALL TO BE AN APOSTLE

HEBER J. GRANT

When President Grant spoke during general conference in October 1942, he was continuing to recuperate from a long illness. "I am grateful beyond my power of expression for the faith and prayers of the people and for the blessings of the Lord in my behalf," he said. "For two and one-half years I have been gaining a little since I became ill. I have been home since that illness overtook me a little longer than two years. . . . My improvement is very remarkable considering the condition I was in, and I attribute it to the prayers of the Saints in my behalf." A year and a half earlier, in April 1941, President Grant related one of the stories also found in this address. A portion of that April 1941 conference talk is included here to provide additional details.

I have decided to tell in detail one or two very remarkable things that have happened in my life.

I was made one of the apostles in October 1882. On October 6, 1882, I met Brother George Teasdale at the south gate of the temple. His face lit up, and he said: "Brother Grant, you and I"—very enthusiastically—and then he commenced coughing and choking, and went on into meeting and did not finish his sentence. It came to me as plainly as though he had said the words: "Are going to be chosen this afternoon to fill the vacancies in the Quorum of the Twelve Apostles."

I went to the meeting and my head swelled, and I thought to myself, "Well, I am going to be one of the apostles," and I was willing to vote for myself, but the conference adjourned without anyone being chosen.

Ten days later I received a telegram saying, "You must be in Salt Lake tomorrow without fail." I was then president of Tooele Stake. The telegram came from my partner, Nephi W. Clayton. When I got to the depot, I said: "Nephi, why on earth are you calling me back here? I had an appointment out in Tooele Stake."

"Never mind," he said; "it was not I who sent for you; it was Brother Lyman. He told me to send the telegram and sign my name to it. He told me to come and meet you and take you to the President's office. That is all I know."

So I went to the President's office, and there sat Brother Teasdale, and all of the ten Apostles, and the Presidency of the Church, and also Seymour B. Young and the members of the Seven Presidents of the Seventies. And the revelation was read calling Brother Teasdale and myself to the apostleship, and Brother Seymour B. Young to be one of the Seven Presidents of the Seventies.

Brother Teasdale was blessed by President John Taylor, and George Q. Cannon blessed me.

After the meeting I said to Brother Teasdale, "I know what you were going to say to me on the sixth of October when you happened to choke half to death and then went into the meeting."

He said, "Oh, no, you don't."

"Yes, I do," and I repeated it: "You and I are going to be called to the apostleship."

He said, "Well, that is what I was going to say, and then it occurred to me that I had no right to tell it, that I had received a manifestation from the Lord." He said, "Heber, I have suffered the tortures of the damned for ten days, thinking I could not tell the difference between a manifestation from the Lord and one from the devil, that the devil had deceived me."

I said, "I have not suffered like that, but I never prayed so hard in my life for anything as I did that the Lord would forgive me for the egotism of thinking that I was fit to be an apostle, and that I was ready to go into that meeting ten days ago and vote for myself to be an apostle."

I was a very unhappy man from October until February. For the next four months whenever I would bear my testimony of the divinity of the Savior, there seemed to be a voice that would say: "You lie, because you have never seen Him." One of the brethren had made the remark that unless a man had seen the Lamb of God—that was his expression—he was not fit to be an apostle. This feeling that I have mentioned would follow me. I would wake up in the night with the impression: "You do not know that Jesus is the Christ, the Son of God, because you have never seen Him," and the same feeling would come to me when I would preach and bear testimony. It worried me from October until the following February.

I was in Arizona in February, traveling with Brigham Young Jr., and a number of other brethren, visiting the Navajo Indians and the Moki Indians. Several of our party were riding in "White Tops" and several on horseback. I was in the rear of the party with Brother Lot Smith. He was on a big, fine, iron-grey horse, and I was on a small mule that I had discovered was the easiest and best riding animal I had ever straddled.

We were going due east when the road changed and went almost north, but there was a trail ahead of us, and I said, "Hold on, Lot; stop."

I said, "Brother Smith, where does this trail lead?"

He said, "It leads to a great gully just a short distance away, and no team can possibly travel over it. We have to make a regular mule shoe of a ride to get to the other side of the gully."

I said, "Is there any danger from Indians if a man were alone over there?"

"None at all."

I said: "I visited the spot yesterday where George A. Smith Jr., was killed by a Navajo Indian, who asked him for his pistol and then shot him with it, and I feel a little nervous, but if there is no danger I want to be all alone, so you go on with the party and I will take that trail."

I had this feeling that I ought not to testify any more about the Savior and that, really, I was not fit to be an apostle. It seemed overwhelming to me that I should be one. There was a spirit that said: "If you have not seen the Savior, why don't you resign your position?" . . .

As I was riding along to meet them on the other side, I seemed to see, and I seemed to hear, what to me is one of the most real things in all my life. I seemed to hear the words that were spoken. I listened to the discussion with a great deal of interest. The First Presidency and the Quorum of the Twelve Apostles had not been able to agree on two men to fill the vacancies in the Quorum of the Twelve. There had been a vacancy of one for two years, and a vacancy of two for one year, and the conferences had adjourned without the vacancies being filled. In this council the Savior was present, my father was there, and the Prophet Joseph Smith was there. They discussed the question that a mistake had been made in not filling those two vacancies and that in all probability it would be another six months before the Quorum would be completed. And they discussed as to whom they wanted to occupy those positions, and decided that the way to remedy the mistake that had been made in not filling these vacancies was to send a revelation. It was given to me that the Prophet Joseph Smith and my father mentioned me and requested that I be called to that position.

I sat there and wept for joy. It was given to me that I had done nothing to entitle me to that exalted position, except that I had lived a clean, sweet life. It was given to me that because of my father's having practically sacrificed his life in what was known as the great reformation, so to speak, of the people in early days, having been practically a martyr, that the Prophet Joseph and my father desired me to have that position, and it was because of their faithful labors that I was called, and not because of anything I had done of myself or any great thing that I had accomplished. It was also given to me that that was all these men, the Prophet and my father, could do for me. From that day it depended upon me and upon me alone as to whether I made a success of my life or a failure.

"There is a law, irrevocably decreed in heaven before the foundations of this world, upon which all blessings are predicated—and when we obtain any blessing from God, it is by obedience to that law upon which it is predicated." (D&C 130:20–21.)

It was given to me, as I say, that it now depended upon me.

No man could have been more unhappy than I was from October 1882 until February 1883, but from that day I have never been bothered, night or day, with the idea that I was not worthy to stand as an apostle, and I have not been worried since the last words uttered by Joseph F. Smith to me: "The Lord bless you, my boy, the Lord bless you; you have got a great responsibility. Always remember this is the Lord's work and not man's. The Lord is greater than any man. He knows whom He wants to lead His Church, and never makes any mistake. The Lord bless you." . . .

I can truthfully say that from February 1883 until today I have never had any of that trouble, and I can bear my testimony that I know that God lives, that Jesus is the Christ, the Savior of the world, and that Joseph Smith is a prophet of the living God; and the evil one does not try to persuade me that I do not know what I am talking about. I have never had one slight impression to the contrary. I have just had real, genuine joy and satisfaction in proclaiming the gospel and bearing my testimony of the divinity of Jesus Christ, and the divine calling of Joseph Smith, the prophet. . . .

May God's blessings be and abide with you, one and all, and all the Saints and all the honest people the world over, is the prayer of my heart, even so. Amen.

Conference Report, October 1942, 24–26; Conference Report, April 1941, 5.

~❦ ❧~

WHEN ARE CHURCH
LEADERS' WORDS ENTITLED
TO THE CLAIM OF SCRIPTURE?

J. REUBEN CLARK JR.

President J. Reuben Clark Jr. delivered this address at
Brigham Young University on July 7, 1954, to help seminary and
institute teachers understand when the words of Church leaders
should be considered the word of the Lord. As the Lord told
Joseph Smith, "Whatsoever they shall speak when moved upon
by the Holy Ghost shall be scripture, shall be the will of the
Lord, shall be the mind of the Lord, shall be the word of the
Lord, shall be the voice of the Lord, and the power of God unto
salvation." (D&C 68:4.)

President Clark explained, "The question is, how shall we
know when the things they have spoken were said as they were
'moved upon by the Holy Ghost'? I have given some thought
to this question, and the answer thereto so far as I can determine, is: We can tell when the speakers are 'moved upon by the
Holy Ghost' only when we, ourselves, are 'moved upon by
the Holy Ghost.' In a way, this completely shifts the responsibility from them to us to determine when they so speak." This
address has been quoted by various General Authorities, including Ezra Taft Benson and Harold B. Lee.

When are the writings and sermons of church leaders
entitled to the claim of being scripture?

I assume the scripture behind this question is the

declaration of the Lord in a revelation given through Joseph primarily to Orson Hyde, Luke S. Johnson, Lyman E. Johnson, and William E. McLellin, who were to engage in missionary work. After addressing a word first to Orson Hyde, the Lord continued:

> And, behold, and lo, this is an ensample unto all those who were ordained unto this priesthood, whose mission is appointed unto them to go forth—
>
> And this is the ensample unto them, that they shall speak as they are moved upon by the Holy Ghost.
>
> And whatsoever they shall speak when moved upon by the Holy Ghost shall be scripture, shall be the will of the Lord, shall be the mind of the Lord, shall be the word of the Lord, shall be the voice of the Lord, and the power of God unto salvation. (D&C 68:2–4.)

The very words of the revelation recognize that the Brethren may speak when they are not "moved upon by the Holy Ghost," yet only when they do so speak, as so "moved upon," is what they say Scripture. No exceptions are given to this rule or principle. It is universal in its application.

The question is, how shall we know when the things they have spoken were said as they were "moved upon by the Holy Ghost"?

I have given some thought to this question, and the answer thereto so far as I can determine, is: We can tell when the speakers are "moved upon by the Holy Ghost" only when we, ourselves, are "moved upon by the Holy Ghost."

In a way, this completely shifts the responsibility from them to us to determine when they so speak.

We might here profitably repeat what Brother Brigham preached. He said:

> Were your faith concentrated upon the proper object, your confidence unshaken, your lives pure and holy, every one fulfilling the duties of his or her calling according to the Priesthood and capacity bestowed upon you, you would be filled with the Holy Ghost, and it would be as impossible for any man to deceive and lead you to destruction as for a

feather to remain unconsumed in the midst of intense heat. (*Journal of Discourses*, 7:277.)

On another occasion he said:

I am more afraid that this people have so much confidence in their leaders that they will not inquire for themselves of God whether they are led by Him. I am fearful they settle down in a state of blind self-security, trusting their eternal destiny in the hands of their leaders with a reckless confidence that in itself would thwart the purposes of God in their salvation, and weaken that influence they could give to their leaders, did they know for themselves, by the revelations of Jesus, that they are led in the right way. Let every man and woman know, by the whisperings of the Spirit of God to themselves, whether their leaders are walking in the path the Lord dictates, or not. (*Journal of Discourses*, 9:150.)

So, we might leave this whole discussion here except that there are some collateral matters involved in the problem that it may not be entirely amiss to consider.

From the earliest days of the Church the Lord has given commandments and bestowed blessings that involved the operation of the principle behind our main question—the determination of whether our Brethren, when they speak, are "moved upon by the Holy Ghost."

Guidance by the Written Word

Speaking to the Prophet, Oliver Cowdery, and David Whitmer (at Fayette) as early as June 1829, the Lord said to Oliver Cowdery regarding the written word: "Behold, I have manifested unto you, by my Spirit in many instances, that the things which you have written are true; wherefore you know that they are true. And if you know that they are true, behold, I give unto you a commandment, that you rely upon the things which are written; for in them are all things written concerning the foundation of my church, my gospel, and my rock." (D&C 18:2–4.)

Thus early did the Lord seem to make clear to Oliver Cowdery that he must be guided by the written word; he was not to rely upon his own ideas and concepts.

Two years later (June 7, 1831), the Lord stressed again the importance of following the written word. Speaking to the Prophet, Sidney Rigdon, Lyman Wight, John Corrill, John Murdock, Hyrum Smith, and several others, the Lord said: "And let them journey from thence preaching the word by the way, saying none other things than that which the prophets and apostles have written, and that which is taught them by the Comforter through the prayer of faith." (D&C 52:9; see also D&C 18:32–33.)

Time and again the Lord told these early Brethren of their duty to spread the Gospel, and in spreading the Gospel, they were to speak with the voice of a trump. (See D&C 19:27; 24:12; 27:16; 28:8, 16; 29:4; 30:5, 9; 32:1; 33:2; 34:5; 35:17, 23; 36:1, 5–6; 37:2; 39:11; 42:6, 11–12; 49:1; 52:9; 58:46, 63–64; 66:5; 68:4; 71:1; 88:77; 93:51; 101:39; 106:2; 107:25–35.)

Not to Teach Sectarianism

In a commandment given to Leman Copley (March 1831), as he went into missionary work among the Shakers, the Lord gave this significant commandment, which has in it a message for all amongst us who teach sectarianism: "And my servant Leman shall be ordained unto this work, that he may reason with them, not according to that which he has received of them, but according to that which shall be taught him by you my servants; and by so doing I will bless him, otherwise he shall not prosper." (D&C 49:4.)

Evil Spirits Not to Be Listened To

To a group of elders (in May 1831), who had been confused by the manifestations of different spirits, the Lord, answering a special request made of him by the Prophet, gave these instructions and commandments:

Wherefore, I the Lord ask you this question—unto what were ye ordained?

To preach my gospel by the Spirit, even the Comforter which was sent forth to teach the truth.

And then received ye spirits which ye could not understand, and received them to be of God; and in this are ye justified?

Behold, ye shall answer this question yourselves; nevertheless, I will be merciful unto you; he that is weak among you hereafter shall be made strong.

Verily I say unto you, he that is ordained of me and sent forth to preach the word of truth by the Comforter, in the Spirit of truth, doth he preach it by the Spirit of truth or some other way?

And if it be by some other way it is not of God.

And again, he that receiveth the word of truth, doth he receive it by the Spirit of truth or some other way?

If it be some other way it is not of God.

Therefore, why is it that ye cannot understand and know, that he that receiveth the word by the Spirit of truth receiveth it as it is preached by the Spirit of truth?

Wherefore, he that preacheth and he that receiveth, understand one another, and both are edified and rejoice together.

And that which doth not edify is not of God, and is darkness.

That which is of God is light; and he that receiveth light, and continueth in God, receiveth more light; and that light groweth brighter and brighter until the perfect day. (D&C 50:13–24.)

This whole revelation (D&C 50) should be read with great care. There is much instruction given in it. But I wish particularly to call your attention to verses 21 and 22, just quoted:

Therefore, why is it that ye cannot understand and know, that he that receiveth the word by the Spirit of truth receiveth it as it is preached by the Spirit of truth?

Wherefore, he that preacheth, and he that receiveth,

understand one another, and both are edified and rejoice together.

Both are "moved upon by the Holy Ghost."

Scope of the Lord's Instructions

I recur to the declaration of the Lord made (November 1831) through the Prophet Joseph to Orson Hyde, Luke S. Johnson, Lyman E. Johnson, and William E. McLellin, as concerned their duties to preach the Gospel as missionaries. I will re-read the passages pertinent to our discussion:

> And, behold, and lo, this is an ensample unto all those who were ordained unto this priesthood, whose mission is appointed unto them to go forth—
>
> And this is the ensample unto them, that they shall speak as they are moved upon by the Holy Ghost.
>
> And whatsoever they shall speak when moved upon by the Holy Ghost shall be scripture, shall be the will of the Lord, shall be the mind of the Lord, shall be the word of the Lord, shall be the voice of the Lord, and the power of God unto salvation.
>
> Behold, this is the promise of the Lord unto you, O ye my servants. (D&C 68:2–5.)

Perhaps we should note that these promises relate, in their terms, to missionary work.

What Missionaries Should Teach

As to missionary work, we will wish to remember that in April of 1829, the Lord, speaking to Joseph and Oliver, said: "Say nothing but repentance unto this generation; keep my commandments, and assist to bring forth my work, according to my commandments, and you shall be blessed." (D&C 6:9.)

The same instruction was given to Joseph and Hyrum a little later (May 1829) in the same words. (D&C 11:9.)

The instruction was repeated a third time (about a year later, March 1830), now to Martin Harris (through a revelation given to him through the Prophet Joseph). In this revelation, the Lord added, after instructing Martin as to his missionary work which was to be prosecuted diligently and "with all humility, trusting in me, reviling not against revilers. And of tenets thou shalt not talk, but thou shalt declare repentance and faith on the Savior, and remission of sins by baptism, and by fire, yea, even the Holy Ghost." (D&C 19:30–31.)

This is repeating some essentials of what the Lord had commanded twice before. Then the Lord said: "Behold, this is a great and the last commandment which I shall give unto you concerning this matter; for this shall suffice for thy daily walk, even unto the end of thy life." (D&C 19:32.)

The Lord seems just a little impatient here. It may be the Brethren had been talking about tenets, about which at that time they were scantily informed. The Church had not yet been organized. Assuming that the revelation regarding the scriptural character and status of the words of the Brethren when "moved upon by the Holy Ghost" referred, at the time, to missionary work, and reminding ourselves of our question—how shall we know when the Brethren so speak?—we should recall the quotation we have just made from an earlier revelation when the Lord said: "Wherefore, he that preacheth and he that receiveth, understand one another, and both are edified and rejoice together"— that is, both are led and inspired by the Comforter, the Spirit of Truth. (D&C 50:22.) Both are "moved upon by the Holy Ghost."

Again considering missionary work, this mutual understanding between preacher and investigator is surely that which brings conversion, one of the prime purposes of missionary work. It would not be easy to preach false doctrines, undetected, on the first principles of the Gospel. So we need say no more about that.

Principle Goes Beyond Missionary Work

However, over the years, a broader interpretation has been given to this passage: "And whatsoever they shall speak when moved upon by the Holy Ghost shall be scripture, shall be the will of the Lord, shall be the mind of the Lord, shall be the word of the Lord, shall be the voice of the Lord, and the power of God unto salvation." (D&C 68:4.)

In considering the problem involved here, it should be in mind that some of the General Authorities have had assigned to them a special calling; they possess a special gift; they are sustained as prophets, seers, and revelators, which gives them a special spiritual endowment in connection with their teaching of the people. They have the right, the power, and authority to declare the mind and will of God to his people, subject to the overall power and authority of the President of the Church. Others of the General Authorities are not given this special spiritual endowment and authority covering their teaching; they have a resulting limitation, and the resulting limitation upon their power and authority in teaching applies to every other officer and member of the Church, for none of them is spiritually endowed as a prophet, seer, and revelator. Furthermore, as just indicated, the President of the Church has a further and special spiritual endowment in this respect, for he is the Prophet, Seer, and Revelator for the whole Church.

Position of the President of the Church

Here we must have in mind—must know—that only the President of the Church, the Presiding High Priest, is sustained as Prophet, Seer, and Revelator for the Church, and he alone has the right to receive revelations for the Church, either new or amendatory, or to give authoritative interpretations of scriptures that shall be binding on the Church, or change in any way the existing doctrines of the Church. He is God's sole mouthpiece on earth for The Church of Jesus Christ of Latter-day Saints, the only true Church. He alone may declare the mind and will of God to his people. No officer of any other church in the world has this high right and lofty prerogative.

So when any other person, irrespective of who he is, undertakes to do any of these things, you may know he is not "moved
upon by the Holy Ghost," in so speaking, unless he has special
authorization from the President of the Church. (D&C 90:1–4, 9,
12–16; 107:8, 65–66, 91–92; 115:19; 124:125; *History of the
Church,* 2:477; 6:363.)

Thus far it is clear.

Interpretations of Scriptures

But there are many places where the scriptures are not too clear,
and where different interpretations may be given to them; there are
many doctrines, tenets as the Lord called them, that have not been
officially defined and declared. It is in the consideration and discussion of these scriptures and doctrines that opportunities arise for differences of views as to meanings and extent. In view of the fundamental principle just announced as to the position of the President
of the Church, other bearers of the Priesthood, those with the special spiritual endowment and those without it, should be cautious
in their expressions about and interpretations of scriptures and doctrines. They must act and teach subject to the overall power and
authority of the President of the Church. It would be most unfortunate were this not always strictly observed by the bearers of this
special spiritual endowment, other than the President. Sometimes
in the past they have spoken "out of turn," so to speak. Furthermore,
at times even those not members of the General Authorities are
said to have been heard to declare their own views on various matters concerning which no official view or declaration has been made
by the mouthpiece of the Lord, sometimes with an assured certainty
that might deceive the uninformed and unwary. The experience of
Pelatiah Brown in the days of the Prophet is an illustration of this
general principle. (*History of the Church,* 5:339–45.)

There have been rare occasions when even the President of
the Church in his preaching and teaching has not been "moved

upon by the Holy Ghost." You will recall the Prophet Joseph declared that a prophet is not always a prophet.

To this point runs a simple story my father told me as a boy; I do not know on what authority, but it illustrates the point. His story was that during the excitement incident to the coming of Johnston's Army, Brother Brigham preached to the people in a morning meeting a sermon vibrant with defiance to the approaching army, and declaring an intention to oppose and drive them back. In the afternoon meeting he arose and said that Brigham Young had been talking in the morning, but the Lord was going to talk now. He then delivered an address, the tempo of which was the opposite from the morning talk.

I do not know if this ever happened, but I say it illustrates a principle—that even the President of the Church, himself, may not always be "moved upon by the Holy Ghost," when he addresses the people. This has happened about matters of doctrine (usually of a highly speculative character) where a subsequent President of the Church and the people themselves have felt that in declaring the doctrine, the announcer was not "moved upon by the Holy Ghost."

How shall the Church know when these adventurous expeditions of the Brethren into these highly speculative principles and doctrines meet the requirements of the statutes that the announcers thereof have been "moved upon by the Holy Ghost"? The Church will know by the testimony of the Holy Ghost in the body of the members, whether the Brethren in voicing their views are "moved upon by the Holy Ghost"; and in due time that knowledge will be made manifest. I refer again to the observations of Brother Brigham on this general question.

Differences of View

But this matter of disagreements over doctrine, and the announcement by high authority of incorrect doctrines, is not new.

It will be recalled that disagreements among Brethren in high places about doctrines made clear appeared in the early days of the Apostolic Church. Indeed, at the Last Supper, "there was also a strife among them, which of them should be accounted the greatest"; this was in the presence of the Savior himself. (Luke 22:24.)

The disciples had earlier had the same dispute when they were at Capernaum. (Mark 9:33; Luke 9:46.) And not long after that, James and John, of their own volition or at the instance of their mother, apparently the latter, asked Jesus that one of them might sit on his right hand and the other on his left. (Matthew 20:20–21; Mark 10:35–37.)

This matter of precedence seems to have troubled the disciples.

There were disputes over doctrine. You will recall that Paul and Barnabas had differences (not over doctrine, however), and says the record, "the contention was so sharp between them, that they departed asunder one from the other." (Acts 15:39.)

Paul had an apparently unseemly dispute with Peter about circumcision. Paul boasted to the Galatians, "I said unto Peter before them all. . . ." (Galatians 2:14.)

Peter, replying more or less in kind, wrote: " . . . even as our beloved brother Paul also according to the wisdom given unto him hath written unto you; as also in all his epistles, speaking in them of these things; in which are some things hard to be understood, which they that are unlearned and unstable wrest, as they do also the other scriptures, unto their own destruction." (2 Peter 3:15–16.)

This same question regarding circumcision became so disturbing to the Church that "the apostles and elders came together for to consider of this matter," in Jerusalem. Paul, Barnabas, and Peter were there and participated in the discussion. The Pharisee disciples stood for circumcision of Gentiles. James delivered the decision against the necessity of circumcising the Gentile con-verts. (Acts 15.)

Conditions after the Passing of the Apostles

So it was with the Apostolic Church. After the passing of the Apostles, bickerings, contentions, strife, rebellion grew apace and ripened in a few generations into the Great Apostasy. I should like to quote here three paragraphs from a work by Dr. Islay Burns (at one time a Professor of Church History, Free Church College, Glasgow). He writes:

> It is the year 101 of the Christian era. The last of the apostles is just dead. The rich evening radiance which in his solitary ministry had for 30 years lingered on the earth when all his companions were gone, has at last passed away, and the dark night settles down again. The age of inspiration is over—that peerless century which began with the birth of Christ, and closed with the death of John—and the course of the ages descends once more to the ordinary level of common time.
>
> It was with the Church now as with the disciples at Bethany, when the last gleam of the Savior's ascending train had passed from their sight, and they turned their faces, reluc-tant and sad, to the dark world again. The termination of the age of inspiration was in truth the very complement and con-summation of the ascension of the Lord. The sun can then only be said to have fairly set, when his departing glory has died away from the horizon, and the chill stars shine out sharp and clear on the dun and naked sky.
>
> That time has now fully come. The last gleam of inspired wisdom and truth vanished from the earth with the beloved apostle's gentle farewell, and we pass at once across the mys-terious line which separates the sacred from the secular annals of the world—the history of the apostolic age from the history of the Christian Church. (Islay Burns, *The First Three Christian Centuries* [London: T. Nelson and Sons, 1884], 49.)

So spoke Burns.

This tragic sunset rapidly deepened into twilight of not too long life, and then came the spiritual darkness of an Apostate night. For the better part of two millenniums men groped about, spiritually stumbling one over the other, vainly seeking even a spark of spiritual light, until, on that beautiful spring morning, a century and a third ago, a pillar of light above the brightness of the noonday sun, gradually fell from the heavens till it enveloped a young boy in the woods praying mightily for spiritual light. As he looked up he saw two persons standing in the light above him, the Father and the Son. The morning of the Dispensation of the Fullness of Times had come, breaking the darkness of the long generations of spiritual night. As in the creation, light was to replace darkness, day was to follow night.

The Church in the Last Dispensation

The Church was organized, named by direct command of the Lord, "The Church of Jesus Christ of Latter-day Saints."

You know its history—the trials, tribulations, hardships, persecutions, mobbings, murders, and final expulsion of its members into the western wilderness. You know the loyalty to death itself of some; the disloyalty almost to the point of murder of others. You know the dissensions, the bickerings, the false witnessing, the disputes, the jealousies, the ambitions, the treachery, that tore at the very vitals of the young Church. You know the apostasies, the excommunications of men in the very highest places, because they did not recognize when men in high places were not "moved upon by the Holy Ghost," in their teachings. These malcontents followed those who had not the guidance of the Holy Ghost. Finally, the machinations of evil men, inside and outside the Church, brought Joseph and Hyrum to a martyr's death. But God's work moved on.

How Revelation and Inspiration Are Given

Preliminary to a little further consideration of the principle involved in being "moved upon by the Holy Ghost," we might call attention to the difficulties some have in conceiving how revelation comes, particularly its physiological and psychological characteristics. Some have very fixed and definite ideas on these matters and set up standards by which they test the genuineness or non-genuineness of revelations which Church members generally and the Church itself accept as revelations.

On that point I would like to call your attention to the experience of Naaman the leper, captain of the host of the King of Syria. A captive Jewish maiden, servant in the house of Naaman, told Naaman's wife there was a prophet in Samaria who could cure Naaman's leprosy. Hearing of this report, the Syrian King ordered Naaman to go to Samaria, and gave him a letter to be delivered to the King of Israel. Naaman went to Samaria with presents, to the great distress and fear of Jehoram, who feared a trick.

Elisha, learning the situation and the King's distress, had Naaman sent to him. When Naaman reached Elisha's home, Elisha did not go to see Naaman, but sent a servant to tell him to wash seven times in the waters of Jordan and he would be healed.

"Naaman was wroth," says the record, and went away, saying he thought Elisha "will surely come out to me, and stand, and call on the name of the Lord his God, and strike his hand over the place, and recover the leper." Humiliated, for he carried a royal commission, Naaman "turned and went away in a rage." But his servants pointed out that if Elisha had asked him to do some great thing, he would have done it, then why not do the simple thing of washing in the Jordan. Mollified at least, perhaps half believing, he went and bathed seven times in the waters of the Jordan, "and his flesh came again like unto the flesh of a little child, and he was clean." (2 Kings 5.)

Read the whole story again; it is interesting and has valuable lessons.

One lesson is—We do not tell the Lord how to do things. He frames his own plans, draws his own blueprints, shapes his own course, conceives his own strategy, moves and acts as in his infinite knowledge and wisdom he determines. When lack-faiths and doubters and skeptics begin to map out the plans, methods, and procedures they would demand that God follow, they would do well to remember God's power, wisdom, knowledge, and authority.

The First Vision

Before noting a few ways in which the inspiration of the Lord and the revelations of his mind and will have come to men, I want to refer to one aspect of the First Vision, that part (on which is hung a charge of epilepsy to discredit and destroy Joseph's inspiration and mission) which relates that as he came out of the vision he found himself lying on his back, looking up into heaven, without strength, though he soon recovered. You might find it interesting to compare this with the account of the condition of Moses after his great theophany (Moses 1:9–10), and of Daniel (Daniel 8:27), also of the incidents connected with the transfiguration on the mount. (Matthew 17:1–9; Mark 9:1–9; Luke 9:28–36.)

I wish to make here one observation about the First Vision.

No man or woman is a true member of the Church who does not fully accept the First Vision, just as no man is a Christian who does not accept, first, the Fall of Adam, and second, the Atonement of Jesus Christ. Any titular Church member who does not accept the First Vision but who continues to pose as a Church member, lacks not only moral courage but intellectual integrity and honor if he does not avow himself an apostate and discontinue going about the Church, and among the youth particularly, as a Churchman, teaching not only lack-faith but faith-destroying doctrines. He is a true wolf in sheep's clothing.

Language of a Revelation

There are those who insist that unless the Prophet of the Lord declares, "Thus saith the Lord," the message may not be taken as a revelation. This is a false testing standard. For while many of our modern revelations as contained in the Doctrine and Covenants do contain these words, there are many that do not. Nor is it necessary that an actual voice be heard in order that a message from our Heavenly Father shall be a true revelation, as shown by revelations given in former dispensations, as well as in our own.

For example: Enos records that while struggling in prayer for forgiveness of his sins, first "there came a voice unto me, saying: . . ." Then, as he continued his struggling in the spirit, he declares, "the voice of the Lord came into my mind again saying. . . ." It is not clear whether the voice was the same on both occasions, or a real voice first and then a voice in the mind. But it does not matter, the message came from the Lord each time. (Enos 1:5, 10.)

In that great revelation, designated by the Prophet as the Olive Leaf, the opening sentence is, "Verily, thus saith the Lord unto you who have assembled yourselves together to receive his will concerning you. . . ." Yet further in the revelation, the Lord says: "Behold, that which you hear is as the voice of one crying in the wilderness—in the wilderness, because you cannot see him— my voice, because my voice is Spirit; my Spirit is truth; truth abideth and hath no end; and if it be in you it shall abound." (D&C 88:1, 66.)

In that glorious vision and revelation recorded as section 76 of the Doctrine and Covenants, the Prophet Joseph records:

By the power of the Spirit our eyes were opened and our understandings were enlightened, so as to see and understand the things of God. . . .

And while we meditated upon these things, the Lord touched the eyes of our understandings and they were opened, and the glory of the Lord shone round about.

And we beheld the glory of the Son, on the right hand of the Father, and received of his fulness. (Vv. 12, 19–20.)

And later, telling of the works of Lucifer and the sufferings of those upon whom he made war and overcame, the record says: ". . . thus came the voice of the Lord unto us: Thus saith the Lord concerning all those who know my power, and have been made partakers thereof . . ." and then are overcome by Satan. (D&C 76:30–31.)

In another revelation, the record reads: "Verily I say unto you my friends, I speak unto you with my voice, even the voice of my Spirit." (D&C 97:1.)

Very early in Church history (April 1829), giving assurance to Oliver Cowdery, the Lord said: "Yea, behold, I will tell you in your mind and in your heart, by the Holy Ghost, which shall come upon you and which shall dwell in your heart. Now, behold, this is the spirit of revelation; behold, this is the spirit by which Moses brought the children of Israel through the Red Sea on dry ground." (D&C 8:2–3.)

A little later, the Lord gave to Oliver the sign of the burning in his bosom when his translations were right, and a stupor of thought when the translations were wrong. (D&C 9:8–9.)

On other occasions, in ancient times and in modern days, the records leave no question but that a real voice was heard, as when the Lord spoke, time and again, to the boy Samuel, a servant to the High Priest Eli, from whose family the Lord took the high office belonging to it, because of the wickedness of his sons, Hophni and Phinehas. (1 Samuel 2–3.)

And in modern days (April 3, 1836), in the great vision of Joseph and Oliver in the Temple at Kirtland, the record reads:

> The veil was taken from our minds, and the eyes of our understanding were opened.
>
> We saw the Lord standing upon the breastwork of the pulpit, before us; and under his feet was a paved work of pure gold, in color like amber.
>
> His eyes were as a flame of fire; the hair of his head was white like the pure snow; his countenance shone above the brightness of the sun; and his voice was as the sound of the rushing of great waters, even the voice of Jehovah, saying:
>
> I am the first and the last; I am he who liveth, I am he

who was slain; I am your advocate with the Father. (D&C 110:1–4.)

Joseph's Work in Revelation and Vision

To close this phase of our talk, I would like to read to you descriptions of how the Prophet received revelations, and how he looked on such occasions. You are probably all familiar with the record.

Elder Parley P. Pratt (speaking of the revelation now printed as section 50 of the Doctrine and Covenants, given in May 1831) describes how the Prophet worked when receiving revelations. He says:

> After we had joined in prayer in his translating room, he dictated in our presence the following revelation:—(Each sentence was uttered slowly and very distinctly, and with a pause between each, sufficiently long for it to be recorded, by an ordinary writer, in long hand.
>
> This was the manner in which all his written revelations were dictated and written. There was never any hesitation, reviewing, or reading back, in order to keep the run of the subject; neither did any of these communications undergo revisions, interlinings, or corrections. As he dictated them so they stood, so far as I have witnessed; and I was present to witness the dictation of several communications of several pages each. . . .) (*Autobiography of Parley Parker Pratt*, Parley P. Pratt Jr., ed. [Salt Lake City: Deseret Book, 1938], 62.)

It seems clear that on this occasion there was no audible voice, though the opening sentence of the revelation reads: "Hearken unto me, saith the Lord your God. . . ."

However, President B. H. Roberts points out that when some of the early revelations were published in the Book of Commandments in 1833, they "were revised by the Prophet himself in the way of correcting errors made by the scribes and publishers; and some additional clauses were inserted to throw increased light upon the subjects treated in the revelations, and

paragraphs added, to make the principles for instructions apply to
officers not in the Church at the time some of the earlier revelations were given. The addition of verses 65, 66, and 67 in sec. XX
of the Doctrine and Covenants is an example." (*History of the
Church*, 1:173, note.)

At Montrose, Iowa, in August 1842 (there is some uncertainty
as to the exact date), the Prophet, attending a Masonic ceremony,
prophesied that the Saints would be driven to the Rocky
Mountains, and declared events incident to the move. Brother
Anson Call describes this scene as quoted in his biography by
Tullidge, as follows:

Joseph, as he was tasting the cold water, warned the
brethren not to be too free with it. With the tumbler still in
his hand he prophesied that the Saints would yet go to the
Rocky Mountains; and, said he, this water tastes much like
that of the crystal streams that are running from the snow-
capped mountains. We will let Mr. Call describe this
prophetic scene:

"I had before seen him in a vision, and now saw while he
was talking his countenance change to white; not the deadly
white of bloodless face, but a living brilliant white. He
seemed absorbed in gazing at something at a great distance,
and said: 'I am gazing upon the valleys of those mountains.'
This was followed by a vivid description of the scenery of
these mountains, as I have since become acquainted with it.
Pointing to Shadrach Roundy and others, he said: 'There are
some men here who shall do a great work in that land.'
Pointing to me, he said, 'There is Anson, he shall go and
shall assist in building up cities from one end of the country
to the other, and you, rather extending the idea to all those
he had spoken of, shall perform as great a work as has been
done by man, so that the nations of the earth shall be aston-
ished, and many of them will be gathered in that land and
assist in building cities and temples, and Israel shall be made
to rejoice.'

"It is impossible to represent in words this scene which is

still vivid in my mind, of the grandeur of Joseph's appearance, his beautiful descriptions of this land, and his wonderful prophetic utterances as they emanated from the glorious inspirations that overshadowed him. There was a force and power in his exclamations of which the following is but a faint echo: 'Oh the beauty of those snow-capped mountains! The cool refreshing streams that are running down through those mountain gorges!' Then gazing in another direction, as if there was a change of locality: 'Oh the scenes that this people will pass through! The dead that will lay between here and there.' Then turning in another direction as if the scene had again changed: 'Oh the apostasy that will take place before my brethren reach that land! But,' he continued, 'the priesthood shall prevail over its enemies, triumph over the devil and be established upon the earth, never more to be thrown down!' He then charged us with great force and power, to be faithful to those things that had been and should be committed to our charge, with the promise of all the blessings that the Priesthood could bestow. 'Remember these things and treasure them up. Amen.'" (Tullidge's Histories, vol. I. History of Northern Utah, and Southern Idaho. Biographical Supplement, 271 et seq.) (*History of the Church*, 5:86, note.)

Brother Pratt affirms he had frequently witnessed the Prophet receiving revelations always in the way he described, and Brother Call says he had before seen the Prophet in a vision.

Stirring records of a glorious event!

One can partly understand how the early Saints clung to Joseph and why the early Brethren followed and protected him even to death itself. Faith and knowledge and love rose to loftiest heights in those early days of tribulation and martyrdom, and jealousy and hate and the spirit of murder, inspired by Satan, sank to the depths of lowest degree, working for the defeat of God's work.

Supremely great is the calling of a Prophet of God to declare the mind and the will of God touching the trials, the vicissitudes, the grievous persecutions that follow the righteous of the children of men, and then to proclaim the glories of the infinite goodness of God, his mercy and love, his forgiveness, his unbounded helpfulness, his divine purposes, his final destiny of man.

Yet we must not forget that prophets are mortal men, with men's infirmities.

Asked if a prophet was always a prophet, Brother Joseph quickly affirmed that "a prophet was a prophet only when he was acting as such." (*History of the Church*, 5:265.)

He pointed out that James declared "that Elias was a man subject to like passions as we are, yet he had such power with God, that He, in answer to his prayers, shut the heavens that they gave no rain for the space of three years and six months; and again, in answer to his prayer, the heavens gave forth rain, and the earth gave forth fruit." (James 5:17–18; *History of the Church*, 2:302.)

On another occasion Joseph quoted the saying of John that "the testimony of Jesus is the spirit of prophecy" (Revelation 19:10) and declared: " . . . if I profess to be a witness or teacher, and have not the spirit of prophecy, which is the testimony of Jesus, I must be a false witness; but if I be a true teacher and witness, I must possess the spirit of prophecy, and that constitutes a prophet." (*History of the Church*, 5:215–16.)

There is not time to say more on this occasion.

I have tried to suggest the meaning of the scripture which says that what the Priesthood says when "moved upon by the Holy Ghost," is itself scripture. I have tried to indicate my own thoughts as to some of the limitations which attend the exercise of this principle, both as to those who are entitled to have their words taken as scripture, and also as to the doctrines that might fall from the lips of those not possessing the special gift and endowment. I have shown that even the President of the Church has not always spoken under the direction of the Holy Ghost, for a prophet is not always a prophet. I noted that the Apostles of the Primitive

Church had their differences, that in our own Church, leaders have differed in view from the first.

I have observed that the Lord has his own ways of communicating his mind and will to his prophets, uninfluenced by the thoughts or views of men as to his proper procedure; that sometimes he evidently speaks with an audible voice, but that at other times he speaks inaudibly to the ear but clearly to the mind of the prophet. I quoted how the Prophet Joseph worked as he received revelations and how his countenance changed in appearance at such times. I have tried to explain briefly how, as Joseph said, a prophet is not always a prophet, but is a prophet only when acting as such, and that this means that not always may the words of a prophet be taken as a prophecy or revelation, but only when he, too, is speaking as "moved upon by the Holy Ghost."

I repeat here some of the elemental rules that, as to certain matters, will enable us always to know when others than the Presiding High Priest, the Prophet, Seer and Revelator, the President of the Church, will not be speaking as "moved upon by the Holy Ghost."

When any one except the President of the Church undertakes to proclaim a revelation from God for the guidance of the Church, we may know he is not "moved upon by the Holy Ghost."

When any one except the President of the Church undertakes to proclaim that any scripture of the Church has been modified, changed, or abrogated, we may know he is not "moved upon by the Holy Ghost," unless he is acting under the direct authority and direction of the President.

When any one except the President of the Church undertakes to proclaim a new doctrine of the Church, we may know that he is not "moved upon by the Holy Ghost," unless he is acting under the direct authority and direction of the President.

When any one except the President of the Church undertakes to proclaim that any doctrine of the Church has been modified, changed, or abrogated, we may know that he is not "moved upon by the Holy Ghost," unless he is acting under the direction and by the authority of the President.

When any man except the President of the Church undertakes to proclaim one unsettled doctrine, as among two or more doctrines in dispute, as the settled doctrine of the Church, we may know that he is not "moved upon by the Holy Ghost," unless he is acting under the direction and by the authority of the President.

Of these things we may have a confident assurance without chance for doubt or quibbling.

God grant us the power so to live that always we may be "moved upon by the Holy Ghost," to the end that we may always detect false teachings and so be preserved in the faith that shall lead us into immortality and eternal life, I humbly pray, in the name of him through whom, only, we approach the Father. Even so. Amen.

Church News, July 31, 1954, 2, 9–11.

⚜

LIVING FLAMES,
NOT DEAD ASHES

S. DILWORTH YOUNG

S. Dilworth Young, a great-grandson of Brigham Young, was called to the First Council of the Seventy in 1945, when he was forty-seven years old. He served until 1978, when he was granted emeritus status. Elder Young, whose early career was as an executive in the Boy Scouts of America's Ogden area council, always had a special love in his heart for the young men and women of the Church; his warmth toward them is clearly evident in this talk.

Elder Young delivered this devotional address to Brigham Young University students on May 17, 1977. The talk's title comes from his observation, "Ashes have no life. Flames are constantly moving, changing, and challenging." In this address, Elder Young cites incidents from his life to show that like the living flame, the Holy Ghost is actively engaged in moving, changing, and challenging us. "You may be sure that if you are doing your normal things in righteousness, there will come to you intuitions, feelings, revelations that will guide you," he said. ". . . It takes a little work to understand when it is there, but you can learn it."

I recall . . . reading somewhere a statement by a French philosopher, a one-sentence statement. I have never read the works of this philosopher—I do not even know his name—but I liked what he said . . . : "From the living flames of our campfires of the past rather than the dead ashes." That is the subject [of my address today].

Ashes have no life. Flames are constantly moving, changing, and challenging. Anybody who sits at a campfire can watch but never tire of the variety of the flames that arise from the burning wood. And after the fire has died down and he has gone through the action of killing it with water or whatever, running his hands through the dead ashes, he finds that the ashes are not very much once they are dead. . . . Here is what I have learned from the living flame.

In righteousness, one may be guided by the spirit of the Holy Ghost in his personal affairs if he seeks such guidance and if these affairs are honorable and honest. I want to call your attention to the fact that there is a place in section 89 of the Doctrine and Covenants that says something like this: "All [those] who . . . keep and do these sayings" (the Lord has been speaking of tobacco and liquor and other noxious substances, as well as wheat and corn and rye and barley—and there might be one added that is not a part of this section: "Retire to thy bed early" [D&C 88:124]), "walking in obedience to the commandments, shall . . . run and not be weary." (D&C 89:18–20.) I have talked to several athletes of my acquaintance who wonder why they are running weary; but they do not seem to realize that they are not walking in obedience to the commandments. We are told in section 93 of the Doctrine and Covenants that if we will do all the things we ought to do, we may see the face of our Savior (see verse 1). On the same basis you may be guided by the Spirit of the Lord, the Holy Ghost, in your personal affairs if you are honorable and honest and keep the commandments.

I have discovered that one is guided sometimes even if he does not ask for it. Nearly all of the occasions in my life when I have had great events foretold me by the Spirit, I have never invited them myself or asked about them. They have just come. I can see why that is: Because every person who joins the Church and is a member of it in good standing has a right to receive the constant companionship of the Holy Ghost. He is given that right at baptism and he keeps that right as long as he is righteous. I have come to the conclusion that this Spirit and whatever influence he uses to reach us is more anxious to help us than we are anxious to be helped. I found that out quite early. So you may be sure that if you are doing your normal things in righteousness, there will come to you intuitions, feelings, revelations that will guide you if you can understand that Spirit and how you're having it. It takes a little work to understand when it is there, but you can learn it.

I found that it is true in that very important thing called marriage. In one case (I have been married twice, as you might know), it came without asking. I did not ask for it, but the guidance came anyhow. In the other case it came after asking, but just as clearly as in the previous case. So I know that if you need guidance, whether or not you seek it, if you are righteous and have not made previous decisions, you will receive guidance. Of course, if you have already made up your mind, you will not; but if you have not made up your mind and are wondering, you will.

I have found that it is true in Church assignments. I knew in 1945, two months before I was called, that I would be a member of the First Council of the Seventy. I can remember my feeling at the time. I was standing near the grave of my mission president, who was a member of that council, paying my respects to his family, and it came to me that I would succeed him. I gave my head a shake and said to myself, "Don't be a fool. No such thing can happen." I fought it, but it didn't do me any good to fight it because the more I fought it the more strongly the impression came. On the day it occurred I could have told you the exact language that would be used in the call, and it proved to be so.

I received a call to preside over the New England Mission, and the method by which I found out had nothing to do with that mission—it was so far removed from it that I could hardly believe it—but a month before I received the call, right out of the clear sky, when I was thinking of something else entirely, I had a very distinct revelation that that would happen.

I name these two incidents not because I am exceptional; I think it is also true of men who become bishops. A woman told me a few days ago that she had a premonition—not a premonition but a warning—that she was going to be made teacher of a certain Sunday School class, and she was. It does not matter what the calling is; you can receive knowledge ahead of time that you are to receive it if you have the Spirit of the Lord in your heart.

I found that it is true in civic affairs, the most noteworthy of which was an occasion when I was to serve on a grand jury. I had every excuse in the world not to serve. If I served, my Boy Scout camp would not open. It could not, because in the days of the Second World War we could not hire a man to help get it ready, for there were no men to hire. So I had to get it ready personally. There were seven or eight hundred boys expecting to come to that camp. When I saw my name in the newspaper among forty others who might serve on the jury, I said to myself, "Well, I won't serve." But as I said it to myself, I knew perfectly well that I would and that no matter what I said to that judge I would not be able to escape it, and that proved true.

I found many times in my life when these things have come to me, with and without asking. But I found out also that if I was not righteous or was not doing righteous things at the moment, it never happened. Whether one asks or not, one must live so the Spirit can dwell in him. That is the key to the whole thing— living so the Spirit can dwell within you. And, of course, you know what that means—that means, in plain, common English: Behave yourselves.

As I look back on my life I see that I have been protected or helped in danger and crisis. I look back, and although at the time I did not see it, now I see that I could not have made it without that assistance. For example, as a boy eight or nine years old, I was standing with some other boys—my brother and two others—in a semicircle, and the boy at the other end of the crescent had a Sears and Roebuck twenty-two caliber single-shot pistol (two dollars and fifty cents with tax), and he was showing us how Buffalo Bill used to shoot. Buffalo Bill was supposed to pull his pistol and fire in this manner [illustrates]; but the spring of this pistol was broken, and my friend had an elastic band around the hammer and around the trigger guard. The way he did it was to pull it back and let it go with his thumb. He was firing this pistol down into City Creek Canyon when all of a sudden I felt my arm go numb. I looked down and saw a red spot forming on my right arm. . . . Then my hand went numb, and I realized that I had been shot. That is what I said as I ran for home; but afterward I thought, had that pistol turned one-sixteenth of an inch farther I would have had it. Now I do not say that the Lord kept that pistol from turning, but something did.

I climbed Longs Peak one time with a group of men. Longs Peak is 14,255 feet high, and as one gets above the thirteen-thousand-foot level, he finds, unless he is used to it, that his legs go numb about every fifth step. One can go four or five steps and then his legs go numb, and he has to wait for them to come alive before he can go farther. It took us about an hour and a half or two hours to go the last thousand feet.

Up on top I noticed that there was a ridge apparently running down in a direction that, if I could get on it, would save me the hours of going around the way we had come. Against the advice of my companions, I decided that I would take that shortcut. So I dropped down off the peak onto a series of ledges that were waist high, just like a giant staircase, and before very long I was a thousand feet down. Then I ran into ice. During the evening before there had been an ice storm up there. It was clear ice; one could not see it on the rocks, and the first thing I knew I slipped. I caught myself and then began to worry; for I could see when I got there that I could not make that ridge. There were glacial cirques on both sides thousands of feet deep, and I was caught. I cannot tell you how panicked I was. I was terribly frightened. I realized that the only way I could escape was to work my way, somehow, back to the top; that meant that one of the men was still up there.

I will not describe the things I went through to start back upward to get out of the particular danger I was in, but finally I got to where I could move. I went up that thousand feet in twenty minutes without even losing my breath. You will say, perhaps, that it was adrenaline, but it was not; and when I got to the top there was Golden Kilburn, a man who was with us, waiting. He said, "I couldn't leave. I knew you were in trouble, so I decided I would not go down this mountain till I found out where you were." And I found out there the value of friendship, too, and of the loyalty and devotion of those who care for you.

One time, on the way to Mexico to attend the funeral of my brother-in-law, we were driving along from Cortez, Colorado, south toward Gallup, New Mexico. It was January, and the thermometer was by the actual count ten below zero. We had a Chevrolet with no heater in it. We were so bundled up in blankets that we could hardly move. There was a ground blizzard, and the snow was drifting across the road so that one could hardly see it. I was going along about fifty miles an hour, the lights penetrating not more than seventy-five or eighty feet in front, when all of a sudden there loomed up in front of me on my side of the highway a horse, with another horse directly behind him, starting across the road.

There was no time to stop. To this day I do not know what happened. All I know is that the horse jerked his head back as I went by on the left side of the road, then I was back into the right-hand side again. My life was spared, and so was that of my wife. I did not do it. There was no time to do it. There was no time to think; but some guiding hand had forced me to turn that car into the left-hand lane and back again, and some guiding hand had kept it from skidding as it went around. By all the laws it should have skidded off into the borrow pit or I should have struck the horse. At ten below zero, we never would have survived.

Sister Young had a stroke two days after we got home from a trip we took to Mexico. It incapacitated her for the rest of her life, and I had the honor and the great pleasure of nursing her for the five or six more years she lived. Had she had the stroke two or three days before in Coatzalcoalcos, Mexico, in the southwest corner of the Gulf of Mexico, we never should have gotten her out alive, but mercifully it waited till she got home.

When I was young, I came home from a mission and needed a job. I got married and was working for a hundred and twenty-five dollars a month when I heard there was a job in Scouting in Ogden. An old friend, Howard McDonald, past president of [Brigham Young University], met me on the street and wanted to know if I wanted that job.

"What is it?" I asked.

He said, "You get paid for being a Boy Scout leader. Lots of fun. You direct the Scout work in a community."

The only thing I had ever done in Scouting was to help my little brother in a fire-by-friction situation. I showed him how to make fire by friction in our kitchen, and all I succeeded in doing was boring a hole through our kitchen linoleum. So I said that I was not interested; but all the way home that night I thought, "Well, why not? Maybe I could do it. I don't know what it's about." So I applied to the president of the local council in such a manner that he was not impressed—anything but impressed. I was frightened, I was stuttering, I was hesitating, I did not know what to say, I could not give him any reason for wanting the job, I did not know what the job was, but I said, "I want it."

He looked at me casually, and finally he said, "Well, we are going to receive written applications, so if you want to write an application we'll read it."

So I wrote the application, and to my surprise I was invited to come to a meeting where I could be interviewed. There were eight candidates, all of whom had had years of experience in volunteer Scouting. I had had none. At the time, however, I suddenly became very calm, very sure of myself. I did not have the least fear. When my turn came to speak—each of the others had taken at least thirty minutes each, so it took nearly all day to hear them, and I was the last one—the president reminded me that they were all tired. So I said, "I don't know a thing about this job, but I know that I can learn to do it rapidly," and then I sat down. To my surprise, I was one of two picked out of that crowd to appear before the board; and with that much of a statement before the executive board, against a man who had had fifteen years of experience, they chose me.

Looking back upon it, I can see the steps by which I was inspired to say the things I said and not say the things I should not have said to get that job. It proved to be good. I had it for twenty-three years before I became a member of the First Council of the Seventy. I am certain as I stand here that the Lord directed me to that job through Howard McDonald and others, and that I was given it, not because of any qualification—not at all—but because somehow I was supposed to have it. I can bear you my witness that you yourselves (only in your case get prepared; this is not 1923) will find the opportunity that will take you to your life's work so that you can have the joy.

Well, the campfire flames mount. I have learned some guideposts in that period of time, and I would like to pass them on to you. The first one is: "One must always tell the truth." Dr. Jeremiah Jenks, a great psychologist of his day, let me have that one time. I was at a big meeting and he was speaking about honor and dignity and truth-telling. Incidentally, you might be interested in knowing that he was the man who was instrumental in seeing to it that the Boy Scout Law contained "A Scout is reverent" and also that the oath had "I will do my duty to God." Otherwise we would have been kind of pagan in our Boy Scout business. He was a great Christian. But he was speaking, and a man in the audience raised his hand and interrupted him and said, "Dr. Jenks, should one always tell the truth?" thinking about the little white lies one tells about how good the dinner was when it wasn't, or "I've got to go somewhere; I've got to quit talking on the phone," or all those other things we do.

Dr. Jenks, aged then about seventy-five, looked out at that man and smiled and said, "Young man, if the truth is told in a courteous manner, the truth may always be told."

I give you a quick illustration that I have told before many times. Many years ago I was driving home late one night from Provo to take care of my sick wife. I was very nervous because I had prepared things for her to last until six o'clock at night, and I was starting home from Provo at eleven o'clock at night, so she had already been without help for five hours. I was fit to be tied. I passed through Salt Lake City (I had not been arrested so far between there and Provo), and started up the highway toward Ogden, got as far as the Farmington junction, and turned off on the hill road, newly paved at that time though not straightened out. With that I stepped on that accelerator and got the car going seventy miles an hour. I passed the road where Hill Field takes off going seventy-two or seventy-three; it was downhill a bit, and going down the hill I think I increased to seventy-eight or eighty. And then I noticed in my rearview mirror the flashing lights of a patrol car. I pulled to a stop and got out and walked back fifteen or twenty feet, extending my hands so he could see I was not armed, and he came up and stopped a few feet away and got out.

"I guess you're arresting me for speeding," I said.

"Yes, you were doing better than sixty miles an hour when you passed the Hill Field road."

"I was doing better than seventy miles an hour when I passed the Hill Field road," I corrected him. "But give me a ticket; I've got to go. My wife's sick, I'm in a hurry, and I'll pay the fine gladly, but let me get out of here. I've got to go home quickly, so just give me the ticket."

He said, "Don't get your shirt off. Stand still a minute. I'm not going to give you a ticket." He had not asked for my name. He just stood there.

I said, "Well, thanks for that."

He continued, "I'm going to give you a warning ticket. That means you don't have to go to court unless you do it again. On one condition."

"What's the condition?" I asked.

"That you drive within the speed limit the rest of the way home, so you will get to your wife."

I said, "I'll do it."

So he gave me the ticket, and when he handed it to me it had my name on it. He smiled, stuck out his hand, and said, "My name's Bybee. I used to be one of your Scouts at Camp Kiesel."

All the way home I said to myself, with each turn of the wheels on my car, "What if I'd lied to him? He knew I was doing seventy. Policemen do. He knew I was going too fast, and he knew I was his Scout executive years before, too." I did not know that he knew any of this, but if I had not told him the exact truth or tried to hedge at all he would have lost respect. He would have given me a ticket, and I would have had no influence on that man ever again.

And so it is with you. You are always doing seventy, no matter where you go or what you are doing, and you had better admit it. Then you will get a reputation for honesty and honor, and it is so great that it will save your life many times. If you get in crises—your word against someone else's word—and if you have a reputation for being truthful, it will save you. That has been my experience.

You must be absolutely honest, of course; that goes along with truth-telling. You cannot afford to do one thing that is not absolutely honest. I commend to you the one thing that many people are not honest in and that is truth-telling in examinations. I do not think that any teacher is ever fooled by the boy who cheats. The boy fools himself. But if he tells the truth, his fifty-percent grade is more honored by the teacher than the ninety percent he might have gotten if he had lied; and what he doesn't know he doesn't know anyhow. That is part of truth-telling.

There are many other phases, of course. You must set your ideals so high . . . well, you have to set your ideals as high as the Lord said to set them: "Be ye . . . perfect, even as your Father . . . in heaven is perfect." (Matthew 5:48.) And then, if you do that and live up to some of them, you will be able to live up to many of them. Some of them you will compromise in spite of yourselves, but you will not compromise enough of them to jeopardize yourselves if you have them high enough. But if you only have them half-high and start compromising, you do not have much, and you are left desolate and barren. So set your ideals as high as you can possibly set them in conduct and handling yourselves and doing what you ought to be doing. If you do that you will find things happening to you that will surprise you.

I can say, now that I am getting to the stage where I am old enough to testify to it, that the greatest thing next to heaven itself is a clear conscience, as far as your personal life is concerned. When one is my age, he looks back upon the things he has done wrong and says to himself over and over again—or I say to myself over and over again—"Why did I do that? Why did I do that?" and there never is an answer. And I suppose that is what hell is like. You never get the answer—and that is futility. But if your conscience is clear, how happy your old age is! It is a time of such rejoicing that you cannot possibly imagine how wonderful it is. You know what things you have to do and what you get if you do them without my naming them over one by one—these become the pearls you count. A man never needs to apologize to any woman for the way in which he treats her or has treated her in the past. He knows his mind is clean, and therefore his speech is clean.

Vulgar talk is such a great temptation. Little half swear words, the *damns* and the *hells*, come easy, I guess. They have done so to me. I punched cattle once and discovered the cattle did not know any of my language, so I tried the language they knew. I wish I had tried my cleaner language on the cattle a little longer. They might have learned something, and I would certainly have saved myself trouble. It is a temptation. Once one of my present associates got irritated and, in saying something over the phone about getting us to move faster, he used a little word with it that made us want to move faster; but to my surprise one of my colleagues, listening on a collective phone, said, "I don't like that. I don't think he ought to use that word. We don't need that here. We'll move without it." And that was just a very simple word. I learned the lesson that there are men in this world and women in this world who want to have clean minds, and want to have clean thoughts, and are insulted if you violate their ideal. You can find them; you don't have to look very far for them. Just be that way and they will gravitate to you.

Live in such a way that you can pray. Most people pray, but I am talking about being able to pray with the assurance that you can be heard. We say our prayers, but are you praying and am I praying with the assurance way down deep that what we are saying is heard where it ought to be heard? That only comes with clean living, with what we call repentance. We must truly repent of our sins, start to make ourselves better, and try to live cleanly; then we are heard. The Lord can hear us and he will hear us and he does hear us, and then what I said in the beginning takes place: the Holy Ghost works on you, whether you want him to or not.

When you do these things, you will have another great compensation come to you. Your life will be such that when you listen to leaders speak—leaders such as the president of the Church or the apostles or the bishop of your ward or your class teachers—you can discern whether that person speaks by the Spirit or not, and that is vital in your life and in mine. We Latter-day Saints can have no other standard than this, that we live in such a way that we will be able to discern when people are speaking by the Spirit. If you have that you have a pearl of great price, and you will understand and know the way by which you may become perfect.

Brigham Young is reported to have said once, "The important thing is not whether I am speaking by the Spirit of the Holy Ghost in conference, but whether or not the congregation can detect the spirit by which I'm speaking." He was more worried that the audience would not have enough spirituality to hear what he was saying by the Spirit than he was that he speak by the Spirit, and I am worried about the same thing right this minute. I hope that I am speaking by the Spirit; and if I am not I hope that you in this congregation will all have enough discernment to know whether I am or am not, or what I am and am not. Anybody who speaks from the pulpit in this university ought to stand that test, and you ought to be the testers and be able to do it.

Brigham Young had a dream once, and I think it is the epitome of what I have been trying to tell you:

> Joseph stepped toward me, and looking very earnestly, yet pleasantly, said, "Tell the people to be humble and faithful, and be sure to keep the Spirit of the Lord and it will lead them right. Be careful and not turn away the small still voice; it will teach them what to do and where to go; it will yield the fruits of the kingdom. Tell the brethren to keep their hearts open to conviction, so that when the Holy Ghost comes to them, their hearts will be ready to receive it. They

can tell the Spirit of the Lord from all other spirits [Now, here's how you can do it, too]; it will whisper peace and joy to their souls; it will take malice, hatred, strife and all evil from their hearts; and their whole desire will be to do good, bring forth righteousness and build up the kingdom of God. [That's how you can know whether or not you have the Spirit.] Tell the brethren if they will follow the Spirit of the Lord, they will go right. Be sure to tell the people to keep the Spirit of the Lord; and if they will, they will find themselves just as they were organized by our Father in Heaven before they came into the world. Our Father in Heaven organized the human family, but they are all disorganized and in great confusion. [And then, finally,] Tell the people to be sure to keep the Spirit of the Lord and follow it, and it will lead them just right." (*Manuscript History of the Church*, February 23, 1847)

Just imagine; the president of the Church has a dream or a vision in which the Prophet Joseph comes to him, and he spends all that time telling him one thing over and over again. That is what it is, brethren and sisters, young folks.

One last thing: I shall tell you how you can measure your spiritual discernment. Nephi became ecstatic one time, and he prayed to the Lord and praised the Lord and sang paeans, psalms, and kept becoming more spiritual and more spiritual, and finally he made a great statement, a great prayer: he said something about "wilt thou do this for me?" "wilt thou keep my soul?" "wilt thou feed me?" and went on like that, "wilt thou do this?" Then, finally, he said, "Wilt thou make me that I may shake at the appearance of sin?" (2 Nephi 4:31.) He was so spiritual that the least deviation from having the Spirit, which is sin, he could discern, and that is what he wanted most of all.

And so with you and me. Let us learn to shake at the very appearance of sin, and we can measure our spirituality by how much we do that. If we do not shake, we are not very spiritual, and if we shake, we are. And the more we shake at the appearance of sin, the more we are spiritual.

After all, the final thing is that the Father and the Son do live and guide us, and the Church established by Joseph Smith is the Church of Christ, the only Church of Christ. That is the great testimony, to know that President [Spencer W.] Kimball is the real prophet of God our Heavenly Father and his Son, and to follow after and keep the commandments of the Lord that our prophet teaches us and to know when he speaks by the Spirit. I know that he does, and I know these things are true, and so do most of you, I suspect. May we all unite together and go forward and earn our place in the kingdom of our God by keeping the Spirit and understanding, I pray in the name of Christ. Amen.

BYU 1977 Devotional Speeches of the Year, 95–101.

~~ ❦ ~~

How to Obtain
Personal Revelation

Bruce R. McConkie

The Prophet Joseph Smith said, "Reading the experience of others, or the revelations given to *them*, can never give us a comprehensive view of our condition and true relation to God. Knowledge of these things can only be obtained by experience through the ordinances of God set forth for that purpose. Could you gaze into heaven five minutes, you would know more than you would by reading all that ever was written on the subject." (*Teachings of the Prophet Joseph Smith*, 324.) Taking that quotation as the theme of this talk, Elder Bruce R. McConkie explained, in his powerful but matter-of-fact way, how any member of the Church may receive such revelation. He gave this talk at a Brigham Young University devotional on October 11, 1966.

As a people, we are in the habit of saying that we believe in latter-day revelation. We announce quite boldly that the heavens have been opened, that God has spoken in our day, that angels have ministered to men, that there have been visions and revelations, and that no gift or grace possessed by the ancients has been withheld—it has all been revealed anew in our day.

But ordinarily when we talk this way, we think of Joseph Smith, Brigham Young, David O. McKay, or some other President of the Church. We think of Apostles and prophets—men called, selected or foreordained to hold the positions which they hold and to do the ministerial service that is theirs. We think of them and of the general principle of the Church itself operating by revelation.

Now, there is no question at all about this: The organization that we belong to is literally the Lord's kingdom. It is the kingdom of God on earth, and is designed to prepare and qualify us to go to the kingdom of God in heaven which is the celestial kingdom. This Church is guided by revelation. I have sat in meetings with the Brethren on many occasions when the President of the Church, who is the prophet of God on earth, has said in humility and with fervent testimony that the veil is thin, that the Lord is guiding and directing the affairs of the Church, and that it is his Church and he is making his will manifest.

There is inspiration at the head, and the Church is in the line and course of its duty; it is progressing in the way that the Lord would have it progress. There is no question that the Church receives revelation all the time. Someone said to Brother John A. Widtsoe, speaking derogatorily, "When did the Church get its last revelation?" He said, "Well, this is Sunday, the last one came last Thursday." And this is just how simple it is. The Brethren get direction and revelation all the time, as they meet to direct the affairs of the Church.

Revelation Not Reserved to a Few

I desire to point attention, however, to the fact that revelation is not restricted to the prophet of God on earth. The visions of eternity are not reserved for Apostles—they are not reserved for the General Authorities. Revelation is something that should come to every individual. God is no respecter of persons (Acts 10:34), and every soul, in the ultimate sense, is just as precious in his sight as the souls of those that are called to positions of leadership. Because he operates on principles of eternal, universal and never-deviating law, any individual that abides the law which entitles him to get revelation can know exactly and precisely what any prophet knows, can entertain angels just as well as Joseph

Smith entertained them, and can be in tune in full measure with all of the things of the Spirit. (Alma 26:21–22.)

Personal Revelation

Joseph Smith said: "Reading the experience of others, or the revelations given to *them*, can never give us a comprehensive view of our condition and true relation to God. Knowledge of these things can only be obtained by experience through the ordinances of God set forth for that purpose. Could you gaze into heaven five minutes, you would know more than you would by reading all that ever was written on the subject." (*Teachings of the Prophet Joseph Smith*, comp. Joseph Fielding Smith [Salt Lake City: Deseret Book, 1938], 324.)

Now note this statement: "Could you gaze into heaven five minutes, you would know more than you would by reading all that ever was written on the subject." I think our concern is to get personal revelation, to know for ourselves, independent of any other individual or set of individuals, what the mind and the will of the Lord is as pertaining to his Church and as pertaining to us in our individual concerns.

Intellectual and Spiritual Fields

We can divide the realm of inquiry into an intellectual field and a spiritual field. In academic halls, we seek knowledge primarily in the intellectual field, which knowledge comes in most instances by reason and through the senses. Somehow, by ordained laws, we have power through reason and through the sense that God has given us, to convey knowledge to the spirit that is within us. "The mind of man," the Prophet said, in effect, "is in the spirit." (See *Teachings of the Prophet Joseph Smith*, 353.) So we say that we learn certain things—that we do this in an intellectual realm. Some knowledge comes to us in this way, and we spend a very great deal of time engaged in this pursuit.

This is tremendously vital and important—and we encourage

and urge it upon all who desire progression, enlightenment, and advancement in their lives.

But we need to devote an increasingly large portion of our time in the actual pursuit of knowledge in the spiritual realm. When we deal with spiritual realities, we are not talking about gaining something by reason alone, we are not talking about conveying in some way knowledge to the mind or the spirit that is within us through the sense alone, but we are talking about revelation. We are talking about learning how to come to a knowledge of the things of God by attuning the spirit that we have to the eternal Spirit of God. Such a course, primarily, is the channel and way that revelation comes to an individual.

It does not concern me very much that somebody writes or evaluates or analyzes from an intellectual standpoint either a doctrinal or Church problem of any sort. No one questions that everything in the spiritual realm is in total and complete accord with the intellectual realities that we arrive at through reason, but when the two are compared and evaluated and weighed as to their relative merits, the things that are important are in the spiritual realm and not the intellectual. The things of God are known only by the Spirit of God. (1 Corinthians 12:3.)

True Religion Requires Personal Involvement

It is true that you can reason about doctrinal matters, but you do not get religion into your life until it becomes a matter of *personal experience*—until you feel something in your soul, until there has been a change made in your heart, until you become a new creature of the Holy Ghost. Providentially, *every* member of the Church has the opportunity to do this because, in connection with baptism, every member of the Church has the hands of a legal administrator placed on his head, and he is given the promise, "Receive the Holy Ghost." He thus obtains "the gift of the Holy Ghost" which, by definition, means that he then has the right to the constant companionship of this member of the Godhead, based upon his personal righteousness and faithfulness.

Now, I say we are *entitled* to revelation. I say that every member of the Church, independent and irrespective of any position that he may hold, is entitled to get revelation from the Holy Ghost; he is entitled to entertain angels; he is entitled to view the visions of eternity; and if we would like to go the full measure, he is entitled to see God the same way that any prophet in literal and actual reality has seen the face of Deity. (D&C 76:1–10; 93:1.)

Each Man a Prophet to Himself

We talk about latter-day prophets; we think in terms of prophets who tell the future destiny of the Church and the world. But, in addition to that, the fact is that every person should be a prophet for himself and in his own concerns and in his own affairs. It was Moses who said: "Would God that all the Lord's people were prophets, and that the Lord would put his spirit upon them." (Numbers 11:29.) It was Paul who said we should "covet to prophesy." (1 Corinthians 14:39.)

A Doctrine of Personal Revelation

Let me take occasion to read a few statements from the revelations given to the Prophet Joseph Smith which, taken together, outline the formula, as it were, by which I as an individual can come to know the things of God by the power of the Spirit.

One thing the Lord said was this: "I will tell you in your mind and in your heart, by the Holy Ghost, which shall come upon you and which shall dwell in your heart. Now, behold, this is the spirit of revelation." (D&C 8:2–3.)

This revelation speaks of spirit speaking to spirit—the Holy Spirit speaking to the spirit within me and in a way incomprehensible to the mind, but plain and clear to spirit understanding—conveying knowledge, giving intelligence, giving truth and giving sure knowledge of the things of God.

Now, this applies to everyone: "God shall give unto you knowledge by his Holy Spirit, yea, by the unspeakable gift of the Holy Ghost, that has not been revealed since the world was until now; which our forefathers have awaited with anxious expectations to be revealed in the last times." (D&C 121:26–27.)

Here is another passage—a glorious one. This is *not* directed to the General Authorities. This is *not* directed to the prophets of God. This is directed to every living soul in the Church. In other words, it is a personal revelation to you:

"For thus saith the Lord—I, the Lord, am merciful and gracious unto those who fear me, and delight to honor those who serve me in righteousness and in truth unto the end.

"Great shall be their reward and eternal shall be their glory.

"And to them [the whole body of the kingdom] will I reveal all mysteries, yea, all the hidden mysteries of my kingdom from days of old, and for ages to come, will I make known unto them the good pleasure of my will concerning all things pertaining to my kingdom.

"Yea, even the wonders of eternity shall they know, and things to come will I show them, even the things of many generations.

"And their wisdom shall be great, and their understanding reach to heaven; and before them the wisdom of the wise shall perish, and the understanding of the prudent shall come to naught.

"For by my Spirit will I enlighten them, and by my power will I make known unto them the secrets of my will—yea, even those things which eye has not seen, nor ear heard, nor yet entered into the heart of man." (D&C 76:1–10.)

We can entertain angels, we can dream dreams, we can see visions, we can see the face of the Lord. Here is one promise in that field: "Verily, thus saith the Lord: It shall come to pass that every soul who forsaketh his sins and cometh unto me, and calleth on my name, and obeyeth my voice, and keepeth my commandments, shall see my face and know that I am." (D&C 93:1.)

No Salvation without Revelation

The Prophet Joseph said that the veil might as well be rent today as any day, provided we come together as the elders of the kingdom in faith and in righteousness and qualify to have the visions of eternity. (*Teachings of the Prophet Joseph Smith*, 9.)

Here is a statement from Joseph Smith:

"Salvation cannot come without revelation [and I am not *now* speaking about the revelation that gave the dispensation in which we live—I am speaking of personal revelation to individuals]; it is vain for anyone to minister without it. No man is a minister of Jesus Christ without being a Prophet. No man can be a minister of Jesus Christ except he has a testimony of Jesus; and this is the spirit of prophecy. Whenever salvation has been administered, it has been by testimony. Men of the present time testify of heaven and hell, and have never seen either; and I will say that no man knows these things without this." (*Teachings of the Prophet Joseph Smith*, 160.)

We are entitled to revelation. Personal revelation is essential to our salvation. The scriptures abound with illustrations of what has happened. Here is one of the things Nephi said: "If ye will not harden your hearts, and ask me in faith, believing that ye shall receive, with diligence in keeping my commandments, surely these things shall be made known unto you." (1 Nephi 15:11.)

There is a Book of Mormon statement about some tremendously successful missionaries, the sons of Mosiah: "They were men of a sound understanding and they had searched the scriptures diligently, that they might know the word of God.

"But this is not all; they had given themselves to much prayer, and fasting; therefore they had the spirit of prophecy, and the spirit of revelation, and when they taught, they taught with power and authority of God." (Alma 17:2–3.)

I shall take time for one more quotation. This is the Prophet Joseph Smith:

"A person may profit by noticing the first intimation of the spirit of revelation; for instance, when you feel pure intelligence flowing into you, it may give you sudden strokes of ideas, so that by noticing it, you may find it fulfilled the same day or soon; (i.e.,) those things that were presented unto your minds by the Spirit of God, will come to pass; and thus by learning the Spirit of God and understanding it, you may grow into the principle of revelation, until you become perfect in Christ." (*Teachings of the Prophet Joseph Smith*, 151.)

We Need Religious Experience

The scriptures say much about this. The Prophet and all of the prophets have said much about it. What it means to us is that we need religious experience; we need to become personally involved with God. Our concern is not to read what somebody has said *about* religion. I read frequently, but primarily for amusement or diversion, what somebody has said in a critical vein about the Church or what some professor of religion has said about the tenets of Christianity. Actually, such views are not of great importance. It is totally immaterial what someone has to say about the Church in a critical vein; or when someone is writing to evaluate from an intellectual standpoint a doctrine or a practice or a so-called program of the Church—it is just totally inconsequential as far as the Church is concerned and as its spiritually inclined people are concerned. Religion is *not* a matter of the intellect.

What We Can Do

I repeat, the better the intellect, the more we are able to evaluate spiritual principles, and it is a marvelous thing to be learned and educated and have insight and mental capacity, because we can use these talents and abilities in the spiritual realm. But what counts in the field of religion is to become a personal participant in it. Instead of reading all that has been written and evaluating all that all the scholars of all the world have said about heaven and hell, we need to do what the Prophet said: gaze five minutes into heaven. As a consequence, we would know more than all that has ever been evaluated and written and analyzed on the subject.

Religion is a matter of getting the Holy Ghost into the life of an individual. We study, of course, and we need to evaluate. And by virtue of our study we come up with some foundations that get us into the frame of mind so that we *can* seek the things of the Spirit. But in the end the result is getting our souls touched by the Spirit of God.

A Formula for Obtaining Revelation

Would you like a formula to tell you how to get personal revelation? My formula is simply this:

1. Search the scriptures.
2. Keep the commandments.
3. Ask in faith.

Any person who will do this will get his heart so in tune with the Infinite that there will come into his being, from the "still small voice," the eternal realities of religion. And as he progresses and advances and comes nearer to God, there will be a day when he will entertain angels, when he will see visions, and the final end is to view the face of God.

Religion is a thing of the Spirit. Use your intellectuality to help you, but in the final analysis, you have to get in tune with the Lord.

The first great revelation that a person needs to get is to know of the divinity of the work. We call that a testimony. When a person gets a testimony, he has thereby learned how to get in tune with the Spirit and get revelation. So, repeating the connection— getting in tune anew—he can get knowledge to direct him in his personal affairs. Then ultimately enjoying and progressing in this gift, he can get all the revelations of eternity that the Prophet or all the prophets have had in all the ages.

A Testimony

To some extent I, along with you, have received revelation. I have received revelation that tells me that this work is true. And as a consequence, I *know* it. And I know it independent of any study and research, and I know it because the Holy Spirit has spoken to the spirit that is within me, and given me a testimony. As a consequence, I can stand as a legal administrator and say in verity that Jesus Christ is the Son of God, that Joseph Smith is his prophet, that the President of the Church wears the prophetic mantle today, and that The Church of Jesus Christ of Latter-day Saints is the only true and living Church upon the face of the whole earth.

And, further, in connection with the matter we are here considering, I can certify and testify that every living soul who will abide the law, search the scriptures, keep the commandments, and ask in faith, can have personal revelation from the Almighty to the great glory and satisfaction of his soul here and to his ultimate salvation in the mansion on high.

New Era, June 1980, 46–50.

SELF-WORTH

❦

"WHO AM I?"

HAROLD B. LEE

Harold B. Lee, with his early professional experience in the field of education, had ample opportunity to observe the youth of the Church. In his later years, he noted an alarming increase in the lack of self-respect among them, as evidenced in "their dress, their manner, and engulfing waves of permissiveness." Concerned about this trend, he gave the matter a great deal of thought and concluded that knowing who we are, in an eternal sense, is vital to understanding our self-worth. In this address he tells of the anguish of those who are confused about their spiritual identity and the peace of mind experienced by those who know of their eternal worth as children of God.

"I would charge you," said President Lee, "to say again and again to yourselves, as the Primary organization has taught the children to sing, 'I am a [son or a daughter] of God,' and by so doing, begin today to live closer to those ideals which will make your life happier and more fruitful because of an awakened realization of who you are."

President Lee gave this address in general conference on October 5, 1973.

May I make some comments about a condition which is of great concern to all of us today. I speak of the shocking lack of self-respect by so many individuals, as is evidenced by their dress, their manner, and engulfing waves of permissiveness which seem to be moving over the world like an avalanche.

We see among us so many who seem to be forsaking standards of decency or an understanding of the meaning of time-honored words which, since the beginning of time, have had real meaning to our forebears; words that have made for strength of character and righteousness and harmony and unity and peace in the world.

There are eternal words which, if understood and taught and practiced, would bring salvation to every man, woman, boy and girl who does now live or has lived or will yet live in the world.

To some it may seem old-fashioned to speak of virtue and chastity, honesty, morality, faith, character, but these are the qualities which have built great men and women and point the way by which one may find happiness in the living of today and eternal joy in the world to come. These are the qualities which are the anchors to our lives, in spite of the trials, the tragedies, the pestilences, and the cruelties of war which bring in their wake appalling destruction, hunger, and bloodshed.

Those who fail to heed the warnings of those who are striving to teach these principles and choose to go in the opposite course will eventually find themselves in the pitiable state which you are witnessing so often among us. The prophet Isaiah described the tragic result most dramatically when he repeated the words of God which came to him as he sought to fortify his people against the wickedness of the world:

> . . . Peace, peace to him that is far off, and to him that is near, saith the Lord; and I will heal him. But the wicked are like the troubled sea, when it cannot rest, whose waters cast up mire and dirt. There is no peace, saith my God, to the wicked. (Isaiah 57:19–21.)

Other prophets have declared likewise, so forcibly as to not be misunderstood, that "wickedness never was happiness." (Alma 41:10.)

As I have prayerfully thought of the reasons why one chooses this course which is dramatically described by the prophet Isaiah—when one who has departed from the path which would have given him peace is like the troubled sea, casting up mire and dirt—it seems to me that it all results from the failure of the individual to have self-respect. Listen to these words of wisdom from those whose lives have been worthy of emulation and who have experienced the realities of the periods of time from which they speak.

"Self-respect—that corner-stone of all virtue."—Sir John Frederick William Herschel.

"Self-respect is the noblest garment with which a man can clothe himself, the most elevating feeling with which the mind can be inspired."—Samuel Smiles.

"Every man stamps his value on himself. The price we challenge for ourselves is given us by others. Man is made great or little by his own will."—Johann von Schiller.

A lovely mother in a nearby community wrote this to me. "I love America, I love my husband, I love my children, I love my God, and why is this possible? Because I truly love myself."

Such are the fruits of self-respect. Conversely, when one does not have that love for himself of which this sister speaks, other consequences can be expected to follow. He ceases to love life. Or if he marries, he has lost his love for his wife and children—no love of home or respect for the country in which he lives—and eventually he has lost his love of God. Rebellion in the land, disorder and the lack of love in the family, children disobedient to parents, loss of contact with God, all because that person has lost all respect for himself.

I recall an invitation I had to speak to men who, for the most part, had not been advanced in the Church because of their lack of desire or their lack of understanding of the importance of conforming to certain standards required for advancement. The subject on which I was to speak was "Who Am I?" As I pondered this subject and searched the word of God to prepare for this assignment, I immediately sensed that I was to talk about a subject that is of first importance to each of us as it was to those men among whom, no doubt, there were some who had not found themselves and who lacked the basis of a solid foundation upon which to build their lives.

The rowdiness of children, the incorrigibility of adolescents are more often than not a bid for a kind of attention or popularity that physical and mental endowments do not invite. So the blasé girl and the unkempt boy are often but a reflection of an individual who is seeking, by superficial adornment or by abnormal conduct (in a strange way), to supply that indefinable quality they may think is charm—a clumsy attempt to draw attention by conduct which certainly reflects that inward frustration because of the lack of understanding of their true identity as a human being.

Well, then, "Who am I?" Those lacking in that important understanding, and, consequently, in some degree those failing to hold themselves in the high esteem which they would have if they did understand, are lacking self-respect.

May I begin to answer that question by posing two questions from scriptural texts which should be impressed upon every soul.

The psalmist wrote:

What is man, that thou art mindful of him? and the son of man, that thou visitest him? For thou hast made him a little lower than the angels, and hast crowned him with glory and honour. (Psalm 8:4–5.)

And the next is the question the Lord posed to Job:

Where wast thou when I laid the foundations of the earth? declare, if thou hast understanding . . . [of] when the morning stars sang together, and all the sons of God shouted for joy? (Job 38:4–7.)

Reduced to more simple language than the words of those

questions from the scriptures, the prophets in these quotations are simply asking each of us, "Where did you come from? Why are you here?"

A great psychologist, MacDougall, once said: "The first thing to be done to help a man to moral regeneration is to restore if possible his self-respect." Also I recall the prayer of the old English weaver, "O God, help me to hold a high opinion of myself." That should be the prayer of every soul; not an abnormally developed self-esteem that becomes haughtiness, conceit, or arrogance, but a righteous self-respect that might be defined as "belief in one's own worth, worth to God, and worth to man."

Now, consider these answers to the searching questions which must be burned into the consciousness of all those who have strayed away or who have not arrived at a true evaluation of themselves in this world of chaos.

The Apostle Paul wrote:

> Furthermore we have had fathers of our flesh which corrected us, and we gave them reverence: shall we not much rather be in subjection unto the Father of spirits, and live? (Hebrews 12:9.)

This suggests that all who live upon the earth, who have their fathers on earth, likewise have a father of their spirits. So did Moses and Aaron, as they fell upon their faces, cry out: "O God, the God of the spirits of all flesh, shall one man sin, and wilt thou be wroth with all the congregation?" (Numbers 16:22.)

Note how they addressed the Lord, " . . . the God [Father] of the spirits of all flesh [mankind]. . . ."

From the revelations through Abraham, we get a glimpse of who and what the spirit is:

> Now the Lord had shown unto me, Abraham, the intelligences that were organized before the world was, and among all these there were many of the noble and great ones;
> And God saw these souls that they were good, and he stood in the midst of them, and he said: These I will make my

rulers; for he stood among those that were spirits, and he saw that they were good: and he said unto me: Abraham, thou art one of them; thou wast chosen before thou wast born. (Abraham 3:22–23.)

There we are told that the Lord promised that those who were faithful in that premortal world would be added upon, by having a physical body in the second estate of this earth's existence and, furthermore, if they would keep the commandments as God taught by the revelations, they would have "glory added upon their heads for ever and ever." (Abraham 3:26.)

Now, there are several precious truths in that scripture. First, we have a definition of what a spirit is, as it relates to our physical body. What did it look like in that premortal world (if we could see it apart from our mortal body)? A modern latter-day prophet gives us an inspired answer:

> . . . that which is spiritual being in the likeness of that which is temporal; and that which is temporal in the likeness of that which is spiritual; the spirit of man in the likeness of his person, as also the spirit of the beast, and every other creature which God has created. (D&C 77:2.)

The next truth we learn from this scripture is that you and I, having been spirits and now having bodies, were among those who passed that first test and were given the privilege of coming to earth as mortal individuals. If we hadn't passed that test, we wouldn't be here with mortal bodies, but would have been denied this privilege and would have followed Satan or Lucifer, as he came to be known, as did one-third of the spirits created in that pre-mortal existence who were deprived of the privilege of having mortal bodies. These are now among us, but only in their spiritual form, to make a further attempt to thwart the plan of salvation by which all who would obey would have the great glory of returning to God our Father who gave us life.

So the Old Testament prophets declared with respect to death: "Then shall the dust [meaning our mortal bodies] return to the

earth as it was: and the spirit shall return unto God who gave it."
(Ecclesiastes 12:7.)

Obviously we could not return to a place where we had never
been, so we are talking about death as a process as miraculous as
birth, by which we return to "our Father who art in heaven," as the
Master taught His disciples to pray.

A further truth is clearly set forth in that scripture (Abraham
3:22–23), that many were chosen, as was Abraham, before they
were born, as the Lord told Moses and also Jeremiah. This was
made still more meaningful by the latter-day prophet, Joseph
Smith, who declared: "I believe that every person who is called to
do an important work in the kingdom of God, was called to that
work and foreordained to that work before the world was." Then
he added this, "I believe that I was foreordained to the work that I
am called to do." (*Documentary History of the Church*, 6:364.)

But now there is a warning: Despite that calling which is spoken of in the scriptures as "foreordination," we have another
inspired declaration: "Behold, there are many called, but few are
chosen. . . ." (D&C 121:34.)

This suggests that even though we have our free agency here,
there are many who were foreordained before the world was, to a
greater state than they have prepared themselves for here. Even
though they might have been among the noble and great, from
among whom the Father declared he would make his chosen
leaders, they may fail of that calling here in mortality. Then the
Lord poses this question: " . . . and why are they not chosen?"
(D&C 121:34.)

Two answers were given: First, "Because their hearts are set
so much upon the things of this world. . . ." And second, they
". . . aspire to the honors of men." (D&C 121:35.)

Now then, to summarize, may I ask each of you again the question, "Who are you?" You are all the sons and daughters of God.
Your spirits were created and lived as organized intelligences before

the world was. You have been blessed to have a physical body because of your obedience to certain commandments in that pre-mortal state. . . .

Now there is another important understanding that we have from the scriptures. We are all free agents, which means to some people who manifest a spirit of rebellion that they are free to do anything they please, but that is not the correct meaning of free agency as the prophets have declared in the scriptures where free agency has been defined:

> Wherefore, men are free according to the flesh; and all things are given them which are expedient unto man. And they are free to choose liberty and eternal life, through the great mediation of all men, or to choose captivity and death, according to the captivity and power of the devil; for he seeketh that all men might be miserable like unto himself. (2 Nephi 2:27.)

The Apostle Paul impressed the sacredness of our individual bodies in this statement:

> Know ye not that ye are the temple of God, and that the Spirit of God dwelleth in you? If any man defile the temple of God, him shall God destroy; for the temple of God is holy, which temple ye are. (1 Corinthians 3:16–17.)

And, again, he said further to those who had been baptized members of the church that they had received the gift of a special endowment known as the Holy Ghost. This was his teaching:

> What? know ye not that your body is the temple of the Holy Ghost which is in you, which ye have of God, and ye are not your own? . . . therefore glorify God in your body, and in your spirit, which are God's. (1 Corinthians 6:19–20.)

If we can get a person to think what those words mean, then we can begin to understand the significance of the words of the renowned psychologist, MacDougall, from whom I have previously quoted, "The first thing to be done to help a man to moral regeneration is to restore, if possible, his self-respect." How better may that self-respect be restored than to help him to fully understand the answer to that question, "Who am I?"

When we see one devoid of respect for himself, as indicated by his conduct, his outward appearance, his speech, and his utter disregard of the basic measures of decency, then certainly we are witnessing the frightening aspect of one over whom Satan has achieved a victory, as the Lord declared he would try to do "to deceive and to blind men, and to lead them captive at his will . . . to destroy the agency of man." (Moses 4:14.) This is the fate of "even as many as would not hearken unto my voice" (Moses 4:4), so declared the Lord to Moses. . . .

The Lord's eternal purpose with respect to His plan of salvation was declared to Moses: "For behold, this is my work and my glory—to bring to pass the immortality and eternal life of man." (Moses 1:39.)

The first goal in that eternal plan was for each of us to come to earth and gain a physical body, and then, after death and the resurrection which would follow, the spirit and the resurrected body would not thereafter be subject to death. All of this was a free gift to every living soul, as Paul declared: "For as in Adam all die, even so in Christ shall all be made alive." (1 Corinthians 15:22.)

What this means to one dying with a malignant malady or to a mother bereft of a child may be illustrated by the expressions of a young mother whom I visited in the hospital some years ago. She said to me, "I have thought all this through. It doesn't make any difference whether I go now or whether I live to seventy, eighty, or ninety. The sooner I can get to a place where I can be active and doing things that will bring me eternal joy, the better for all concerned." She was comforted by the thought that she had lived such a life as to be worthy to enter into the presence of God, which is to enjoy eternal life.

The importance of taking advantage of every hour of precious time allotted to each of us here was impressed forcibly upon me by an incident in my own family. A young mother came with her beautiful flaxen-haired six-year-old daughter to her grandparents. The mother asked if we would like to hear a beautiful new children's song the daughter had just learned in her Primary class. While the little mother accompanied her, she sang:

> I am a child of God,
> And He has sent me here,
> Has given me an earthly home
> With parents kind and dear.
>
> I am a child of God,
> And so my needs are great;
> Help me to understand His words
> Before it grows too late.
>
> I am a child of God,
> Rich blessings are in store;
> If I but learn to do His will
> I'll live with Him once more.
>
> (Chorus)
> Lead me, guide me, walk beside me,
> Help me find the way.
> Teach me all that I must do
> To live with Him some day.
> (*Hymns*, no. 301)

Her grandparents were in tears. Little did they know then that hardly before that little girl would have had the full opportunity for her mother to teach her all that she should know in order to return to her heavenly home, the little mother would be suddenly taken away in death, leaving to others the responsibility of finding the answer to the pleadings of that childhood prayer, to teach and train and to lead her through the uncertainties of life.

What a difference it would make if we really sensed our divine relationship to God, our Heavenly Father, our relationship to Jesus

Christ, our Savior and our Elder Brother, and our relationship to each other.

Contrasted with the sublime peace to one such as that wonderful sister I visited in the hospital is that terrifying state of those who do not, as they approach death, have that great comfort, for as the Lord has told us plainly: "And they that die not in me, woe unto them, for their death is bitter." (D&C 42:47.)

It was George Bernard Shaw who said, "If we all realized that we were the children of one father, we would stop shouting at each other as much as we do."

Now, I trust that I might have given to you, and to others who have not yet listened to such counsel, something to stimulate some sober thinking as to who you are and whence you came; and, in so doing, that I may have stirred up within your soul the determination to begin now to show an increased self-respect and reverence for the temple of God, your human body, wherein dwells a heavenly spirit. I would charge you to say again and again to yourselves, as the Primary organization has taught the children to sing, "I am a [son or a daughter] of God," and by so doing, begin today to live closer to those ideals which will make your life happier and more fruitful because of an awakened realization of who you are.

God grant that each of us here today may so live that all among us, and with us, may see not us, but that which is divine and comes from God. With that vision of what those who have lost their way may become, my prayer is that they may receive strength and resolution to climb higher and higher and upward and onward to that great goal of eternal life and also that I may do my part in seeking to show by example, as well as by precept, that which will be the best of which I am capable of doing.

I again bear my solemn witness to the great truth of the Master's profound words to the sobbing Martha: "I am the resurrection, and the life: he that believeth in me, though he were dead, yet shall he live." (John 11:25.)

I thank God that I too can say, with the same spirit as did Martha, who bore her testimony as the Spirit witnessed to her from the depths of her soul: "Yea, Lord: I [too know] that thou art the Christ, the Son of God, which [came] into the world." (John 11:27.)

"Understanding Who We Are Brings Self-Respect," *Ensign*, January 1974, 2–6.

❦ ❧

IN HIS STRENGTH

MARVIN J. ASHTON

This oft-quoted address was given in general conference in April 1973. In it, Elder Marvin J. Ashton cites instances showing that "nobody is a nobody." His belief in the intrinsic eternal worth of each soul was a result not only of his testimony of the gospel but also of his longtime efforts to assist the youth of the Church, including prison inmates and others considered less worthy. "Worthiness is a process," he said in one conference address, "and perfection is an eternal trek. We can be worthy to enjoy certain privileges without being perfect." (*Ensign*, May 1989, 20.)

He later noted, "When we have a yearning and don't know what it is for, perhaps it's our soul longing for its heartland, longing to be no longer alienated from the Lord and the pursuit of something much higher, better, and more fulfilling than anything this earth has to offer," he said in his last general conference address. "May our yearning for home be the motivation we need to so live that we can return to our heavenly home with God our Father on a forever basis." (*Ensign*, November 1992, 23.)

———————————

A few weeks ago on a day when this area was experiencing one of its worst snowstorms, . . . a handsome young serviceman and his beautiful bride-to-be encountered extreme difficulty in getting to the Salt Lake Temple for their marriage appointment. She was in one location in the Salt Lake Valley and he was to come from another nearby town. Heavy snows and winds had closed the highways during the night and early morning hours. After many hours of anxious waiting, some of us were able to help them get to the temple and complete their marriage plans before the day was over.

How grateful they, their families, and friends were for the assistance and concern in their keeping this most important appointment. My friend—we will call him Bill—expressed his deep gratitude with, "Thank you very much for all you did to make our wedding possible. I don't understand why you went to all this trouble to help me. Really, I'm nobody."

I am sure Bill meant his comment to be a most sincere compliment, but I responded to it firmly, but I hope kindly, with, "Bill, I have never helped a 'nobody' in my life. In the kingdom of our Heavenly Father no man is a 'nobody.'"

This tendency to wrongfully identify ourselves was again brought to my attention the other day during an interview with a troubled wife. Her marriage is in great difficulty. She has tried earnestly to correct the communication blocks with her husband but with little success. She is grateful for the time her bishop has spent in counseling. Her stake president has also been most patient and understanding in his willingness to try and help.

All of her problems are not resolved, but she is making progress. Her many contacts with properly channeled priesthood direction have left her not only grateful, but somewhat amazed. Her concluding observation the other day was, "I just don't understand all of you people giving so much time and showing so much concern. After all, I'm really 'nobody.'"

I am certain our Heavenly Father is displeased when we refer to ourselves as "nobody." How fair are we when we classify ourselves a "nobody"? How fair are we to our families? How fair are we to our God?

We do ourselves a great injustice when we allow ourselves, through tragedy, misfortune, challenge, discouragement, or whatever the earthly situation, to so identify ourselves. No matter how or where we find ourselves, we cannot with any justification label ourselves "nobody."

As children of God we are somebody. He will build us, mold us, and magnify us if we will but hold our heads up, our arms out, and walk with him. What a great blessing to be created in his image and know of our true potential in and through him! What a great blessing to know that in his strength we can do all things!

Ammon taught a great lesson not only to his brother Aaron, but to all of us in this day, in Alma 26:10–12:

"And it came to pass that when Ammon had said these words, his brother Aaron rebuked him, saying: Ammon, I fear that thy joy doth carry thee away unto boasting.

"But Ammon said unto him: I do not boast in my own strength, nor in my own wisdom; but behold, my joy is full, yea, my heart is brim with joy, and I will rejoice in my God.

"Yea, I know . . . as to my strength I am weak; therefore I will not boast of myself, but I will boast of my God, for in his strength I can do all things; yea, behold, many mighty miracles we have wrought in this land, for which we will praise his name forever."

As grievous as labeling ourselves as a "nobody" is man's tendency to classify others as a "nobody." Sometimes mankind is prone to identify the stranger or the unknown as a nobody. Often this is done for self-convenience and an unwillingness to listen. Countless numbers today reject Joseph Smith and his message because they will not accept a 14-year-old "nobody." Others turn away from eternal restored truths available today because they will not accept a 19-year-old elder or a 21-year-old lady missionary or a neighbor down the street because they are "nobody," so they may suppose.

There is no doubt in my mind that one of the reasons our Savior Jesus Christ was rejected and crucified was because in the eyes of the world he was blindly viewed as a "nobody," humbly born in a manger, an advocate of such strange doctrine as "Peace on earth, good will toward men."

I bear witness to you and the world that Joseph Smith knew with earth-shattering impact he was "somebody" when, in answer to humble prayer, God appeared with his Son, Jesus Christ, and spoke unto Joseph, calling him by name. God through the centuries has often chosen what the world would classify as a "nobody" to bear his truths. Listen to Joseph Smith's thoughts and self-analysis in this area:

"It caused me serious reflection then, and often has since, how very strange it was that an obscure boy, of a little over fourteen years of age, and one, too, who was doomed to the necessity of obtaining a scanty maintenance by his daily labor, should be thought a character of sufficient importance to attract the attention of the great ones of the most popular sects of the day, and in a manner to create in them a spirit of the most bitter persecution and reviling. But strange or not, so it was, and it was the cause of great sorrow to myself.

"However, it was nevertheless a fact that I had beheld a vision. . . ." (JS–H 1:23–24.)

May I remind all of us that Joseph Smith referred to himself as "an obscure boy" but never as a "nobody." Joseph Smith was sustained all the days of his perilous life by the knowledge that in God's strength he could accomplish all things.

God help us to realize that one of our greatest responsibilities and privileges is to lift a self-labeled "nobody" to a "somebody," who is wanted, needed, and desirable. Our first obligation in this area of stewardship is to begin with self. "I am nobody" is a destructive philosophy. It is a tool of the deceiver.

It is heartbreaking when youth in difficulty look up and respond to offered guidance with, "What does it matter? I'm nobody."

It is just as disturbing when a questioned student on campus responds with, "I am no one special on campus. I'm just one of the thousands. I'm really nobody."

May we learn an important lesson from a missionary recently interviewed. This elder, in answer to the question, "How often do you receive letters from your parents?" responded with, "Very, very seldom."

"What are you doing about it?" I asked.

"I'm still writing them every week."

Here is a young man who may have had some excuse to pity himself with a "nobody" label when his parents don't bother to write, but he is having no part of this kind of attitude. Further conversation with him emphatically convinced me that here is a young man who is really someone. If his parents don't write, that is their responsibility. His responsibility is to write, and that is just what he is doing with enthusiasm. I have never met this missionary's mother or father, probably never will, but wherever they are, in my mind they are "somebody" just to have him for their son. This missionary will succeed because he knows he is someone and is conducting himself accordingly.

More than once during the past few months President Harold B. Lee has called me to his office to listen with him to someone he has invited to share a suggestion, concern, bewilderment, or heartache. Some might well conclude for President Lee that he just doesn't have time for the least of these his brethren, but he knows well the worth of every soul in the kingdom. I recall one saying to President Lee at the time of departure, "I can't believe you would take the time to listen to someone like me."

To mothers, fathers, husbands, wives, and children everywhere, we declare that regardless of your present station in life you are someone special. Remember, you may be an obscure boy, girl, man, or woman, but you are not a "nobody." Please enjoy with me one of the truly great parables in all of the holy scriptures as we think along this subject.

A certain man had two sons:

And the younger of them said to his father, Father, give me the portion of goods that falleth to me. And he divided unto them his living.

And not many days after the younger son gathered all together, and took his journey into a far country, and there wasted his substance with riotous living.

And when he had spent all, there arose a mighty famine in that land; and he began to be in want.

And he went and joined himself to a citizen of that country; and he sent him into his fields to feed swine.

And he would fain have filled his belly with the husks that the swine did eat: and no man gave unto him.

And when he came to himself, he said, How many hired servants of my father's have bread enough and to spare, and I perish with hunger!

I will arise and go to my father, and will say unto him, Father, I have sinned against heaven, and before thee,

And am no more worthy to be called thy son: make me as one of thy hired servants.

And he arose, and came to his father. But when he was yet a great way off, his father saw him, and had compassion, and ran, and fell on his neck, and kissed him.

And the son said unto him, Father, I have sinned against heaven, and in thy sight, and am no more worthy to be called thy son.

But the father said to his servants, Bring forth the best robe, and put it on him; and put a ring on his hand, and shoes on his feet:

And bring hither the fatted calf, and kill it; and let us eat, and be merry:

For this my son was dead, and is alive again; he was lost, and is found. And they began to be merry.

Now his elder son was in the field: and as he came and drew nigh to the house, he heard music and dancing.

And he called one of the servants and asked what these things meant.

And he said unto him, Thy brother is come; and thy

father hath killed the fatted calf, because he hath received him safe and sound.

And he was angry, and would not go in: therefore came his father out, and intreated him.

And he answering said to his father, Lo, these many years do I serve thee, neither transgressed I at any time thy commandment: and yet thou never gavest me a kid, that I might make merry with my friends:

But as soon as this thy son was come, which hath devoured thy living with harlots, thou has killed for him the fatted calf.

And he said unto him, Son, thou art ever with me, and all that I have is thine.

It was meet that we should make merry, and be glad: for this thy brother was dead, and is alive again; and was lost, and is found. (Luke 15:11–32.)

Brothers and sisters, think well again on these points, if you will. "Father, divide your goods and give me my share. I am going off on my own." In the days ahead he wasted his possessions with riotous living. He became so low, so hungry, he lived with the swine. "Father, I have sinned against heaven, and in thy sight, and am no more worthy to be called thy son." His heart was crying out, "I am lower than the low. I am now absolutely nothing—I am absolutely nobody."

Please weigh the impact of the father's response once more. He saw the son coming; he ran to him; he kissed him; he placed his best robe on him; he killed the fatted calf; and they made merry together. This self-declared "nobody" was his son; he was "dead, and is alive again; he was lost, and is found."

In the father's joy he also taught well his older, bewildered son that he too was someone. "Son, thou art ever with me, and all that I have is thine." Contemplate, if you will, the depth—yes, even the eternal proportions—of "all that I have is thine." I declare with all the strength I possess that we have a Heavenly Father who claims and loves all of us regardless of where our steps have taken us. You are his son and you are his daughter, and he loves you.

Do not allow yourself to be self-condemning. Avoid discouragement. Teach yourself correct principles and govern yourself with honor. Appropriately involve yourself in helping others. As we develop proper self-image in ourselves and others, I promise you the "nobody" attitude will completely disappear. Ever remember wherever you are today within the sound of my voice that you are someone.

God lives. He too is someone—real and eternal—and he wants us to be someone with him. I bear witness that in his strength we can become like him. I leave you this my witness and my testimony humbly and in the name of Jesus Christ. Amen.

Ensign, July 1973, 25–27.

SPIRIT WORLD

~≪ ≫~

SPIRITUAL COMMUNICATION

PARLEY P. PRATT

This address was given in general conference, April 7, 1853. In it, Elder Parley P. Pratt set forth some of the glorious gospel principles pertaining to the postmortal world and the beings who inhabit it. Those who dwell in the spirit world, he taught, remain in ignorance of gospel truths until someone teaches them. "Who, then, is prepared, among the spirits in the spirit world, to communicate the truth on the subject of salvation, to guide the people, to give advice, to confer consolation, to heal the sick, to administer joy, and gladness, and hope of immortality and eternal life, founded on manifest truth? . . . Peter, James, Joseph, Hyrum, Father Smith, any, or all of those ancient or modern Saints who have departed this life, who are clothed upon with the power of the eternal Apostleship or Priesthood, who have gone to the world of spirits, not to sorrow, but as joyful messengers, bearing glad tidings of eternal truth to the spirits in prison—could not these teach us good things? Yes."

Four years after giving this message, Elder Pratt was murdered at the young age of fifty, thus going to join his fellow Apostles in their missionary labors in the world of the spirits.

————————

I was led to reflection on this subject, not only by my acquaintance with the present state of the world, and the movements and powers which seem new to many, but because this text, written by Isaiah so many centuries since, and copied by Nephi ages before the birth of Jesus Christ, seemed as appropriate, and as directly adapted to the present state of things, as if written but yesterday, or a year since.

"Should not a people seek unto their God, for the living to hear from the dead?" is a question by the Prophet, and at a time when they shall invite you to seek unto those familiar with spirits, and to wizards, etc., or in other words, to magnetizers, rappers, clairvoyants, writing mediums, etc. When they shall say these things unto you, then is the time to consider the question of that ancient Prophet—"Should not a people seek unto their God, for the living to hear from the dead?"

We hear much, of late, about visions, trances, clairvoyance, mediums of communication with the spirit world, writing mediums, etc., by which the world of spirits is said to have found means to communicate with spirits in the flesh. They are not working in a corner. The world is agitated on these subjects. Religious ministers are said to preach, editors to write and print, judges to judge, etc., by this kind of inspiration. It is brought into requisition to develop the sciences, to detect crime, and in short to mingle in all the interests of life.

In the first place, what are we talking about, when we touch the question of the living hearing from the dead? It is a saying, that *dead men tell no tales.* If this is not in the Bible, it is somewhere else; and if it be true, it is just as good as if it were in the Bible.

The Sadducees in the time of Jesus, believed there were no such things as angels or spirits, or existence in another sphere; that when an individual was dead, it was the final end of the workings of his intellectual being, that the elements were dissolved, and mingled with the great fountain from which they emanated, which was the end of individuality, or conscious existence.

Jesus, in reply to them, took up the argument from the Scriptures, or history of the ancient fathers, venerated by reason of antiquity, in hopes, by this means, to influence the Sadducees, or at least the Pharisees and others, by means so powerful and so well adapted to the end in view.

Said he, God has declared Himself the God of Abraham, Isaac, and Jacob. Now God is not the God of the dead, but the God of the living; as much as to say that Abraham, Isaac, and Jacob were not dead, but living; that they had never been dead at all, but had always been living; that they never did die, in the sense of the word that these Sadducees supposed, but were absolutely alive.

Now if intelligent beings, who once inhabited flesh, such as our fathers, mothers, wives, children, etc., have really died, and are now dead in the sense of the word, as understood by the ancient Sadducees, or modern Atheist, then it is in vain to talk of converse with the dead. All controversy, in that case, is at an end on the subject of correspondence with the dead, because an intelligence must exist before it can communicate. If these individuals are dead, in the sense that the human body dies, then there is no communication from them. This we know, because of our own observation and experience. We have seen many dead bodies, but have never known of a single instance of any intelligence communicated therefrom.

Jesus, in his argument with the Sadducees, handled the subject according to the strictest principles of ancient and modern theology, and true philosophy. He conveyed the idea in the clearest terms, that an individual intelligence or identity could never die.

The outward tabernacle, inhabited by a spirit, returns to the element from which it emanated. But the thinking being, the individual, active agent or identity that inhabited that tabernacle, never ceased to exist, to think, act, live, move, or have a being; never ceased to exercise those sympathies, affections, hopes, and aspirations, which are founded in the very nature of intelligences, being the inherent and invaluable principles of their eternal existence.

No, they never cease. They live, move, think, act, converse, feel, love, hate, believe, doubt, hope, and desire.

But what are they, if they are not flesh and bones? What are they, if they are not tangible to our gross organs of sense? Of what are they composed, that we can neither see, hear, nor handle them, except we are quickened, or our organs touched by the principles of vision, clairvoyance, or spiritual sight? What are they? Why, they are organized intelligences. What are they made of? They are made of the element which we call spirit, which is as much an element of material existence, as earth, air, electricity, or any other tangible substance recognized by man; but so subtle, so refined is its nature, that it is not tangible to our gross organs. It is invisible to us, unless we are quickened by a portion of the same element; and, like electricity, and several other substances, it is only known or made manifest to our senses by its effects. For instance, electricity is not always visible to us, but its existence is made manifest by its operations upon the wire, or upon the nerves. We cannot see the air, but we feel its effects, and without it we cannot breathe. . . .

It is true that this subtle fluid or spiritual element is endowed with the powers of locomotion in a far greater degree than the more gross or solid elements of nature; that its refined particles penetrate amid the other elements with greater ease, and meet with less resistance from the air or other substances, than would the more gross elements. Hence its speed, or superior powers of motion.

Now let us apply this philosophy to all the degrees of spiritual element, from electricity, which may be assumed to be one of the lowest or more gross elements of spiritual matter, up through all the gradations of the invisible fluids, till we arrive at a substance so holy, so pure, so endowed with intellectual attributes and sympathetic affections, that it may be said to be on a par, or level, in its attributes, with man.

Let a given quantity of this element, thus endowed, or capacitated, be organized in the size and form of man, let every organ be developed, formed, and endowed, precisely after the pattern or model of man's outward or fleshly tabernacle—what would we call this individual, organized portion of the spiritual element?

We would call it a spiritual body, an individual intelligence, an agent endowed with life, with a degree of independence, or inherent will, with the powers of motion, of thought, and with the attributes of moral, intellectual, and sympathetic affections and emotions.

We would conceive of it as possessing eyes to see, ears to hear, hands to handle; as in possession of the organ of taste, of smelling, and of speech.

Such beings are we, when we have laid off this outward tabernacle of flesh. We are in every way interested, in our relationships, kindred ties, sympathies, affections, and hopes, as if we had continued to live, but had stepped aside, and were experiencing the loneliness of absence for a season. Our ancestors, our posterity, to the remotest ages of antiquity, or of future time, are all brought within the circle of our sphere of joys, sorrows, interests, or expectations; each forms a link in the great chain of life, and in the science of mutual salvation, improvement, and exaltation through the blood of the Lamb.

Our prospects, hopes, faith, charity, enlightenment, improvement, in short, all our interests, are blended, and more or less influenced by the acts of each.

Is this the kind of being that departs from our sight when its earthly tabernacle is laid off, and the veil of eternity is lowered between us? Yes, verily. Where then does it go?

To heaven, says one; to the eternal world of glory, says another; to the celestial kingdom, to inherit thrones and crowns, in all the fulness of the presence of the Father, and of Jesus Christ, says a third.

Now, my dear hearers, these things are not so. Nothing of the kind. Thrones, kingdoms, crowns, principalities, and powers, in the celestial and eternal worlds, and the fulness of the presence of the Father, and of His Son Jesus Christ, are reserved for resurrected beings, who dwell in immortal flesh. The world of resurrected beings, and the world of spirits, are two distinct spheres, as much so as our own sphere is distinct from that of the spirit world.

Where then does the spirit go, on its departure from its earthly tabernacle? It passes to the next sphere of human existence, called the world of spirits, a veil being drawn between us in the flesh, and that world of spirits. Well, says one, is there no more than one place in the spirit world? Yes, there are many places and degrees in that world, as in this. Jesus Christ, when absent from his flesh, did not ascend to the Father, to be crowned, and enthroned in power. Why? Because he had not yet a resurrected body, and had therefore a mission to perform in another sphere. Where then did he go? To the world of spirits. . . . The thief on the cross, who died at the same time, also went to the same world, and to the same particular place in the same world, for he was a sinner, and would of course go to the prison of the condemned, there to await the ministry of that Gospel which had failed to reach his case while on the earth. . . . "This day shalt thou be with me in Paradise," said Jesus, or, in other words, this day shalt thou be with me in the next sphere of existence—the world of spirits.

Now mark the difference. Jesus was there, as a preacher of righteousness, as one holding the keys of Apostleship, or Priesthood, anointed to preach glad tidings to the meek, to bind up the brokenhearted, to preach liberty to the captive, and the opening of the prison to them that were bound. What did the thief go there for? He went there in a state of ignorance, and sin, being uncultivated, unimproved, and unprepared for salvation. He went there to be taught, and to complete that repentance, which in a dying moment he commenced on the earth.

He had beheld Jesus expire on the cross, and he had implored him to remember him when he should come into possession of his kingdom. The Saviour under these extreme circumstances, did not then teach him the Gospel, but referred him to the next opportunity, . . . in the spirit world. If the thief thus favoured continued to improve, he is no doubt waiting in hope for the signal to be given, at the sound of the next trump, for him to leave the spirit world, and to re-enter the fleshly tabernacle, and to ascend to a higher degree of felicity. Jesus Christ, on the other hand, departed from the spirit world on the third day, and re-entered his fleshly tabernacle, in which he ascended, and was crowned at the right hand of the Father. Jesus Christ then, and the thief on the cross, have not dwelt together in the same kingdom or place, for this eighteen hundred years, nor have we proof that they have seen each other during that time.

To say that Jesus Christ dwells in the world of spirits, with those whose bodies are dead, would not be the truth. He is not there. He only stayed there till the third day. He then returned to his tabernacle, and ministered among the sons of earth for forty days, where he ate, drank, talked, preached, reasoned out of the Scriptures, commissioned, commanded, blessed, etc. Why did he do this? Because he had ascended on high, and been crowned with all power in heaven and on earth, therefore he had authority to do all these things.

So much then for that wonderful question that has been asked by our Christian neighbors, so many thousand times, in the abundance of their charity for those who, like the thief on the cross, die in their sins, or without baptism, and the other Gospel ordinances.

The question naturally arises—Do all the people who die without the Gospel hear it as soon as they arrive in the world of spirits? To illustrate this, let us look at the dealings of God with the people of this world. "What can we reason but from what we know?" We know and understand the things of this world, in some degree, because they are visible, and we are daily conversant with them. Do all the people in this world hear the Gospel as soon as they are capable of understanding? No, indeed, but very few in comparison have heard it at all.

Ask the . . . Lamanites who have, with their fathers before them, inhabited these mountains for a thousand years, whether they have ever heard the Gospel, and they will tell you nay. But why not? Is it not preached on the earth? Yea, verily, but the earth is wide, and circumstances differ very greatly among its different inhabitants. The Jews once had the Gospel, with its Apostleship, powers, and blessings offered unto them, but they rejected it as a people, and for this reason it was taken from them, and thus many generations of them have been born, and have lived and died without it. So with the Gentiles, and so with the Lamanites. God has seen proper to offer the Gospel, with its Priesthood and powers, in different ages and countries, but it has been as often rejected, and therefore withdrawn from the earth. The consequence is that the generations of men have, for many ages, come and gone in ignorance of its principles, and the glorious hopes they inspire.

Now these blessings would have continued on the earth, and would have been enjoyed in all the ages and nations of man, but for the agency of the people. They chose their own forms of government, laws, institutions, religions, rulers, and priests, instead of yielding to the influence and guidance of the chosen vessels of the Lord, who were appointed to instruct and govern them.

Now, how are they situated in the spirit world? If we reason from analogy, we should at once conclude that things exist there after the same pattern. I have not the least doubt but there are spirits there who have dwelt there a thousand years, who, if we could converse with them face to face, would be found as ignorant of the truths, the ordinances, powers, keys, Priesthood, resurrection, and eternal life of the body, in short, as ignorant of the fulness of the Gospel, with its hopes and consolations, as . . . [are the spiritually uneducated in this mortal life].

And why this ignorance in the spirit world? Because a portion of the inhabitants thereof are found unworthy of the consolations of the Gospel, until the fulness of time, until they have suffered in hell, in the dungeons of darkness, or the prisons of the condemned, amid the buffetings of fiends, and malicious and lying spirits.

As in earth, so in the spirit world. No person can enter into the privileges of the Gospel, until the keys are turned, and the Gospel opened by those in authority, for all which there is a time, according to the wise dispensations of justice and mercy.

It was many, many centuries before Christ lived in the flesh, that a whole generation, eight souls excepted, were cut off by the flood. What became of them? I do not know exactly all their history in the spirit world. But this much I know—they have heard the Gospel . . . , and have the privilege of being judged according to men in the flesh. . . .

How long did they wait? You may reckon for yourselves. The long ages, centuries, thousands of years which intervened between the flood of Noah and the death of Christ. Oh! the weariness, the tardy movement of time! the lingering ages for a people to dwell in condemnation, darkness, ignorance, and despondency, as a punishment for their sins. For they had been filled with violence while on the earth in the flesh, and had rejected the preaching of Noah, and the Prophets which were before him.

Between these two dispensations, so distant from each other in point of time, they were left to linger without hope, and without God, in the spirit world; and similar has been the fate of the poor Jew, the miserable Lamanite, and many others in the flesh. Between the commission and ministry of the Former- and Latter-day Saints, and Apostles, there has been a long and dreary night of darkness. Some fifteen to seventeen centuries have passed away, in which the generations of man have lived without the keys of the Gospel.

Whether in the flesh, or in the spirit world, is this not hell enough? . . . Think of those swept away by the flood in the days of Noah. Did they wait a long time in prison? Forty hundred years! O what a time to be imprisoned. What do you say to a hundred, a thousand, two thousand, three or four thousand years to wait? Without what? Without even a clear idea or hope of a resurrection from the dead, without the broken heart being bound up, the captive delivered, or the door of the prison opened. Did not they wait? Yes they did, until Christ was put to death in the flesh.

Now what would have been the result, if they had repented while in the flesh at the preaching of Noah? Why, they would have died in hope of a glorious resurrection, and would have enjoyed the society of the redeemed, and lived in happiness in the spirit world, till the resurrection of the Son of God. Then they would have received their bodies, and would have ascended with him, amid thrones, principalities, and powers in heavenly places.

I will suppose, in the spirit world, a grade of spirits of the lowest order, composed of murderers, robbers, thieves, adulterers, drunkards, and persons ignorant, uncultivated, etc., who are in prison, or in hell, without hope, without God, and unworthy as yet of Gospel instruction. Such spirits, if they could communicate, would not tell you of the resurrection or of any of the Gospel truths, for they know nothing about them. They would not tell you about heaven, or Priesthood, for in all their meanderings in the world of spirits, they have never been privileged with the ministry of a holy Priest. If they should tell all the truth they possess, they could not tell much.

Take another class of spirits—pious, well-disposed men; for instance, the honest Quaker, Presbyterian, or other sectarian, who, although honest, and well disposed, had not, while in the flesh, the privilege of the Priesthood and Gospel. They believed in Jesus

Christ, but died in ignorance of his ordinances, and had not clear conceptions of his doctrine, and of the resurrection. They expected to go to that place called heaven, as soon as they were dead, and that their doom would then and there be fixed, without any further alteration or preparation. Suppose they should come back, with liberty to tell all they know? How much light could we get from them? They could only tell you about the nature of things in the world in which they live. And even that world you could not comprehend, by their description thereof, any more than you can describe colours to a man born blind, or sounds to those who have never heard.

What, then, could you get from them? Why, common chit-chat, in which there would be a mixture of truth, and of error and mistakes, in mingled confusion: all their communications would betray the same want of clear and logical conceptions, and sound sense and philosophy, as would characterize the same class of spirits in the flesh.

Who, then, is prepared, among the spirits in the spirit world, to communicate the truth on the subject of salvation, to guide the people, to give advice, to confer consolation, to heal the sick, to administer joy, and gladness, and hope of immortality and eternal life, founded on manifest truth?

All that have been raised from the dead, and clothed with immortality, all that have ascended to yonder heavens, and been crowned as Kings and Priests, all such are our fellow servants, and of our brethren the Prophets, who have the testimony of Jesus; all such are waiting for the work of God among their posterity on the earth.

They could declare glad tidings if we were only prepared to commune with them. What else? Peter, James, Joseph, Hyrum, Father Smith, any, or all of those ancient or modern Saints, who have departed this life, who are clothed upon with the power of the eternal Apostleship or Priesthood, who have gone to the world of spirits, not to sorrow, but as joyful messengers, bearing glad tidings of eternal truth to the spirits in prison—could not these teach us good things? Yes, if they were permitted so to do.

But suppose all spirits were honest, and aimed at truth, yet each one could only converse of the things he is privileged to know, or comprehend, or which have been revealed to his understanding, or brought within the range of his intellect.

If this be the case, what then do we wish, in communicating with the eternal world, by visions, angels, or ministering spirits? Why, if a person is sick they would like to be visited, comforted, or healed by an angel or spirit! If a man is in prison, he would like an angel or spirit to visit him, and comfort or deliver him. A man shipwrecked would like to be instructed in the way of escape for himself and fellows from a watery grave. In case of extreme hunger a loaf of bread brought by an angel would not be unacceptable.

If a man were journeying, and murderers were lying in wait for him in a certain road, an angel would be useful to him in telling him of the circumstance, and to take another road.

If a man were journeying to preach the Gospel, an angel would be useful to tell the neighbors of his high and holy calling, as in case of Peter and Cornelius. Or would you not like to have angels all around you, to guard, guide, and advise you in every emergency?

The Saints would like to enter a holy temple, and have their President and his assistants administer for their dead. They love their fathers, although they had once almost forgotten them. Our fathers have forgotten to hand down to us their genealogy. They have not felt sufficient interest to transmit to us their names, and the time and place of birth, and in many instances they have not taught us when and where ourselves were born, or who were our grandparents, and their ancestry. Why is all this? It is because of that veil of blindness which is cast over the earth, because there has been no true Church, Priesthood, or Patriarchal order, no holy place for the deposit or preservation of the sacred archives of antiquity, no knowledge of the eternal kindred ties, relationship, or mutual interests of eternity. The hearts of the children had become estranged from the fathers, and the hearts of the fathers from the children, until one came in the spirit and power of Elijah, to turn the keys of these things, to open communication between worlds, and to kindle in our bosoms that glow of eternal affection which lay dormant.

Suppose our temple was ready, and we should enter there to act for the dead, we could only act for those whose names are known to us. And these are few with the most of us Americans. And why is this? We have never had time to look to the heavens, or to the past or future, so busy have we been with the things of the earth. We have hardly had time to think of ourselves, to say nothing of our fathers.

It is time that all this stupidity and indifference should come to an end, and that our hearts were opened, and our charities extended, and that our bosoms expanded, to reach forth after whom? Those whom we consider dead! God has condescended so far to our capacity, as to speak of our fathers as if they were *dead*, although they are all living spirits, and will *live for ever*. We have no dead! Only think of it! Our fathers are all living, thinking, active agents; we have only been taught that they are dead!

Shall I speak my feelings, that I had on yesterday, while we were laying those Corner Stones of the Temple? Yes, I will utter them, if I can.

It was not with my eyes, not with the power of actual vision, but by my intellect, by the natural faculties inherent in man, by the exercise of my reason, upon known principles, or by the power of the Spirit, that it appeared to me that Joseph Smith, and his associate spirits, the Latter-day Saints, hovered about us on the brink of that foundation, and with them all the angels and spirits from the other world, that might be permitted, or that were not too busy elsewhere.

Why should I think so? In the first place, what else on this earth have they to be interested about? Where would their eyes be turned, in the wide earth, if not centered here? Where would their hearts and affections be, if they cast a look or a thought towards the dark speck in the heavens which we inhabit, unless to the people of these valleys and mountains? Are there others who have the keys for the redemption of the dead? Is any one else preparing a sanctuary for the holy conversation and ministrations pertaining to *their* exaltation? No, verily. No other people have opened their hearts to conceive ideas so grand. No other people have their sympathies drawn out to such an extent towards the fathers.

No. If you go from this people, to hear the doctrines of others, you will hear the doleful sayings—"*As the tree falls, so it lieth. As death leaves you, so judgment will find you. There is no work, nor device, nor knowledge in the grave, etc., etc. There is no change after death, but you are fixed, irretrievably fixed, for all eternity. The moment the breath leaves the body, you must go to an extreme of heaven or of hell, there to rejoice with Peter on thrones of power in the presence of Jesus Christ in the third heavens, or, on the other hand, to roll in the flames of hell with murderers and devils.*" Such are the doctrines of our sectarian brethren, who profess to believe in Christ, but who know not the mysteries of godliness, and the boundless resources of eternal charity, and of that mercy which endureth forever.

It is here, that the spirit world would look with an intense interest, it is here that the nations of the dead, if I may so call them, would concentrate their hopes of ministration on the earth in their behalf. It is here that the countless millions of the spirit world would look for the ordinances of redemption, so far as they have been enlightened by the preaching of the Gospel, since the keys of the former dispensation were taken away from the earth.

Why? If they looked upon the earth at all, it would be upon those Corner Stones which we laid yesterday; if they listened at all, it would be to hear the sounds of voices and instruments, and the blending of sacred and martial music in honour of the commencement of a temple for the redemption of the dead. With what intensity of interest did they listen to the songs of Zion, and witness the feelings of their friends. They were glad to behold the glittering bayonets of the guards around the temple ground, and they longed for the day when there would be a thousand where there is now but one. They wish to see a strong people, gathered and united, in sufficient power to maintain a spot on earth where a baptismal font might be erected for the baptism for the dead.

It was here that all their expectations were centered. What cared they for all the golden palaces, marble pavements, or gilded halls of state on earth? What cared they for all the splendor, equipage, titles, and empty sounds of the self-styled great of this world, which all pass away as the dew of the morning before the rising sun? What cared they for the struggles, the battles, the victories, and numerous other worldly interests that vibrate the bosoms of men on either side? None of these things would interest them. Their interests were centered here, and thence extended to the work of God among the nations of the earth.

Did Joseph, in the spirit world, think of anything else, yesterday, but the doings of his brethren on the earth? He might have been necessarily employed, and so busy as to be obliged to think of other things. But if I were to judge from the acquaintance I had with him in his life, and from my knowledge of the spirit of Priesthood, I would suppose him to be so hurried as to have little or no time to cast an eye or a thought after his friends on the earth. He was always busy while here, and so are we. The spirit of our holy ordination and anointing will not let us rest. The spirit of his calling will never suffer him to rest, while satan, sin, death, or darkness, possesses a foot of ground on this earth. While the spirit world contains the spirit of one of his friends, or the grave holds captive one of their bodies, he will never rest, or slacken his labours.

You might as well talk of Saul, king of Israel, resting while Israel was oppressed by the Canaanites or Philistines, after Samuel had anointed him to be king. At first he was like another man, but when occasion called into action the energies of a king, the spirit of his anointing came upon him. He slew an ox, divided it into twelve parts, and sent a part to each of the tribes of Israel, with this proclamation—"So shall it be done to the ox of the man who will not come up to the help of the Lord of hosts."

Ye Elders of Israel! you will find that there is a spirit upon you which will urge you to continued exertion, and will never suffer you to feel at ease in Zion while a work remains unfinished in the great plan of redemption of our race. It will inspire the Saints to build, plant, improve, cultivate, make the desert fruitful, in short, to use the elements, send missions abroad, build up states and kingdoms and temples at home, and send abroad the light of a never-ending day to every people and nation of the globe.

You have been baptized, you have had the laying on of hands, and some have been ordained, and some anointed with a holy anointing. A spirit has been given you. And you will find, if you undertake to rest, it will be the hardest work you ever performed. I came home here from a foreign mission. I presented myself to our President, and inquired what I should do next. "Rest," said he.

If I had been set to turn the world over, to dig down a mountain, to go to the ends of the earth, or traverse the deserts of Arabia, it would have been easier than to have undertaken to rest, while the Priesthood was upon me. I have received the holy anointing, and I can never rest till the last enemy is conquered, death destroyed, and truth reigns triumphant.

May God bless you all. Amen.

Journal of Discourses, 1:6–15.

SPIRITUALITY

SPIRITUAL AWAKENING

DAVID O. MCKAY

In beginning this address, President David O. McKay said, "It is over fifty years since I stood here for the first time as one of the General Authorities of the Church. I remember well then my trembling and humility at facing such an audience and accepting a position as one of the leaders. The passing of a half a century has made it no easier to face this vast audience and to realize the responsibility that one holds in discharging such a responsibility. This morning, as then and during the intervening years, I solicit your sympathy and your prayers."

These sentiments echoed what President McKay said in his first conference address, given in October 1906, when he was a young, thirty-three-year-old Apostle: "Along with the enjoyment of the spirit of this conference, my soul has had a struggle with a feeling of dread of this moment, and if I am not able to make you hear, my brethren and sisters, it is because a great deal of my energy has been expended in suspense. I pray for your sympathy, and for your faith and prayers, that the words which I utter may conform to the spirit of this conference."

In this April 1958 conference talk, President McKay repeated an expression he used nine times in conference talks, in different variations (the first instance was in 1936; the last was in 1969): "Spirituality, our true aim, is the consciousness of victory over self, and of communion with the Infinite. Spirituality impels one to conquer difficulties and acquire more and more strength. To feel one's faculties unfolding, and truth expanding in the soul, is one of life's sublimest experiences."

———————

It has been difficult for me to put even in outline the message that I have had in my heart for the people of the Church and the people of the world. There is a saying by Paul, that "to be carnally minded is death; but to be spiritually minded is life and peace." (Romans 8:6.)

Carnal relates, as you know, to the physical. It includes sensual. But we have in mind this morning the physical surroundings and our animal instincts, the anger that comes to us, the unpleasant words that are spoken, making life unpleasant, rather than emphasizing the spiritual side, the real side of our nature.

The text was suggested several weeks ago, particularly emphasized at that time, by a report that came to me of unpleasantness in a home, and I wondered why we cannot emphasize spiritual attitudes in our homes instead of unpleasant attitudes; why, having before us all the admonitions of the Lord, all the opportunities offered by the Church, we cannot express spiritual attitudes every day of our lives. What good is religion if it does not make our daily lives better? Why need there be emphasis put upon the carnal side of our natures? True, that is the natural reaction for all animals. But having in our possession the high principles of the gospel as revealed through Christ, why cannot members of the Church at least in the home, in school, in all their associations, emphasize the spiritual side of their natures instead of the carnal side?

I learned through a letter of a condition which I think, so far as members of the Church are concerned, is absolutely inexcusable. A husband and wife quarreling—the husband demeaning himself to such an extent as to curse his wife, and in a mad fit of anger overturning a table spread with dishes—a creature in the form of a man harboring the nature of an animal! A man in such a mental state that the anger itself does him more harm than the condition which aroused his anger, and in reality, brothers and sisters, he suffers more from the vexation than he does from the acts that aroused that vexation.

I wonder how long it will take us to realize that in matters of temper nothing can bring us damage but ourselves—we are responsible for what helps us and for what injures us—that the harm that each one sustains he carries about with him, and never is he a real sufferer but by his own fault. I think you get that thought, and yet the tendency of each one is to blame somebody else, the wife blaming the husband, the husband blaming the wife, children finding fault with the parents when the fault lies with themselves. If in the dignity of manhood such a man would cease to magnify his troubles; would face things as they really are; recognize blessings that immediately surround him; cease to entertain disparaging wishes for another; how much more of a man he would be, to say nothing about being a better husband and a more worthy father! A man who cannot control his temper is not very likely to control his passion, and no matter what his pretensions in religion, he moves in daily life very close to the animal plane.

Religion is supposed to lift us on a higher level. Religion appeals to the spirit in man, the real person, and yet how often notwithstanding our possessing a testimony of the truth, we yield to the carnal side of our nature. The man who quarrels in his home, banishes from his heart the spirit of religion. A mother in this Church who would light a cigarette in the home is yielding to the carnal side of her nature. How far below the ideal of the Church! Any quarreling in the home is antagonistic to the spirituality which Christ would have us develop within us, and it is in our daily life that these expressions have their effect.

Man is making great progress in science and invention, greater perhaps than ever before, but is not making comparable progress in character and spirituality.

I read a while ago of a remark of General Omar N. Bradley,

formerly Army's Chief of Staff, who on one occasion said: "With the monstrous weapons man already has, humanity is in danger of being trapped in this world by its moral adolescence. Our knowledge of science has clearly outstripped our capacity to control it.

"We have too many men of science; too few men of God. We have grasped the mystery of the atom and rejected the Sermon on the Mount. Man is stumbling blindly through a spiritual darkness while toying with the precarious secrets of life and death.

"The world has achieved brilliance without wisdom, power without conscience. Ours is a world of nuclear giants and ethical infants. We know more about war than we know about peace, more about killing than we know about living."

Our living comes hourly and daily in the home, in our association in business affairs, in our meeting strangers. It is the attitude of the person during the daily contacts by which we show whether we are appealing to the carnal or to the spiritual within us and within those with whom we associate. It is a daily matter. I do not know whether we can get the thought over or not. And it is within the power of each one, especially members of the Church who make such pretensions. You cannot imagine a real, true Christian, and especially a member of the Mormon Church, swearing at his wife. Why, it is inconceivable that such a thing as that could be in a home and especially with children around. How can anyone justify parents quarreling in front of children! In the instance to which I have referred the man (I should say the brute) even struck his wife. Such a thing should never be. That is out of the life of Church members.

Christ has asked us to develop the spiritual within us.

Man's earthly existence is but a test as to whether he will concentrate his efforts, his mind, his soul upon things which contribute to the comfort and gratification of his physical nature or whether he will make as his life's purpose the acquisition of spiritual qualities.

Every noble impulse, every unselfish expression of love, every brave suffering for the right; every surrender of self to something higher than self; every loyalty to an ideal; every unselfish devotion to principle; every helpfulness to humanity; every act of self-control; every fine courage of the soul, undefeated by pretense or policy, but by being, doing, and living of good for the very good's sake—that is spirituality.

The spiritual road has Christ as its ideal—not the gratification of the physical, for he that will save his life, yielding to that first gratification of a seeming need, will lose his life, lose his happiness, the pleasure of living at this present time. If he would seek the real purpose of life, the individual must live for something higher than self. He hears the Savior's voice, saying: "I am the way, the truth, and the life." (John 14:6.) Following that voice he soon learns that there is no one great thing which he can do to attain happiness or eternal life. He learns that life is made up not of great sacrifices or duties, but of little things in which smiles and kindness and small obligations given habitually are what win and preserve the heart and secure comfort.

Spirituality, our true aim, is the consciousness of victory over self, and of communion with the Infinite. Spirituality impels one to conquer difficulties and acquire more and more strength. To feel one's faculties unfolding, and truth expanding in the soul, is one of life's sublimest experiences.

"The thing a man does practically lay to heart," says Carlyle, "and know for certain concerning his vital relations to this myste-rious Universe, and his duty and destiny there, that is in all cases the primary thing for him, and creatively determines all the rest. . . . And, I say, if you tell me what that is, you tell me to a very great extent what the man is, what the kind of thing he will do is."

The man who sets his heart upon the things of the world, who does not hesitate to cheat his brother, who will lie for gain, who will steal from his neighbor, or, who, by slander, will rob another of his reputation, lives on a low, animal plane of existence, and either stifles his spirituality or permits it to lie dormant. To be thus carnally minded is to be spiritually dead.

On the other hand, keeping in mind our daily vocations, the man who tills the soil, garners his fruit, increases his flocks and his herds, having in mind making better the world in which he lives, desiring to contribute to the happiness of his family and his fellows, and who does all things for the glory of God, will, to the extent that he denies himself for these ideals, develop his spirituality. Indeed, only to the extent that he does this will he rise above the plane of the animal world.

Years ago we read in school the following from Rudolph Eucken:

"I cannot," he says, "conceive of the development of a powerful personality, a deep-rooted, profound mind, of a character rising above this world, without his having experienced a divinity in life above, beyond the world of sensible reality, and as surely as we create in ourselves a life in contrast to pure nature, growing by degrees and extending to the heights of the true, the good, and the beautiful, we may have the same assurance of that religion called universal."

Paul, you will remember, expresses it more specifically:

"But if ye bite and devour one another, take heed that ye be not consumed one of another.

"This I say then, Walk in the Spirit, and ye shall not fulfil the lust of the flesh.

"For the flesh lusteth against the Spirit, and the Spirit against the flesh: and these are contrary the one to the other: so that ye cannot do the things that ye would.

"But if ye be led of the Spirit, ye are not under the law.

"Now the works of the flesh," he says, "are manifest, which are these; Adultery. . . ."

The young man who leaves his home at night having in mind anything that would injure either the character or the life or the reputation of a young woman with whose company he is entrusted, is carnal-minded instead of spiritual-minded.

".... fornication, uncleanness, . . .

".... hatred, variance, emulations . . . strife, seditions. . . .

"Envyings, . . . drunkenness, revellings, and such like: of the which I tell you before, as I have also told you in time past, that they which do such things shall not inherit the kingdom of God.

"But the fruit of the Spirit is love, joy, peace, longsuffering, gentleness, goodness, faith,

"Meekness, temperance: against such there is no law.

"And they that are Christ's have crucified the flesh with the affections and lusts.

"If we live in the Spirit, let us also walk in the Spirit," daily, hourly. (Galatians 5:15–25.)

It can be done, and it should be done in every home of the Latter-day Saint Church.

With all our boasted civilization there never was a time when spiritual awakening and spiritual ideals were more needed. Civilization has grown too complex for the human mind to visualize or to control. Unless mankind come to a speedy realization that the higher and not the baser qualities of man must be developed, the present status of civilization is in jeopardy. Life on the animal plane has as its ideal the survival of the fittest, crush or be crushed, mangle or be mangled, kill or be killed. For man, with his intelligence, this is a sure road to anguish and death.

About fifty years ago, Lord Balfour, Prime Minister of Great Britain, delivered a lecture in the McEwen Hall of the University of Edinburgh on the subject, "The Moral Values Which Unite the Nations." In an interesting and convincing manner, the gentleman presented four fundamental ties that unite the different nations of the world: (1) "Common Knowledge"; (2) "Common Commercial Interests"; (3) "The Intercourse of Diplomatic Relationship"; (4) "The Bonds of Human Friendship." The audience greeted his masterful address with a great outburst of applause.

As the presiding officer arose to express his appreciation and that of the audience, a Japanese student who was doing graduate work at the university stood up, and leaning over the balcony, said, "But, Mr. Balfour, what about Jesus Christ?"

Mr. Robin E. Spear, to whom Professor Lang related this incident, writes:

"One could have heard a pin drop in the hall. Everyone felt at once the justice of the rebuke. The leading statesman of the greatest Christian empire in the world had been dealing with the different ties that are to unite mankind, and had omitted the one fundamental and essential bond. And everyone felt, too, the dramatic element in the situation—that the reminder of his forgetfulness had come from a Japanese student from a far-away non-Christian land."

Life, brethren and sisters, is an ever-flowing river on which one embarks at birth and sails, or is rowed, for fifty, seventy, eighty, or more years. Every year that passes goes into an eternity, never to return; yet each carries with it into the past no personal weakness, no bodily ailment, no sorrow, no laughter, no thought, no noble aspirations, no hope, no ambition: all these with every trait of character, every inclination, every tendency, remain with each individual. In other words, our lives are made up of daily thoughts and actions. We may resolve to let all our sorrows and weaknesses go with the passing time, but we know that every thought, every inclination has left its indelible impression upon our souls, and we shall have to deal with it today.

So live, then, that each day will find you conscious of having wilfully made no person unhappy. No one who has lived a well-spent day will have a sleepless night because of a stricken conscience. Daniel Webster once said that the greatest thought that had ever occupied his mind was the realization of the fact that, and I quote, "there is no evil we cannot face or flee from but the consequences of duty disregarded. A sense of obligation pursues us ever. It is omnipresent like the Deity. If we take to ourselves the wings of the morning and dwell in the uttermost parts of the sea, duty performed, or duty violated is still with us, for our happiness or our misery. If we say that night shall cover us, in the darkness as in the light, our obligations are yet with us. We cannot escape their power nor fly from their presence. They are with us in this life, will be with us at its close, and in that scene of inconceivable solemnity which lies yet farther on, we shall find ourselves followed by the consciousness of duty—to pain us forever if it has been violated, and to console us so far as God has given us grace to perform it. Weighed against conscience the world itself is but a bubble. For God himself is in conscience lending it authority."

Mankind needs a spiritual awakening, brethren and sisters; the carnal minded are causing heartaches and threatening the extinction of the race.

But the sun of hope is rising. Thinking men and women are recognizing the need of man's looking up towards the heavens instead of groveling in response to the animal instinct. One man, commenting upon this, said that if all the destroyers of civilization could be eliminated, and the traits of the rest of us that come from destructive strains could be eliminated, an approach to the millennium some hundred years hence is by no means inconceivable.

"Can you imagine," he continues, "what this country would be like if ten or twenty billion dollars a year" (that is the amount expended to take care of our criminals) "were added to our national income? That would mean five hundred dollars, or one thousand dollars per family; but the average today, even if we include Henry Ford, is only twenty-five hundred, or three thousand dollars. What would happen if that sum were increased by twenty or even forty percent all around? Even if you cannot imagine the result, do you realize what it would be like to feel no need of locking doors and windows, no fear of leaving your car unprotected, no danger that your wife or daughter would be insulted, or you yourself sandbagged if you went out at night, no fear that you would have any uncollectible bills except through accident or unpreventable misfortune, no fear that in political election there would be any bribery, or in politics any graft, and no fear that anyone anywhere was trying to 'do you'—can you imagine all that? It would almost be heaven on earth. Of course, it cannot happen" (someday it will have to happen) " . . . and yet if all the destroyers of civilization could be eliminated, and if the traits of the rest of us that come from destructive strains could be eliminated, an approach to such a state some hundred years hence is by no means inconceivable."

Spiritual awakening in the hearts of millions of men and women would bring about a changed world. I am hopeful, my brethren and sisters, that the dawning of that day is not far distant. I am conscious, as I hope all of you are, that the responsibility to try to bring about such a day rests upon the priesthood of the Church of Jesus Christ and upon the membership and upon husbands and wives and upon children in Mormon homes.

May that message be felt throughout the conference that we are now holding. We cannot just come and meet and talk about good things and then go home and express our feelings, the feelings of our carnal nature.

My faith in the ultimate triumph of the gospel of Jesus Christ assures me that a spiritual awakening must come. It will come through the acceptance of Jesus Christ and obedience to his gospel and in no other way completely. I believe there never was a time in the history of the world when there was such a need for a united, determined stand to uphold Christ and the restoration of the gospel through the Prophet Joseph Smith as there is today.

God bless you here assembled that we may sense as never before the efficacy of the restored gospel and that we hold as a duty our application of spiritual traits in our daily association with one another in home, in business, in society, I pray in the name of Jesus Christ. Amen.

Conference Report, April 1958, 4–9.

THE LIGHT OF CHRIST

MARION G. ROMNEY

In this doctrinally significant address given at the priesthood session of general conference in April 1977, Elder Marion G. Romney discussed the light of Christ, which is given to all mankind; the gift of the Holy Ghost; and the more sure word of prophecy.

Elder Romney taught that the conscience is synonymous with the light of Christ. Of the Holy Ghost, he said, "One is born again by actually receiving and experiencing the light and power inherent in the gift of the Holy Ghost." Regarding the more sure word of prophecy, or the making of one's calling and election sure, Elder Romney testified, "I know that everyone who, following the whisperings of the Spirit, develops faith, is baptized, and receives the Holy Ghost through the laying on of hands by those having authority, may, by compliance with the teachings of the gospel, receive the gifts and the power of the Holy Ghost."

My brethren, I pray, and ask you to join in that prayer, that while I speak we will enjoy the Spirit of Christ. If we don't enjoy it, we won't enjoy these remarks, because my topic is "The Light of Christ." There are three phases of the light of Christ that I want to mention.

The first one is the light which enlighteneth every man that cometh into the world;

The second phase is the gift of the Holy Ghost;

And the third is the more sure word of prophecy.

In the eighty-eighth section of the Doctrine and Covenants, the Lord says, "The light of Christ . . . proceedeth forth from the presence of God to fill the immensity of space." (D&C 88:7, 12.)

In another revelation, it is written that this light, which is "the Spirit of Jesus Christ . . . giveth light to every man that cometh into the world; and the Spirit enlighteneth every man through the world, that hearkeneth to the voice of the Spirit." (D&C 84:45–46.)

This Spirit is, no doubt, the source of one's conscience, which Webster defines as "a knowledge or feeling of right and wrong with a compulsion to do right."

Mormon was alluding to this Spirit when he wrote to his son Moroni that "every thing which inviteth and enticeth to do good, and to love God, and to serve him, is inspired of God.

"Wherefore, take heed, my beloved brethren, that ye do not judge that which is evil to be of God, or that which is good and of God to be of the devil.

"For behold, my brethren, it is given unto you to judge, [and that gift is because the light of Christ enlighteneth every man that cometh into the world], that ye may know good from evil; and the way to judge is as plain, that ye may know with a perfect knowledge, as the daylight is from the dark night.

"For behold, the Spirit of Christ is given to every man, that he may know good from evil." (Moroni 7:13–16.)

President Joseph F. Smith says that this Spirit of Christ "strives with . . . men, and will continue to strive with them [if they will resist the enticings of Satan], until it brings them to a knowledge of the truth and the possession of the greater light and testimony of the Holy Ghost." (*Gospel Doctrine* [Deseret Book, 1973], 67–68.)

Now, this statement of President Smith's brings us to a consideration of the second phase of our subject: the gift of the Holy Ghost.

The Holy Ghost is a person, a spirit, the third member of the

Godhead. He is a messenger and a witness of the Father and the Son. He brings to men testimony, witness, and knowledge of God the Father, Jesus Christ His Son, and the truths of the gospel. He vitalizes truth in the hearts and souls of men.

"There is a difference," said the Prophet Joseph Smith, "between the Holy Ghost and the gift of the Holy Ghost. Cornelius received the Holy Ghost before he was baptized, which was the convincing power of God unto him of the truth of the Gospel, but he could not receive the gift of the Holy Ghost until after he was baptized. Had he not [been baptized], the Holy Ghost which convinced him of the truth of God, would have left him." (*Teachings of the Prophet Joseph Smith*, 199.) That's not my statement; that's the statement of the Prophet Joseph Smith. But I know it's true.

The gift of the Holy Ghost confers upon one, as long as he is worthy, the right to receive light and truth.

Obtaining the gift of the Holy Ghost is preceded by faith, repentance, and baptism. Retaining the spirit, power, and guidance of the Holy Ghost requires a righteous life—a dedicated effort to constantly comply with the laws and ordinances of the gospel.

The Holy Ghost is, as we have said, the third member of the Godhead. Of Him the Prophet Joseph said:

"The Holy Ghost has not a body of flesh and bones [as we know that God and Jesus Christ have], but is a personage of Spirit." (D&C 130:22.)

The Holy Ghost is the great witness of, the messenger for, and testifier of the Father and the Son. The Savior, speaking of Him as the "Spirit of truth," said:

"When he, the Spirit of truth, is come, he will guide you into all truth: for he shall not speak of himself; but whatsoever he shall hear, that shall he speak: and he will shew you things to come.

"He shall glorify me: for he shall receive of mine, and shall shew it unto you." (John 16:13–14.)

By the witness and power of the Holy Ghost we receive personal testimonies of the truths of the gospel, including knowledge of God the Father and His beloved Son, Jesus Christ, our Savior and Redeemer.

Notwithstanding the availability of the gifts of the Holy Ghost, there are many people who live within reach of them who fail to see them. Concerning such tragedy, the Lord said:

"Behold, I am Jesus Christ, the Son of God. I am the same that came unto mine own, and mine own received me not. I am the light which shineth in darkness, and the darkness comprehendeth it not." (D&C 6:21.)

All three of the synoptic Gospel writers record the following classic illustration of the difficulty one in darkness has in comprehending the light. Matthew's version reads:

"When Jesus came into the coasts of Caesarea Philippi, he asked his disciples, saying, Whom do men say that I the Son of man am?

"And they said, Some say that thou art John the Baptist: some, Elias; and others, Jeremias, or one of the prophets." (Matthew 16:13–14.)

Now, the people who expressed these opinions were Christ's contemporaries. Their conclusions evidenced the fact that they knew something about His mighty works. No doubt they were aware of His claim that He was the Son of God. Their minds, however, were opaque to the light of His true identity. Although the light was shining brightly about them, they "comprehended it not."

Having heard their answer as to who men said He was, Jesus directed to His disciples the question, "But whom say ye that I am?" (Matthew 16:15.)

Then Peter, speaking for himself and presumptively for the others, answered, "Thou art the Christ, the Son of the living God." (Matthew 16:16.) In this declaration, Peter evidenced the fact that he and his fellow disciples did comprehend the light shining in the world of spiritual darkness around them.

In His response to Peter's answer, Jesus declared a truth understood only by those who comprehend the light by and through the gift and power of the Holy Ghost, for Jesus' answer was:

"Flesh and blood hath not revealed it unto thee," He said, "but my Father which is in heaven, . . . and upon this rock"—meaning, upon the rock of revelation, which comes by means of the Holy Ghost—"I will build my church; and the gates of hell shall not prevail against it." (Matthew 16:17–18.)

How difficult it is to get one in darkness to comprehend the light or to believe that there is such light is illustrated by John's account of the interview between Jesus and Nicodemus.

"There was," says John, "a man of the Pharisees, named Nicodemus, a ruler of the Jews:

"[Who] came to Jesus by night, and said unto him, Rabbi, we know that thou art a teacher come from God: for no man can do these miracles that thou doest, except God be with him.

"Jesus answered and said . . . Verily, verily, I say unto thee, Except a man be born again, he cannot see the kingdom of God.

"Nicodemus saith unto him, How can a man be born when he is old? can he enter the second time into his mother's womb, and be born?

"Jesus answered, Verily, verily, I say unto thee, Except a man be born of water and of the Spirit, he cannot enter into the kingdom of God." (John 3:1–5; see also John 3:6–10.)

One is born again by actually receiving and experiencing the light and power inherent in the gift of the Holy Ghost.

Now, concerning the third phase of our theme, "the more sure word of prophecy" (D&C 131:5), which is obtained by making one's "calling and election sure" (2 Peter 1:10), the Prophet Joseph said:

"After a person has faith in Christ, repents of his sins, and is baptized for the remission of his sins and receives the Holy Ghost, (by the laying on of hands) . . . then let him continue to humble himself before God, hungering and thirsting after righteousness, and living by every word of God, and the Lord will soon say unto him, Son, thou shalt be exalted. When the Lord has thoroughly proved him, and finds that the man is determined to serve Him at all hazards, then the man will find his calling and his election made sure, then it will be his privilege to receive the other Comforter, which the Lord hath promised the Saints, as is recorded in the testimony of St. John." (*Teachings of the Prophet Joseph Smith*, 150.)

In the eighty-eighth section of the Doctrine and Covenants is recorded a revelation in which the Lord, addressing some of the early Saints in Ohio, said:

"I now send upon you another Comforter, even upon you my friends, that it may abide in your hearts, even the Holy Spirit of promise; which other Comforter is the same that I promised unto my disciples, as is recorded in the testimony of John.

"This Comforter is the promise which I give unto you of eternal life, even the glory of the celestial kingdom." (D&C 88:3–4.)

I should think that all faithful Latter-day Saints "would want that more sure word of prophecy, that they were sealed in the heavens and had the promise of eternal life in the kingdom of God." (*History of the Church*, 5:388.)

As I read the sacred records, I find recorded experiences of men in all dispensations who have had this more sure anchor to their souls, this peace in their hearts.

Lehi's grandson Enos so hungered after righteousness that he cried unto the Lord until "there came a voice unto [him], saying: Enos, thy sins are forgiven thee, and thou shalt be blessed." (Enos 1:5.) Years later Enos revealed the nature of this promised blessing when he wrote:

"I soon go to the place of my rest, which is with my Redeemer; for I know that in him I shall rest. And I rejoice in the day when my mortal shall put on immortality, and shall stand before him; then shall I see his face with pleasure, and he will say unto me: Come unto me, ye blessed, there is a place prepared for you in the mansions of my Father." (Enos 1:27.)

To Alma the Lord said, "Thou art my servant; and I covenant with thee that thou shalt have eternal life." (Mosiah 26:20.)

To His twelve Nephite disciples, the Master said:

"What is it that ye desire of me, after that I am gone to the Father?

"And they all spake, save it were three, saying: We desire that after we have lived unto the age of man, that our ministry, wherein thou hast called us, may have an end, that we may speedily come unto thee in thy kingdom.

"And he said unto them: Blessed are ye because ye desired this thing of me; therefore, after that ye are seventy and two years old ye shall come unto me in my kingdom; and with me ye shall find rest." (3 Nephi 28:1–3.)

As Moroni labored in solitude abridging the Jaredite record, he received from the Lord this comforting assurance:

"Thou hast been faithful; wherefore, thy garments shall be made clean. And because thou hast seen thy weakness thou shalt be made strong, even unto the sitting down in the place which I have prepared in the mansions of my Father." (Ether 12:37.)

Paul, in his second epistle to Timothy, wrote:

"I am now ready to be offered, and the time of my departure is at hand.

"I have fought a good fight, I have finished my course, I have kept the faith:

"Henceforth there is laid up for me a crown of righteousness, which the Lord, the righteous judge, shall give me at that day." (2 Timothy 4:6–8.)

In this dispensation many have received like assurances. In the spring of 1839, while the Prophet Joseph and his associates were languishing in Liberty Jail, Heber C. Kimball, our president's grandfather, labored against great odds caring for the Saints and striving to free the brethren who were in jail. On the sixth of April he wrote:

"My family having been gone about two months, during which time I heard nothing from them; our brethren being in prison; death and destruction following us everywhere we went; I felt very sorrowful and lonely. The following words came to mind, and the Spirit said unto me, 'write,' which I did by taking a piece of paper and writing on my knee as follows: . . .

"Verily I say unto my servant Heber, thou art my son, in whom I am well pleased; for thou art careful to hearken to my words, and not transgress my law, nor rebel against my servant Joseph Smith, for thou hast a respect to the words of mine anointed, even from the least to the greatest of them; *therefore*"—listen to this—"*thy name is written in heaven, no more to be blotted out for ever.*" (Orson F. Whitney, *Life of Heber C. Kimball,* Bookcraft, 1975, 241; italics added.)

To the Prophet Joseph Smith the Lord said:

"I am the Lord thy God, and will be with thee even unto the end of the world, and through all eternity; *for verily I seal upon you your exaltation, and prepare a throne for you in the kingdom of my Father, with Abraham your father.*" (D&C 132:49; italics added.)

Now my beloved brethren, by way of summary and conclusion, I bear witness to the verity of these great truths. I know that the Spirit of Christ enlighteneth "every man that cometh into the world; and [that] the Spirit enlighteneth every man through the world, that hearkeneth to the voice of the Spirit." (D&C 84:46.)

I know that everyone who, following the whisperings of the Spirit, develops faith, is baptized, and receives the Holy Ghost through the laying on of hands by those having authority, may, by compliance with the teachings of the gospel, receive the gifts and the power of the Holy Ghost.

And I bear further witness that every such person who, having come this far, will follow the Prophet's admonition to "continue to humble himself before God, hungering and thirsting after righteousness, and living by every word of God" (*Teachings of the Prophet Joseph Smith*, 150), may obtain the more sure word of prophecy.

That the Lord will bless all of us priesthood bearers that we will so understand these great truths, that in the end we shall, by making our calling and election sure, enjoy the full light of Christ, I humbly pray, in the name of Jesus Christ, our Redeemer. Amen.

Ensign, May 1977, 43–45.

TEMPLE

~❧ ❧~

THE PEARL OF GREAT PRICE

JOSEPH FIELDING SMITH

This talk, which explains the inestimable value of eternal life, was given at a meeting of the high priests of the Salt Lake Stake on Sunday, October 20, 1920, in the Seventeenth Ward chapel. At the time, Elder Joseph Fielding Smith was a member of the Quorum of the Twelve.

Again, the kingdom of heaven is like unto treasure hid in a field; the which when a man hath found he hideth, and for joy thereof goeth and selleth all that he hath, and buyeth that field.

"Again, the kingdom of heaven is like unto a merchant man, seeking goodly pearls: Who, when he had found one pearl of great price, went and sold all that he had, and bought it." (Matthew 13:44–46.)

A great many of the members of the Church evidently do not realize the importance of the blessings we receive in the temples of the Lord. I wish we all loved the gospel to the extent that we would be willing to do anything the Lord asks of us irrespective of what the world thinks or does. Why cannot the Latter-day Saints uphold the standards and the regulations of the Church with united effort notwithstanding what the world might do or think? With some of us it is the custom to do very much as the world does. We dress as the world does. We seek its pleasures; we follow its customs; and there is no question in my mind that these things do bring us somewhat in conflict with things the Lord has taught and commanded us to do.

Blessings Come Through Obedience to Law

The Lord says that when we obtain any blessing it is based upon obedience to the law upon which that blessing is predicated. (D&C 130:20–21.) We cannot get a blessing from him in any other way and this is according to that which was "decreed in heaven before the foundation of this world." I wonder if we have thought of this seriously?

The Lord, when speaking to some of the elders of the Church in the beginning, said: "And they who remain"—when rewards are given and men are assigned to the place where they belong—"shall be quickened; nevertheless they shall return again to their own place, to enjoy that which they are willing to receive, because they were not willing to enjoy that which they might have received." (D&C 88:32.)

He has revealed to us things pertaining to the celestial kingdom, the terrestrial kingdom and the telestial kingdom, and how those who inherit these kingdoms will come forth in the resurrection to receive their rewards; then he says, "And they who remain shall also be quickened"—those who do not belong to any of these kingdoms—"to enjoy that which they are willing to receive, because they were not willing to enjoy that which they might have received. For what doth it profit a man if a gift be bestowed upon him, and he receive not the gift? Behold, he rejoices not in that which is given unto him, neither rejoices in him who is the giver of the gift."

Heirs of the Kingdom

The Lord offers us what? A place in his kingdom, where we can be heirs, in other words sons and daughters, possessing and receiving the fulness of that kingdom, through obedience to the principles and ordinances of the gospel as we are required to take that obedience upon us in the temple of the Lord. If we will not receive these blessings then we do not rejoice in them, neither in the Giver of this great gift.

In one of the parables by the Savior he likens the kingdom of God to a treasure of great price which a man discovered in a field and, who, when he discovered it, sold all that he had and purchased that field. In other words, he was willing to forsake all for the kingdom of God. *So we should be willing to give up everything in this world for the sake of the kingdom of God.* This doctrine Jesus taught emphatically, saying that we are not worthy of him if we are not willing to do so for his sake.

He has offered us the fulness of his kingdom and to make us heirs to receive all that the Father has, if we will receive it through obedience to his commandments. The Lord said to John, "He that overcometh shall inherit all things; and I will be his God, and he shall be my son." (Revelation 21:7.) There are other expressions of similar nature in the Bible, but the people of the world do not understand them. In the revelations given to the Prophet Joseph Smith this promise is enlarged upon, or made more clear. For instance, in that wonderful revelation known as "The Vision" we read:

> And again, we bear record, for we saw and heard, and this is the testimony of the gospel of Christ, concerning them who come forth in the resurrection of the just:
>
> They are they who received the testimony of Jesus, and believed on his name and were baptized after the manner of his burial, being buried in the water in his name, and this according to the commandment which he has given—
>
> That by keeping the commandments they might be washed and cleansed from all their sins, and receive the Holy Spirit by the laying on of the hands of him who is ordained and sealed unto this power;
>
> And who overcome by faith, and are sealed by the Holy Spirit of promise, which the Father sheds forth upon all those who are just and true.

They are they who are the church of the Firstborn.

They are they into whose hands the Father has given all things—

They are they who are priests and kings, who have received of his fulness, and of his glory;

And are priests of the Most High, after the order of Melchizedek, which was after the order of Enoch, which was after the order of the Only Begotten Son.

Wherefore, as it is written, they are gods, even the sons of God—

Wherefore all things are theirs, whether life or death, or things present, or things to come, all are theirs and they are Christ's and Christ is God's.

And they shall overcome all things. (D&C 76:50–60.)

All Things Are Theirs

These are the promises the Lord makes to all those who come into his Church in the waters of baptism and then, by keeping his commandments, remain washed and cleansed from all their sins, and receive the Holy Spirit of Promise by obedience to the requirements made in the temples of the Lord. "All things are theirs." They become sons and daughters of God and are made heirs in that kingdom. That is what salvation means to us. I am using the term "salvation" in the full sense of exaltation. The world has a very vague idea of salvation. The great majority of men most everywhere believe that you are either saved in heaven or you are in an extremely bad place. If you get into heaven there is nothing much for you to do. You rest from your labors, being saved; no work to perform; no responsibility upon your shoulders, only to sing, or play a harp. If you are damned you are in eternal torment where you are to remain forever. They have very little idea of the exaltation which the Lord has prepared for the faithful in the mansions of the Father. The Lord has revealed it to us, and these are our privileges on conditions of faithfulness according to the law decreed in the heavens upon which these blessings are predicated.

No Exaltation without Fulness of Priesthood

There is no exaltation in the kingdom of God without the fulness of priesthood. How could a man be an heir in that kingdom without priesthood? While the sisters do not hold the priesthood, they share in the fulness of its blessings in the celestial kingdom with their husbands. These blessings are obtained through obedience to the ordinances and covenants of the House of the Lord. The Prophet Joseph Smith once said: *"If a man gets a fulness of the priesthood of God, he has to get it . . . by keeping all the commandments and obeying all the ordinances of the house of the Lord."* To obtain the fulness of the priesthood does not mean that a man must become president of the Church. Every man who is faithful and will receive these ordinances and blessings obtains a fulness of the priesthood, and the Lord has said that "he makes them equal in power, and in might, and in dominion." Only one man at a time on the earth holds the keys of the priesthood; only one man at a time has the power to receive revelations for the Church; but the Lord has made it possible for every man in this Church, through his obedience, to receive the fulness of the priesthood through the ordinances of the temple of the Lord. This cannot be received anywhere else.

So being ordained an elder, or a high priest, or an apostle, or even president of the Church, is not the thing that brings the exaltation, but obedience to the laws and the ordinances and the covenants required of those who desire to become members of the Church of the Firstborn as these are administered in the House of the Lord. *To become a member of the Church of the Firstborn, as I understand it, is to become one of the inner circle.* We are all members of The Church of Jesus Christ of Latter-day Saints by being baptized and confirmed, and there are many who seem to be content to remain such without obtaining the privileges of exaltation. *The Lord has made it possible for us to become members of the Church of the Firstborn by receiving the blessings of the House of the Lord, and* "*overcoming all things.*" Thus we become heirs, "priests and kings, who have received of his fulness, and of his glory," who shall "dwell in the presence of God and his Christ forever and ever," with full exaltation. Are such blessings worth having?

I have said that only one man at a time on the earth holds the keys of this sealing power of priesthood, but he may, and does, delegate power to others and they officiate under his direction in the temples of the Lord. No man can officiate in these sealing ordinances until he receives the authority to do so by being set apart by the one who holds the keys, notwithstanding he may hold the priesthood. All the authority exercised in the temples, is then, after all, the authority centered in one man. He has the power and calls upon others to officiate and they *seal upon us the keys and powers which, through our obedience, entitle us to become sons and daughters, and members of the Church of the Firstborn, receiving all things in the kingdom.* This is what we can get in the temple, so that we become *members of the family, sons and daughters of God, not servants.*

Sons and Daughters of God

You know what it says about servants in the scriptures. Those who become servants are those who are not willing to receive these blessings in the House of the Lord and abide in them. They are not sons, they are not daughters. They are children of God, it is true, for all men are his children. But they do not inherit, and therefore remain servants throughout all eternity because they were not willing to receive that which they might have received, and the gift which was bestowed upon them or offered to them. They not only rejected the gift, but the Giver of the gift. There will be a great many servants, but there will not be many heirs, "Because strait is the gate, and narrow is the way, which leadeth unto life, and few there be that find it." (Matthew 7:14.)

Having put this matter before you in this way, endeavoring to impress you with the importance of these blessings obtained in the temples, I would like to ask you a question. Are these blessings to be desired? The question answers itself. Now let me ask another. When the Lord offers us these great blessings, are we justified in saying, "It is all right, we want them, but we want to put them off just as long as we can before we receive them, so that we can live as the world lives"? Is there any sincerity in that? Is there any spirit of humility or repentance, or faith in such an attitude?

I have known of mothers saying to their daughters, "I do not want you to go to the temple now. Wait a little while. When you get older you may go to the temple, but now have a good time while you are young." Well, of course, if a girl is going to enter into covenants in the temple which she does not intend to keep, it is better for her not to go there. Far better for her to stay out. But is there any blessing the Lord offers us that we are justified in post-poning because we feel that it will interfere with our having a good time, or indulging in the customs and fashions of the world? Is it right for us to feel that we are justified in seeking the things of the world until we are along in years and then we will repent and turn unto the Lord? Should we not seek to obtain these important blessings just as soon as we can, consistently and in reason?

The Pearl of Great Price

Children should not go to the temple until they are old enough to understand the purpose of their going. They should be taught the principles of the gospel and to have faith in God and in the mission of Jesus Christ, and should gain a testimony of the truth before they receive the blessings of the temple. I believe that a young man or woman should seek after these blessings in the temple and just as soon as they are old enough to understand the meaning of temple ordinances they should have them. Moreover, they should not go to the temple until they do have a testimony of the truth and a knowledge of the gospel, no matter how old they may be. It is not intended that these sacred covenants should be given to those who do not have faith and who have not proved themselves worthy by obedience to the gospel.

After we have received these covenants we should sacredly observe them even if it should cost us the association and good will of all the world. Why? *Because we have found the pearl of great price, the kingdom of God.* We are on the road to receive all that the Father has, all that he can give—exaltation. If others are not willing to receive these blessings let them take their course, but for us, let us walk in the light of the truth and forsake the world.

I do not think because girls go through the temple they will necessarily be ostracized socially by friends and companions. I know of mothers, however, who have made their daughters feel that they would be, and that they could not make themselves attractive if they went to the temple and kept the covenants made there, for they would not be able to dress according to the fashion. Such a doctrine may mean the damnation of that precious daughter in whose welfare you have such an interest if you feel that way.

Power from on High

The Lord has not offered us these blessings that we might receive them just before we die or when we are old or crippled. What are these blessings for? Not only for eternity, but to be a guide to us and a protection through the struggle of life. Do you understand why our missionaries go to the temple before they are set apart for their mission fields? This is a requirement made of them whether they are eighteen years of age, or twenty, or older, because the Lord has said it should be done. He called all the missionaries to Kirtland in the early days of the Church to receive endowments in the temple erected there. He said this was so that they could go out with greater power from on high and with greater protection. Zion was not to be redeemed until endowments were given. These are the words of the Lord:

Therefore in consequence of the transgression of my

people, it is expedient in me that mine elders should wait for a little season for the redemption of Zion—

That they themselves may be prepared, and that my people may be taught more perfectly, and have experience, and know more perfectly concerning their duty, and the things which I require at their hands.

And this cannot be brought to pass until mine elders are endowed with power from on high.

For behold, I have prepared a great endowment and blessing to be poured out upon them, inasmuch as they are faithful and continue in humility before me. (D&C 105:9–12.)

Speaking of the building of the temple at Kirtland the Lord further said:

Yea, verily I say unto you, I gave unto you a commandment that you should build a house, in the which house I design to endow those whom I have chosen with power from on high.

For this is the promise of the Father unto you; therefore I command you to tarry, even as mine apostles at Jerusalem. (D&C 95:8–9.)

The endowment received now is greater than that given in Kirtland, for the Lord has revealed additional covenants and obligations for us to keep. If we go into the temple we raise our hands and covenant that we will serve the Lord and observe his commandments and keep ourselves unspotted from the world. If we realize what we are doing then the endowment will be a protection to us all our lives—a protection which a man who does not go to the temple does not have.

I have heard my father say that in the hour of trial, in the hour of temptation, he would think of the promises, the covenants that he made in the House of the Lord, and they were a protection to him. He was but fifteen years of age when he received his endowments and went forth into the mission field. This is exceptional, I know, and I do not recommend that our sons and our daughters go to the temple as young as that, but that they go as soon as they are prepared. This protection is what these ceremonies are for, in part. They save us now and they exalt us hereafter, if we will honor them. I know that this protection is given for I, too, have realized it, as have thousands of others who have remembered their obligations.

The Greatest Blessing of Life

And yet mothers and fathers will say: "Oh, let the children have a good time, let them do as the world does and when their charms are gone, then they can go to the temple." Therefore many procrastinate the day of their repentance, which is a very dangerous thing to do. These blessings insure to us, through our faithfulness, the pearl of great price the Lord has offered us, for *these are the greatest blessings we can receive in this life*. It is a wonderful thing to come into the Church, but you cannot receive an exaltation until you have made covenants in the House of the Lord and received the keys and authorities that are there bestowed and which cannot be given in any other place on the earth today.

You have read what the Prophet has written in the Pearl of Great Price. He has given us some of the interpretations of the Egyptian characters in the writings of Abraham and we learn that Abraham wrote things and sealed them up that they cannot be read, saying: "They cannot be revealed unto the world but are to be had in the holy temple of God." They are certain keys and blessings that are obtained in the house of the Lord that we must have if we are to obtain exaltation.

The Need of Repentance

What we need in the Church, as well as out of it, is repentance. We need more faith and more determination to serve the Lord. Do not get the impression from what I have said that I feel that we should keep aloof from everybody outside of the Church and not associate with them. I have not said that, but I do want us to be consistent Latter-day Saints, and if the people of the world walk in darkness and sin and contrary to the will of the Lord, there is the place for us to draw the line.

Why should we not uphold the standards of our faith? Why should we not walk in strict accord with the regulations of the Church notwithstanding what the world may think? The Lord has revealed the fulness of his gospel. We have been fully informed regarding all of its principles pertaining to salvation. Is it worthwhile for us to maintain our integrity and prove faithful to every trust? *Is the pearl of great price—the fulness of the glory, honor and eternal life in the presence of the Father and the Son—worth the sacrifice we may be called upon to make? Are we, as the man spoken of in former times, willing to sell all that we have in order that we may buy this field which will bring to us everlasting joy and exaltation as sons and daughters of God?* I pray that we are, in the name of our Redeemer. Amen.

Utah Genealogical and Historical Magazine, July 1930, 97–104.

~☙ ❧~

TEMPLE WORSHIP

JOHN A. WIDTSOE

"Temple Worship" was given as a lecture under the auspices of the Genealogical Society of Utah at the Assembly Hall in Salt Lake City on October 12, 1920. At the time, John A. Widtsoe, scientist, author, and educator, was president of the University of Utah. He was called as an Apostle a few months later, on March 17, 1921, serving under President Heber J. Grant. One of the finest summaries of temple worship ever published, this talk has been widely quoted, particularly these words: "We live in a world of symbols. No man or woman can come out of the temple endowed as he should be, unless he has seen, beyond the symbol, the mighty realities for which the symbols stand."

I f an apology were needed for speaking on temple worship, I would simply call your attention to section 2 of the Doctrine and Covenants, the first recorded revelation of the Lord in these latter days, through the Angel Moroni to Joseph Smith.

"Behold I will reveal unto you the Priesthood, by the hand of Elijah the prophet, before the coming of the great and dreadful day of the Lord;

"And he shall plant in the hearts of the children the promises made to the fathers and the hearts of the children shall turn to their fathers;

"If it were not so, the whole earth would be utterly wasted at his coming."

Some day, no doubt, this Society will call us together and devote one evening or more to a discussion of this magnificent revelation and its meaning, historical and doctrinal. Almost the first words of the Lord to the Prophet Joseph Smith, when as a boy he was called to restore the gospel of Jesus Christ, dealt with the subject that we are discussing throughout this week; and almost the last words spoken by God to the Prophet before the Prophet's death, as far as we can tell, dealt with the same subject.

Present Increased Interest in Temple Work

There is at present an unusual increased interest in temple activity. Our temples are crowded. The last time I attended the Salt Lake Temple I was a member of the third company. One started early in the morning, one late in the forenoon, and my company started about two o'clock in the afternoon. It was about 6 P.M. before we had completed the day's work.

The number of temples is also increasing. The Hawaiian temple has only recently been dedicated; the Cardston temple is being rushed to completion; the Arizona temple is being planned and numerous communities in the Church are anxiously waiting and praying for the time that they may have temples.

There is a renewed spirit in behalf of temple work, not because people are wealthier than they were before, nor because temples are more accessible, but because the time has come for more temple work to be done. The spirit is abroad among the people, and those who are honest in heart and understand the Gospel of Jesus Christ are willing to give their time and means more liberally in behalf of temple work.

Opposition and Blessings from Temple Work

In view of this great temple activity, we may well prepare ourselves for opposition. There never yet has been a time in the history of the world when temple work has increased without a corresponding increase in the opposition to it. Some three or four years after the pioneers came to this valley, President Brigham Young said it was time to begin the building of a temple; and some of the old timers here will probably remember that thousands of the Saints dreaded the command, because they said, "Just as soon as we lay the cornerstone of a temple, all hell will be turned loose upon us and we will be driven out of the valleys." President Young thought that was true, but that they also would have, if temple work were undertaken, a corresponding increase in power to overcome all evil. Men grow mighty under the results of temple service; women grow strong under it; the community increases in power; until the devil has less influence than he ever had before. The opposition to truth is relatively smaller if the people are engaged actively in the ordinances of the temple.

Temple Work for All the People

We need more workers to accomplish the wonderful work. . . . Even three companies a day in each temple will not be enough; we shall have to organize four, or five, and for all I know, the day may come, unless we build more temples, when we shall keep the temples open twenty-four hours a day. We need more converts to temple work, drawn from all ages, from the young, from the middle-aged, and from the rich and poor, from among the busy and those of leisure. The time has come, I verily believe, in this new temple movement, to bring into active service all the people, of all ages. From the children doing baptisms, to the aged grandparents doing endowments for the dead, all the members of the family, if we do our duty well, must be brought into the work. Temple work is quite of as much benefit to the young and the active, as it is to the aged, who have laid behind them many of the burdens of life. The young man needs his place in the temple even more than his father and his grandfather, who are steadied by a life of experience; and the young girl just entering life needs the spirit, influence and direction that comes from participation in the temple ordinances. If I say nothing else tonight that will linger, I hope you will remember that temple work is for the young and for the middle-aged and for the aged—for all and not for one specialized, separated class within the Church organization.

Historical Distribution of Temples

What is a temple? According to the ordinary definition, it is any place set apart for sacred purposes and dedicated to a sacred purpose—a house of God.

All people of all ages have had temples in one form or another. When the history of human thought shall be written from the point of view of temple worship, it may well be found that temples and the work done in them have been the dominating influence in shaping human thought from the beginning of the race. Even today political controversies are as nothing in determining the temple of a people, as compared with religious sentiments and convictions, especially as practiced in the temples of the people.

In every land and in every age temples have been built and used. In China, age old with four thousand years of written history; in India; on the islands of the sea; in South America; in North America; in Africa and in Australia; everywhere there are evidences of the existence and use of temples.

Temples of the Priesthood

There is a fairly complete history of some of the temples of the priesthood, the temples built by the chosen people of God. There are evidences that even in patriarchal days, in the days of Adam, there was the equivalent of temples, for the priesthood was held in its fulness, as far as the people needed it; and there is every reason to believe that from Adam to Noah, temple worship was in operation. After the flood the holy priesthood was continued; and we have reason to believe, in sacred places, the ordinances of the temple were given to those entitled to receive them.

When Israel was in Egypt, the priesthood was with them, and we may believe from certain sayings of the scriptures that Israel had in Egypt a temple or its equivalent, the mysterious "testimony." When Israel was in the wilderness temple worship was provided for, for the Lord said to the Prophet Joseph (D&C 124:38):

"For, for this cause I commanded Moses that he should build a tabernacle, that they should bear it with them in the wilderness, and to build a house in the land of promise, that those ordinances might be revealed which had been hid from before the world was."

In the tabernacle (or temple) of the wilderness, the ordinances of God's house were given to a certain extent, as least, as we give them today.

I need not review with you the history of the temples of Israel, the temple of the wilderness or "tabernacle of the congregation," later placed at Shiloh; the temple of Solomon; the temple of Zerubbabel after the captivity; the restoration of this temple by Herod, and so on. We need simply remember that the story of ancient Israel, the chosen people of God, centers upon their temples.

The Book of Mormon indicates that from about 600 B. C. until about 35 or 40 years A.D., temples, under the authority of the holy priesthood, were found on this continent. Nephi says distinctly that he proceeded to gather up all the precious things of the people and to build a temple according to the pattern of the temple of Solomon.

Temple Worship Eternally a Part of the Gospel

When Joseph Smith was commissioned to restore the Gospel and to re-establish the Church of Jesus Christ, the building of temples and temple worship became almost the first and last issue of his life. The temple site in Independence, dedicated shortly after the organization of the Church; the building and completion of the Kirtland temple and the wonderful things that happened there; the building of the Nauvoo temple and the giving of endowments in the temple after the death of the Prophet; the dedication of other temple sites and many revelations concerning temples indicate, altogether, that the main concern of the Prophet Joseph Smith in the restoration of the Gospel in these latter days was the founding, building, and completion of temples in which the ordinances "hid from before the foundation of the world" might be given. In fact, the Lord declared repeatedly to the Prophet that unless temples were built and used, the plan of salvation could neither be in full operation nor fully accomplished.

Let me suggest that the reason why temple building and temple worship have been found in every age, on every hand, and among every people, is because the gospel in its fullness was revealed to Adam, and that all religions and religious practices are therefore derived from the remnants of the truth given to Adam and transmitted by him to the patriarchs. The ordinances of the temple in so far as then necessary, were given, no doubt, in those early days, and very naturally corruptions of them have been handed down through the ages. Those who understand the eternal nature of the gospel, planned before the foundation of the earth, understand clearly why all history seems to revolve about the building and use of temples.

Eternal Nature of Man

To understand the meaning of temple worship, it is necessary to understand the plan of salvation and its relation to temple worship. The human race were "in the beginning with God," and were created spiritual beings in a day before their arrival upon this earth. Mankind is here because of its acceptance of the plan of salvation, and satisfactory pre-existent lives. We have won the right to be here; we have not been forced to come here; we have won our place upon the earth. We shall pass into another sphere of existence, and shall continue upward and onward forever and forever, if we obey the high laws of eternal existence.

The plan of salvation for eternal beings involves the principle that God's work with respect to this earth will not be complete until every soul has been taught the Gospel and has been offered the privilege of accepting salvation and the accompanying great blessings which the Lord has in store for his children. Until that is done the work is unfinished.

Men frequently ask when the last day shall come and when the earth shall go through its great change. Men attempt uselessly to figure out the dates of the coming events from the sayings of Daniel and the other prophets. We know that the Lord will come when we are ready to receive him; that is when we have done the work he required of us; not before, not later; but when the labor of the day has been accomplished, the present day will end and a new stage of action will be set. When the work assigned to the earth's children has been done in accordance with the plan of salvation, the Lord will remember his promises, and the end of the earth, which is the beginning of a new day of advancement, will occur.

We who travel the earth journey are working out an eternal problem. An endless journey is ours, and earth life is a fraction of it; the purpose is unending.

Conditions of Eternal Progress

It has been ordained that to follow the path God has laid out for us, we must have faith, we must repent, and we must show our obedience by going into the waters of baptism, and then as our great reward we shall receive the gift of the Holy Ghost. Some people, having obeyed these first principles, believe their work done. They have found entrance into the Church, they are members of God's chosen people; what more need they? In fact, however, the gift of the Holy Ghost, according to the Prophet Joseph Smith, is a promise of increasing intelligence, it is a beginning of things to be. It is a promise of larger, fuller knowledge, of something new, more wonderful, and vaster, in its intent and purpose than anything that we have known before. It is a promise of growth into a larger life and a larger condition of life. In my opinion, the gift of the Holy Ghost, which implies a promise of added intelligence, is realized in part at least in the worship and ordinances of the temples of the Lord. The request of the soul, which leads a man into obedience of the first principles, is answered by one method through the institution of the eternal ordinances which all the faithful may enjoy.

Salvation vs. Exaltation

Through obedience to the first principles of the Gospel, and a subsequent blameless life, a person may win salvation for himself. But in God's kingdom are many gradations, which lead to exaltation upon exaltation. Those who hunger and thirst for righteousness and labor for the fulfillment of the promise involved in the gift of the Holy Ghost will advance farther than those who placidly sit by with no driving desire within them. Temple worship is an avenue to exaltation in God's kingdom.

God's Definition of a Temple

God's definition of a temple is given over and over again in this good book, the Doctrine and Covenants. A temple is a place in which those whom he has chosen are endowed with power from on high. And what is power? Knowledge made alive and useful, that is intelligence; and intelligence in action, that is power. Our temples give us power, a power based on enlarged knowledge and intelligence, a power from on high of a quality with God's own power.

Purposes of Temples

This is accomplished through the various purposes of temples. A temple is a place where God will come; a place where the pure in heart shall see God; a place where baptisms for the dead are performed; a place where the endowment of the priesthood is given; a place where the keys of the priesthood are committed in abundance; and a place where many other wonderful things may occur and should occur and in fact do occur.

Communion of God and man. It is a great promise that to the temples God will come, and that in them man shall see God. What does this promised communion mean? Does it mean that once in a while God may come into the temples, and that once in a while the pure in heart may see God there; or does it mean the larger thing, that the pure in heart who go into the temples, may, there by the Spirit of God, always have a wonderfully rich communion with God? I think that is what it means to me and to you and to most of us. We have gone into these holy houses, with our minds freed from the ordinary earthly cares, and have literally felt the presence of God. In this way, the temples are always places where God manifests himself to man and increases his intelligence. A temple is a place of revelation.

Baptisms for the dead. The ordinance of baptism for the dead fits into the scheme of salvation. It is an acknowledgement of itself that the whole plan is eternal, and that the past, the present and the future are parts of one continuous whole. Were the life of man discontinuous there would be no need of labors for the dead.

Sealings. Sealings, for time and eternity, have the purpose of tying together father and son, mother and daughter, the living and the dead, from age to age. In addition it emphasizes the authority of the priesthood. No merely earthly power could accomplish a union of a condition of this earth with a condition beyond this earth; a person of this life with a person of the life hereafter, or of the life before. When man contemplates the full meaning of the sealing ordinance, if I may call it an ordinance, he is overwhelmed with the boundless power that it implies and the weight of authority that it represents. The mere words of sealing may be easily spoken at the altars of the holy temples, but they are so full of meaning that any man with even a particle of imagination who witnesses or participates in the sealing ordinance must be overcome with the feeling of responsibility and opportunity and enjoyment that it carries with it.

The endowment. In the wonderful section 124 of the Doctrine and Covenants, the Lord has described the work to be done in the temples, including the holy endowment:

"For a baptismal font there is not upon the earth, that they, my saints, may be baptized for those who are dead—

"For this ordinance belongeth to my house, and cannot be acceptable to me, only in the days of your poverty, wherein ye are not able to build a house unto me. . . .

"For therein are the keys of the holy priesthood ordained, that you may receive honor and glory. . . .

"And again, verily I say unto you, how shall your washings be acceptable unto me, except ye perform them in a house which you have built to my name?

"For, for this cause I commanded Moses that he should build a tabernacle, that they should bear it with them in the wilderness, and to build a house in the land of promise, that those ordinances might be revealed which had been hid from before the world was.

"Therefore, verily I say unto you, that your anointings, and your washings, and your baptisms for the dead, and your solemn assemblies, and your memorials for your sacrifices by the sons of Levi, and for your oracles in your most holy places wherein you receive conversations, and your statutes and judgments, for the beginning of the revelations and foundation of Zion, and for the glory, honor, and endowment of all her municipals, are ordained by the ordinance of my holy house, which my people are always commanded to build unto my holy name."

At first reading the full meaning may not be clear, yet in these few verses lie the germs of practically everything that belongs to and is done in the house of the Lord. Dr. James E. Talmage, under authority of the Church, has also discussed the meaning of endowment, in the book called *The House of the Lord*. I will read a part of it.

"The Temple Endowment, as administered in modern temples, comprises instruction relating to the significance and sequence of past dispensations, and the importance of the present as the greatest and grandest era in human history. This course of instruction includes a recital of the most prominent events of the creative period, the condition of our first parents in the Garden of Eden, their disobedience and consequent expulsion from that blissful abode, their condition in the lone and dreary world when doomed to live by labor and sweat, the plan of redemption by which the great transgression may be atoned, the period of the great apostasy, the restoration of the Gospel with all its ancient powers and privileges, the absolute and indispensable condition of personal purity and devotion to the right in present life, and a strict compliance with Gospel requirements.

"As will be shown, the temples erected by the Latter-day Saints provide for the giving of these instructions in separate rooms, each devoted to a particular part of the course; and by this provision it is possible to have several classes under instruction at one time.

"The ordinances of the endowment embody certain obligations on the part of the individual, such as covenant and promise to observe the law of strict virtue and chastity, to be charitable, benevolent, tolerant and pure; to devote both talent and material means to the spread of truth and the uplifting of the race; to maintain devotion to the cause of truth; and to seek in every way to contribute to the great preparation that the earth may be made ready to receive her King the Lord Jesus Christ. With the taking of each covenant and the assuming of each obligation a promised blessing is pronounced, contingent upon the faithful observance of the conditions.

"No jot, iota, or tittle of the temple rites is otherwise than uplifting and sanctifying. In every detail the endowment ceremony contributes to covenants of morality of life, consecration of person to high ideals, devotion to truth, patriotism to nation, and allegiance to God. The blessings of the house of the Lord are restricted to no privileged class; every member of the Church may have admission to the temple with the right to participate in the ordinances thereof, if he comes duly accredited as of worthy life and conduct."

In no part of the temple service is the spirit of the purpose of temple worship so completely shown as in the endowment.

Internal Evidence of Veracity

I desire to leave with you as the next thought that the work done in temples brings to those of pure and sincere hearts the evidence of its veracity. This is said in view of the question so often asked: Is there anything in the temple ordinances themselves that speaks for their truth?

The temple ordinances encompass the whole plan of salvation as taught from time to time by the leaders of the Church, and elucidate matters difficult of understanding. There is no warping or twisting in fitting the temple teachings into the great scheme of salvation. The philosophical completeness of the endowment is one of the great arguments for the veracity of the temple ordinances. Moreover, this completeness of survey and expounding of the Gospel plan, makes temple worship one of the most effective methods of refreshing the memory concerning the whole structure of the Gospel.

Another fact has always appealed to me as a strong internal evidence for the truth of temple work. The endowment and the temple work as revealed by the Lord to the Prophet Joseph Smith (see also Dr. Talmage's *The House of the Lord*) fall clearly into four distinct parts: the preparatory ordinances; the giving of instructions by lectures and representations; covenants; and, finally, tests of knowledge. I doubt that the Prophet Joseph, unlearned and untrained in logic, could of himself have made the thing so logically complete. The candidate for the temple service is prepared, as in any earthly affair, for work to be done. Once prepared he is instructed in the things that he should know. When instructed, he covenants to use the imparted knowledge, and at once the new knowledge, which of itself is dead, leaps into living life. At last, tests are given him, whereby those who are entitled to know may determine whether the man has properly learned the lesson. The brethren and sisters who go through the temple should observe all these things and recognize the wonderful coherence and logical nature of the carefully worked out system, with a beginning and an end, fitting every known law of God and nature, which constitutes temple worship.

The wonderful pedagogy of the temple service, especially appealing to me as a professional teacher, carries with it evidence of the truth of temple work. We go to the temple to be informed and directed, to be built up and to be blessed. How is all this accomplished? First by the spoken word, through lectures and conversations, just as we do in the class room, except with more elaborate care; then by the appeal to the eye by representations by living, moving beings; and by pictorial representations in the wonderfully decorated rooms (as any one may see in Dr. Talmage's book). Meanwhile the recipients themselves, the candidates for blessings, engage actively in the temple service as they move from room to room, with the progress of the course of instruction. Altogether our temple worship follows a most excellent pedagogical system. I wish instruction were given so well in every school throughout the land, for we would then teach with more effect than we now do.

For these reasons, among many others, I have always felt that temple work is a direct evidence of the truth of the word re-established by the Prophet Joseph Smith. It may be that the temple endowment and the other temple ordinances form the strongest available evidence of the divine inspiration of the Prophet Joseph Smith.

Objections to Temple Worship

I said near the beginning of this address that with any increase in temple activity we must expect a new and vigorous opposition to temple work, from evil forces, which however will be wholly subdued if the work is continued. This opposition will not wholly come from without; some will come from within the Church. Unfortunately, that is also a natural law. Young people and sometimes older people will question this or that thing about the temple service. "Is this or that necessary?" "Is this or that thing reasonable?" "Why should I do this or that?" Even though such questions should be needless, it is best to answer them, especially if they are asked by those who are untrained and inexperienced, and therefore unable to think clearly for themselves.

Why a House?

The objection is sometimes raised that a house is not needed for temple worship. "Why should a house be required, when God is everywhere, the God who made the trees and the mountains and the valleys?" "Why should God require the poor saints in Illinois and Ohio and Missouri to build temples at tremendous expense?" Of course the Lord does not need a house, and temple work may be done elsewhere than in a house. The Lord has specifically stated that under certain conditions the temple endowment may be given on the tops of the mountains, but as men multiply upon the face of the earth, it will be increasingly difficult to conduct temple worship, except in especially dedicated places away from the multitude and the chaos and the rattle and the disturbance of ordinary life.

The holy endowment is deeply symbolic. "Going through the temple" is not a very good phrase; for temple worship implies a great effort of mind and concentration if we are to understand the mighty symbols that pass in review before us. Everything must be arranged to attune our hearts, our minds, and our souls to the work. Everything about us must contribute to the peace of mind that enables us to study and to understand the mysteries, if you choose, that are unfolded before us. We would not give our family dinners out of doors, in the crowd; why should anyone ask us to do our most sacred work in the face of the crowd?

Sacred vs. Secret

Some young persons do not like temple work "because the things done in it are secret, and we do not believe in secret things; we want to stand in the sunshine." In fact, there is nothing secret about the temple. I have found nothing secret in or about our temples; I have found many things that are sacred. There is a vast difference between things secret and things sacred—the thing [secret, which is] hidden away from the light; and the thing sacred, which plays in the light and is protected from darkness and impurity and all unworthy conditions.

God has declared that he will not enter a defiled temple, whether that temple be the body of a man or a dedicated grove or a mountain top, or a house, like the temple on these grounds. The Holy Spirit will withdraw from a defiled place. People who have no faith in temple worship, who desire simply as tourists to inspect unsympathetically our holy house, in spite of themselves, defile it. We desire to present our temple ordinances to those who are believers. Moreover, visitors in temples would interfere with the procedure of the work. Of itself there is no reason why at proper times the temple may not be inspected.

Covenants and Promises

Many young people object to temple work because, "We must make covenants and promises and we do not like to be tied; we want full freedom." This objection arises from a misunderstanding of the meaning of covenants. Knowledge becomes serviceable only when it is used; the covenant made in the temple, or elsewhere, if of the right kind, is merely a promise to give life to knowledge, by making knowledge useful and helpful in man's daily progress. Temple work, or any other work, would have no meaning unless accompanied with covenants. It would consist simply of bits of information for ornament; the covenant gives life to truth, and makes possible the blessings that reward all those who use knowledge properly, or the penalties that overtake those who misuse knowledge. That knowledge of itself is valueless, and that its use or misuse brings about inevitable results are the A B C of every scientific laboratory. The electric current properly used lights this building; improperly used, it may go through the body of the man and leave death behind. Unused, the electric current is to the man as if it were not. Penalties and rewards hang upon the use of knowledge.

Lack of Beauty

Others say that the temple ordinances are unbeautiful. Some young man ready for a mission, or some young lady just married says, "It is unbeautiful; I did not enjoy it." Again the misunderstanding. They have gone through the temple looking at the outward form and not the inner meaning of things. The form of the endowment is of earthly nature, but it symbolizes great spiritual truths. All that we do on this earth is earthly, but all is symbolic of great spiritual truths. To build this temple, earth had to be dug, wood had to be cut; stone was quarried and brought down the canyon. It was dusty and dirty work and made us sweat; it was of this earth, yet it was the necessary preparation for the mighty spiritual ordinances that are carried on daily in this magnificent temple. The endowment itself is symbolic; it is a series of symbols of vast realities, too vast for full understanding. Those who go through the temple and come out feeling the service is unbeautiful have been so occupied with the outward form as to fail to understand the inner meaning. It is the meaning of things that counts in life.

Symbolism

This brings me to a few words concerning symbolism. We live in a world of symbols. We know nothing, except by symbols. We make a few marks on a sheet of paper, and we say that they form a word, which stands for love, or hate, or charity, or God or eternity. The marks may not be very beautiful to the eye. No one finds fault with the symbols on the pages of a book because they are not as mighty in their own beauty as the things which they represent. We do not quarrel with the symbol G-o-d because it is not very beautiful, yet represents the majesty of God. We are glad to have symbols, if only the meaning of the symbols is brought home to us. I speak to you tonight; you have not quarreled very much with my manner of delivery, or my choice of words; in following the meaning of the thoughts I have tried to bring home to you, you have forgotten words and manner. There are men who object to Santa Claus, because he does not exist! Such men need spectacles to see that Santa Claus is a symbol; a symbol of the love and joy of Christmas and the Christmas spirit. In the land of my birth there was no Santa Claus, but a little goat was shoved into the room, carrying with it a basket of Christmas toys and gifts. The goat of itself counted for nothing; but the Christmas spirit, which it symbolized, counted for a tremendous lot.

We live in a world of symbols. No man or woman can come out of the temple endowed as he should be, unless he has seen, beyond the symbol, the mighty realities for which the symbols stand.

Corruptions of Temple Worship

Many apostates have tried to reveal the ordinances of the house of the Lord. Some of their accounts form a fairly complete and correct story of the outward form of the temple service; but they are pitiful failures in making clear the eternal meaning of temple worship and the exaltation of the spirit that is awakened by the understanding of that meaning. Such attempts are only words; symbols without meaning. Is anything more lifeless than a symbol of an unknown meaning?

Such attempted improper revelations of temple worship have led in all ages to corruptions of temple ordinances. The fact that such corruptions of ordinances and ceremonies have always existed is a strong evidence of the continuity of temple worship, under the priesthood, from the days of Adam. Sister Gates handed me this afternoon a quotation from a book that she had picked up, in which it is related that Moses adopted a holy garment from Jethro, which he wore, and in turn communicated it to his brother Aaron, who adopted it and who in turn communicated it to the priests of Israel, from whom in turn it was taken in some form by the priests of false gods. Such corruptions of temple worship are found every-where, but they are poor lifeless imitations, symbols from which the meaning has been wrested.

The Revelation of the Temple

If we are correct in believing that the blessings obtained in the temples of the Lord are a partial fulfillment, at least, of the promise made when the Holy Ghost, who is a Revelator, is conferred upon man, it would be expected that temple ordinances would be in the nature of a revelation to those who participate. Certainly the temple is a place where revelations may be expected.

But whether in the temple or elsewhere, how do men receive revelations? How did the Prophet Joseph Smith obtain his first revelation, his first vision? He desired something. In the woods, away from human confusion, he summoned all the strength of his nature; there he fought the demon of evil, and, at length, because of the strength of his desire and the great effort that he made, the Father and the Son descended out of the heavens and spoke eternal truth to him. So revelation always comes; it is not imposed upon a person; it must be drawn to us by faith, seeking and working. Just so; to the man or woman who goes through the temple with open eyes, heeding the symbols and the covenants, and making a steady, continuous effort to understand the full meaning, God speaks his word and revelations come.

The endowment is so richly symbolic that only a fool would attempt to describe it; it is so packed full of revelations to those who exercise their strength to seek and see, that no human words can explain or make clear the possibilities that reside in the temple service. The endowment which was given by revelation can best be understood by revelation; and to those who seek most vigorously, with pure hearts, will the revelation be greatest.

I believe that the busy person on the farm, in the shop, in the office, or in the household, who has his worries and troubles, can solve his problems better and more quickly in the house of the Lord than anywhere else. If he will leave his problems behind and in the temple work for himself and for his dead, he will confer a mighty blessing upon those who have gone before, and quite as large a blessing will come to him, for at the most unexpected moments, in or out of the temple will come to him, as a revelation, the solution of the problems that vex his life. That is the gift that comes to those who enter the temple properly, because it is a place where revelations may be expected. I bear my personal testimony that this is so.

In temple worship, as in all else, we probably gain understanding according to our differing knowledge and capacity; but I believe that we can increase in knowledge and enlarge our capacity, and in that way receive greater gifts from God. I would therefore urge upon you that we teach those who go into the temples to do so with a strong desire to have God's will revealed to them, for comfort, peace, and success in our daily lives, not for publication, or for conversation, but for our own good, for the satisfying of our hearts.

Preparation for Temple Worship

Colonel Willard Young said last night, in casual conversation, that we should give more attention to preparing our young people and some of the older people, for the work they are to do in the temple. He is undoubtedly right in his view. It is not quite fair to let the young girl or young man enter the temple unprepared, unwarned, if you choose, with no explanation of the glorious possibilities of the first fine day in the temple. Neither is it quite fair to pass opinion on temple worship after one day's participation followed by an absence of many years. The work should be repeated several times in quick succession, so that the lessons of the temple may be fastened upon the mind.

Conclusion

The beginning and the end of the Gospel is written, from one point of view, in section 2 of the Book of Doctrine and Covenants. If I read this section correctly, the work which in part has been committed by the Church to this Society is the keystone of the wonderful gospel arch. If this center stone is weakened and falls out, the whole arch falls into a heap of unorganized doctrinal blocks. It is a high privilege for young or old to be allowed to enter the house of the Lord, there to serve God and to win power.

I hope that temple worship will increase in our midst, that we shall have a finer understanding of its meaning, and that more temples may be built to supply the demands of the living and the dead, and to hasten the coming of the great day of the Lord.

May the Lord bless us in this work, I ask in the name of Jesus. Amen.

Utah Genealogical and Historical Magazine, April 1921, 49–64.

TITHING

~⚘~

THE LAW OF TITHING

LORENZO SNOW

President Lorenzo Snow gave this address to the Saints in St. George, Utah, on May 17, 1899. In the middle of the address, President Snow received a revelation on the law of tithing. His son, LeRoi C. Snow, explained the circumstances surrounding the revelation:

> President Snow, after his call as Church president, humbly admitted that he did not know just what he would do; but he was confident that the Lord would show him, and he placed such dependence upon the promptings of God's spirit, and was so sure that he would follow those instructions that he said: "My administration will not be known as mine, but as God's administration through me."
>
> The day after President John Taylor's funeral, proceedings for the confiscation of Church property were begun in the United States Court (because of plural marriage in the Church). All the property of the Church was seized, and for nearly ten years tedious and expensive litigation continued. Then, too, for several years the General Authorities had been compelled, by prosecution under the Edmunds-Tucker Law, to remain from home. Therefore, during this period, the business interests of the Church suffered greatly.
>
> These are but two of the several contributing causes which brought about serious financial distress. . . . I well remember my father's approaching his personal clerk, James Jack, with the warning, "Brother Jack, we must raise

some money. Go through all the securities we have and see if you can find something we can sell to make some money." . . .

One prominent businessman presented a plan to solicit contributions from the entire Church membership. He suggested a "one thousand dollar club" to include all who would contribute one thousand dollars each, a "five hundred dollar club," etc., but President Snow shook his head and said: "No, that is not the Lord's plan." The Lord had not yet shown his servant just how the problem was to be solved, but he revealed the plan a little later.

One morning my father said he was going to St. George in Southern Utah. I was much surprised at the thought of his making this long and hard trip. Mother expressed considerable surprise, but asked no questions.

Upon entering the President's office, father informed Secretary George F. Gibbs of the contemplated trip to St. George. Brother Gibbs at once asked how soon President Snow expected to leave and who would be in the party. The reply was that he would leave just as soon as arrangements could be made, and that he would take as many of the General Authorities as could be spared from the important work at home. . . .

President Snow stood the trip exceptionally well, but was very tired on reaching St. George. . . .

He had the most painful and anxious expression on his face that I had ever seen, and he must have been going through intense mental suffering. After pacing up and down the floor several times, he commenced talking aloud as follows: "Why have I come to St. George, and why have I brought so many of the Church authorities, when we are so much needed at home to look after the important affairs of the Church? Haven't I made a mistake? Why have I come here?"

When the Lord instructed his servant to go to St. George, the purpose of the journey was withheld.

President Snow answered the call to go, and then wondered and worried until further light was given.

He finally went to bed and rested very well during the
night, appearing to feel very much better the following
morning. It was Wednesday, May 17, the day on which the
special conference opened in the tabernacle in St. George.
It was during one of these meetings that President Snow
received the revelation on tithing. I was sitting at a table
on the stand, recording the proceedings, when all at once
father paused in his discourse.

Complete stillness filled the room. I shall never forget
the thrill as long as I live. When he commenced to speak
again his voice strengthened, and the inspiration of God
seemed to come over him, as well as over the entire assembly. His eyes seemed to brighten and his countenance to
shine. He was filled with unusual power. Then he revealed
to the Latter-day Saints the vision that was before him.

God manifested to him there and then not only the
purpose of the call to visit the Saints in the South, but also
Lorenzo Snow's special mission, the great work for which
God had prepared and preserved him. And he unveiled
the vision to the people. He told them that he could see,
as he had never realized before, how the law of tithing had
been neglected by the people; also that the Saints, themselves, were heavily in debt, as well as the Church. And
now through strict obedience to this law—the paying of a
full and honest tithing—not only would the Church be
relieved of its great indebtedness, but through the blessings of the Lord this would also be the means of freeing the
Latter-day Saints from their individual obligations. And
they would become a prosperous people.

Directly on tithing President Snow said:

"The word of the Lord is: The time has now come for
every Latter-day Saint, who calculates to be prepared for
the future and to hold his feet strong upon a proper foundation, to do the will of the Lord and to pay his tithing in

full. That is the word of the Lord to you, and it will be the word of the Lord to every settlement throughout the land of Zion."

President Snow then referred to the terrible drought which had continued so severely for three years in the South. The Virgin River and all its tributaries were virtually dry. . . .

President Snow said . . . :

"All through Dixie we found everything dying out. The stock were dying by hundreds; we could see them as we traveled along, many of them being nothing but skin and bones, and many lying down never, I suppose, to get up again."

In speaking of these serious drought conditions President Snow told the people that if they would observe the law of tithing from then on, and pay a full and honest tithing, that they might go ahead, plough their land and plant the seed. And he promised them, in the name of the Lord, that the clouds would gather, the rains from heaven descend, their lands would be drenched, and the rivers and ditches filled, and they would reap a bounteous harvest that very season.

Many of the people had become so discouraged that they were not willing to risk the seeds of another planting, and many had not even ploughed their fields. Cattle everywhere were dying, and the country was parched. It was now getting very late in the planting season in that southern country, and here the prophet of the Lord made this wonderful prediction. Everyone present in that vast congregation knew that he was speaking under the inspiration of the Holy Spirit.

That evening, father, mother, and I were again in the room together and father walked up and down the floor as he had done the previous night, but there was a sweet expression of happiness and joy on his face. He talked aloud again, as he did the night before, and this is what he said:

"Now I know why I came to St. George. The Lord sent me here, and he has a great work for me to perform. There is no mistake about it. I can see the great future for the Church, and I can hardly wait to get back to Salt Lake City to commence the great work."

When the returning party reached Nephi, where we were to take train for home, President Snow called the members all together in a meeting which will never be forgotten by those who were present. He commissioned every one present to be his special witness to the fact that the Lord had given this revelation to him. He put all the party under covenant and promise not only to obey the law of tithing themselves, but also that each would bear witness to this special manifestation and would spread the tithing message at every opportunity. He made wonderful promises to those who would be faithful to these admonitions. He was filled with great power and inspiration and spoke with such feeling that Elder Francis M. Lyman says in his journal: "I was almost overcome, could hardly control my feelings."

President Snow, with his party, returned to Salt Lake City, Saturday, May 27, 1899. During his absence of eleven days, he visited sixteen settlements, held twenty-four meetings, delivered twenty-six addresses. . . .

President Snow gathered and compiled data regarding the tithes being paid by the people, but kept especially in mind the Saints in the south. He called for a daily report showing the exact amount of tithing received from those settlements. I well remember handing him one of these reports. After looking it over carefully he said, "Wonderful, wonderful. The good people in Dixie are not only paying one-tenth of their income, but they must be giving all they have to the Lord's work!"

But the rains did not come, and the drought was not

broken. President Snow had the daily weather report placed on his desk, which he carefully looked over, but there was no indication of any storms moving in the direction of southern Utah. Week after week passed, and the only word was that southern Utah was burning up under the hot weather, and there seemed to be no prospect of any change.

One morning, as I was going up the stairway leading to father's bedroom, I was surprised to hear him talking to someone. I did not know that anyone had preceded me to the room that morning, but not wanting to disturb him, I walked quietly up the heavily carpeted stairway leading to his room. The door was open, and as I reached it, there I saw this aged, grey-haired prophet, down on his knees before his bedside, in the manner of praying, but seeming to talk to the Lord as if he might have been right in His very presence. He was pouring out his heart and pleading for the Saints in the south. I stood at the open door for a few moments and heard him say:

"Oh Lord, why didst thou make those promises to the good people in St. George if they are not to be fulfilled? Thou didst promise them, if they would accept the command to obey the law of tithing, thou wouldst send the rains from heaven and bless them with a bounteous harvest. These good people accepted thy word and are not only paying a tenth of their income, but they are offering all they have to thee. Do keep thy promise and vindicate the words of thy servant through whom thou didst speak."

I could not bear to hear any more. I turned from the door with my heart bleeding and went down the stairs.

When father came into his office that morning, I noticed that he looked discouraged and seemed to have little interest in his work. [There was] still no report of rain in St. George. Several days passed. One day there was a knock at the door. Brother Gibbs, the secretary, being out, I answered the call. It was a messenger boy with a telegram.

I signed for it, opened the telegram, and as I was approaching father's desk I could see on the face of the telegram: "Rain in St. George." I was so happy I could not wait, but cried out: "Father, they have had rain in St. George."

"Read it, my boy, read it," he said, and I read the telegram telling of a great rain that had come to the people there, filling the river and its tributaries and the canals and reaching the entire country. . . .

Father took the telegram from my hand, read it very slowly, and after a few moments, got up from his desk and left the office.

A little while afterwards I followed him into the house and asked mother where he was. When she told me she had not seen him, I knew he must have gone to his room. I walked quietly up the stairway and before reaching the top I heard him talking, as I had on the other occasion. I went to his room and there he was again, down on his knees pouring out his heart in gratitude and thanksgiving to the Lord. He said:

"Father, what can I do to show my appreciation for the blessing which thou hast given to the good people in St. George? Thou hast fulfilled thy promise to them and vindicated the words spoken through thy servant. Do show me some special thing I can do to prove my love for thee."

This faithful servant of the Lord, who had devoted all his long life in beautiful and unwavering service to God, felt that he had not done enough and wanted to do more. There he was in the presence of his Heavenly Father, overcome with joy and happiness. The last words I heard, as I was returning down the stairs, were: "Thou canst not ask anything of me that I am not willing to do, even though it be the offering of my life, to prove my love for thee."

When father returned to his office, his face was filled with happiness, and I am very sure that his heart was lightened and his difficult task made much easier. . . .

During the MIA conference in 1899, at one of the

officers' meetings, President Snow spoke on tithing. At the conclusion of his address the following resolution was presented by Elder B. H. Roberts:

"Resolved: That we accept the doctrine of tithing, as now presented by President Snow, as the present word and will of the Lord unto us, and we do accept it with all our hearts; we will ourselves observe it, and we will do all in our power to get the Latter-day Saints to do likewise." (*Improvement Era*, July 1938, 400–401, 439–42.)

I come here now my brethren that you may understand what is required of you as a people under the peculiar conditions in which the Church is now placed. It is the word of the Lord to you, my brethren and sisters, that you should conform to that which is required of you as a people who have these glorious prospects of exaltation and glory before you. What is it? Why it is something that has been drummed into your ears from time to time until you perhaps have got tired of hearing it. I need the faith and the prayers of every Latter-day Saint; no man needs them any more than I do; and it is unpleasant for me to say things that would in any way diminish the exercise of your faith and prayers in my behalf. But the Lord requires me to say something to you, and since I commenced to labor in His interest, I have never failed, thank the Lord, to do that which He has required at my hands; and I shall not do it today, nor any other day, the Lord being my helper.

The word of the Lord to you is not anything new; it is simply this: THE TIME HAS NOW COME FOR EVERY LATTER-DAY SAINT, WHO CALCULATES TO BE PREPARED FOR THE FUTURE AND TO HOLD HIS FEET STRONG UPON A PROPER FOUNDATION, TO DO THE WILL OF THE LORD AND PAY HIS TITHING IN FULL. That is the word of the Lord to you, and it will be the word of the Lord to every settlement throughout the land of Zion.

After I leave you and you get to thinking about this, you will see yourselves that the time has come when every man should stand up and pay his tithing in full. The Lord has blessed us and has had mercy upon us in the past; but there are times coming when the Lord requires us to stand up and do that which He has commanded and not leave it any longer. What I say to you in this Stake of Zion I will say to every Stake of Zion that has been organized. There is no man or woman that now hears what I am saying who will feel satisfied if he or she fails to pay a full tithing.

I could reason with you upon this, but what need is there of showing why we should do these things. We receive from different Stakes of Zion requests for help, some to build meeting houses and some for other purposes. Well, we feel that we ought to help them, because they are deserving of help; but we cannot do it. I do not think I will say much about the financial condition of the Church. The Church, of course, is very much in debt. And I do not know that anybody is to blame for it being in debt. It has been partially explained today by the brethren, and I will leave it that way. But we are going into debt no longer. All the enterprises that we have gone into have been for the benefit of the people.

Well, I do not care to talk about this. It is sufficient to say to the Latter-day Saints that we must now pay our tithing. I have scarcely ever talked about tithing. I have said it was the duty of the Latter-day Saints to pay tithing, but I have never made it a business like some of my brethren have. You will not hear much from me now in regard to tithing. I simply tell you the truth straight out; and I have faith in the Latter-day Saints to believe and know that they will respond to this.

Brethren and sisters, I feel and know that you are a good people. I do not flatter you when I say this. I simply tell the facts. The Lord has helped you, as He has helped other portions of the people in Zion. He has done this, not because they have done right under all circumstances, not because they have paid their tithing properly, but because they have paid it partially and have done some good. But when the voice of the Lord comes to us and His will is expressed, then is the time for us to act.

Now, I have shaken hands with over 800 children, and I want to see those children grow up and become 80, 90, 100 or 140 years of age; and this will surely be the case if you will teach them these things that I am talking to you about today. Teach them to pay their tithing while they are young. You mothers, teach your children that when they get any money they should pay one-tenth of it to the Lord, however little it may be. Educate them to pay their tithing in full. . . .

President Smith was talking yesterday about the land of Zion. Yes, surely, this entire continent is the land of Zion, and the time will come when there will be Temples established over every portion of the land, and we will go into these Temples and work for our kindred dead night and day, that the work of the Lord may be speedily accomplished, that Jesus may come and present the kingdom to His father. He is coming soon, too. . . .

Now we should make preparation for this. We are not only going to have Zion throughout this continent, but we will have it over the whole earth. The whole earth is the Lord's. The time will come when it will be translated and be filled with the spirit and power of God. The atmosphere around it will be the spirit of the Almighty. We will breathe that Spirit instead of the atmosphere that we now breathe. But now it is for us to make the preparation, that we may be worthy to be called into the house of the Lord and receive our second blessings. I do not want the presidents of Stakes to send any person to our Temples to receive the highest blessings that have ever been bestowed upon man since the world began, until it can be said of him, "He pays his full tithing."

Millennial Star, 61:532–33, 545–46.

WEALTH

❧ ❦

THE DUTY OF MAN

BRIGHAM YOUNG

This discourse was delivered in the Old Tabernacle in Salt Lake City on February 3, 1867. Without a loudspeaker system, President Brigham Young and others often found it challenging to be heard. At the beginning of this address, he said, "If the people can hear me as well as I can hear their noise walking, there will not be much difficulty in my making myself understood. This walking carelessly with heavy boots makes quite a confusion in the hall."

President Young taught that if we are faithful we can enjoy the guidance and assistance of the Spirit in all our doings—including our temporal labors: "No matter what the person is called to do, if it is to build up the kingdom of God on the earth, if he cheerfully performs the duty, he is entitled to the Spirit of the Lord—the Spirit of Truth—the Holy Ghost; and will most assuredly possess the same. There is a time for preaching, for praying, for sacrament meetings, for labor, and when we are attending to any or all of these, in the season thereof, we are entitled to the purifying influence of the Spirit of God."

I n addressing the Saints, whether by the word of exhortation, admonition, correction or in doctrine, it requires good attention for a person to retain even a small portion of that which they hear. This is why it is so necessary for us to be talked to and preached to so much. If we read the Bible, it soon goes from us; we gather principles and have the pleasure of perusing the experience of others who have lived in former days; but we soon forget them. Our own cares and reflections, and the multitude of thoughts that pass through our minds take away from our recollections that which we hear and read, and our minds are upon present objects—our woes, our trials, our joys, or whatever seems to be present with us and directly in the future, and we forget what we have heard.

When I address the Latter-day Saints, I address a people who wish to be Saints indeed. I look upon my brethren and sisters, and I think, what have you come here for? What brought you here into this territory—this mountainous country—into these wild regions? Why, the answer is, at once, "I came here because I was a Latter-day Saint, I wanted to gather with this people; my heart was with those who had embraced the Gospel, and I wished to be with the Saints." There are none who have done so but would like to gather.

What for? What is the object of being a Saint? For the express purpose of enjoying the blessings of the pure in heart—of those who will be prepared to dwell in the presence of the Father and the Son. For this I have left my all—left, perhaps, father, mother, sisters, brothers, friends, relatives, a good home; in many instances left a wife, left a husband, left our children for the sake of the society of the Saints.

And when we are gathered together we can look around and inquire of ourselves, if we are really what we profess to be; do we walk in that path that is marked out for the faithful and obedient as strictly and as tenaciously as we should, devoting ourselves entirely to the service of God, for the building up of his kingdom, and the sanctifying of ourselves—striving to overcome every evil passion, every unhallowed appetite; seeking to the Lord for strength to subdue every obnoxious weed that seems to grow in our affections, and overcome the same to that degree that we may be sanctified? We can examine ourselves, and decide upon this question, without asking the counsel of bishop, or presiding elder, or Apostle or any man or woman in this church. We are capable of deciding this for ourselves.

If any of the Latter-day Saints would like to have the path of duty pointed out to them in plainness and simplicity, and the road that leads to perfection marked before them so as to travel therein with ease, they should seek unto the Lord and obtain his spirit—the Spirit of Christ—so that they can read and understand for themselves. Do they love God with all their hearts? Do they keep his commandments? Do we know whether we do love the Lord? Do we know whether we keep his commandments? Do we know whether we are walking in the path of obedience or not?

There is a trait in the character of man which is frequently made manifest in the Saints. It is simply this—to see faults in others when we do not examine our own. When you see people, professing to be Latter-day Saints, examining the faults of others, you may know that they are not walking in the path of obedience as strictly as they should. For this simple reason—it is all that you and I can do as individuals, as members in the Church and Kingdom of God, to purify ourselves, to sanctify our own hearts, and to sanctify the Lord God in our hearts.

It may be observed, or the question may be asked: "Are we never to know the doings of others? Are we never to look to see how others are walking and progressing in this Gospel? Must we for ever and for ever confine our minds to thinking of ourselves, and our eyes to looking at ourselves?" I can merely say that if persons only understand the path of duty and walk therein, attending strictly to whatever is required of them, they will have plenty to do to examine themselves and to purify their own hearts; and if they look at their neighbors and examine their conduct, they will look for good and not for evil. . . .

. . . No matter what the person is called to do, if it is to build up the kingdom of God on the earth, if he cheerfully performs the duty, he is entitled to the Spirit of the Lord—the Spirit of Truth—the Holy Ghost; and will most assuredly possess the same. There is a time for preaching, for praying, for sacrament meetings, for labor, and when we are attending to any or all of these, in the season thereof, we are entitled to the purifying influence of the Spirit of God.

If a man is called to go and farm, and he goes faithfully about it, because he is directed to do so by the authorities that are over him, and he raises his grain, his cattle, and brings forth his crops to sustain man and beast, and does this with an eye single to the glory of God and for the building up of his kingdom, he is just as much entitled to the Spirit of the Lord, following his plough, as I am in this pulpit preaching, according to the ministry and calling, and the duties devolving upon him.

If a man is called to deal in merchandise for the benefit of the people of God; in traveling to buy his goods, and looking after them and their safety until they reach their place of destination, and distributing those goods to the Saints and taking his pay for them, let him act with an eye single to the glory of God and the upbuilding of his kingdom on the earth, and he is as much entitled to the Spirit of the Lord and the Holy Ghost as a man is preaching.

If a man is called to raise stock, and to procure machinery to manufacture the clothing that is necessary for the Saints, and he goes at that business with his eye single to the building up of the kingdom of God on the earth he is entitled to the Spirit of the Holy Gospel, and he will receive and enjoy it just as much as if he were preaching the Gospel. Will he have the spirit of teaching and expounding the Scriptures? No, he has the spirit to know how to raise sheep, to procure the wool, to put machinery in operation to make the clothing for the advancement, benefit and building up of the people of God on the earth. And the Spirit of the Lord is here in these labors—farming, merchandizing and in all mechanical business just as much as it is in preaching the Gospel, if men will live for it.

Suppose we bring a few illustrations in regard to the present feelings and knowledge of the elders of Israel. We need not go back to Nauvoo or Kirtland, to find illustrations among our merchants, but take them as we find them here. If they enter upon their business without God in their thoughts, it is, "How much can I get for this? And how much can I make on that? And how much will the people give for this and for that? And how fast can I get rich? And how long will it take me to be a millionaire?"—which thoughts should never come into the mind of a merchant who professes to be a Latter-day Saint.

But it should be, "What can I do to benefit this people?" And when they live, act, and do business upon this principle, and think, "What can I do to benefit the kingdom of God on the earth, to establish the laws of this kingdom, to make this kingdom and people honorable, and bring them into note, and give them influence among the nations so that they can gather the pure in heart, build up Zion, redeem the House of Israel, and . . . prepare for the coming of the Son of Man?" and labor with all their might for their own sanctification and the sanctification of their brethren and sisters, they will find that the idea of "How much can I make this year? Can I make sixty-thousand dollars? Can I make in my little trade a hundred thousand dollars?" never would enter their minds; they never would think of it.

But I am sorry to say they do not. Our merchants may turn round and ask us if we expect them to make anything. Yes, we are perfectly willing they should get rich; no matter how rich they are, but what will you do with those riches? The question will not arise with the Lord, nor with the messengers of the Almighty, how much wealth a man has got, but how has he come by this wealth and what will he do with it?

I can reveal things to the people, if it would do any good; give them the mind of the Lord if they could hear and then profit by it, with regard to wealth. The Lord has no objection to his people being wealthy; but he has a great objection to people hoarding up their wealth and not devoting it, expressly, for the advancement of his cause and kingdom on the earth. He has a great objection to this.

And our mechanics [those who construct machines, furniture, etc.], do they labor for the express purpose of building up Zion and the kingdom of God? I am sorry to say that I think there are but very few into whose hearts it has entered, or whose thoughts are occupied in the least with such a principle; but it is, "How much can I make?" If our mechanics would work upon the principle of establishing the Kingdom of God upon the earth, and building up Zion, they would, as the prophet Joseph said, in the year 1833, never do another day's work but with that end in view. In that year a number of Elders came up to Kirtland; I think there were some twenty or thirty Elders. Brother Joseph Smith gave us the word of the Lord; it was simply this: "Never do another day's work to build up a Gentile city; never lay out another dollar while you live, to advance the world in its present state; it is full of wickedness and violence; no regard is paid to the prophets, nor the prophesyings of the prophets, nor to Jesus nor his sayings, nor the word of the Lord that was given anciently, nor to that given in our day. They have gone astray, and they are building up themselves, and they are promoting sin and iniquity upon the earth; and," said he, "it is the word and commandment of the Lord to his servants that they shall never do another day's work, nor spend another dollar to build up a Gentile city or nation."

Now, if any one is disposed to ask whether Brother Brigham has ever, since then, worked a day, or half a day, or an hour, to build up a Gentile city or the Gentile world, he will most emphatically tell the Latter-day Saints that he never has.

I could illustrate by circumstances, and could relate if I were disposed to give them to you, the providences of God, and how favorable they are to those who walk humbly before him. In the summer of 1833, in July, Brother Joseph gave the word of the Lord to the Elders, as I have been telling you. I returned east; and in September Brother [Heber C.] Kimball and I went up together with our little families. When we arrived in Kirtland, if any man that ever did gather with the Saints was any poorer than I was—it was because he had nothing. I had something and I had nothing; if he had less than I had, I do not know what it could be. I had two children to take care of—that was all. I was a widower. "Brother Brigham, had you any shoes?" No; not a shoe to my foot, except a pair of borrowed boots. I had no winter clothing, except a home-made coat that I had had three or four years. "Any pantaloons?" No. "What did you do? Did you go without?" No; I borrowed a pair to wear till I could get another pair.

I had traveled and preached and given away every dollar of my property. I was worth a little property when I started to preach; but I was something like [John] Bunyan—it was "life, life, eternal life," with me, everything else was secondary. I had traveled and preached until I had nothing left to gather with; but Joseph said: "Come up"; and I went up the best I could, hiring Brother Kimball to take my two little children and myself and carry us up to Kirtland.

In those days provisions and clothing were as dear as they are now in this place; and a mechanic in that country who got a dollar a day and boarded himself was considered rather an extra man. A dollar a day! And my brethren when they have three or five dollars a day, and have worked a year, will be sure to come out four or five or six hundred dollars in debt if they can get it. We did not live so in that country; we never used anything more than our means. When I reached Kirtland I went to work as soon as the word was that I could work and not preach. I knew that I could get plenty; for I knew how; I always could gather around me and make property.

There were some thirty or forty Elders gathered to Kirtland that fall; but there was only one mechanic in the entire number whom I knew that did not go to Cleveland and the neighboring towns to work during the winter—for the simple reason, that they thought they could not get one day's work and get their pay for it, in the place Joseph was trying to build up—and that exception was your humble servant. I made up my mind that I would stay in Kirtland, and work if I never got a farthing for it; and I went to work for Brother [Reynolds] Cahoon, one of the Trustees of the Temple, to build his new house. I worked all winter, and when spring came, was called upon to go to Missouri—a tramp of a thousand miles on foot—and a thousand back.

Before going, the brethren gathered in who had been to the surrounding places during the winter—joiners, painters, masons and plasterers. I asked some of the brethren how much they had made? I had worked there through the winter, and at its commencement had not the least prospect of getting twenty-five cents for my winter's work. I told Brother Cahoon I would work whether I could get anything for it or not, "for," said I, "the word of the Lord is for me to work, to build up Zion, and poor as I am I shall do it." But the Lord opened the way; and I gained Brother Cahoon's heart to that degree that if he received anything he always came to me, and said, "Brother Brigham, I have so and so, and I will divide it with you." Brother William F. Cahoon and I kept to work at the house until his father got into it. When we had finished the house, he had paid me all that was coming to me. The Lord had opened the way. This work finished, another job came, and then another, and when the spring opened, I can safely say that there was not any four, nor perhaps any six or ten of the brethren who had gone elsewhere to work who could produce as much property, made by them through that winter, as I had made.

You can see from this the providences of God, with one winter's work in Kirtland, when it was one of the hardest places that ever mortal man had to get a living in, and that too, when I had to work for nothing and find myself, that is, seemingly so, to all outward appearance.

I had my pants and coats, two cows, a hired house and a wife in the meantime. And I was better off than any other man who came to Kirtland the fall before, according to the property that we came with, and I had enough to live with my family and leave them comfortable, and my gun and sword and money enough to pay my expenses. If I had no work to do, and there was nobody to hire me, there was plenty of timber and I made some bedsteads or stands, and if anybody wanted such things they would come along and say, I will give you a little oats or a little corn, or something or other for them, and so the Lord opened the way most astonishingly.

I tell this, because it is an experience I am acquainted with, for it is my own. I am not so well acquainted with the providences of God in the experience of others, as I am with my own, except by faith and the visions of the Spirit.

I stayed in Kirtland from 1833 till 1837; I preached every summer. Here are brethren who know what I am saying. I traveled and preached, and still went back [to] nothing; but was willing to exchange, deal, work and labor for the benefit of my brethren and myself, with the kingdom and nothing else before me all the time. When I left there for Missouri I left property worth over five thousand dollars in gold, that I got comparatively nothing for. I could travel along, with regard to my experience, to this valley. I left my property in Nauvoo, and many know that I left a number of good houses and lots and a farm, and came here without one farthing for them, with the exception of a span of horses, harness and carriage, that Almon W. Babbit let me have for my own dwelling-house that my family lived in; and when I arrived here I owed for my horses, cows, oxen and wagons.

Now, the brethren say: "Why, Brother Brigham you are rich." I simply relate this to show you how I have lived and what I have been doing, and the result, that God, and not I, has brought forth. Now, I have some four or five grist mills, besides saw mills and farms; and let anyone ask my clerks if they ever hear me mention them from one year's end to another, unless somebody comes into the office and alludes to them; but my mind is upon increasing the wealth and advancing the interests of this people, and upon the spread of the Gospel on the continents and the islands of the sea. Ask my clerks and my closest associates if they ever hear me mention my individual property unless somebody speaks about it. I own property, and I employ the best men I can find to look after it. If God does not give it to me, I do not want it; if he does I will do the very best I can with it; but as for spending my own time in doing it, or letting my own mind dwell upon the affairs of this world, I will not do it. I have no heart to look after my own individual advantage, I never have had; my heart is not upon the things of this world.

Excuse me for referring to myself. But I know that there is no man on this earth who can call around him property, be he a merchant, tradesman, or farmer, with his mind continually occupied with: "How shall I get this or that; how rich can I get; or, how much can I get out of this brother or from that brother?" and dicker and work, and take advantage here and there—no such man ever can magnify the priesthood nor enter the celestial kingdom. . . .

"I do not know," says one, "how to do better than I do." The Lord has given you and me the privilege of gathering up from among the wicked. "Come out of her, my people," are some of the last words revealed through his servant John in the last of the revelations given in the New Testament. And one of the last writers we have here in this book—John the Revelator—looking at the Church in the latter days, says: "Come out of her, my people"—out of Babylon, out of this confusion and wickedness, which they call "civilization." Civilization! It is corruption and wickedness of the deepest dye. It is no society for you, my people; come out of her.

Gather out where you can pray, where you can have meetings and sacraments; where you can meet, associate, and mingle together; where you can beautify the earth and gather around you the necessaries of life, and make everything as beautiful as Zion, and begin to establish Zion on the earth; sanctify yourselves, sanctify your houses, the lands that you live upon; your farms, the streams of water that flow through your cities, country places and farms; sanctify your hills and mountains and valleys, and the land around about, and begin to build up Zion. Now, "come out of her, my people," for this purpose, "and partake not of her sins, lest ye receive of her plagues." . . .

. . . I do not care whether a man is a merchant or a beggar, whether he has much or little, he must live so that neither the things of this world, nor the cares of this life will becloud his mind, nor exclude him from the revelations of the Lord Jesus Christ; but all, whether merchants or preachers, tradesmen or farmers, and mechanics and laborers of every kind, whether they work in the ditch, or building post and rail fence, must live so that the revelations of the Lord Jesus are upon them; and if they live not according to this rule, they will miss the kingdom they are anticipating.

You may think this is pretty hard talk; but recollect the saying of one of the Apostles, when speaking about getting into the kingdom of heaven, that "if the righteous scarcely be saved, where shall the ungodly and the sinner appear?" The best man that ever lived on this earth only just made out to save himself through the grace of God. The best woman that ever lived on the earth has only just made her escape from this world to a better one, with a full assurance of enjoying the first resurrection. It requires all the atonement of Christ, the mercy of the Father, the pity of angels and the grace of the Lord Jesus Christ to be with us always, and then to do the very best we possibly can, to get rid of this sin within us, so that we may escape from this world into the celestial kingdom. This is just as much as we can do, and there is no room for that careless-ness manifested by too many among us. . . .

Now, we are here to build up the kingdom of God, and for nothing else; but here are our enemies determined that the king-dom of God shall not be built up. I have often thought that I ought not to blame them so much. They have had possession of this earth some six thousand years; the devil has reigned tri-umphant, and without a rival has held possession; the wicked rule all over the earth, and they have had possession of this little farm, called earth, so long that they think they are the rightful heirs, and inherit it from the Father. But the Lord has said that the Saints should possess it. And when Joseph translated the Book of Mormon, and revealed the Gospel as it was among God's children on this continent anciently, that was the starting point. The Lord said, "I am going to establish my kingdom; my open foe has had possession of this earth long enough, and I am going to show all the inhabitants of the earth, saint and sinner, good and bad, that it is time for Jesus, according to his promise, sufferings and death to commence to redeem the earth and those who will hearken to his counsel, and bring them forth to enjoy his presence."

The enemy has had possession of the earth a great while, and they really feel as though it is their right, and that they are the legal heirs.

If the gospel goes to the uttermost parts of the earth and ful-fills its destiny as predicted by the Prophets, by Jesus and by the Apostles, it will eventually swallow up all the good there is on the earth; it will take every honest, truthful and virtuous man and woman and every good person and gather them into the fold of this kingdom, and this society will enlarge, spread abroad and multiply. . . .

As I said here, once, with regard to preaching the Gospel, a very simple person can tell the truth, but it takes a very smart per-son to tell a lie and make it appear like the truth. Go into the sectarian world with their systems called religion now before the people; it requires a very learned and talented man to make it appear anyway commendable to the hearts of the honest, so far as doctrine is concerned. When we come to the doctrines that Jesus taught, they are what can save the people, and the only ones on the face of the earth that can. In conversation not long since with a visitor who was about returning to the Eastern States, said he, "You, as a people, consider that you are perfect?" "Oh, no," said I, "not by any means. Let me define to you. The doctrine that we have embraced is perfect; but when we come to the people, we have just as many imperfections as you can ask for. We are not perfect; but the Gospel that we preach is calculated to perfect the people so that they can obtain a glorious resurrection and enter into the presence of the Father and the Son."

Our doctrine embraces all the good. It descends to the capacities of the weakest of the weak; it will teach the girl how to knit, and to be a good housekeeper, and the man how to plant corn. It will teach men and women every vocation in life; how they should eat; how much to eat; how to feed, clothe, and take care of themselves and their children; how to preserve themselves in life and health. But you will ask, how? By close application, and learning from others, and obtaining all the knowledge possible from our surroundings, and by the assistance of the Spirit, as all who have introduced art and science into the world by the aid of revelation. . . .

Now let us . . . prove to the heavens that our minds are set on beauty and true excellence, so that we can become worthy to enjoy the society of angels, and raise ourselves above the level of the wicked world and begin to increase in faith, and the power that God has given us, and so show to the world an example worthy of imitation.

May the Lord bless you. Amen.

Journal of Discourses, 11:291.

Treasures in Heaven

Orson Hyde

An early convert to the Church, Orson Hyde was called in 1835 as one of the first Apostles of the modern dispensation. In 1839, during a brief period of disillusionment (which John Taylor kindly suggested was sickness "with a violent fever"), Elder Hyde signed an affidavit against the Saints and was dropped from the Quorum of the Twelve. He repented later that same year and was again sustained to the quorum. Elder Hyde served faithfully for the remainder of his life and was known for his missionary work, colonization efforts, and eloquence in public speaking.

In this address, Elder Hyde contrasts the riches of the world with the blessings God gives to those who put his kingdom first. "I recollect when we were forced away from Nauvoo, at the point of the bayonet," he said, "and when we crossed the river to the Iowa side there were hundreds of our people camped along the shore, and what had they to eat, or to make themselves comfortable with, in the scorching sun and burning with fevers? Nothing. We wanted meat and other comforts, but we had not the means to procure them, and the Lord in mercy sent clouds of quails right into camp. They came into the tents, flew into the wagons, rested on the wagon wheels, ox yokes and wagon tongues, and our little children could catch them, and there was an abundant supply of meat for the time being."

He chastised those who, bent on obtaining the riches of the world, neglect the things of God: "Said the Savior, 'It is easier for a camel to go through the eye of a needle than for a rich man to enter into the kingdom of God.' This is a saying which very few people who live now seem to believe, for, apparently, the main object for which most people labor is to get rich, and hence, according to the saying of Jesus, to keep themselves out of the kingdom of God."

This address, later printed in the *Journal of Discourses*, was delivered in the Fourteenth Ward assembly rooms in Salt Lake City on Sunday evening, February 8, 1874.

I rejoice very much, brethren and sisters, at the opportunity we enjoy tonight of meeting together to worship the Lord our God, and to wait upon him, that we may renew our strength. It is the desire of my heart to do all I can to inspire in you a living faith in God, and I am sorry to say that there are those in our midst, against whom I have no particular charge to make, but who, by reason of the favors which fortune or this world has bestowed upon them, have become weak and sick in the faith, and who, I may say, have almost no faith at all. I feel on this occasion that if wealth would destroy what little faith I have I would rather that it would take to itself wings and fly beyond my reach. I have no faith to boast of, but what little faith I may possess I think more of than I do of the wealth of this world, for the wealth of this world will not carry me successfully through the dark valley of the shadow of death; it will not open to me the portals of bliss, but real and genuine faith in God will accomplish this.

I remember once, in Nauvoo, when we felt ourselves happy and fortunate if we could get half a bushel of meal to make mush of, the Prophet Joseph Smith, talking to some of us at the house of brother John Taylor, said, "Brethren, we are pretty tight run now, but the time will come when you will have so much money that you will be weary with counting it, and you will be tried with riches"; and I sometimes think that perhaps the preface to that time has now arrived, and that the Saints will soon be tried with riches; but if riches would kill our prospects of eternal life by alienating us from the Priesthood and kingdom of God, I say it would be far better for us to remain like Lazarus, and that all our fine things should perish like the dew, and we come down to the bedrock of faith, and trust in the true and living God.

The question is whether we have to come there in order to inherit eternal life. I will read a little of the words of our Savior, as recorded in the sixth chapter of Matthew. Said he: "Take no thought, saying what shall we eat or what shall we drink, or where-withal shall we be clothed, for after all these things do the Gentiles seek, for your Heavenly Father knoweth ye have need of these things, but seek ye first the kingdom of God and his righteousness, and all these things shall be added unto you. Take therefore no thought for the morrow, for the morrow shall take thought for the things of itself. Sufficient unto the day is the evil thereof." (Matthew 6:25.)

There are many Saints at this time who are laboring to acquire wealth; and the kingdom, in the hearts of a good many, has become a secondary consideration; if we were to reverse this order of proceeding and seek the kingdom of God first, we could then put our Heavenly Father to the proof whether all these things shall be added to us, and thus also test the truth of our religion, and I believe that this would be a legitimate way to test it to our satisfaction.

I have heard several very able discourses, by good men, showing that unless our exports equal our imports, we are not making headway financially. This is all very good so far as it goes, but reasoning of that kind is not our Savior's; it is the reasoning of this world, and so far as this world is concerned, their reasoning, if correct, is just as good as any other reasoning; but if it is not correct, and we are swerved by its force and power from the line marked out for us to walk by, we shall become the losers. I wish now to refer you to certain events that have transpired in days gone by, and then any of you may tell me by what financial calculations these things happened, and whether they were brought down to the very nicety of worldly reasoning, or whether they were left open to the providences of our God.

Once on a time there was a great famine in Samaria, and so sore was that famine that a mule's head sold for four score pieces of silver in the market, and a cab of dove's dung sold for food in the market; I can not recollect how much. We should consider it pretty much of a task or penalty to be compelled to use an article like that for food; but the people of Samaria were sorely distressed with famine, and which way to turn to save themselves they knew not.

About this time, the King of Syria, with a large army, came to besiege the city, and there was a mighty host of them, and they brought everything in the shape of food that was necessary for the comfort and happiness of man; and although the famine was so sore among the Samaritans, the old Prophet, Elisha I think it was, told them that on the next day meal should be sold in the gate of their city at very low figures, lower than it had ever been known to be sold before. A certain nobleman, who heard the prophecy of Elisha expressed his doubt of its truth, and he said that if the windows of heaven were opened and meal poured down from above it could not fall to such low figures. Now see what he got by doubting the words of the Prophet. Said Elisha to him, "Your eyes shall see it, but you shall not taste it."

That night the Lord sent forth the angels of his presence and they made a rustling in the trees, and sounds like horses' hoofs and chariots, as if the whole country had combined to go out to battle against the Syrians, and they did not know what to make of it, and they were frightened, and fled, leaving almost every thing they had brought with them in the borders of the town; and as they went, the rustling of the trees and the noise of the horses and chariots seemed to pursue them, and in order to make their burdens as light as possible, they threw away everything they had with them, and their track was strewed with everything good and desirable. The next morning the people of Samaria went out and brought the spoils into the market, and it was overstocked with provisions, and the word of the Lord through the Prophet was fulfilled.

Now, you see, the Lord knew they had eaten mules' heads long enough, and that they had need of something more palatable; he had had the matter under advisement, no doubt, when the crusade was inaugurated against the people of Samaria, and he, in all probability, inspired them to take abundant supplies, that they might feel all the more confident on account of their great numbers being so well provided for. They no doubt calculated that they had the sure thing, little thinking that God was making them pack animals to take to his people what they needed. Their Father in Heaven knew that they had need of them, and he sent them, and the people of Samaria brought them into market, and behold and lo the multitude rushed together just as hungry people will, and this nobleman came out also, and he was trodden down under foot and stamped to death—he saw it but he never tasted it.

That is the reward of those who disbelieve the Prophets of God; it was so then, and if the same thing does not occur in every instance, something of a similar character is sure to take place. There was no living faith in that man; he could not believe the testimony of the Prophets, and in this he was like some of our— what shall I say?—great men whose faith is weak and sickly, and they think they know it all, and can chalk out right and left that which would be best for building up the kingdom of God.

Well, after the flight of Sennacherib and his hosts, the starving multitudes of Samaria had an abundant supply of food. By what financial calculation was this brought about? Was it by worldly financiering, or was it by the bounteous dispensation of kind Heaven, who, disregarding worldly technicalities, sent a full supply to administer to and supply the wants of those who put their trust in him, for at that time the people of Samaria stood fairly before him, and he pled their cause.

Said the Savior, "Take no thought what ye shall eat or what ye shall drink, or wherewithal ye shall be clothed, for after all these things do the Gentiles seek." Have the Gentiles come here to make money and to become wealthy? They say they have; I am told that that is their sole errand. I have not the least objection to it, but I have an objection to my brethren and sisters adopting their spirit by which their faith withers and becomes like a dried reed.

The Lord said to Joseph Smith once: "As I live, saith the Lord, I give not unto you that ye shall live after the manner of the world." Are we seeking to live after the manner of the world by our trading and trafficking? I do not know, however, that there is anything objectionable about legitimate, honorable trading, and I am not going to speak against it; but in these days it is a pretty rare thing to find an honorable dealer. There may be, and undoubtedly there are, men who do nothing but honorable business transactions, but most business men are eager to lay up a fortune, and to get rich in a short time. Some of our merchants think they ought to get rich in from five to ten years, and then retire; but in honorable business transactions it takes almost a lifetime to amass a fortune. I will not, however, speak of things that occurred in old times, but will come down to our own experience.

I recollect when we were forced away from Nauvoo, at the point of the bayonet, and when we crossed the river to the Iowa side there were hundreds of our people camped along the shore, and what had they to eat, or to make themselves comfortable with, in the scorching sun and burning with fevers? Nothing. We wanted meat and other comforts, but we had not the means to procure them, and the Lord in mercy sent clouds of quails right into camp. They came into the tents, flew into the wagons, rested on the wagon wheels, ox yokes and wagon tongues, and our little children could catch them, and there was an abundant supply of meat for the time being. Who financiered that, and by what calculation of two and two make four did it happen? It was the mercy and generosity of kind Providence.

After the people arrived here in Salt Lake, they had pretty hard times. I was not one of the honored ones first here, but I arrived soon after, and I can recollect very well hearing of the hard times, when the brethren and sisters were forced to dig roots, and boil up thistletops, and anything that could be converted in the seething pot into food for the stomach. In those days the rations of our people were very short indeed. The Lord was aware of the position of the Saints in those times, he knew that they craved and had need of the necessaries and comforts of life, and he provided a way for them to obtain them. He opened the mines of California, and he caused the news to fly eastward, and this inspired the people of the East, almost en masse, to go to the El Dorado of the West to secure the precious metals.

I happened to be on the borders at the time the excitement was in progress, and having crossed the plains once or twice, people came to me to know what they should load with. I told them to take plenty of flour, for that would be good anyhow, and if they took more than they could carry they could trade it with the Indians to good advantage for something that they needed. I also told them to take plenty of bacon, the very best that they could bring; plenty of sugar, and also plenty of coffee and tea, we were not quite so conscientious in those days about using tea and coffee as we profess to be now. I also told them to take plenty of clothing, such as shirts, overcoats, blankets and everything that would keep the body warm; and I told them that tools of every kind would be very convenient and almost indispensable, such as spades, shovels, planes, saws, augurs, chisels, and everything that a carpenter needs, for said I, "When you get to the end of your journey you may not find everything to your hand that you want,

and these things will be very convenient for you to build with."
And I gave them this counsel in good faith, for I thought if they
did not feel disposed to carry all these things through, they could
very readily exchange them in our valley for something that our
folks could spare and which the emigrants would find useful.

Well, they fitted up train after train with these staple articles,
and to use a steamboat phrase, they loaded to the very guards, and
when many of them reached here, having been retarded by their
heavy loads, it was so late that they said, "If we attempt to go
through to California with this outfit, we shall be swamped in the
snows of the Sierra Nevada Mountains, and so we must leave it
here." They had brought it just where God wanted it, for said he,
"I knew you had need of these things"; and while many of those
who brought them along were good, honorable men, it so happened in the providence of God that his people were abundantly
supplied.

Did not Brother Kimball prophesy here once, in a time of the
greatest strait, that goods and merchandize of every kind would be
so cheap and plentiful within a certain time, that they would have
to be piled up on the wayside? Yes, and his prediction came true,
and the merchandize had to be placed by the wayside because
there were not houses enough to put it in. Well, when the emigrants got here with their jaded teams, they were glad to trade
them off. Said they, "Here, gentlemen, are the dry goods, merchandize, tools, and other things we have brought along; they are
at your service; give us a pack mule and a pack-saddle, a lariat and
a pair of spurs that we may go on our way." This was the way matters were arranged in many instances, and there was no fault to
find; we did the best we could under the circumstances, and they
did the best they were obliged to for us.

Who financiered that? Was that on the principle of two and
two make four? I do not object at all to that principle, but one is
the result of human skill and wisdom, the other is based upon

unshaken faith in God. That is what I am coming to—unshaken faith in God, which in this case, in our own experience, brought deliverance to the Saints, for they were well supplied with tools, wagons, clothing and all they needed to make them comfortable. Our community was small then, a few trains heavily laden were sufficient to supply it, but now it would take a number of railroad trains. We are growing and increasing beyond our faith; we are taking thought for tomorrow too much.

To illustrate this matter I will suppose that I say to my sons, "Here, my boys, I want you to go and plough, take care of the stock, or make the garden beautiful"; and they reply, "Father, we want some boots, pants and hats." I tell them I know they have need of these things, but I want them to attend to what I require of them without first receiving the boots, pants and hats. What would you think of these boys if, because their father did not give them what they thought they needed just at the time, they should say, "We will strike out on our own hook, for we must have, and are determined to have, these things"?

How many of us are there now who feel as though we could chalk out and financier our own course irrespective of what the Prophet says? Perhaps some would be grieved if their faith in the ordinances of the Gospel and in the servants of God were questioned; but, as I said in the start, to come down to the bedrock, leaving fiction out of the question, how many of us are there who are ready to strike hands with the Prophet of God and to hang on to him blow high, or blow low, come coarse or come fine?

There are some men who have acquired fortunes and who are rich, and I have reason to believe, though perhaps good men in every other respect, there will be a divorce between them and their silver and gold, or I fear they may not enter the kingdom of God. The rich man may say, "Divorced! Is it possible that I must be divorced from that to which I am so devotedly attached—my riches—in order that I may obtain life everlasting?"

In further illustration of the subject we have under consideration, I will quote the saying of the Savior, "Lay not up for yourselves treasures upon earth, where moth and rust doth corrupt, and
where thieves break through and steal: but lay up for yourselves
treasures in heaven, where neither moth nor rust doth corrupt, and
where thieves do not break through nor steal." (Mathew 6:19–20.)
If heaven be beyond the bounds of time and space, as some of our
religious friends believe, it would require a long arm to deposit our
treasures there; but I apprehend that the heaven here referred to
is not so far away. I believe it is near, and that when I yield my
treasures to the powers that govern the kingdom of God I lay up
treasure in heaven. Whenever I see the hungry and feed him, the
naked and clothe him, the sick and distressed and administer to
their wants, I feel that I am laying up treasure in heaven. When I
am educating my children and embellishing their minds and fitting them for usefulness, I am laying up treasures in heaven.

I would ask that little boy, who is well educated and well
trained, "What thief can enter in and steal the knowledge you
have got?" It is beyond the power of the thief to steal; it is out of
his reach; that treasure is laid up in heaven; for where is there a
place more sacred than the hearts of the rising generation which
beat with purity, and with love to their parents, and with love to
God and his kingdom? What better place can you find in which to
deposit treasures than that? But all our obligations are not pointing
to one source or quarter, there are many ways in which we can lay
up treasures in heaven by doing good here on the earth.

The Bible says, "Take no thought beforehand, what ye shall eat
or what ye shall drink, or wherewithal ye shall be clothed." Says
one, "If we are to take no thought beforehand, I would like to
know how the farmer will ever contemplate sowing his seed if he
does not look with an eye to harvest, if he does not take some fore-
thought?" I do not see any necessity for this. I know that the times
and seasons roll around, and when Spring comes my natural senses

tell me then is the time to plough, and I go and plough, because I know it is my duty to plough. I keep on ploughing day after day until I get through, and then I commence sowing seed. It is no use for me to give myself any anxiety about the harvest—I have no control over that. As the Scriptures say, Paul may "have planted, [and] Apollos watered; but God gave the increase" (1 Corinthians 3:6), and I, with all my figuring, can not swell the kernels of wheat and cause them to germinate.

I can do my duty in the time and the season thereof, but I must leave the issue with God. When I see that the grain wants watering I can turn on the water, but never mind tomorrow; let that take care of itself. As each day rolls around I can do the duties thereof, but tomorrow is beyond my reach or control.

We, however, are looking to great results from our present labors as Latter-day Saints, and perhaps there is no particular harm in this; but it is far safer for us to do the duties of today than to neglect them by dreaming of the glory that is to be revealed in the future. That is in safe-keeping. The hands of the Lord are strong and true; they will keep the reward in reserve for the faithful; and none can rob them of it. Let us do the work of today, then, and our Heavenly Father knoweth that we have need of all these things.

There is one very peculiar saying of our Savior in the New Testament which I believe I will quote. Said the Savior, "It is easier for a camel to go through the eye of a needle, than for a rich man to enter into the kingdom of God." (Matthew 19:24.) This is a saying which very few people who live now seem to believe, for, apparently, the main object for which most people labor is to get rich, and hence, according to the saying of Jesus, to keep themselves out of the kingdom of God. I know men in this Church whom I would have gladly seen here tonight, but I do not see them. I suppose they have so much riches they have no time to attend meeting. Maybe they are here. I hope so. My sight is not very keen, and I can not see all over the room; but I do hope and pray that I shall never get so much wealth that I shall have no time to attend meetings, or so much as to keep me busy taking care of it, so that I shall not have time to enrich my heart with the knowledge of the Lord our God by putting myself in the way to obtain it. "Easier for a camel to enter the eye of a needle than for a rich man to enter into the kingdom of God." Said the disciples, "Who then can be saved?" The Savior answered, "That which is impossible with man is possible with God."

Now I want to look a little at the possibilities and impossibilities of the matter, not that I claim to understand everything, but sometimes a train of thought comes through my mind which cheers and does me good. That man who claims to be under the jurisdiction of an authority that he professes to believe is paramount with God, and yet is engaged in this way, that way and the other way, in getting rich so that he has no time to honor it, the question is, Can that man enter into the kingdom of God? I am not going to say, but I will bring up another case that, perhaps, may have a bearing on, and serve to illustrate, this subject.

There was a certain rich man who fared sumptuously every day. He had abundance of everything that was good. Then there was a poor man named Lazarus, who lay at his gate, and the dogs came and licked his sores. This poor man would have been glad of the crumbs that fell from the rich man's table. By and by poor Lazarus died and was carried by angels into Abraham's bosom. . . . I suppose he has a pretty large bosom and a large heart, large enough to embrace all the faithful from his day down to the end of time, for in him and his seed shall all the families of the earth be blessed.

By and by the rich man died, and it is said that he lifted up his eyes in hell, or in torment, and he saw Abraham afar off with Lazarus in his bosom. Said he, "Father Abraham, send Lazarus that he may dip the tip of his finger in water that he may cool my tongue, for I am tormented in this flame." Abraham replied, and he spoke to him very kindly and fatherly, "Son, remember that thou in thy lifetime receivedst thy good things, and likewise Lazarus evil things, but now he is comforted and thou art tormented. And besides all this, between us and you there is a great gulf fixed, so that they who would pass from hence to you cannot; neither can they pass to us who would come from thence." (Luke 16:24–26.)

Here, then, we see illustrated the fate of the man who obtained wealth independent of the Lord Almighty. He obtained wealth and enjoyed it, and down he went to hell, while that poor man who, in this life, lay at the rich man's gate and desired to be fed with the crumbs that fell from his table, was carried by angels into Abraham's bosom. Probably, in life, this rich man had oppressed and dealt wrongfully by that poor man; I cannot tell how that was, but at any rate he went to hell.

Now, let me ask you who the man is who may be rich, and still enter into the kingdom of God? There was father Abraham himself; none of you will dispute that he was a rich man while here, yet there he was, on the other side of the great gulf, prepared to welcome Lazarus to happiness and heaven. But how did Abraham get rich? Was it by cheating and defrauding, by calculating and financiering? Or did he get it by doing his duty and trusting in God to bestow upon him what he saw fit? He trusted in the Lord, and the Lord gave to him all the Land of Canaan for an everlasting possession and promised him that his seed should be as numerous as the stars in the sky, or the sands on the seashore. The Lord made Abraham rich, Abraham did not do it himself; he did not cheat anybody, but in the providences of God he was elevated and made rich.

Why, there are some men who can not sleep nights for laying plans to get rich, but I would advise them, if they want to get riches that will last for ever, just to lay plans to build up the kingdom of God, or in other words to take the advice of Jesus: "Seek first the kingdom of God, and his righteousness; and all these things shall be added unto you." (Matthew 6:33.)

I used to think—I can not get married until I get rich, for I can not support a wife; and it was not half so hard to support a wife in the days when I married as it is now, because there was not half the pride or fashion to support then that there are now. Then I did not make money very fast, and I thought that if I waited until I got rich before I married I should wait too long, and finally I concluded that I would marry and take hold with my wife and we would work together.

Well, then, I would give the same advice to my young brethren and sisters that I acted upon myself, and that is: Get married and get rich afterwards, and dispense with this fashion that so many are anxious to follow.

We cannot very well, unless we are born princes, heirs or millionaires, support the fashion of the present day and prosper, and we had better dispense with it. I like to see everybody clean and comfortable, but all this display and paraphernalia that fashion demands of its votaries seems to me like clogging the wheels and creating discomfort rather than comfort. When I was in the old country, I recollect hearing a lady say, "Some people wrap themselves up and put on so much that they are completely clogged. If you draw a net over a fish, how can it swim in the water? It is freedom they want, and it is a light covering we want, especially in warm weather." I like to see persons neat and clean, and would rather see them thus than adorned in fine feathers, dresses, caps and jewelry. I believe God's people will be so. I have no particular fault to find; I am only telling what I think would be good.

The man that goes along and does his duty, and, without straining a point, picks up honestly and fairly the blessings and means that God strews in his pathway, can appreciate and do good with his means; and as long as he keeps an open heart and is willing to do good, God will continue to put wealth in his way, and wealth obtained in this way, no matter how much, if it swells as large as the mountains on the east here, can not keep its possessor out of the kingdom, because it is the gift of God, and not the fruits of over-reaching dishonesty. God is not going to keep me out of his kingdom because I have wealth, no matter how much, if I obtain it honestly in his sight, and strive continually to do good with it.

The reason why men of God were rich in old times was that they were willing and desirous that God should rule, govern and control them and their means, while the miserable calculators after the fashion of the world shut God out of the question altogether. Such men are a stink in the nostrils of the Almighty, and he will hurl them from his presence, and they will find that it is easier for a camel to go through the eye of a needle than for them to enter into His kingdom.

This is my faith, and I hope it will last me all the way through and for ever, that if we will keep the commandments of God, build up his kingdom, and lay up treasure in heaven by doing good with whatever means and ability God may entrust us with here, wealth will roll in upon us from quarters we are not aware of, and in a way that eye has not seen nor ear heard, neither has it entered into the heart of man to conceive. All the world is for the Saints, and if they only take the right course and do as they are required, wealth will roll in upon them and cannot go anywhere else.

The world says the Latter-day Saints are the lowest of all people, and just for argument's sake we will grant it; but then, if we are so, that fact is only a proof of our excellence, for everything that has weight and worth rolls down and finds the center; the froth only rises to the top. I will venture to say that if you take a dollar and place it on the edge of a nice washbasin, it will roll down to the center, and if we are there, we shall all be in the right place. It is the meek and lowly who are to inherit the earth and the kingdom of God, and enjoy the gifts of heaven.

I have spoken once today before pretty freely, and I begin to feel a little sore about the sides, and I do not think I shall talk to you much longer on this occasion. I was talking this afternoon about the ante-diluvians. How strong they were in their own estimation! They were able to carve out their own destiny, and to amass and spend their own fortunes; but when the flood came they and their wealth went together. They were not in the ark; they had no interest in it whatever. I suppose they were a good deal as some people are at the present day. I saw a little ticket out here—I did not stop to read it—but in passing I read the words: "Not one cent for Tithing." I suppose that was the motto of the ante-diluvians. "Not one cent for Tithing," not one iota to build up the kingdom of God. Well, they went to destruction.

I wish to say to my brethren, I have had considerable experience in the kingdom of God, and I have had some experience that a man never ought to have, and let me here ask my brethren and sisters if everything could be arranged to suit all, where under the heavens would there be any trial of our integrity? There would be no such thing. As [some] say, "When I can read my title clear to mansions in the skies," and neither stumbling-block nor obstacle in the way, I shall begin to think that I am on the wrong road, for I do know that in the way of exaltation and eternal life there are stumbling-blocks and difficulties to overcome. . . .

"Take no thought for the morrow, what ye shall eat, or what ye shall drink, nor wherewithal shall ye be clothed," but go to, and do just as God, through your brethren, tells you, and never be the means of administering a blow or doing one act that shall cause a division among the Saints of God, for says Jesus, "Except you are one you are not mine," and how many are there in this city and throughout the country who are kind of half Jew and half Ashdod, and more Ashdod than Jew in many instances? Do not understand me to apply this to the body of the Saints, but to them that are pairing off, the disaffected and dissatisfied, and those who seem as if they had just swallowed a dose of fishhooks, and were choking over it. I would advise such to grease it well, and it will go down. Let the oil of the grace of God be applied, and there is no obstacle that we can not overcome. I say then, let us never allow ourselves to be the entering wedge to divide the people of God. If we cannot overcome a little difficulty or a little trial, how much faith have we got? Not much. I say to my brethren, God bless you; and to the weak, the Lord, through the Prophet, says, "Be strong." . . . If we have the right spirit, the more strength we need the more we shall have, but keep the fire burning, and may the Lord God of heaven bless you.

. . . Then let us . . . keep ourselves unspotted from the world and live to the honor and glory of God, that when we have got through, having really complied with the will of heaven, we may see opening before us fields of everlasting bliss, and crowns and dominions beyond calculation opening in the wide expanse of eternity. Oh, shall we come short, or shall we not?

Brethren and sisters, live to God, and may God bless you. I want to live until the power of God will be felt and acknowledged in this world, and that day is not far remote. May God bless us for ever, is my prayer in the name of Jesus. Amen.

Journal of Discourses, 17:4–14.

WISDOM

~❦ ❧~

WHERE IS WISDOM?

STEPHEN L RICHARDS

Elder Stephen L Richards, as a member of the Quorum of the Twelve, delivered this commencement address at the Utah State Agricultural College (now Utah State University, in Logan, Utah) in 1948, just a few years after World War II ended. He told the graduates, "The really important things in life are relatively few, at least a very limited number of classifications will embrace them. There are your body, family, property, and relationship to fellow man and God. . . . Where then is wisdom about these important things?" Elder Richards then gave the graduates his advice about those areas, his wisdom from nearly seventy years of experience.

I t was only two or three weeks ago that I picked up a morning paper in Oakland, California, and was struck by a headline which read: "Materialism is unintelligent, says Scientist Robert A. Millikan." I was immediately called away and did not get time to read the article, but I was intrigued by the thought projected in this heading, especially coming from a world-famed physicist now in his eightieth year and once winner of the Nobel Prize.

This statement, my friends, is but indicative of the thoughtful observations of many students of trends and conditions manifest in the world today and challenges our attention to numerous problems. I assure you it is not my purpose to attempt a solution of such problems on this occasion, but I would like to set before you, if I can, some items that may intimately touch your lives as you set out from this commencement to achieve the goals you have set for yourselves. This I shall attempt to do under the caption: "Where Is Wisdom?"

Wisdom is defined as "the power of true and just discernment, sound judgment, and a high degree of knowledge." I have a preference for my own definition. I define wisdom as being the beneficent application of knowledge in decision. I think of wisdom not in the abstract but as functional. Life is largely made up of choices and determinations. That at least is true of intelligent living, and I can think of no wisdom that does not contemplate the good of man and society. Wisdom is more than prudence, more even than judgment which is less exalted in character, and far more than skill. Wisdom is true understanding, and we are told in Proverbs:

"She is more precious than rubies: and all the things thou canst desire are not to be compared unto her.

"Length of days is in her right hand; and in her left hand riches and honour.

"Her ways are ways of pleasantness, and all her paths are peace.

"Happy is the man that findeth wisdom." (Proverbs 3:15–17, 13.)

Now, the really important things in life are relatively few, at least a very limited number of classifications will embrace them. There are your body, family, property, and relationship to fellow man and God. With a little stretching I think you can get almost everything under these headings—health, housing, marriage, children, economics, industry, capital, labor, government, international relations, spirituality, philosophy of life, education, and almost everything else about man in the universe could be grouped in the few classifications I have mentioned. Where then is wisdom about these important things? Surely a search for it is justified.

Where is wisdom about the body? We cannot contemplate happy, successful living without healthy, physical equipment. Every once in a while we hear wonderful stories which touch our hearts about the courage and accomplishments of the physically handicapped. But averagely we need health for success, and surely it is wisdom to strive for the largest possible measure of it.

I think wisdom about the body lies largely in our fundamental concept of it. I don't mean mere knowledge of its organic structure and chemistry although these are highly important. What I have in mind is the larger understanding of the origin and purpose of this physical structure which is you and I. I am sure it makes a great deal of difference whether it be regarded as a mere piece of earthy substance integrated into a living organism that eats and sleeps and thinks for a brief period and then disintegrates into the great heap of inorganic material from which it was made or whether, on the other hand, it be looked upon as a noble creation in the very similitude of the Creator himself to house the eternal spirit within it.

It makes a great difference, my young friends, which understanding you have. If these bodies of yours are, in your estimation, merely element and chemistry, it is not improbable that you will try to get out of them all you can while they last, all the fun, all the satisfaction of appetite that they will afford. If, however, you invest them with spiritual quality and purpose, they will become sacred to you. You will conserve your bodily strength as a means to a great end. You will know that you cannot violate the laws of health with impunity and that you cannot pollute your bodies without conscious offense to your self-respect and your Creator. I am sure that this concept will be helpful to you. It would be a boon to all men if they would accept it. Why, scarcely a week goes by that I do not learn of tragedies resulting from infractions of the laws of health and bodily care—loss of positions, marital difficulties, and disgrace resulting from drink, riotous living, and the abuse of the body. I hope you will pardon me, my dear young friends, if I charge you in kindness and firmness not to drink intoxicating liquors. There is dynamite in the practice. If any of you is indulging, my appeal and my counsel to you is to stop and stop quickly. For many years I have been in a position to see what drink does for men in business and professional circles. While it is true that some exercise control, many do not have that power, and the results are disastrous.

I caution you, also, against any perversion of the physical attributes and powers with which you have been blessed. Ever bear in mind the exalted statement of Paul: "Know ye not that ye are the temple of God, and that the Spirit of God dwelleth in you?" (1 Corinthians 3:16.) Here is wisdom about the body.

And now, the family—where is wisdom about this mighty institution which shapes the destiny of the world? This college is situated in and largely supported by a community which for generations has laid great emphasis on the home. The college itself, as I understand it, has majored in education for homebuilding, and I have no doubt that you graduates are leaving the school with an exceptionally fine foundation for successful homemaking. I am glad that you have had this training because I am sure that it will not only develop the skills essential to make beautiful home surroundings, but it will also have enhanced the importance and dignity of this elemental institution in your estimation. You can't appraise it too highly. A noble nation of ignoble households is impossible and many of our most far-reaching and perplexing national problems today center in and around the home. Here our fundamental concepts about home and family and marriage are the determining factors in our attitudes and practices. I am aware that I put a strain on your patience when I repeat some ideas about this institution that are generally known among you, but I cannot point out where wisdom lies in this matter without doing so.

True marriage is a sacrament. There are four parties to it—the man, the woman, the state, and the Church. It is true the Church is not indispensable under the law, but the law contemplates Church participation and makes provision for it. The proportion of marriages performed without ecclesiastical authority, I believe, has increased in recent years. I regard this as regrettable but not more regrettable than the evident decline in understanding and respect of and for the Church ceremony. When God is taken into the compact it is far more likely to endure the irritations and strains that are put upon it and reach the high purposes he has set for the wedded life.

I know of nothing more stabilizing to this now seemingly precarious institution which only survives about two-thirds of its trials than a full compensation of its sacred nature and lofty purposes the Lord has set for the race. "To replenish the earth" is his word proclaimed in the very dawn of creation when man and woman were placed in the world. Marriage and homes are for families and not merely for social convenience and showy housing. Family is a collective word without limitation as to number. It is unfortunate when it is interpreted to mean only the two principals or three or four or any number less than unselfish devotion to the ideals of home and providence may dictate. My dear young friends, I most earnestly hope that none of you will ever consider it vulgar to have a large family. I hope, too, that you will not permit economics to be the arbitrary dictator of the size of your families. Of course, families cost a lot, but they are worth a lot, and when well brought up, they make the finest contribution any of you can make to the well-being of society.

Goodness itself is largely a matter of propagation. Good people come from good homes as I might well illustrate if time permitted. And then, too, aside from this great altruistic undertaking of making a home and rearing a family with all the trials, sacrifices, and deprivations it entails there is more genuine, enduring happiness and satisfaction in it than anything else which will come into your lives. It will establish a real partnership in marriage. It will bring mutual respect and common interest, and it will keep husband and wife together and stem the tide of this awful flood of divorces which threatens to inundate our whole nation with disasters greater than those of war. Here is wisdom—God's wisdom about the divinely appointed institution of marriage and home.

And now comes property! I suppose we all hope it will come, and when it comes, I hope it will not come to plague us but to bless us. Perhaps, in that thought lies wisdom about it and it is likely that something of that nature is what Dr. Millikan had in mind when he said: "Materialism is unintelligent." It is said that Jesus had more to say about man's attitude toward money and property than about any other one thing. In sixteen of thirty-eight parables Jesus made this his theme. We all need to make a living, but a living does not always make a life. Money is a means to an end, not a worthy end in itself. And money alone is not security. It may be that enough of it will keep the wolf from the door but not from the heart.

Now please do not suppose that I am impractical enough to expect that you can enter your various vocations and acquire property and means sufficient for your needs without giving a major portion of all your time and energies to the enterprise. There isn't a person here who will attain success without working for it, hard and persistently. Property and means are acquired as a reward for useful service. Don't forget that all the money and wealth is owned by somebody. The only way you can get a portion of it is by exchanging something you have for that which somebody else has. Even the things you take out of the earth or out of the air have pecuniary value only as you may be able to trade or sell them for somebody else's property, except perhaps the small amount you may eat and drink.

I regard the idea of exchange in the acquisition of property as being important because from it is readily discerned the necessity of fairness and integrity in all trade relations, and here is where character comes in. Unless a reputation can be established for fair and honest exchange of services, skills, and goods, a man is in a poor way to succeed in any business or employment. That is why gambling is morally and economically wrong. It is not a fair and honest exchange of values, and I warn you against it, my friends, in all its vicious and enticing forms. I might take a long time, if it were available, to tell you of tragedies that have come under my own observation in a rather extended experience in a number of businesses attributable to this venturesome spirit of trying to get something for nothing. We have a rule in one of our institutions that if we catch an employee at it he is discharged. We can't trust our own and other people's property to those who corrupt their sense of fair dealing and integrity with such practices.

There is another aspect of this matter of property I must mention. There is a scripture setting forth the word of the Lord on this subject. "Behold, all these properties are mine. . . . And if the properties are mine, then ye are stewards." (D&C 104:55–56.)

This principle of stewardship in ownership is a very salutary one. It invests all ownership with benevolence. That does not mean that everything a man acquires he is to give away, but it does mean that all his goods are impressed with a trust for the benefit of others and good causes and that ultimately all will be required to give an accounting of their use and disposition of the things of earth committed to their custody. Do you think that if such a noble understanding of property were prevalent in the world today we would have any such spectacle of greed and avarice and industrial and international contention and bitterness as now confronts us? I am sure we would not. I am sure, too, that this doctrine of stewardship of property will take from materialism its power to enslave men and rob them of their altruistic ideals. Ever bear in mind that when money becomes your master, the joys of ownership will be gone. I can think of no more elemental wisdom about property.

And now, what of our relationship to our fellow men and to God—sociology, in its broadest sense, government, and religion?

Where is wisdom about these vitally important matters? Here I revert again, as by now you would expect me to do, to fundamental concepts. I don't know that I can do better in epitomizing the underlying principles than to borrow the statement of a man whom I once heard address a national conference of social workers in New Orleans:

> God is a Father.
> Man is a brother.
> Life is a mission
> And not a career.

The doctrine of the brotherhood of man is a common theme in the world today. It is proclaimed so widely, and seemingly so generally accepted it seems strange that it does not make more progress in application. I don't know that I can give an explanation which you would regard as adequate, but I have a few suggestions. There can be no fraternity without paternity, that is in a genetic sense. Without a complete recognition of the Fatherhood of God there is little hope of establishing a sense of filial obligation and community of interest among his children. Now the kind of recognition which is necessary involves not only an acknowledgement of his universal supremacy but a submission also to his will as Lawgiver and Judge. There are many thousands of good people in the world who admire the teachings of the Savior, and many who make honest endeavor to incorporate in their lives the virtues he gave to mankind—neighborliness, generosity, and unselfish consideration for others. Such virtues are highly commendable, but unfortunately they do not always carry with them complete recognition of the divine Lordship of Jesus Christ. Only when his law becomes the criterion by which all things are measured and judged will the recognition become complete.

And man must consciously know that he is a son of God. Do you think the boys and young men of the nations could ever have been cannon fodder in the lethal operations of the last few decades if there had been a deep-seated respect for the majesty and dignity of man as a divine son of a divine Parent? I tell you that conversion to that principle is indispensable to bring peace to this stricken world. It is also essential for an understanding of true liberty, and it is the issue which divides peoples of the world today.

Unfortunately, many who support the cause of the dignity of man in public do not support it in their private lives. That's the real trouble with our nation. We are trying desperately to sell the peoples of the world our concepts of liberty, of equity, and justice in our way of life. We know these principles are right and conform to divine law, but we are using poor ways in teaching them to others. I saw it recently in South America. We try to tell in our broadcasts (expensive broadcasts, too; the people of this state could afford to pay something to keep some of them off the air)— we try to tell about the excellence of American life, our marvelous industries, our great agriculture, our beautiful homes, our education, and our free government. And while we are telling them these things, spending enormous sums to promote the good neighbor policy, our Hollywood picture shows are depicting on the screens in South America lurid scenes of marital infidelity, broken homes, licentiousness, gangsterism, revolting crime in all its forms, immodesty, extravagance, and obscene jokes. For everyone who hears the expensive broadcast of the Department of State, there are a hundred or a thousand who see the pictures. And then, too, the press play up sensational stories of crime and degradation in North America, sometimes with premeditated design to prejudice their peoples against us.

Well, how much progress do you think we can make in promoting the brotherhood of the world with these methods? Why, with the facilities now at our command, there could be spread all over the earth in most appealing form the virtues and the higher concepts and joys of good living if there were but the disposition and courage to do so. But behind such a project must live a background of righteousness in the homes and lives of the people themselves. No man can really be a good brother in the community of men however generous he may be with his money or civic service, unless he sets an example of decent, righteous living. There is a widespread disposition today evidenced particularly in public figures to want to disassociate public utterances and actions from private living. I don't believe it can be successfully done, however much some men seem to want it. The only way we can judge character is to look behind the career to the individual, and in the end we must depend on character in all our associations.

It goes without saying that altruistic service is essential to the promotion of brotherhood in the world. To care for the needs of the hungry, the sick, and the distressed will ever be a challenge to the best and noblest impulses within us. Your country and your community and your church will always need your help and devotion. You will never regret giving generously to good causes. Enduring happiness will come to you in such endeavor. But even more than this I am sure that wisdom dictates the highest contribution a man can make to the brotherhood of the race is to live as a son of God, proud of his noble lineage, shedding the divine light within him on his fellow men in works of virtue and truth.

Where now is wisdom about our intimate selves, our faith, our religion? I feel a little delicacy about discussing this personal matter with you, my young friends. I don't want you to feel that I have anything to impose on you, nor do I wish unduly to intrude on your private, personal philosophy, but I cannot conclude a discussion of the important things of life without mention of religion. I know that it involves personal feelings, experiences, and convictions about spiritual forces and God, and I know, too, something of the influence that religion exerts on the lives of people. I have been engaged in making those observations for many years.

I hope you have all reached the conclusion that there is a spiritual nature in man. If you have, I am sure it will enable you to understand many manifestations in life and nature that are otherwise most difficult of understanding, and I am sure, too, that a recognition of the divinity in your lives will bring purpose, security, and great happiness.

There is in a recent issue of the *Reader's Digest* an article entitled "The Quest of Our Lives." I wish all would read it. The author discusses security, the attainment of which seems to be the national ambition today. She asserts that "a greater menace even than the atomic bomb is . . . the feeling that material things can satisfy our unrest and unhappiness . . . and the belief that an individual's incapacity to deal with this limitless threatening universe may be assuaged in mass organization." She says there is a "secret citadel . . . within all men and women of good will," and that "to find it is an individual quest—the most urgent, significant quest of our lives."

This "secret citadel" of which she speaks is our inner spiritual selves. It is the divine within us. In its discovery and promptings lie our only safeguard against discouragement and despair in the battle of life. It is in fact our only reliable security. More than anything else, my young friends, I want you to have this priceless endowment of the spirit. It will bring an inner strength to resist all temptation. It will enlarge the vision and purpose of your lives. Comfort, peace, and reconciliation will come in times of trial, and wisdom, a beneficent wisdom beyond your mortal capacities, will attend you all your days.

Where Is Wisdom? 65–77.

~❦~

Sources

Benson, Ezra Taft. *A Witness and a Warning*. Salt Lake City: Deseret Book, 1988.

Brigham Young University 1981–82 Fireside and Devotional Speeches. Provo, Utah: University Publications, 1983.

BYU 1977 Devotional Speeches of the Year. Provo, Utah: Brigham Young University Press, 1978.

Clark, J. Reuben, Jr. *Charge to Religious Educators*. Edited by the Church Educational System. Salt Lake City: The Church of Jesus Christ of Latter-day Saints, 1977.

Clark, James R., comp. *Messages of the First Presidency of The Church of Jesus Christ of Latter-day Saints*. 6 vols. Salt Lake City: Bookcraft, 1965–75.

Collected Discourses. 5 vols. Edited by Brian H. Stuy. Woodland Hills, Utah: B.H.S. Publishing, 1987–92.

Conference Reports of The Church of Jesus Christ of Latter-day Saints. Salt Lake City: The Church of Jesus Christ of Latter-day Saints, 1898–.

Cowley, Matthew. "Miracles." In *BYU Speeches of the Year*. Provo, Utah: BYU University Press, 18 February 1953.

Hunter, Howard W. *That We Might Have Joy*. Salt Lake City: Deseret Book, 1994.

Hymns of The Church of Jesus Christ of Latter-day Saints. Salt Lake City: The Church of Jesus Christ Latter-day Saints, 1985.

Journal of Discourses, 26 vols. London: Latter-day Saints' Book Depot, 1854–1886.

Kimball, Spencer W. *Faith Precedes the Miracle*. Salt Lake City: Deseret Book, 1972.

———. "Tragedy or Destiny." In *BYU Speeches of the Year*. Provo, Utah: BYU University Press, 6 December 1955.

Richards, Stephen L. *Where Is Wisdom?* Salt Lake City: Deseret Book, 1955.

Smith, Joseph. *History of The Church of Jesus Christ of Latter-day Saints*. 7 vols. 2d ed. rev. Edited by B. H. Roberts. Salt Lake City: The Church of Jesus Christ of Latter-day Saints, 1932–51.

———. *Lectures on Faith*. Salt Lake City: Deseret Book, 1985.

———. *Teachings of the Prophet Joseph Smith*. Selected by Joseph Fielding Smith. Salt Lake City: Deseret Book, 1976.

Smith, Joseph Fielding. *Take Heed to Yourselves*. Salt Lake City: Deseret Book, 1966.

~❦

~⁀❦ ❦⁀~

PERMISSIONS

Permission has been granted by copyright holders to use all copyrighted materials in this book.

The following talks are © by Intellectual Reserve, Inc.:

"An Anchor to the Souls of Men," by Howard W. Hunter

"The Book of Mormon—Keystone of Our Religion," by Ezra Taft Benson

"The Meaning of Repentance," by Theodore M. Burton

"Born of God," by Ezra Taft Benson

"'Stand Ye in Holy Places,'" by Harold B. Lee

"The False Gods We Worship," by Spencer W. Kimball

"'No Less Serviceable,'" by Howard W. Hunter

"What Is True Greatness?" by Howard W. Hunter

"The Purifying Power of Gethsemane," by Bruce R. McConkie

"When the World Will Be Converted," by Spencer W. Kimball

"How to Obtain Personal Revelation," by Bruce R. McConkie

"'Who Am I?'" by Harold B. Lee

"In His Strength," by Marvin J. Ashton

"The Light of Christ," by Marion G. Romney

~⚜~

BIOGRAPHICAL NOTES

Marvin J. Ashton

Born May 6, 1915, at Salt Lake City, Utah, Marvin Jeremy Ashton was the son of Marvin O. Ashton, who served as first counselor in the Presiding Bishopric under LeGrand Richards. Elder Marvin J. Ashton was sustained as an Assistant to the Quorum of the Twelve in October 1969 and ordained an Apostle in December 1971. He died February 25, 1994, at the age of seventy-eight.

Melvin J. Ballard

Born February 9, 1873, at Logan, Utah, Melvin Joseph Ballard was ordained an Apostle in January 1919. He died July 30, 1939, at the age of sixty-six. Elder Ballard was a grandfather of Elder M. Russell Ballard, currently a member of the Quorum of the Twelve.

Ezra Taft Benson

Born August 4, 1899, at Whitney, Idaho, Ezra Taft Benson was a great-grandson of the earlier Apostle by the same name. He was ordained an Apostle in October 1943. During his service as an Apostle, he simultaneously served for eight years in the cabinet of President Dwight D. Eisenhower, as U.S. secretary of agriculture. Elder Benson was ordained president of the Church in November 1985. He died May 30, 1994, at the age of ninety-four.

Hugh B. Brown

Born October 24, 1883, at Granger, Utah, Hugh Brown Brown was sustained as an Assistant to the Quorum of the Twelve in October 1953 and was ordained an Apostle in April 1958. He served as a counselor to President David O. McKay from 1961 to 1970. He died December 2, 1975, at the age of ninety-two.

Theodore M. Burton

Born March 27, 1907, at Salt Lake City, Utah, Theodore Moyle Burton was sustained as an Assistant to the Quorum of the Twelve in October 1960, sustained to the First Quorum of the Seventy in October 1976, and named an emeritus General Authority in October 1989. He died December 22, 1989, at the age of eighty-two.

J. Reuben Clark Jr.

Born September 1, 1871, at Grantsville, Utah, Joshua Reuben Clark Jr. was ordained an Apostle October 11, 1934. He served as a counselor to presidents Heber J. Grant, George Albert Smith, and David O. McKay from 1933 to 1961. A lawyer and a statesman, President Clark served as U.S. State Department solicitor, under secretary of state, and ambassador to Mexico. He died October 6, 1961, at the age of ninety.

Oliver Cowdery

Born October 3, 1806, at Wells, Vermont, Oliver Cowdery became the primary scribe for Joseph Smith as he translated the Book of Mormon and later became one of the Three Witnesses. Along with Joseph Smith, he received the Melchizedek Priesthood at the hands of Peter, James, and John in May 1829. He was sustained as Second Elder of the Church on April 6, 1830, was ordained assistant president of the High Priesthood in December 1834, and was sustained as a counselor in the First Presidency in September 1837. He was excommunicated in April 1838, was rebaptized in November 1848, and died March 3, 1850, at the age of forty-three.

Matthew Cowley

Born August 2, 1897, at Preston, Idaho, Matthew Cowley was the son of Matthias Cowley, a member of the Twelve. Matthew was ordained an Apostle in October 1945. He was widely known for his stories of the great faith of the Maoris of New Zealand, among whom he had served as a missionary. He died December 13, 1953, at the age of fifty-six.

Richard L. Evans

Born March 23, 1906, at Salt Lake City, Utah, Richard Louis Evans was sustained as a member of the First Quorum of the Seventy in October 1938 and ordained an Apostle in October 1953. Long known and beloved as the voice behind the radio broadcast *Music and the Spoken Word*, he died November 1, 1971, at the age of sixty-five.

Heber J. Grant

Born November 22, 1856, at Salt Lake City, Utah, Heber Jeddy Grant was the only son of Jedediah Morgan Grant, who was serving in the First Presidency under President Brigham Young at the time of his son's birth. Elder Grant was ordained an Apostle in October 1882 and was ordained president of the Church in November 1918. He died May 14, 1945, at the age of eighty-eight.

Howard W. Hunter

Born November 14, 1907, at Boise, Idaho, Howard William Hunter was ordained an Apostle in October 1959 and was set apart as president of the Church in June 1994. During his presidency he emphasized temple work and invited less-active members to return to full Church participation. He died nine months after becoming Church president, on March 3, 1995, at the age of eighty-seven.

Orson Hyde

Born January 8, 1805, at Oxford, Connecticut, Orson Hyde was ordained an Apostle on February 1835 under the hands of the Three Witnesses to the Book of Mormon (Oliver Cowdery, David Whitmer, and Martin Harris) at Kirtland, Ohio. In 1841 he took an arduous journey to Jerusalem, where, atop the Mount of Olives, he dedicated the Holy Land for the return of the Jews. He died November 28, 1878, at the age of seventy-three.

Heber C. Kimball

Born June 14, 1801, at Sheldon, Vermont, Heber Chase Kimball was one of the original Twelve Apostles of this dispensation. He was ordained an Apostle in February 1835 under the hands of the Three Witnesses to the Book of Mormon (Oliver Cowdery, David Whitmer, and Martin Harris). Elder Kimball was sustained as first counselor to President Brigham Young in December 1847. He served in that position until his death on June 22, 1868, at the age of sixty-seven. Elder Kimball was a grandfather of Spencer W. Kimball, who also is represented in this book.

Spencer W. Kimball

Born March 28, 1895, at Salt Lake City, Utah, Spencer Woolley Kimball was ordained an Apostle in October 1943 and became president of the Church in December 1973. He was known for his love of the American Indians, his admonition to "lengthen your stride," and his worldwide vision for the mission of the Church. He was also known for the revelation that made it possible for every worthy male Church member to hold the priesthood. He died November 5, 1985, at the age of ninety.

Harold B. Lee

Born March 28, 1899, at Clifton, Idaho, Harold Bingham Lee was ordained an Apostle in April 1941. He briefly served as a counselor to President Joseph Fielding Smith, and he was ordained president of the Church in July 1972. He is best known for his establishment of the Church's correlation program and its welfare program, which had its beginnings in his stake when, as a young man, he served as a stake president. He died December 26, 1973, at the age of seventy-four.

Bruce R. McConkie

Born July 29, 1915, at Ann Arbor, Michigan, Bruce Redd McConkie was sustained to the First Council of the Seventy in October 1946 and was ordained an Apostle in October 1972. A student of the scriptures and a prolific writer, Elder McConkie was best known for his book *Mormon Doctrine* and for *The Mortal Messiah* series. He died April 19, 1985, at the age of sixty-nine.

David O. McKay

Born September 8, 1873, at Huntsville, Utah, David Oman McKay was ordained an Apostle in April 1906. He served as second counselor to Presidents Heber J. Grant and George Albert Smith from 1934 to 1951. He was sustained as president of the Church in April 1951. He died on January 18, 1970, at the age of ninety-six. His service as an Apostle and Church president totaled nearly sixty-four years, more than any other man in this dispensation.

Orson Pratt

Born September 19, 1811, at Hartford, New York, Orson Pratt was one of the original Twelve Apostles of this dispensation. He was ordained an Apostle in April 1835 under the hands of the Three Witnesses to the Book of Mormon (Oliver Cowdery, David Whitmer, and Martin Harris). Elder Pratt briefly grew disaffected from the Church and was excommunicated in August 1842, but he was rebaptized the following January and reordained an Apostle. He died October 3, 1881, at the age of seventy. Elder Pratt was a younger brother of Parley P. Pratt, who also is represented in this book.

Parley P. Pratt

Born April 12, 1807, at Burlington, New York, Parley Parker Pratt was one of the original Twelve Apostles of this dispensation. He was ordained to the apostleship in February 1835 by Joseph Smith, Oliver Cowdery, and David Whitmer. His younger brother, Orson Pratt, was ordained an Apostle two months later. Elder Pratt was assassinated on May 13, 1857, near Van Buren, Arkansas, at the age of fifty.

LeGrand Richards

Born February 6, 1886, at Farmington, Utah, LeGrand Richards was a son of George Franklin Richards and a grandson of Franklin Dewey Richards, both of whom had also served in the Quorum of the Twelve. LeGrand Richards served as Presiding Bishop of the Church from 1938 to 1952; in April of 1952, he was ordained an Apostle. Elder Richards's *A Marvelous Work and a Wonder*, still in print after more than fifty years, has influenced the lives of countless members and investigators of the Church. He died on January 11, 1983, at the age of ninety-six.

Stephen L Richards

Born June 18, 1879, at Mendon, Utah, Stephen Longstroth Richards served as a counselor in the Sunday School General Superintendency from 1908 to 1934. He was ordained an Apostle in January 1917 and became a counselor to President David O. McKay in April 1951. An attorney and businessman, he was a grandson of Willard Richards, who was with Joseph Smith at the Martyrdom in the Carthage Jail. He died May 19, 1959, at the age of seventy-nine.

Marion G. Romney

Born September 19, 1897, at Colonia Juarez, Mexico, Marion George Romney was sustained as the Church's first Assistant to the Quorum of the Twelve in April 1941 and was ordained an Apostle in October 1951. He served as counselor to Presidents Harold B. Lee and Spencer W. Kimball from 1972 until the death of President Kimball in 1985. Elder Romney then served as president of the Quorum of the Twelve Apostles for the last two and a half years of his life. He died on May 20, 1988, at the age of ninety.

George Albert Smith

Born April 4, 1870, at Salt Lake City, Utah, George Albert Smith was a grandson of George A. Smith, an Apostle and counselor to President Brigham Young, and a son of John Henry Smith, an Apostle and counselor to President Joseph F. Smith. George Albert Smith was ordained an Apostle in October 1903. He served as president of the Church from May 1945 until his death on April 4, 1951, at the age of eighty-one.

Joseph Smith

Born December 23, 1805, at Sharon, Vermont, Joseph Smith witnessed the First Vision in 1820, wherein the Father and the Son appeared to him, ushering in the dispensation of the fulness of times. He was ordained to the Melchizedek Priesthood by Peter, James, and John in May 1829, was sustained as First Elder of the Church at the organization of the Church on April 6, 1830, and was sustained as president of the High Priesthood in January 1832. He was martyred at Carthage Jail in Carthage, Illinois, on June 27, 1844, at the age of thirty-eight.

Joseph F. Smith

Born November 13, 1838, at Far West, Missouri, Joseph F. Smith (whose full name was Joseph Fielding Smith) was a son of Hyrum Smith. He was ordained an Apostle in July 1866. He served as a counselor to presidents Brigham Young, John Taylor, Wilford Woodruff, and Lorenzo Snow. He was ordained president of the Church in October 1901. He is well known for his vision of the redemption of the dead, which is published as section 138 of the Doctrine and Covenants. He died November 19, 1918, at the age of eighty. President Smith was the father of Joseph Fielding Smith, who also is represented in this book.

Joseph Fielding Smith

Born July 19, 1876, at Salt Lake City, Utah, Joseph Fielding Smith was a grandson of Hyrum Smith and a son of President Joseph F. Smith. He was ordained an Apostle in April 1910. He was sustained as a counselor in the First Presidency in 1965. Following the death of President David O. McKay, Joseph Fielding Smith served as president of the Church from January 1970 to July 2, 1972, when he died at the age of ninety-five. A prolific writer, President Smith was the author of two dozen books and countless magazine articles.

Lorenzo Snow

Born April 3, 1814, at Mantua, Ohio, Lorenzo Snow was baptized at Kirtland, Ohio, in June 1836. Elder Snow was ordained an Apostle in February 1849 and was sustained as president of the Church in September 1898. During his presidency he saved the Church from bankruptcy by his inspired emphasis of the law of tithing. He died October 19, 1901, at the age of eighty-seven.

James E. Talmage

Born September 21, 1862, at Hungerford, England, James Edward Talmage was ordained an Apostle in December 1911. The author of the classic works *Jesus the Christ, The Articles of Faith,* and *The House of the Lord,* he died July 27, 1933, at the age of seventy.

John Taylor

Born November 1, 1808, at Milnthorpe, England, John Taylor was ordained an Apostle in December 1838. He was wounded in the Carthage Jail during the martyrdom of Joseph and Hyrum Smith. His book *The Mediation and Atonement* has become a classic in the Church. Sustained as president of the Church in October 1880, he died July 25, 1887, at the age of seventy-eight.

Orson F. Whitney

Born July 1, 1855, at Salt Lake City, Utah, Orson Ferguson Whitney was ordained an Apostle in April 1906. Elder Whitney was the author of a biography of Heber C. Kimball, as well as doctrinal works and many poems. He died May 16, 1931, at the age of seventy-five.

John A. Widtsoe

Born January 31, 1872, at Daloe, Island of Foyen, Norway, John Andreas Widtsoe was a scientist who specialized in agriculture and wrote books on dry farming and irrigation techniques. Known for his question-and-answer column in the *Improvement Era* and his book *A Rational Theology,* he was ordained an Apostle in March 1921. He died November 29, 1952, at the age of eighty.

Wilford Woodruff

Born March 1, 1807, at Avon, Connecticut, Wilford Woodruff was baptized a member of the Church in 1833. He subsequently became a courageous and dedicated missionary, baptizing more than two thousand people on his missions. He was ordained an Apostle in April 1839 and was sustained as president of the Church in April 1889. As president of the Church he received the revelation that led to the Manifesto included in the back of the Doctrine and Covenants. He died September 2, 1898, at the age of ninety-one.

Brigham Young

Born June 1, 1801, at Whitingham, Vermont, Brigham Young was one of the original Twelve Apostles of this dispensation. He was ordained an Apostle in February 1835 under the hands of the Three Witnesses to the Book of Mormon (Oliver Cowdery, David Whitmer, and Martin Harris). He was sustained as president of the Church in December 1847. He led the Saints on their trek from Nauvoo, Illinois, to the Great Basin of Utah, where he established Church headquarters in the area of the Great Salt Lake. He died August 29, 1877, at the age of seventy-six.

S. Dilworth Young

Born September 7, 1897, at Salt Lake City, Utah, Seymour Dilworth Young was the grandson of Seymour Bicknell Young, who had been a member of the First Council of the Seventy. S. Dilworth Young was sustained to the First Council of the Seventy in April 1945, sustained to the First Quorum of the Seventy in October 1976, and named emeritus General Authority on September 30, 1978. He died July 9, 1981, at the age of eighty-three.

INDEX

blind child, 100; of lame man, 130–31
Health, 528–30
Heaven, 166–67, 170
Heirs in kingdom, 458–59, 462–64
Helaman, 146–47
Heroes: unsung, 146–54, 190–92; of the world, 187
Herschel, Sir John Frederick William, 404
Hezekiah, 11
Himni, 149
Holy Ghost: belongs to the faithful, 65–66, 117, 455, 499–501; understanding things of, 73–74; testifies of Christ, 196–97, 200, 204; receiving gift of, 278–79, 409; as guide to perfection, 294, 443–44; confirms knowledge of God, 324–27; inspiration through, to man, 343–46, 378–91; moves men to speak will of the Lord, 355–57; discerning truth through, 358–63, 366, 389–90; receiving revelations through, 366–75, 396–401; identity of, 449–50; gift of, as promise of larger knowledge, 474, 484–86
Holy Spirit of Promise, 460
Homes, 178–85
Honesty, 242, 385–87, 524
Hong Kong, 260
Horses, story of, 382–83
Howell, Rulon, 270
Hubbard, Brother, 342
Human nature, changing, 55
Humor: of Hugh B. Brown, 14; of Matthew Cowley, 91
Hunter, Howard W.: on life's adversities, 23–31; on unsung heroes, 146–54; on achieving true greatness, 186–93
Hyde, Orson: with Wilford Woodruff, 344; revelation to, 355, 359; on building kingdom of God, 510–12;

on providence of God, 513–18; on treasures in heaven, 519–26

"I Am a Child of God," 411–12
Icarianism, 327–29
Identity, man's immortal, 308–14, 405–13, 414–21, 424–37
Idolatry, 139–45
Ignorance, 109
Illnesses, 3–4
Independence, Missouri, 472
Infant, analogy of, 321
Inspiration, 90–91, 96–97
Intellectualism, 77–78
Intelligence, of man, 310, 425
Isaac, 210–11
Isaiah, 165
Ishmael, 148–49
Israel, 471–72

Jack, James, 487–88
Jacob, 38, 165
James, 432
James, William, 181
Jarom, 38
Jehoshaphat, King, 143
Jenks, Jeremiah, 384
Jesus Christ, life of: learns from suffering, 4; instructs faithful spirits in spirit world, 8; bears witness to Book of Mormon, 34–35; makes full commitment to his Father, 47–48; heals us through our repentance, 49, 50; choosing to follow, 52–57; will not allow his Church to be led astray, 61–62, 64; literal resurrection of, 69, 206–7, 428; having true faith in, 143–44; as separate from God the Father, 164–65; as Creator, 167–68; being joint heirs with, 169–70; sacrifice of, 210–13; foretells of his Second Coming, 227–28; directs apostles to teach all nations, 247–52; will open doors for missionary work, 253–54; to present